THE MEDIA SWIRL

THE MEDIA SWIRL
Politics, Audiovisuality, and Aesthetics

CAROL VERNALLIS

Duke University Press   Durham and London   2023

© 2023 DUKE UNIVERSITY PRESS
All rights reserved

Designed by Matthew Tauch
Typeset in Untitled Serif and IBM Plex Sans
by Westchester Publishing Services

Library of Congress Cataloging-in-Publication Data
Names: Vernallis, Carol, author.
Title: The media swirl : politics, audiovisuality, and aesthetics / Carol Vernallis.
Description: Durham : Duke University Press, 2023. | Includes bibliographical references and index.
Identifiers: LCCN 2022039204 (print)
LCCN 2022039205 (ebook)
ISBN 9781478019060 (paperback)
ISBN 9781478016427 (hardcover)
ISBN 9781478023692 (ebook)
Subjects: LCSH: Mass media and culture. | Mass media—Social aspects. | Mass media—Political aspects. | Spectacular, The, in motion pictures. | Music videos—Social aspects. | Digital media—Social aspects. | Social media and society. | BISAC: SOCIAL SCIENCE / Media Studies | MUSIC /Genres & Styles / Pop Vocal
Classification: LCC P94.6 .V466 2023 (print) | LCC P94.6 (ebook) | DDC 302.23—dc23/eng/20221121
LC record available at https://lccn.loc.gov/2022039204
LC ebook record available at https://lccn.loc.gov/2022039205

Cover art: Dua Lipa during the MTV Europe Music Awards 2019. Doug Peters / Alamy Stock Photo. Color grading by Aubrey Woodiwiss.

For Charlie and Beatrice/Bea the bee

Contents

xi   ACKNOWLEDGMENTS
xiii   A NOTE ON THE COVER

1   Introduction

I Post-Classical Cinema at the Limit

27   1   Partying in *The Great Gatsby*: Baz Luhrmann's Audiovisual Sublime

48   2   Shattered Pleasures: Michael Bay's *Transformers: Age of Extinction*

II Music Video and the Art-Video Border

71   3   Beyoncé's Overwhelming Opus; or, the Past and Future of Music Video

97   4   Avant-Gardists and the Lure of Pop Music

122   5   Beyoncé's *Lemonade*: She Dreams in Both Worlds
                  Carol Vernallis, Lisa Perrott, and Holly Rogers

138   6   Tracing the Carters through the Galleries: "APES**T/APESHIT" and the Louvre

154   7   Storytelling on the Ledge: Lady Gaga and Jonas Åkerlund's "Paparazzi"

III Music Video's Late Late Style

175	8	How to Analyze Music Videos: Beyoncé and Melina Matsoukas's "Pretty Hurts"
196	9	Dave Meyers's Moments of Audiovisual Bliss
211	10	Janelle Monáe's "You Make Me Feel" and Anderson .Paak with Kendrick Lamar's "Tints": Getting Up in My [Rearview] Mirror

IV Audiovisual Aesthetics Online

| 231 | 11 | Who Needs Music Documentaries When There's TikTok and *Carpool Karaoke*? |
| 247 | 12 | TikTok and Costume-Drama Mashups on YouTube |

V New Modes of Analysis: Industry

| 265 | 13 | The Art of Color Grading
Carol Vernallis, Jonathan Leal, Eric Weidt, and Aubrey Woodiwiss |
| 290 | 14 | Music Video Directors, Production Houses, and the Media Swirl |

VI New Modes of Analysis: Neuroscience

| 307 | 15 | Music Video's Multisensory |
| 319 | 16 | Tracing the Asset: Humanistic and Quantitative Approaches to Cybercrime Film Trailers (Snowden and Bourne) |

VII	**New Modes of Analysis: Politics and Vernacular Culture**
335	17 New Technologies, Social Justice, and the Future in Beyoncé's Audiovisual Albums
356	18 Fox News, COVID-19, Brief Media Aesthetics, and Historical Resonances

369	Afterword
373	NOTES
403	BIBLIOGRAPHY
429	INDEX

Acknowledgments

Charles Kronengold, Jim Buhler, Holly Rogers, Selmin Kara, Jonathan Leal, Lisa Perrott, Lori Burns, Alan Cameron, Martine Beugnant, Arild Fetveit, Joseph Tompkins, Walter Carl Metz, Jarek Kapuscinski, Lanier Anderson, Steve Shaviro, Ken Wissoker, Margaret Vernallis, Joan Friedman, Tom Grey, Aubrey Woodiwiss, Eric Weidt, Jonas Åkerlund, Abteen Bagheri, Colin Tilley, Alan Ferguson, David Fincher, Joseph Kahn, Kevin Kerslake, Marc Klasfeld, Francis Lawrence, Melina Matsoukas, Mark Mayr, Dave Meyers, Emil Nava, Marcus Nispel, Mark Pellington, Floria Sigismondi, Oliver Stone, Dan Hallin, George Lipsitz, Jann Pasler, Tommy Labuda, Stan Hawkins, Jason King, Maeve Sterbenz, Gabriel Ellis, Gabrielle Lochard, Daniel Oore, Eric Lyon, Kyra Gaunt, Dale Chapman, Lauren McLeod Cramer, Anders Liljedahl, Eduardo Viñuela, Maxwell Joseph Suechting, Sarah Wood, Ian Forrester, Becky Waring, Dana Gorzelany-Mostak, Noah Fram, Paul Skokowski, Brian Knutson, Justin Gardner, Anthony Wagner, Kalanit Grill-Spector, and Jay McClelland.

A Note on the Cover

The cover image of Dua Lipa reflects this book's arguments. In what follows I claim that spectacle forms the core of our entertainment economy. And I give special attention to women dancing in formation. Historically, the image of dancing women bears a kinship to what Sigmund Kracauer called the mass ornament (as realized in Busby Berkeley's 1930s musicals). Equally important, this image pops, partly by drawing on saturated reds and yellows, a phenomenon I discuss in chapter 13, on color grading. The media swirl includes so much content that an individual object can only cut through by projecting intensity. The svelte, beautiful women surrounded by others suggests the swirl; a common music video scheme also places a lead singer among undefined background figures. We might seek other images to suggest the swirl.

Introduction

SPECTACLE GETS A BAD RAP. This book makes a case for it. There are good reasons to resist the pull of spectacle. On consecutive Fourths of July, then-President Donald Trump threatened to roll tanks down Pennsylvania Avenue; fortunately the streets couldn't bear the weight, and his parade didn't happen. Spectacle has been understood as a way of maintaining a passive public, often with torture and death as part of the show: Christians thrown to the lions, floggings, the guillotine in the public square. In *Triumph of the Will* (1935), Adolf Hitler's cross-like plane casts a shadow over crowds marching in lockstep. Some of the North Korean public extravaganzas are frightening images of people en masse.

Spectacle often assumes a more benign aspect today, but it still may foreground threatening features. Richard Dyer, one of few scholars who both celebrates and theorizes spectacle, notes that Hollywood musicals at least offered a sense of what utopia can feel like, if not the means to get there.[1] One of my favorite wondrous, elysian film sequences is Busby Berkeley's Depression-era "By a Waterfall," from *Footlight Parade* (1933). For me, the women's private watery spaces—their framed, art-deco-latticed architecture, and partially submerged formations of bodies forming chrysanthemums and DNA—crossfade toward increasing gender fluidity. Though scholars have identified reactionary elements in this number (women matched, as the director said, "like a string of pearls" to be molded into abstract shapes),[2] I embrace the sequence's close with its two pools, and a giant terraced fountain in the back, decorated with women squirting water like sculptures of peeing young boys. Ingénue Ruby Keeler's warbling soprano nestled in orchestral strings works as a siren's call.

What I'm calling "the media swirl" reflects the ways that spectacle saturates everything we experience. We might first think of arena-staged pop concerts and football halftime shows with their skyscraper-like walls of projections, flashpots, and lasers, and drones' bird's-eye sweeps over the concave architecture, a close-up of the star, who winks, and then immersion again within the crowds, a view obscured by hands and arms wielding cellphones, held high. But Caryl Flynn has also found something similar in brief media, noting that YouTube has realized pop-up, pocket-sized musicals.[3] I'd say that music videos—a genre with a nearly unfathomable reach (three billion views is unremarkable)—now give us pocket-sized spectacles, scaled for one viewer and one performer.

Ariana Grande's video "Breathin" (2018) is a good example. Grande sings while standing in a studio space, steam billowing in from the frame's sides as if to encircle her. In a complementary space, the steam obscures her head alone. She walks through a train station among crowds streaming at different speeds around her, mostly blurred. She sings while sitting on a pile of stacked suitcases under a light, floating motes illuminated by its spot. Then suddenly she's apotheosized, cutting back and forth through the sky on a gigantic swing, surrounded by enormous, gorgeous, cumulus clouds, like some sort of grand Tiepolo-inspired painting. It's a "Wow." How did we get here? We might turn to the soundtrack, with its evocations of a heartbeat, and its unusually rhythmicized phrases that leave space for Grande's breaths. Still, the clip is surprisingly hard to gauge, because in some ways it's so minimal. It's just Ariana with amorphous swirling stuff—just her and us.

And if I squint, I can locate spectacle in even shorter media, like Instagram and TikTok. Beyoncé's Instagram posts of her pregnancy with twins seemed to radiate through the web. A thirteen-second TikTok cellphone video of a wide-eyed cat, multiplied nine times, clapping its paws, and arcing through the top of the screen seemingly crowned by a ceiling fan (and hoisted from behind by its owner) to the Chordettes 1954 pop song "Mr. Sandman," belongs to the realm of maximum cute-adorable-charismatic (though the tune also casts an ominous tone; it had accompanied the closing credits for John Carpenter's 1978 *Halloween*). "Mr. Sandman" was shot by a twelve-year-old girl as her first upload, and it's the best of hundreds of TikTok's "Mr. Sandman Cats." Is this where I want to park my attention?

Yes, I value the merits of my fellow scholars' negative assessments of spectacle, and I know this is a hard-to-resolve dissonance, but I still hold on to many instantiations of it. Guy Debord rightly says that "spectacle is the nightmare of imprisoned modern society which ultimately expresses nothing more than its desire to sleep"; with spectacle, "the real world changes into simple images."[4] According to Theodor Adorno, "The culture industry perpetually cheats its consumers of what it perpetually promises . . . all [spectacle] actually confirms is that the real point will never be reached, that the diner must be satisfied with the menu."[5] And as Jonathan Crary notes, "No moment, place, or situation now exists in which one cannot shop, consume, or exploit networked resources, there is a relentless incursion of the nontime of 24/7 into every aspect of social or personal life."[6] Virginia Heffernan claims that the irreality of the digital produces a "hyperinflation of not cash, but values . . . increasingly bewildering levels of abstraction distort ordinary experience: a flesh-and-blood friend becomes a wink, an emoji, a $20 bill, a Venmo swipe, no wonder we turn to soil and blood a là Trump." Heffernan claims that "billions of people have passed through the looking glass from reality to the internet."[7]

But I'd add that we might still engage, no matter the distractions or our sense of disorientation. Participation can be time-consuming and numbing. Sometimes I've played a game with my students where we follow YouTube links based on curiosity and Google's algorithms. Sometimes we wind up in good places, but more often than once some place dark, like a less-than-sympathetic clip about a father with Tourette's syndrome. But there are ways to ameliorate or circumvent such experiences, including pressuring Google to more carefully curate its collection. The company, for example, should offer simultaneously encountered, engaging clips that support media literacy and participation—here is one of several strong reasons to participate in the media swirl.

I think Dyer would agree with me that spectacle should be but one component of a life (perhaps apportioned like screen time for young children—I try to make sure my daughter watches no more than forty-five minutes a day). It could use both celebration and deflation (*Vogue*'s seductive YouTube series *73 Questions* calls for serious analysis; I discuss it in a chapter on today's music documentaries). I often feel invigorated after watching spectacle. More able to engage with the world; less alone. Spectacle may be progressive. Stanley Cavell suggests that media move us because a viewer can contemplate what's before her without feeling an immediate pressure to intercede—it's there for her as possibility and reserve—and this can be hopeful.[8] Elias Canetti argued that the objects in spectacles can stand in for people (including sparkly lights and columned rows)—they're a representation of community itself.[9] Perhaps it's that we haven't built the right structures around spectacular entertainment. Perhaps we haven't learned how to read it.

Spectacle has been defined as a phenomenon to be looked at. I'll take this and add "listened to." It can evoke a sense of wonder, but it's human-built (its seams often peek through). Art theorists often contrast spectacle with nature's sublime—Niagara Falls or a tornado may simultaneously appear beautiful and terrifying. Our responses to spectacle and the sublime have long overlapped. The spectacle's senses of wonder and charm connect to the sublime's sense of being overwhelmed, and its association with nature's capacity to induce fear. But today, with 24/7 work speedup, global capital's acceleration, and new technologies, the borders between these two aesthetic categories are becoming even more porous. An aurora borealis or eclipse can resemble a human-staged light show in today's media-saturated culture, and not always to ill effect. On August 21, 2017, many of us pulled out our protective glasses—bought from Amazon's vendors before they began price-gouging, or freely obtained after waiting in lines at local public libraries—to gaze at the great solar eclipse at midday. Standing in the driveway, peering through clear grey plastic and cardboard, I'd soon find that the almost instantaneously uploaded corresponding YouTube and *New York Times* content would deepen my experience, making the event more tangible for me, and, I felt, for others too. An example where media tilts toward the sublime might be certain audiovisual moments in *Avengers: Infinity War* (2018). When the monster/God Thanos opines, against the background of multiple galaxies, about obliterating half of them, his words resound as a portent of global warming and our Anthropocene. In December 2019, close to Christmas, Trump released a political ad with his head superimposed on Thanos. Twitter responded with questions about whether his campaign knew what this was all about—another reason to be engaged with this spectacle. I found the clip clumsy but striking.

It has been argued that the political Left is more frightened of spectacle than is the Right.[10] The Left hopes to gain ground through rational appeals, especially arguments derived from Jürgen Habermas, Immanuel Kant, Karl Marx, and John Rawls. Frenzied masses of people overcome by Dionysian affects can seem threatening, at risk of falling under fascism's sway. The chaste, even dainty depictions of crowds in Bernie Sanders's and Hillary Clinton's 2006 presidential campaign ads contrast Donald Trump's raucous, unruly ones (e.g., Sanders's "America," Clinton's "Pantsuit Flashmob," and Trump's "C'Mon Ride the Train" and "Argument for America").[11] But the Left might learn how to read and embrace spectacle, especially of images of crowds, because the masses' strong drives are often bound up with desires for change. (Images of utopia and sci-fi may work similarly.)

Spectacle has joyous aspects, then, but also precarious and ominous ones. Film theory's concept of the gaze, that in strong work, part of the image (or soundtrack) stares threateningly back at you, is useful here.[12] Hans Holbein's painting *The Ambassadors*, with its anamorphic painted skull nestled at its base that suddenly coalesces into a vision of your death, is one example. What instances of audiovisual spectacle both charm and frighten us? (Perhaps some of Billie Eilish's music videos, or the opening of James Bond's *Spectre*?)

Of course, the media swirl is impossibly big. One could devote a scholarly career either to Instagram or to TikTok. I'd claim nearly everything on the internet seems tinged by spectacle, because the content almost always creates links beyond itself. Spectacle and the media swirl overlap here. The swirl's large and small objects (many web-based), too many to take in, tenuously linked, recombinant and malleable, as a total experience, feel spectacular. When I watch a brief, intimate clip of Taylor Swift at her living-room piano I experience not just Swift, but also her and others' archives (Beyoncé, Dua Lipa, Billie Eilish, and Trump do this for me too—they appear across so many platforms). This book takes on a narrower set of cases, and then, toward the end, it heads elsewhere, to embrace the swirl's syncretism through investigations of industry, science and technology, and politics. While this book is largely devoted to a collection of objects I find worth considering, it probably differs from yours. Unable to cover everything, I don't analyze video games and long streaming series, and I focus on American media in part to better consider US politics. Brief media I consider include many kinds of objects: music videos, commercials, political ads, scenes from movies, trailers, and TikTok posts. But this book also considers longer forms, because in the digital era, when sound and image can be modulated as flexible and interchangeable data, forms and genres intermingle—contracting and expanding in scale: Beyoncé's *Lemonade* (2016), a string of music videos with interstitial material, becomes a complete work for us; Michael Bay's *Transformers: The Last Knight* (2017) calls for a brief overview, and then we can zoom in on a single autobot's fight.

I've got skin in the game, a chip on my shoulder, an enthusiast's zeal. I'd like us to participate in new forms of interdisciplinarity and to share theorizations of sound and image. We live in an audiovisually intensified culture, and most media scholarship focuses on the moving image. While there's some work on film soundtracks, these don't place the image and soundtrack in relation. We could use a new field of study on audiovisuality.

Brief media, too, have their own aesthetics: they work differently than narrative films, documentaries, and streaming series.

Here's a brief description of the book's structure. Chapters 1 and 2 open with prismatic, layered Hollywood films like Baz Luhrmann's *The Great Gatsby* (2013) and Michael Bay's *Transformers 4* (2014). Some theorists predicted that the speed and density of postclassical films would hit an upper limit because viewers would become unable to assimilate the content. I've doubted these claims as I've tracked postclassical, audiovisually intensified films, but they may be right. The films considered here, which I think best exemplify the intensified style, are a bit older. *Transformers 4* and *The Great Gatsby* contain sequences that are cousins to music video, as my close analysis reveals.

Chapter 2 considers music video's widening domain. Many forces have made this possible, including the migration from MTV and other satellite services to online delivery, and the more permissive structures for including sex, violence, product placement, and interrupting the song. The aim of clips differ now too—many recent artists are concerned first with ticket sales, merchandising, and licensing songs for commercials than with record sales. With the internet, performers sense that any clip could find an audience. Here, music video dallies with classical Hollywood and high-art aesthetics.

Chapter 3 also questions whether the postclassical film aesthetic maps onto music video. Here, the genre's "late" styles and norms have become established, and we recognize its well-wrought forms. An upper limit of density, self referentiality, and intertextuality has been reached. The clips I analyze are by today's top music video directors—Dave Meyers, Alan Ferguson, Colin Tilley, and Melina Matsoukas. Chapter 4 considers YouTube's aestheticization and shifting boundaries. I look at three phenomena: 1) the constellations formed by YouTube clips of stars (their music videos, late-show performances, *Carpool Karaoke* appearances, and short quasi-documentaries); 2) the success of TikTok as a genre; and 3) romantic costume-drama mashups with pop songs on YouTube, hundreds of clips that constitute a unique genre with surprising aesthetics. These mashups (or "mixes") work on a different register from the book's other content, and from the audiovisual aesthetics scholars have analyzed; they complicate assumptions about audiovisuality.

Part II (with chapters 5–7) pivots to questions of where we go from here. As I note in the first half, I've developed techniques for responding to texts that can't be plumbed by existing methods (one favorite is a mixing, matching, and schematizing approach employing YouTube).

I've also worked closely with others in consortiums. I hope part II's new trajectories, its explorations in industry studies, neuroscience, and politics, will enrich the field.

This book has pushed my abilities to meet and analyze objects in ways I haven't encountered. I now feel better able to interpret novel media. This book's objects include odd sound/image juxtapositions (like the Gatsby party sequence) along with reactionary examples (*Transformers*, Lady Gaga's "Paparazzi," and Fox News). Considering a slice of the swirl makes new connections possible. I was surprised to find that both the grand and the small can feel oppressive. Postclassical blockbusters, like Michael Bay's *Transformers*, are so bombastic there's little way to place oneself in them—they can make our lives feel puny. But the intimate miniatures of TikToks and mashups leave me feeling I've failed to experience lived moments in rich ways.

Francesco Casetti claims that our mediascape has always possessed bad objects, though today much seems subsumed by late capitalism.[13] But we might consider that the field and its eras aren't uniform. When new consumer technologies first appear, openings for resistance can also—such as citizen participation tied to ham radio, Polaroids, Super 8 film, ½- and ¾-inch videotape, prosumer digital video cameras, cellphones, and now, yes, even TikTok.[14] Director Abteen Bagheri recently told me people couldn't tell his iPhone footage from that of a fancy Alexa camera (once both were printed to film). And even the worst objects can inform us about ourselves. This book's instances of music/image relations have shaped my views so profoundly that I believe my thoughts about *real people* have changed (see chapter 12).

Part II, with its first look at industry studies, neuroscience, and politics, might leave readers thinking "why not more?" But there's little in these areas, and a start is worthwhile. The Society of Cinema and Media Studies has a large industry studies interest group, but no journal in the academic databases is devoted to media industries. A search through these databases for color grading brings up nothing; there's also almost nothing on music, color, and moving media, and hardly anything on neuroscience and audiovisual aesthetics. There's little on politics and audiovisual aesthetics. I hope to keep pursuing these areas with the aim of understanding why sound and image moves us.

Toward this introduction's close, I'll turn again to the darker side of the media swirl—the ways late capitalism, technologies, and entertainment interpenetrate—but let me first, mirroring the book proper, build toward there.

As mentioned, *The Media Swirl* aims to help readers become more skilled at reading audiovisual content and committed to the discipline. It also hopes readers will reevaluate their political commitments and actively participate in the commons. Many alternate paths forward are possible and each of us, still making a helpful contribution, may not find ourselves in the same place. Let me follow one trajectory.

The book's first half focuses on honing skills in audiovisual studies. For those unfamiliar, let me provide a brief introduction to or glimpse of the field, drawing on predecessors like Nicholas Cook, Philip Tagg, Claudia Gorbman, and Michel Chion. Cook claims that when music and image are placed in relation, isolated elements within the sound and the image form new meanings through metaphor. Often the blended characteristics share similarities with the original object's elements: in a Citroen commercial, Mozart's music might suggest continuity and drive, while the car itself reflects craft; the two together might suggest not-yet-experienced qualities of technical excellence. But other elements wouldn't be taken up and would recede. Relations between music and image might be based on conformance, congruence, gap-making, or contrast.[15] Tagg's close attention to sound and image is among the most masterful, and his methods for analyzing work through a process of substitution produce strong results. Consider, for example, a brief media object's different musical or visual arrangement—for example, a Pantene shampoo commercial with an oompah performed by a polka band or set in a rural Nordic village.[16] Gorbman notes the ways that the film's soundtrack can disappear from view, and several reasons why we might wish it to do so.[17] Chion draws attention to the many ways sound performs unusual roles in audiovisual contexts. When offscreen, it can adopt a kind of ghostly presence. Sometimes an instantaneous meld comprised of sound plus image forges a sync point, what he's termed a "synchresis." Often sound becomes a property of the image.[18]

Can we take this scholarship on audiovisuality further? Since our culture is so saturated with and influenced by genres and platforms like YouTube, streaming series, Hollywood blockbusters, commercials, and political advertisements, audiovisual literacy is needed, but the discipline faces strong obstacles. Academia could engage even more with popular culture and lend more support for faculty wishing to cross disciplines. A scholar, to analyze audiovisual relations, also needs some chutzpah. That person must be open to addressing music, image (including moving bodies, cinematography, and editing), lyrics, and the relations among them. (This might include looking at a dance gesture against a harmonic shift and an edit, and asking how these might relate to one another.)[19]

I'd like to take a stretch to describe the ways my research contributes to our understanding of audiovisual aesthetics. The work of Claudia Gorbman, Michel Chion, Annabel Cohen, and even to some extent Nicholas Cook's insights apply best for film soundtracks (e.g., sound is absorbed by the image, the film's soundtrack is often unheard, congruence most often claims the viewer's attention, and sound-image relationship pair into complement, contest, and gap making).[20] But these effects tend to be tied to narrative cinema: soundtracks are most often designed, like editing, cinematography, lighting, and camera, to not detract from film's primary aim, which is to immerse the viewer in the story. All parameters tend to render themselves seamless, or, in other words, invisible. But this doesn't hold as true for much of the content we experience today—from TikTok, prosumer-created clips, political advertising, intensified cinematic, postclassical film segments, film trailers, to music videos. Scholars like David Ireland, Robynn Stilwell, Jeff Smith, and others have also made claims about audiovisual aesthetics, diegetic relations, and levels of incongruity that hold better for narrative films than for these forms.[21] *The Media Swirl*, I believe, provides new insights into this content.

Each genre has its own features, but for this introduction, let me stay with the music video, which is a sibling to these brief forms but which also possesses unique features. It's hard to fix a definition for it as it's changed platforms and contexts across four decades (today on YouTube, a postclassical audiovisually intensified film segment, the children's musical limerick "The Llama Song," and "Autotune the News," where newscasters "sing" their stories accompanied by Fruity Loops tracks, might all be called music videos). Still, if we focus on commercial pop clips, we might note that a clip most often comes out of a collaboration among musicians, industry practitioners, and record personnel. The visual track is designed to sell the song. They're often short and must accomplish many things: highlight the star, draw attention to the lyrics, and underscore the music. To teach listeners what's memorable about a song, the image might emphasize the shift from verse to chorus, or showcase an unusual timbre, rhythm, or melodic contour. The visual track might point to one or two musical features at a time, like a guide. For while music envelops us, visual features more often focus our attention momentarily, especially if they're showcasing the song. So, as opposed to immersion, our attention is divided among music, image, and text. Music videos are capable of eliciting a sense of being "alongside." (Music videos may be said to create a viewer-encounter that resembles a dancer's exploration of herself and others, for example, she might attend to her body in motion, while tracking its unfolding in relation to others.)

This engagement differs from narrative cinema's modes of absorption and immersion. Characteristic terms for music video include "brief," "open," "heterogeneous," "elliptical," "poetic," or "strange."

Music videos often draw us in, but they also keep us at a distance. Enticing a viewer, clips present much to attend to—momentary instances across sound, image, and text—for example, "Oh a snippet of the lyrics," or "bass line!" A viewer may trace a path through the video. If she likes the song and/or the imagery, she can find a moment of attunement, of well-judged comportment. A viewer needs to piece out the music, poetic lyrics, performers, settings, camera movement, and editing, and place them in relation. Gaps among lyrics, music, and image can encourage a viewer to circulate within the video and trace her unfolding experience; she can then judge it alongside the video's unfolding.

But then, music videos also proffer distance. Their materials—sounds, lyrics, and images—tend to be fleeting, and, to some extent, empty. Music can be described as resembling a yearning, or, stated differently, a non-linguistic utterance directed toward something undefined.[22] (Music, it's been claimed, can't point to real objects or express emotions like envy that take targets.[23]) Pop music lyrics are also vague; for instance, who's "my baby?" Music video's images could be said to provide targets for these unnamed desires or drives, but they also step away from them, and the best ones often show us that the task of representing the song is impossible. The Chainsmokers' "Mean What You Say" contains ambiguous lyrics: in a bath of overdubbed synths, "break me off like a cigarette, it's not you, it's me" might suggest the band's relations to its fans, its name, or an introspective moment. Models eat jewelry from platters with chopsticks, and a band member directs a hairdryer at an ice cream cone held by a model's outstretched arm. This last shot recurs, multiplied as a mise-en-abyme of stripes and bathtubs. Another model walks up to the camera, stands still, and then drops several lemons from her clear plastic purse.

But this indeterminacy also offers the viewer several entry points. Clips frequently seem to be on the cusp of getting things started. They show people in a context, and how they might begin to feel and respond. The imagery can help us find a way into a song, and conversely the song can help us connect with the imagery. A listener might embrace Sam Smith's and Demi Lovato's celebratory LGBTQIA+ song, "I'm Ready" (2020), with Smith's airy falsetto alongside Lovato's full-throated belting, and its Broadway-like choruses. From there the imagery can further interpolate a viewer into a less-familiar context—male sprinters wearing flouncy hats and mustaches, and male divers in high heels, women's one-piece bathing suits, and lipstick. Psychologists and neuroscientists have noted that musical performance can create a rapport between performers and groups of listeners. Like pop records, musical performance often aims to build a rapport between performers and groups of listeners—as do pop records: "Music, bodily movement, or any recurrent rhythmic pattern can be something we entrain to."[24]

Several devices can interpolate the viewer:

1. the music: As Suzanne Langer has stated, a song allows us to track the movement of sentiment. A tune isn't feeling per se, but it bears the shape of feeling. When I'm listening to music, I sense emotions, even when attachments seem vague.[25]
2. the charismatic body: watching music video with a performer in motion, I experience kinesthetic expansions and contractions, as well as imagined reachings forward, which can then be projected onto performers (like viewers' projections of figures into Mather's series of filmed moving dots).[26] Through entrainment, a link forms between the viewer, the performers' bodies, the unfolding spaces, and the music's course.
3. the body within a complex, mutating space: tethered to and sometimes at a distance from the performer's body, the viewer navigates through rapid editing, changing speeds, and shifting scales. Though not locked in, she might stay close, so as not to skip an edit, and jump into empty space. If a musical or visual trope comes upon a viewer quickly and the performing body is jerked, the viewer too feels pulled. If the performer's body slows down, one tries to meet it.
4. the camera's assertiveness: music video's cinematic address has become increasingly sophisticated, mirroring narrative cinema's developments.[27] Today, cameras track characters, often through close-ups, partially encircling them, as well as swiftly interpolating them into new contexts.
5. phantasmagoric worlds: with a song number, a film musical's real-time narrative usually bows out. Performers break into dance, and props can become dancing partners, as Jane Feuer points out.[28] In music video, however, both a real world and a heightened, phantasmagoric audiovisual world can exist at once.[29] If a musician draws a sword from a stone, this performer becomes heroic for straddling real-time, lived space as well as heightened audiovisual space.

Not only is the genre's strangeness tied to the effects just described; it also is closely linked to music videos' and pop songs' structure and modes of production.

Music video clips often intimate that music is the ultimate cause of their inner dynamics. This stems from a pop song's production. The pop song is often shaped through nuanced soundscapes and fine details created during recording and postproduction. To set the imagery, directors, musicians, and industry personnel turn to the song as a source to generate ideas. On set, song playback puts performers, costumes, and props in motion, thereby making music the causal agent for visual materials. Perhaps in an effort to sell the song and to encourage repeated listenings and viewings, a network of visual signs also often traces back to the song's authority (to prompt a viewer's care for the song and hopefully buy it). By way of contrast, Hollywood cinema's depictions of causes reside within protagonists who wield a strong sense of agency, and who transcend the obstacles they encounter.

Another odd artifact: the lead performers are often charismatic, but the silent background figures often become uncanny—those stony mannequin-like people, service workers, or robotic figures dancing in formation. Mute or robotic performers, however, often also serve musical purposes. They fill in temporalities and speeds spanning from stillness to rapid motion, which help to illuminate the song's various rhythmic strata (e.g., the star dancing briskly with falling glitter, against the more static backdrop of furniture and background figures).

Music video's imagery also mimics the song's attributes—a clip's figures and settings might form circles or spread out like a brass instrument's bell, for example, and performers turn both toward sonic sources as well as receptively toward viewers. Many videos have an inclusive quality.

Pop songs' emphasis on recurrence also shapes a clip's structure and its ethics. A pop song's sections are segmented and built on recurring verses, choruses, and bridge. Briefer materials like a melodic hook, rhythmic pattern, or timbral quality also repeat in a cyclical fashion. With so much recurrence, music-video imagery tends not to foreground a prototypical narrative. Rather, materials cycle in and out, reappearing with subtly mutated features.

And most music videos lack a prototypical narrative: we can't take the events they depict and arrange them according to their presumed causal relations, chronological order, duration, frequency, and spatial locations.[30] Nonnarrative videos can fail to provide consistency or yield a satisfying resolution because 1) each shot can possess its own truth value that cannot be undermined by another shot's; and 2) each shot has only a vague temporality. Here, the image follows musical unfoldings; for example, a flute motive and/or timbral hook that comes to the fore and resubmerges. Because of these ambiguities concerning veracity and temporality—and because a pop song's form and lyrics can't undermine one another's authority—the viewer is hard-pressed to decide a video's ultimate meaning.

With so few cues to hold on to, we may search surprising places for meaning. If we're feeling poetic, we might even think all parameters act upon one another as affective agents. I locate some meaning in what I call the "audiovisual seam," or the joining of a song and images (seen best, perhaps, while squinting). That seam resembles what Rudolf Arnheim has claimed about the power of the center within paintings. In paintings one finds the microtheme lodged in the frame's middle, perhaps in the ways hands cradle one another, or hold a flower or glass.[31] In George Michael's music video "Father Figure," the inflexible technologies from the 1980s shape "Father Figure"'s song-image seam (1-inch videotape slipped frames, and telecine-shifted color only as uniform blocks). Yet this roughness fits well with George Michael's brusque, impassioned vocals and the story of a working-class cabby's aspirational love for a high-paid model.

With music videos, I've come to argue that sound and image can resemble human relations. When you've known a long-term couple as a single entity for a while, you may identify the couple with a quality tangibly different from one attributed to either partner. The relationship isn't a metaphor, but rather one more basic—an amalgam—that exudes a kind of scent. As Lars von Trier says, sound and image create "such a beautiful cocktail."[32] The flavors emulsify. And like romantic partners, relationships between sound and image may not only blend, but also become disparate. Fraught, image and sound may tussle, with one dominating. Perhaps the media critic resembles a therapist: What's going on with this dynamic? Is this about fluid or unrequited desire?

Music videos can hold ambiguity in suspension. I'd like to claim that some music videos can also thereby teach us an expanded model of persons—videos can represent people as multiple. As neuroscientist Jay McClelland has claimed, our brain might be structured through neural nets enabling some states to come to the fore and others at another moment, all close to the surface.[33] Scientists note that we perceive but a small portion of the world, and make further guesses about it based on Bayesian inferences. In music videos, elements like characters can come forward and back (a phenomenon E. Ann Kaplan characterized as "Madonna 1" and "Madonna 2" in Madonna's 1986 "Papa Don't Preach," and that Steve Shaviro describes as "Leibnizian monads").[34] Our engagements with brief audiovisual material can expand our constructs of persons and lead us to ethical positions. Music videos as microcosms may also mirror the obscure dynamics of post-Taylorist, neoliberalism.

I sense that my previous description makes music video appear complicated and opaque, but I believe if many of us devote attention to the genre, it'll become as facile and transparent for us as narrative cinema. *The Media Swirl*'s part I features close analysis, exploring a variety of brief audiovisual material from music videos and film segments to TikTok clips. Here, often, as an analyst, I've felt bereft, wondering whether I was gathering anything. Later chapters, I think, build steam. Pop music is heterogeneous, and scholars can trace different paths through an audiovisual work.[35] Collaborators here have sometimes helped me gather broader perspectives.[36]

Part II takes on new areas not yet well explored—industry studies, ethics and media, neuroscience, and politics. It opens with a discussion of the industry, because in order to traverse the media swirl, its objects might be made more tangible; to do this we need to grasp how these objects are made. Most likely many of us still hold onto some sort of image of the studio system, but the field is now different: small production houses with their stables of directors and freelance production practitioners produce media across many forms, genres, platforms, and media—from commercials, music videos, films, documentaries, to long-form streaming series—under just-in-time labor conditions. The most successful directors and practitioners have strong audiovisual skills.

The ways the production industry has shifted in the last decade has not been well chronicled. When the internet first took off, many traditional production companies didn't know how to adapt, and those skilled at producing music videos and commercials broached the gaps. These houses could offer rapid turnarounds, because they had stables of versatile directors, in-house production services, and external networks of practitioners in reserve. Often the client companies' talent were athletes or pop music stars who preferred these production houses' directors, because they specialized in pop music's new sounds and visual styles. Often the owners of and producers for these houses were also former music video directors (e.g., David Fincher's Anonymous Content and Michel Gondry's Partizan). Production houses like Caviar and Somesuch have global offices, including Los Angeles, New York, and London, which affords 24/7 turnarounds with tight synchronization.

The Media Swirl devotes time to the makers themselves and their relation to digital technologies, audiovisuality, and production practices today. Over several years I've interviewed many directors who've worked across music videos, commercials, and film, including Jonas Åkerlund, Abteen Bagheri, Colin Tilley, Alan Ferguson, David Fincher, Joseph Kahn, Kevin Kerslake, Marc Klasfeld, Francis Lawrence, Melina Matsoukas, Dave Meyers, Emil Nava, Marcus Nispel, Mark Pellington, and Floria Sigismondi. My sense is that their experiences have helped forge a new style for today's moving media. Other directors I discuss in this collection, like Michael Bay and Baz Luhrmann, are good exemplars of this style. Still others, like David Lynch, Wes Anderson, and Lars von Trier, are analyzed in my coedited volume *Transmedia Directors: Artistry, Industry, and New Audiovisual Aesthetics*.[37] All bring a new sensibility to media-making that's driven by the soundtrack and music video–like aesthetics.

Critics have long pointed to a music video style that has infiltrated filmmaking, but I'm identifying a richer back-and-forth across forms and genres.[38] When making a music video a director learns how to bring the soundtrack to the fore, to place images against the music and lyrics, and to create a sense of flow. Commercials teach a director to be meticulous and concise (e.g., to quickly bring a well-framed close-up front and center). With film (including long-form streaming media), the director practices world-building and ways to suggest a past and a future that stretches beyond the quotidian. Many of these directors also hone their style through branching out into other media forms. Their experiments with virtual reality and gaming encourage them to reconsider viewers' subjective and objective perspectives and sense of embodiment. Participating in social media like Instagram and Twitter facilitates new imaginaries about one's fans and other artists and practitioners, and helps hone one's voice for instant recognition. To cope with the media swirl's frenzied activity and sense of impermanence, many directors also build out to real-world artifacts and contexts: David Lynch has placeware and furniture; Wes Anderson has restaurants; Michael Bay has an amusement-park ride; and Lars von Trier, besides devoting time to cutting diamonds, has a museum exhibit of a house constructed from stacked wax corpses. These gestures may reflect a desire to touch a material shore.

The new transmedial style derives not only from participating in forms and genres; technological and socioeconomic factors matter as well. Digital technologies make sound, image, forms, and genres more malleable and interchangeable.[39] In today's neoliberal, post-Fordist global relations, directors and their collaborators are forced to work ever harder. From my interviews with directors, I've surmised that these artists are a bit more charming and charismatic than us, but—and this might seem surprising—also more anxious. Some worry they're like the last gladiators in the ring, whose techniques will be ripped off by others; others are concerned that if they don't keep producing, their names will be forgotten. (The capacity to see one's own and competitors' techniques dissected on YouTube is surely an intensifier as well.) Many directors are also affiliated with production houses: working in a consortium, too, influences one's identity and style. The most powerful production houses, with their global offices, seek cheap labor (e.g., commercials are often shot in South America or South Africa with local workers and a few practitioners and actors flown in, the latter predominantly European American). Transmedia directors like Jonas Åkerlund and Joseph Kahn are skilled at dropping swiftly in and out of global contexts, as well as negotiating jet lag. (Kahn shared that for many years he only got five hours of sleep, mostly on planes.)[40]

Director Francis Lawrence's *Dior* commercial "Joy" (2018) with actress Jennifer Lawrence foregrounds this new style. Its sense of movement, editing, and line seems drawn from music video (Lawrence started in music videos to then direct the *Hunger Games* and *Red Sparrow*). The sense of a world around actress Jennifer Lawrence may come out of filmmaking. Chatty three-minute docs surrounding the clip establish a sense of an actress's world, a technique borrowed from social media. Lawrence's entrancing close-ups may stem from intimacy gained from the Lawrences' earlier collaborations, but also again from social media's norms. Similar examples appear not just in commercials, but also in feature films. The jewel-like micro-moments of narrative and spectacle in Marvel's *Infinity War* also come out of the media swirl.

Tracking agents, causes, sources, and influences can be hard. Perhaps we'll discover that ad designers are the true drivers of the new style. (*Dior* has a similar ad for Natalie Portman; perhaps the agency has lit on a template.) Perhaps the real exchange is between music video directors who also work in commercials, and more traditionally oriented film directors who dip in and out.

How, after considering audiovisual aesthetics and the industry, do we move to politics, technology, and science? The next step is to pause and take time to look at morals and values. Why might some of us want to participate in today's commons? Whose values resonate or contrast with ours? What can skills with audiovisual interpretation offer? It may be because of global warming, Trumpism, accelerated technological change, discrimination, and extreme income inequality, but I, and perhaps you too, want to make a contribution. Spectacle creates the hope that people can coordinate around a common goal. Knowing more about one's commitments in relation to others can facilitate future alliances. Colleagues and I have debated whether art can serve moral instruction.[41] My intuition is that the sum of interactions with media objects, even though they often reinscribe ideology, also illuminates the contingencies of others' lives, and this can lead us to a greater investment in others (though algorithms for YouTube and TikTok can also now herd us into affective and political cul-de-sacs). These claims are hard to measure. But on this, however, my interlocutors and I agree. Stating claims and rationales can be beneficial. *The Media Swirl* seeks to place claims and rational arguments in relation to the aesthetics of embodied, affective media. This should be a persuasive mode, for such an approach enlists somatic, affective, and cognitive networks of the brain and body. I adopt this tack most directly in chapter 17, on Beyoncé's oeuvre, turning to Kimberle Crenshaw, Marx, and Rawls.

In this book I analyze objects that could be considered progressive and/or reactionary, and I aim to withhold judgment until I've completed an analysis. Even after, I like to remain open to the work. I hope this is a model for treating persons—that we can reach out to those with beliefs and orientations different from our own (see chapters 3, 7, 10, and 18).

It's probably easier to be receptive to a media object than a family member or friend, but this potential for relationships still holds. As an example of how we might remain open to a work's meaning, we might look back historically and consider what several feel is problematic about the 1930s screwball comedies that Cavell analyzes: these films' celebration of the rich. But while Cavell acknowledged this problem, he also noted that the film characters' freedom from financial worries allowed them to explore wider modes of possibility with one another, especially in terms of roles as a couple, and their discoveries (new forms of companionate marriage) might be useful for many.[42] Though I would prefer working-class characters, I then saw something new—the characters' daftness and dream-like contexts could create an opening for imaginative roleplay. Here, for me, entertainment and culture could be placed in relation. When I taught in the Midwest (farm country), my students felt discomfort with these films, but I was surprised to find that ones like Howard Hawks's *Bringing Up Baby* (1938) lent an opportunity to explore citizens' roles.

In the first half of this book, we can begin with a question that's highly contested in America—the roles of contingency and free will, and, as I will show, neuroscience can help us here. Through my own introspection, I've adopted a perspective: that health, meaningful work that's valued by others, sympathy from and with the community, respect in one's family, location, and other such goods, help form a good life. These goods can be contingent and hard to secure. While I desire more—youth, health, excitement, recognition, community—and a restlessness accompanies me, as it does for others under neoliberalism—I also, however, experience gratitude for the ways my life has unfolded lately.[43] Having experienced precarity and contingency, it's hard for me not to grieve that I didn't have more of these goods earlier, to hope that this life's passage will continue, and to wish for and to imagine the possibility of everyone having good lives.

Just as I aim to imagine other lives in media, I think I can picture how other citizens in the United States might have different commitments. I've taught in red states, and worked closely with community members whose worldviews diverge from mine. If I had grown up in a rural area with fewer economic possibilities—say if I owned a hardware store or a beauty salon, and I imagined that most of what I created came from my astute choices and labor (which others failed to deploy), and most of the goods and services arrived from places that felt remote to me—I might experience the world differently. What would it mean to have that context, and to say we are all connected, that we might want everyone to have good lives, and that freedom from economic precarity is a good first step?

I spend time with media and neuroscience here because I think these can help us form a better democracy. Neuroscience shows us that experience is inscribed both on the body and brain. Forms of knowledge are concrete and not easily transferrable (e.g., think of the difference between knowing H_2O as a concept and as water running through fingers). Each person must have her own embodied experiences to know plentitude, precarity, and contingency. Our selves are multiple and come to the surface based on the scripts we've been asked to play. It's hard for me to share with friends and coworkers in red states what different lives might look like. But conversation, as well as making and participating with media, can help establish some common ground.

How can media help us find common ground? Many scholars believe that when we participate in media, we experience traces of others—their voices, gestures, whiffs of thought and mood. As we move through a work, we get a taste of others' experiences and modes of being.[44] Again, Cavell claimed we enjoy film because we can watch the world without feeling a pressure to intervene. This gives us greater freedom to contemplate and more deeply experience events unfolding before us, because we won't be called upon to act. Neuroscientists studying the brain's processing have shown that when we participate in media, we simulate external occurrences through brain modules devoted to theories of mind. These processes are even located within specific brain cells, identified as "mirror cells." As Uri Hasson has shown, we sync ourselves to phenomena.[45]

Disclosing something personal about me, I find neuroscience valuable because several family members were psychologists, and we shared the belief that one's unconscious desires to harm oneself and one's relationships. Neuroscience isn't uniform, but I find freeing Jay McClelland's notion that neural nets enable some states to come to the fore and others at another moment, all bubbling below the surface.[46] One's biology and context also shapes who we are. Scientists note that we perceive but a small portion of the world, and make further guesses about it based on Bayesian inferences. They acknowledge the roles of bias and faulty thinking. Cognitive and affective processes are partly sociocultural.

It's been demonstrated that in the stream of cognitive processing, as a viewer traces a path through a media object, ideology steps in. Magnetic resonance imaging studies have shown that both music and moving media encourage a participant's mental constructs, eliciting maps linked to one's own and/or imagined others' experiences. Empathy, once initiated, can be blocked, however, particularly if the participant perceives that the representations belong to an "outsider" group.[47] If a participant watches someone experiencing poverty, for example, and her model is that an individual's choices are self-made and the poor will always be with us, she may not experience care for the other. A viewer who perceives life as contingent, on the other hand, may want to help. The latter's belief system is more in accordance with one I'm affirming—while some self-made Horatio Alger types might be rewarded for their efforts to some extent—this stressful mode of living should not be required. While free will plays a role, gifts and inheritances can play even larger ones. Utopia might be imagined as everyone having good lives.

Here are seven points for envisioning a way forward, but they needn't be yours. Perhaps they may help clarify your commitments.

- The United States is a wealthy country. We have the world's best soil, other rich natural resources, and impressive human capital.
- We're shaped by inheritances and gifts. Inheritances include biological traits, which are unique to each of us; gifts include the contexts in which we flourish or don't.
- Neuroscientists will probably continue to confirm that free will plays some role, but not as much as we currently believe it does.
- We're highly connected and social. No one succeeds or fails apart from the rest of us.

- Though some truths remain uncertain, we can still feel grateful that we're here. A sense of theistic or nontheistic gratitude can lead to a commitment to others.
- Our commitment could be to everyone having good lives.
- The grounds for ensuring this includes freedom from precarity: access to healthcare, education, economic security, respect, and community.

After reflecting on morals and ethics in relation to media, aesthetics, and the state of media practice, how do we get to politics, science, and technology? We just jump. Seriously—we step across. Even our skills at close readings can be useful for looking at content in other disciplines. (And other disciplines can provide new perspectives on our own as well; note chapters 15 and 16.) While there's much to discuss—for example, if we engage with psychometrics, are we validating such practices? What if we admire a media object and know it's objectionable?—we might engage. The costs of not doing so seem too high.

The second half of the book includes forays I hope others will also pursue. I'll provide considerations of psychometrics, facial recognition, and cybersurveillance trailers, as well as close readings of political and news advertising. Alongside this book, my coedited collection *Cybermedia: Explorations in Science, Sound, and Vision* aims to blend media studies with science.[48] *Cybermedia*'s focus comes out of a perspective many humanities scholars share—that media reflects contemporary society's fears, hopes, fantasies, memories, and regrets. These media also suggest how we might orient ourselves in relation to shifting technological and economic forces. Many frames (e.g., from sci-fi and blockbusters) are constructed through a sketchy knowledge of science. Work that links facts with embodied experience, especially experiences of entertainment, can enable a richer understanding of how our worldviews materialize. New connections can become visible. We might then be better able to address the issues we're facing, including climate change, repressive social structures, and responsibilities of the self and community.

Recent neuroscience research provides a backdrop for *The Media Swirl*. Justin Gardner argues that contexts shape our decision-making. Sometimes, we're almost like Bayesian optimists (using a predetermined algorithm that weights previous experiences in relation to a current likelihood); in others we use cruder heuristic reasoning, which can draw on only part of the data, including samples or averages.[49] This makes evolutionary sense. This book's first half includes close readings. Readers may wonder, "Do

I want to know so much about the *Transformers* movies?" Perhaps. For when we quickly and casually encounter a media object, we may know it only through a rough schema. With a slower, more careful reading that attends to multiple sensory sources, and the ways our affective responses shift, we can produce richer descriptions that help us identify a work's progressive and reactionary features, and grasp how it relates to genre, platform, and medium. Several chapters in *The Media Swirl* explore this kind of gap between a rough summary and moment-by-moment experience, such as "Paparazzi," "Tints," and *Transformers*.

Brian Knutson notes that these models should account for emotion, which is variable and contingent.[50] I wish to know whether media literacy can change how we understand media objects, especially strongly politically partisan ones. While neuroscientists can't yet provide these rich mathematical equations, they should be able to do so soon."

Let me turn briefly again to media's dark side, a discussion of how capitalism, politics, and entertainment connect. I also want to consider where media and society might go from here.

My fellow scholar Steve Shaviro and I have been trying to track audiovisual aesthetics and media for a while.[51] Shaviro finds some of the best limit cases, like obscure music videos (with view-counts in the thousands rather than millions) that employ recent pre- and postproduction technologies and that function as riddles, or present something cognitively difficult. Considering his clips gives a picture of what the media landscape will look like and how we can respond. His analysis of Tkay Maidza's "Where Is My Mind? (Pixies Cover)" discusses the way this clip pulls viewers in too many directions to biologically assimilate. Media objects often reflect our moment.[52] Examples like "Where Is My Mind?" connect to the lived sense that there are too many concurrent yet unchartable processes shaping our lives, over which we have little control. We can neither adequately track these threads nor place them in relation to one another. Unproductive but relatable responses might include anxiety, depersonalization, and passivity.

Our moment's unfolding processes feel overwhelming, as this partial list of examples suggests:

1. Global climate change and the planet's degradation, which occur at different rates.
2. The pandemic, with variants multiplying, against a race for an easily disseminated vaccine, with the Global North and South protected unequally.

3   Global finance, run by futures trading and algorithms that move faster than human analysis.
4   Artificial intelligence, with its neural nets and algorithms that reweight their flows.
5   Advances in technological and scientific techniques, including CRISPR, hybrid chimerical creatures, prosthetic brain interfaces, and algorithmically based surveillance.
6   Corporations and the rich seizing power through political influence and dark money to corrode communities.
7   The recurrence of racism, which returns us to an initial moment of theft.
8   Entertainment, disseminated in many ways (large streaming services and smaller single-tiered websites, emerging celebrities, auxiliary mouthpieces), and that elicits staggered scales of attention, and in many forms (from a ten-hour series like *The Underground Railroad* to brief media like TikTok videos and Instagram posts).

Entertainment flows can overlap and influence each other through contagion. Artists, entrepreneurs, scientists, politicians, performers, and musicians cross these landscapes, perturbing them with scandals and long chains of associations. It can feel as if capitalism subsumes all.[53] This is what Lauren Berlant calls living without a ballast.[54] It can leave one feeling powerless, as if one's contribution would make little difference, even though we can watch players as spheres of influence or nodes across all these different scales. Where will we find ourselves? Many experience a sense of precarity. Especially after several years of the COVID-19 pandemic, one can feel isolated and adrift.

The level of interpenetration between politics and audiovisual styles and genres can feel dizzying. Let me share a few manifestations (or symptoms) of the interpenetration of politics and entertainment in 2021.

When I watched the Capitol insurgency of January 6, I was surprised by how many moments felt like art cinema. I couldn't quite believe it. I thought I was dreaming—it was often so audiovisually dramatic (will we ever know how much of it was rehearsed and staged?). Many critics cited Sergei Eisenstein's *Battleship Potemkin* (1925). I continued in this vein, drawing connections between the crowds from Fritz Lang's *Fury* (1936) and the mad second bananas from F. W. Murnau's *Nosferatu* (1922) and James Whale's *Frankenstein* (1931)—they look like the insurgents rifling through papers. The insurrectionists scrambling over and under the seats in the Senate chamber reminded me of the slanderous scenes of Black legislators in D. W. Griffith's *Birth of a Nation* (1915), or the vagabonds squatting in a mansion from Luis Buñuel's *Viridiana* (1961). The screening of video documentation (comprised primarily out of cellphone footage) in the House hearings drew from classic film aesthetics, as David Bordwell has pointed out.[55] Montage carried spots of blood across shots toward moments of culmination. The Lincoln Project, too, worked evocatively, posting YouTube clips akin to music videos. Later, Joe Biden's inauguration was derivative of music video. Katy Perry's performance of "Fireworks" before the Lincoln Memorial might take pop fans back to her original music video, directed by Dave Meyers. Demi Lovato's "Brand New Day" showcased the star against a backdrop of circular panoramic screens that drew heavily on aesthetics that had been developed in music videos produced during the pandemic.

But I suspect that no single media object reflects all these interlocking structures, influences, and pressures: shifts distribute unequally across a landscape, as Shane Denson has noted.[56] Nevertheless, I think we'll see more of what Denson describes as discorrelated media: content produced by digital cameras and algorithmic image-processing technologies that is no longer "calibrated to our embodied senses."[57]

Two major forces driving change include computer-based technologies like digital workstations, and new industrial organizations such as the collaboration of major online streaming services with boutique production houses that maintain inhouse stables of directors and practitioners who are facile with audiovisually intensified forms (including commercials, music videos, documentaries, and long dramatic streaming series).[58] But these processes have been in play for some time. So while I can't promise a new frame can be quickly gleaned from this book, I hope it will help readers develop interpretive skills, reconsider political engagements, and become inspired to further the discipline. In sum, music video, YouTube, and audiovisual aesthetics seem to have infiltrated almost everything (consider glitch-based TikToks, though objects less affected by these centrifugal forces include the film *Nomadland* from 2020, with its echoes of Terrence Malick). In general objects and events seem more porous, with materials creating a swirl, or what John Landreville describes as a slurry, with glancing or tenuous relations between nodes that are continually reformed.[59] And see my note on Lil Nas X, the film *Call Me By Your Name*, and Armie Hammer, which discusses moments so volatile and fleeting they might remain out of the body text. The note shows how scholars can be driven to conniptions in response to glance aesthetics.[60]

The Media Swirl attempts to cover a lot—and I'm hoping fellow scholars will continue to explore the following:

1. New methods for analyzing audiovisual content.
2. A review of today's audiovisual theory and ways to deepen and extend it.
3. A discussion of today's entertainment media and the ways they connect to ideology and socioeconomic questions.
4. A picture of today's entertainment industries, accompanied by interviews with practitioners.
5. Close readings of today's transmedia auteurs and their work.
6. Engagement with reactionary and progressive media objects.
7. Music video's history in relation to other forms, including postclassical cinema.
8. Explorations of particular genres (e.g., the costume-genre mashup, TikTok) in all their uniqueness.
9. A cross-section of objects in the media swirl, from the most grand and intensified to the smallest and most intimate.
10. An exploration of how today's media genres have interpenetrated one another.
11. A consideration of "high" and "low" media.
12. A foray into new fields, including neuroscience, big data, and collaborative authorship as they inform audiovisual aesthetics.
13. A call for a field of audiovisual studies that stretches beyond the film soundtrack, especially toward brief media.
14. An engagement with progressive politics, and a possible path for getting there from entertainment media.

I've had the good fortune where I teach to cross-disciplines, and take courses in philosophy, neuroscience, computer science, and symbolic systems. Nevertheless, I'm aware of my dilettantism, and I'm sure many stakeholders will be roughed up by it. But *The Media Swirl* argues that today musical spectacles are all around us, and worth our engagement. I think it's worthwhile to try to be in touch with as much of a larger picture as possible, and then participate in what we can accomplish (I wish we could coordinate especially around global warming and issues of socioeconomic justice). It's easy to feel overwhelmed—that's what the swirl is all about. But I also embrace Cornel West's reminder that forces are powerful, and the only way for survival may be forward.[61]

I Post-Classical Cinema at the Limit

1

Partying in *The Great Gatsby*: Baz Luhrmann's Audiovisual Sublime

THE GREAT GATSBY'S (2013) "arcadian" party sequence counts as one of the most opulent, densely articulated, and extravagant in film history.[1] On its release critics noted its "frenetic beauty," "orgasmic pitch," and "Vincente Minnelli–style suavity with controlled vertigo."[2] Décor, costuming, sound, movement, and color come to the fore because the sequence's spatial layout cannot be determined. The mélanged soundtrack refuses to grant the viewer a sense of ground: Who is performing and who is not? To which period and community does this music speak? Why this snippet against that? Sound-sources and imagined locations seem to cross and overlap in elaborate vectors. Against a finely wrought sonic barrage, densely articulated visual details make every instant potentially riveting: within swarming crowds, every extra's head-turn and feather boa seem carefully considered. Fairy-tale tableaux of hired performers merge with party guests who mimic these tableaux. Ornaments, from paper birds to balloons, are thrown up as complicating scrims. A sense of musicality is carefully established: background performers pop up or flare their arms in response to musical cues, and the speed of moving bodies showcases the music. But even within the spectacle, story both recedes and advances: the crowd's engagement builds to a moment of class solidarity, but moneyed patriarchy (Gatsby) is offered as a substitute. Meanwhile, Black performers and music appear to be prized but linked to an underclass.[3] Expertly realized by an arsenal of technicians, the scene's excessive display speaks to today's neoliberal order; its extravagant rhetoric serves as a useful reminder of our unfortunate gilded age (fig. 1.1).[4]

Indeed, *Gatsby*'s director, Baz Luhrmann, and others like him, are arguably suited to our current moment of fluid global capital and post-Fordist,

1.1 Spectacular effects.

neo-liberal, just-in-time labor.[5] Luhrmann is one of several emerging impresarios: artists with multiple skill sets, the charisma to engage talented fellow practitioners, an ability to work across platforms and markets, and a style that carries across media. He has worked in sound production, and with dance, opera, commercials, music videos, department store windows, and more. His aesthetic approach is both an expression and an excavation of the multifarious, highly commercialized mediascape that plays host to these formats and genres.

Some close analysis considers musical-film numbers in which digital technologies shape both sound *and* image.[6] None considers the kind of opulent aesthetics Luhrmann flaunts. I will show the ways a multitude of techniques in concert present an unassimilable "too-muchness," even *jouissance*—an overload of pleasure and pain to the point of unbearability. Sensations offered to viewers are both so subtle and fleeting that they sneak in beneath the attentional threshold, and so overwhelming and massive that they stretch beyond it.

Musical spectacles have long embodied a kind of surplus that Richard Dyer argues is comprised of abundance, energy, play, intensity, excitement, transparency, clarity, community, and immediacy (the *Gatsby* party sequence possesses these features too, with clarity and transparency delegated to the lead characters).[7] We might trace the party sequence's lineage from the Tiller Girls and Busby Berkeley through Minnelli, Fosse, and Bollywood. The sheer excess of this sequence contends with these and others. Other postclassical films, musical though not belonging within "the musical," share some of this scene's aesthetics: the highway battle in Michael Bay's *Transformers: Age of Extinction* (2014); the quaaludes-party scene in Martin Scorsese's *Wolf of Wall Street* (2014); and the Mexico City sequence in Sam Mendes's *Spectre* (2015). But these examples lack the density of unfolding material and the integration of musical cues; they're not really that close.[8]

The scene's kaleidoscopic, overwhelming aesthetics are enabled by Luhrmann's concerted honing of his "red curtain style" and his longstanding collaborations with his wife Katherine Martin on set and costume design, and friends Craig Pearce and Anton Monsted for scriptwriting and soundtrack design.[9]

The Great Gatsby's development was atypically synergetic. Martin and the other crafts departments began design while the script was being written, and the soundtrack was built before the image. Just as crucially, the heavy use of pre-vis (pre-visualization), 3D, and compositing technologies enabled what has been called machinic vision. As Steen Christiansen has said: Instead of a cinema based on human perceptual structures, we now have a "post" cinema based on nonhuman perceptual structures. Motion capture cameras, virtual cameras, and synth cameras all produce images that go beyond the human sensorium and reconfigure it in the same process.[10] This scene is much more than a first- or even a twentieth-time viewer can absorb. Its difficulties offer readers a challenge—if we can analyze *The Great Gatsby's* party scene, we can grasp many other texts.

The film's strategies for what Mark Wolf has called "world-building" also contribute to the scene's overwhelming, sublime aesthetics.[11] Its transmedial approach draws from many external sources and reconfigures them. Luhrmann fastidiously adapted Fitzgerald's book, for example, using the original dialogue for Nick Carraway's introduction to Jay Gatsby at that first extravagant party in Gatsby's mansion. Luhrmann and his team referenced jazz-era sound recordings, films, and photographs as well as drawing on academics and the general public (the latter through a website that solicited feedback and comments). Through these contributions Luhrmann was able to create a responsive historical document. But he was just as willing to distort—the costumes have been contemporized, and hip-hop and EDM have been mashed up with jazz. Careful reproduction along with the willingness to displace contributes to the scene's disorienting effects.

Analyzing this scene provides secondary gains: an opportunity to extend the growing field of audiovisual relations, from writings on commercials, music videos, television title-sequences, and narrative-film soundtracks, to the more purely spectacular. The *Gatsby* sequence seems unique, but it may augur a new style. Some of my approaches and methods—both parametric and temporal, developed for music video, postclassical cinema, and YouTube analysis—can be applied to this scene, but not all. I've claimed that music video's image aims to draw our attention to aspects of a song: "Here's what's special about a rhythmic detail, a timbre, a hook." Now it feels as if to analyze music video is to harvest low-hanging fruit.[12]

Unlike with music video, Luhrmann's sequence aims for barrage and bedazzlement. It buries its processes and techniques, especially those meant to establish audiovisual relations. Still, a parametrically based approach lends insight. I will spend the bulk of this chapter describing the ways nineteen techniques pull the viewer affectively and proprioceptively in different directions. Toward the chapter's end I'll aim to place these techniques in relation to each other with a particular attention to moments when things come forward temporally, but I encourage readers, as they move through the chapter, to try to do so as well. How much weight does a particular technique carry at a particular moment? I am often unsure; for me, finding the structure for the party sequence has often felt like being the security person watching the X-rays of suitcases go by. It can be difficult to find patterns. Many features contribute simultaneously to a texture that can only be understood in retrospect, if ever. Perhaps technologies like eye-tracking and facial recognition, GSR (galvanic skin response measures), fMRI (functional magnetic resonance imaging) and EEG (electroencephalography), for both new and repeat viewers, might tell us something. But remove one or more of these nineteen techniques and my guess is we would not have our effect. We would have something blunter, more like a scene directed by Michael Bay, Peter Jackson, or Martin Scorsese. We would lose that overwhelming "wow" that fixates us, for ten long minutes, like a deer in headlights.

On the Surface: Spectacular Overload

Gatsby's first party sequence showcases a dazzling variety of ornamentation: snowflake-speckled orbs, enormous white balloons, pastel-colored confetti, metallic streamers and drizzling glitter, paper birds, girls on swings and girls pouring wine, fans of water and fans of feathers, ostentatiously dressed faux-sailors and navigators, lovers and revelers peering out of windows and archways ornamented with ivy, fully dressed partiers diving into pools with inflatable zebras, a few older women, virtually no Black males, and, one notes, too many white, elderly, privileged men—with young ladies to assist them. In the moments when these amass, viewers-experiencers may perceive a blurring of vision (fig. 1.2).

1.2 Spectacular overload.

The Monumental, the Miniature, and the Stochastic

This scene foregrounds three deformations of classical spatial relations: 1) some of the background's details resemble the miniaturized tableaux of Fabergé eggs; 2) large chunks of architecture and human forms loom in the foreground; and 3) between the large and the small, the overall swirl of paper and confetti, streamers and miniature cut-out butterflies, along with multitudes of people, pushes the scene toward the stochastic.[13] The viewer cannot shift perspectives quickly enough, subsequently experiencing a sense of aural and visual fixation as well as misdirection.

A Prismatic Landscape

The depiction of Gatsby's chateau contributes to a sensation of kaleidoscopic overload. "It's like an amusement park," says Nick, "wow." The mansion's long rectangular ballroom abuts an impossibly long entrance hallway; one of the ballroom's lengthy sides connects to this main entrance and the other provides an exit to the bay. Once inside, it seems we are led straight back—past the winged and pedestalled woman—to the organist. In truth we veer sharply right. Before we can orient ourselves, we cut quickly to three performers—a Cab Calloway–like band leader and twin dancers—whom we might assume are performing in the hall. But here we've somehow been transported outside the home onto a lower patio. Suddenly we're ferried down again, to a patio with a pool ringed by an orchestra, and the pool's center, a small musical ensemble that inexplicably vanishes. From there a vertiginous drop leads to the bay. Next, up again, to a second-story library. The camera shifts unpredictably among five tiers. The party's terrain does not become clear until nearly dawn, when the servants, Nick, and Gatsby are left to survey the evening's wreckage.[14]

Both steadying and disorienting the viewer, the camera cuts away repeatedly and briefly to a new location before we shift to it. During Nick's name-checking of the grand hall, two gossip columnists dance on the pool's star-patterned mosaic, but not yet having seen the pool, we cannot get our bearings. Some of Nick's and Jordan's trajectories are also confusing. The two walk to the patio and then decide to search for Gatsby. Suddenly they are two floors up, with "Owl Eyes" in the library, and then three flights down at the pool. Transported? Absolutely.[15]

Many side patios and antechambers cannot be placed in clear spatial relation. A steadying moment seems to appear at the midpoint, when the camera makes one rapid downward tilt, but the scene's content is too ornate. The four flights of Gatsby's chateau appear veiled behind lace and nets comprised of various-sized butterflies, spangles, miniature lights, larger orbs, and spider web–like tree branches—a fairy-tale-like Amazonian jungle with its own produce, plants and birds, densely entwined.[16] And how many revelers are in attendance? A "jelly beans in a jar" approximation might suffice, but the jar's size cannot be determined (fig. 1.3).

Still, by the scene's end, formal divisions based on stylistic approach and location might be determined. These work in contradictory ways based on a viewer's attention.

Reading 1: Starting from the clip's end and reading backward, *Gatsby*'s bay is a site of drowning, desire, and loss. The poolside provides possibili-

1.3 The mansion: layout cannot be determined until the scene's end.

ties for decadence and sexuality. The performance patio and great hall are a space for community and engagement. The high library stands for social climbing, knowledge, and patriarchy.

Reading 2: An audience-member might notice the ways sections have themes and their abutments generate a frisson. The drive to the mansion and the revelers tumbling out of cars could be said to be like a Warner Brothers cartoon; the name-checking of revelers in the grand hall has a nineteenth-century feel, with small-town folk viewed through stereoscopes; the first patio is more modern (the Cab Calloway ensemble), and the instant when Jordan and Nick first meet is more urban still (note the Noel Coward references); the patio below suggests old money and East Coast primness (a kind of display that might steal Jordan away). The pool is kaleidoscopic and decadent.[17] This sequence resembles director George Cukor's famous parties, when, after the industry brass had headed home, the gay and socially progressive guests would get drunk in his pool. The scene's closing brings lead actors and crowds into more ordered formations.

Audiovisual Trajectories (Large-Scale)

The camera and soundtrack take paths that reassure and disorient us. At the scene's opening the camera tracks behind cars, and over a ring of trees. A crescendo of organ, drums, and trumpets speeds past them until it is overwhelmed by the jazzy wail of a single trumpet. A similar climb closes the scene: we make our way up a tremendous flight of stairs, to Gatsby's introduction of "I'm Gatsby," Gershwin's *Rhapsody in Blue,* and a trumpet's split note. We also swoop up to the dubious descendant of Beethoven, organist Ewing Klipspringer, and to our sudden meeting of Owl Eyes on top of a ladder in the upstairs library. There's Jordan's and Nick's climb to the grand hall's high balcony, and dancer Gloria Gray's luminous entrance established more aurally than visually.[18] Audiovisual drops feel even more vertiginous (e.g., alongside the crane shots and overheads of the pool).

Splintered Narratives

Narrative unfolds within the spectacle, realized primarily as struggles for status.[19] Nick Carraway, the only reveler to receive an invitation, *must* find Gatsby: "Why me?" he wonders, as he searches among the crowds. Jordan materializes as a potential lover, and she and Nick flirt, but then she's stolen quickly by a rich man. Perhaps Nick's bruised ego can be salvaged if he deciphers the party's mysteries. How is it that, like the enchanted monster from "Beauty and the Beast," Gatsby has not been seen by anyone, and everyone from all of New York can party every weekend at his home, in his absence? As Nick watches, the partygoers' dance unfolds with a radical potential for social transformation—a new classless solidarity. How might the rapscallions and ne'er-do-wells introduced at the scene's opening help facilitate this transmutation? Who is "Owl Eyes," lurking in Gatsby's library and inciting Jordan and Nick to ever more Scooby-Doo-like investigations? After Jordan has been stolen away, and the crowd's moment passes, is Gatsby the paternalistic figure who will bind Nick's wounds?

And what about other narrative trajectories—those white bankers and their Black mistresses? The clutch of gay men gathered by the pool? The gamblers, senators, and executives who might make secret deals that entangle everyone, or the vice squad that might shut everything down? Will all become distracted by the faux movie stars? Multiple branching narratives can disorient a viewer. Is she attending to the best one?

A Postmodern Soundtrack

The soundtrack contributes additional layers of phrasing, the strongest pulling toward four orgasmic explosions: 1) "Bang!" and the whiteout of the chandelier; 2) "Shot my baby, bang!" and the camera's rocketing over East Egg's peninsula; 3) Fergie's "A Little Party Never Hurt Nobody," and bursting streamers over at the pool; and 4) Gatsby's, "I'm Gatsby" and the trumpeter's split note.

Complicating the image, *Gatsby*'s soundtrack suggests a celebration of the potential power of the masses, the hope for democracy and community. Many musical styles coexist—baroque, classical, EDM, rap, pop, honky-tonk, Dixieland, modern jazz. Though cuts between musical segments are often sharpened and jarring (an "extra" 2/4 measure appears unpredictably),[20] added sonic details and heightened audiovisual relations grant the segments equal play. The descending melodic line into Fergie's "A Little Party Never Killed Nobody" suggests a search for a habitus, where everyone might participate; the split note before *Rhapsody in Blue* takes away some of its overblown grandiosity; the lowered volume of the Dixieland music ameliorates the showy displays of wealth on the patio; "A Little Party Never Killed Nobody"'s hard four-on-the-floor beat might overwhelm listeners, but the arrangement breaks down in the library scene.

Musical segments also share material, creating a sense of conviviality. The organ cheerily takes up a countermelody against Nicole Scherzinger's tune "Bang, Shot My Baby," and the Dixieland clarinet and trumpet continue to riff on it. The soundtrack's musical samples foreground odd, misplaced details that create an additional charge; when one abuts another, the lack of clear genre boundaries adds an edge. Alongside the famous Bach toccata in D minor that heralds our entrance to Gatsby's chateau, ululations appear uncharacteristically in the mix. Scherzinger's "Bang" sample devolves into a nervous, reiterating "ang," as if both the singer and the sample had become infected. Several musical cues accompanying the grand hall's notorious guests belong to the carnival, and one becomes so parodic it sounds like a hurdy-gurdy.

The soundtrack is haunted by the specter of automation. Especially at section endings, a sample speeds up and repeats, as if jammed in a mechanical device (Scherzinger's "bang, bang, bang" vocal fragments before the camera takes flight over East Egg; or the sudden "whir-whir-whir" as flapper Gloria Gray takes center stage). We are not watching a party scene, but rather a mechanical phantasmagoria.

Musical cues can also reassure the viewer: in the grand hall, generic associations with musical cues inform relations between notorious guests. With music, Klipspringer becomes more clearly ridiculous; boss Walter Chase seems more comical; the heiresses comparing inheritances are cunning and modern; the high school dropouts and morality protectors become more quaint and absurd.

Viewers experience a kind of hide-and-seek with the mysterious soundtrack as they 1) see and hear performers, 2) hear music without seeing performers, and 3) see performers playing instruments not on the soundtrack. Music often leapfrogs the performers, reaching us from distant locations. Musical cues also collide in midair, as if *Gatsby*'s sonic space might need a sonic air-traffic controller: the poolside performing group soars over Cab Calloway's music to reach the organist in the grand hall, for example, while we remain on the patio.

The visible and audible trumpeters on the patio provide the clearest sense of stability (their music connects with the scene's opening blare, as we swoop up to Gatsby's chateau, and later to Gatsby's self-introduction and Gershwin's *Rhapsody in Blue*). The organist Klipspringer might seem like our guide, but his uncanny goofiness discredits him. (Music arrives from outside his aural peripheries—the patios—and his riffing feels beyond the performerly virtuosic; he thereby seems cartoonish. Nondiegetic drums pound underneath him.)[21]

The images of musicians who perform but lack sound are disorienting: a flutist, banjoist, and harpist, and the small ensemble with a handsome singer, who appear in the pool's center, to then quickly vanish. Also ghostly are the musicians we do not see—a pianist on an out-of-tune bar piano and a ukuleleist—but especially the female divas. (Where might Scherzinger and Fergie perform? Large mics in front of the Cab Calloway figure and small ensemble's bandleader suggest that sounds carry, but we never discover where they go.) Though we might assume that Fergie's "A Little Party Never Killed Nobody" is a live event, like the EDM music playing by the driveway and the upstairs library, it has no verifiable source.

The mash-up of musical materials may contribute to the viewer's sense of being under barrage; the indeterminate sourcings of sound can also elicit a viewer's anxiety that she's attending to the wrong events.

Emphatic, Sing-Song Dialogue

Dialogue is repetitive, alliterative, and phrased to resemble song lyrics embedded within a music video.[22] Over time, dialogue winnows to "I'm Gatsby." Our quest to know Gatsby provides a recurring goal, but as John Belton has noted, Nick's first voice-over resembles the news reporter's description of *Citizen Kane*'s Xanadu. We seek a man who lacks a center.[23]

Nick says of the crowd, "Billionaire playboy publishers, and their blond nurses . . . Heiresses comparing inheritances . . . My boss, Walter Chase, losing money at the roulette tables."

Later, revelers proclaim: "He was a German spy during the war . . . No, no, no, no. He's the Kaiser's assassin . . . I heard he killed a man once."

Owl Eyes muses: "You won't find him . . . ! This house and everything in it, are all part of an elaborate disguise. But Mr. Gatsby doesn't exist."

Then Nick says, "They say he's third cousin to the Kaiser and second cousin to the devil," and Gatsby replies, "I'm afraid I'm not a very good host, old sport . . . I'm Gatsby."

Daubed Color

The scene's color arc, described schematically, includes a background of teal blue and blueish green, an early instance of a very large blot of bright, yellowy orange, dabs of magenta purple with pink, crossing into the scene's end with a darker, congealed blood-red (also featured a bit in the beginning). White sets off sections and establishes phrasing. At the scene's end, the color palette reduces to white and gold with a spot of blue. As such, the scene moves from energy to quietude. Dabs of color create flow and visual interest. The oomph of the tracking shot with its corresponding line of millionaire trust-fund women with their orange martini glasses and fans projects because suddenly, at the previous shot's end, a woman with a fantastical, ornate Egyptian headdress in bright orange momentarily steps into view. The late-evening varied reds around the pool are also striking. Suddenly an obese woman in a deep red bathing suit and cap, a more brilliant and brighter red-dressed couple on a raft, and the performers' dark red masonic hats appear. Often color patches seem out of reach, perhaps encouraging the viewer to strain past where she is (while the green silk wallet a woman presses to her breast as she gazes at Gatsby seems close, the iridescent green dancing on the bay's surface is much further away—Gatsby's green light). It takes a lot of blue, white, silver, and gold to close the scene and the color arc's trajectory. Overall, color helps tell time (from a night that is young to one that is past). Color dabs also create a sense of futurity; the viewer's eye reaches out to grasp them.

Cinematographic Rhythm

The multiangled shots are rapidly edited. As the seemingly weightless camera drifts while it subtly reframes, it seems slightly dazed. But when striking musical material comes forward (the bass line against the appearance of heiresses, or the horns filling in the arrangement of Fergie's "A Little Party Never Hurt Nobody"), the camera suddenly snaps to, tugging a bit harder and showboating with a tracking or moving crane shot. This is what I've called mixing board aesthetics, a stylistic approach common in music video and much postclassical film. Here audiovisual elements unpredictably come to the fore and recede, suddenly claiming a viewer's attention, much as a record producer brings elements forward and back by raising and lowering faders at the audio mixing board.[24] The uncertainty of unfolding events can itself elicit a viewer's engagement with both the image and the soundtrack.

Emergent Tableaux

One of the party sequence's most striking features, the deployment of crowds, can be understood more deeply through two overlapping, nonsimultaneous perspectives: as collections grouped into larger crowds, smaller groups of people, pairs, and individuals; and as tableaux and the people around them. Here I define a tableau as an allegorical and/

or picturesque disposition of people and objects. These tableaux momentarily crystallize and then disappear. Let me discuss tableaux first.

Fairy-tale tableaux are staged, with musicians playing instruments appearing on the soundtrack or not. Other employees, dressed in bird or marine-themed costumes, pose or perform brief routines. A giant, female firebird at the scene's beginning beckons guests. Near stairs, a magenta and pink peacock-dressed ballerina spills glitter from a giant champagne bottle. Two women with headdresses ride blown-up balloons of white geese and wear darting silver fish around their necks. In the far distance, blue-green mermaids—or sirens—perch on rocky outcrops. But then the party guests engage with tableaux in ways that lend them a fairy-tale ambience too. A tanned blonde androgyne of Gatsby who says "I heard he killed a man once" steps back with two upper-crust boys into a tableau. These guests suddenly look like they're posed on a parade float.

Tableaux contribute to a sense of charm, romance, and magic. In the grand hall, female twins encircle and then pass an elderly gentleman, while another man looks on enviously. Behind this scene of unrequited desire, a giant sculpture of a woman's head underscores the women's allure. When two frat-boys in pinstripe suits run past a waiter, another two wield an overhanging garland-frame behind them; next to them, three ingénues dance in formation, as if echoing Botticelli's *Spring* (or a Victorian restaging thereof).[25]

The boundaries between tableaux and the crowds are porous. Tableau elements disperse and mingle among the crowd. Next to the bird-woman who pours glitter are two more revelers with hats resembling whole birds nesting on their heads. A woman's fantastic orange-bird headdress also appears, suddenly suggesting a miniature aviary. One of Nick's name-checked guests, the movie star, wears a spiked headdress so enormous that she seems to become one of the ornamental displays. Behind her, in the recesses of a smaller room, are her Black ladies-in-waiting. For a moment we sense we've peered into a private world.

Tableaux also adopt larger forms. In the grand hall, guests line-dance in giant S-shaped patterns, and on the patio, the audience masses and builds up to a circular, centripetal, tiered structure topped by a bird-winged woman. A multispoked constellation! This image of celebratory community is wide. Additional resonance is gained through the soundtrack's retro disco swoops.[26]

Most densely articulated is Nick's fantastical climb to see Gatsby, like in Hitchcock's *Saboteur* (1942), with Gatsby resembling the Statue of Liberty. Nick ascends as partiers stream downstairs, but the upward sweep

1.4 Tableaux momentarily crystallize.

remains prominent. Nick must bypass a cluster of four women, some with silver caps and silver shawls, like minarets. In the distance the bandleader encourages him on with gesticulations of "up, up!" while wielding his baton; musicians pop out of their chairs and a streak of white light cuts a path toward them. A man with an unbuttoned white shirt raises his bottle emphatically toward the sky. Upward and out, the scene moves toward closure as crowds stand in more regularized formation with arms raised skyward. Throughout the scene, tableaux, as they crystallize, create momentary senses of enchantment (fig. 1.4).

Narrative Emerging Out of Tableaux

A more modern sexuality becomes available to Nick and Jordan as narrative elements cross between them and events in the background. In an alcove, a gentleman surrounded by folds of white fabric jumps up as if he's had his pants pulled down; next, a woman on a swing comes forward with her legs splayed. Jordan confirms this bequeathed sexuality by languorously lifting her veil before her eyes, while an elderly white businessman tenderly draws a woman of color closer to him.

Later on the patio three incidents in the background bring Jordan and Nick even closer together: 1) an exoticized, seemingly torso-less woman (the camera's framing reveals hips and legs only) wearing zebra-striped tights, appears on a ledge (though these legs may instead be enormous, artificial leaves); 2) a Black woman, with eyelids painted silver, regally passes next to them, as revelers criss-cross behind her; she also wears the scene's only other iteration of the silent film star's dress; 3) head-dressed dancers next to the bandleader cross their legs directly over his lap, creating one three-figured composite. Jordan and Nick now seem like predestined lovers.

The party scene's merging of tableaux and attendees is facilitated through contagion, repetition, and foreshadowing.

Contagion

Music video's aural and visual elements often seem to seep across borders. There might be a band performing followed by an inset narrative featuring a couple's trials. Suddenly, the color or a prop next to the band might appear in the inset narrative. It seems as if the music could be responsible for these permeable boundaries.[27] In music video I call this process contagion.

In the party sequence, champagne bubbles poured on the ground turn to gold. Floating up and morphing into gigantic orbs, they reassert themselves as enormous sky-placed ovaries, fertilized by the fireworks behind Gatsby, to then take leave through the night. Martini glasses tinkle like the piano's keys. Confetti assists with narration. A gentleman lands a blue piece of glitter when he finds a young miss; similarly Jordan, dabbed with a red blotch of metal, grieves over Barton's theft of her (why might confetti tell a story?). Revelers and employees also seem to shift racial categories. The Cab Calloway figure should be Black, but he's white. There should be some Black musicians playing (they're on the soundtrack and many perform at Gatsby's second party, but they remain unseen). One Black male wears a stovetop hat, an accessory typed as European American. The organist is dubiously descended from Beethoven, but really belongs in a Looney Tunes cartoon. Yet the elements within the evening's end turns solid—glitter and fireworks shift to gold and silver, and even the tubas' open bells and the jellyfish-like umbrellas bobbing on the horizon become more shinily metallic. The first half of *Rhapsody in Blue* is digital rather than performed by live musicians. Miniature beachcombers are digitally composited in. Everything hardens into currency.

Foreshadowing and Underscoring

The modes of what theorists and I term "foreshadowing" and "underscoring" ground and yet destabilize the viewer. Because they work in the service of form these techniques feel authorial, yet they also bewilder because they unfold near or below the level of conscious perception.[28]

Luhrmann acknowledges the effectiveness of partially revealing a motif before its primary appearance (foreshadowing). Gatsby's spectacular entrance at the close of the party scene is prepped for by many devices, including not only his ring (and a corresponding metallic sound), his female lookalike (who says, "I heard he killed a man once") and dialogue, but also additional subtle effects.

At the scene's opening, pinstriped men toss hats back and forth. The flat straw hats, and many waiters' platters hoisted above the crowd, prepare for Gatsby's palming of a waiter's silver dish. A white directional light often appears in key moments in the scene, as does a "whiteout" of the full frame. The great displays of light before and behind Gatsby upon his spectacular appearance seem prefigured.

Other touches also provide continuity for the scene. Martini glasses piled up in tiers on books on the library's table seem like a memory of the multileveled spaces below. The "orb theme" (culminating in those fertilized sky-bound ovaries) continues through the library scene (a large orb-like sculpture stands behind the table).

Enormous feather fans of the pedestalled bird-woman wave in-sync with activities in the foreground (underscoring). As the party scene closes, fan-shaped fireworks appear over the lake. As the camera turns back to the chateau and we spy a duplicate of Jordan heading out of the door and another duplicate, this time of Gatsby in the other direction, the fountain's fans embrace us from both sides. A little earlier, men with red-striped jackets had seemed to enclose the viewer in a "cupping" gesture. Now, gazing at Gatsby, a woman pulls a green purse to her chest. On the other side, the lake takes on the same soft green—the narrator's green light. In multiple ways, we're embosomed. Gatsby tells Nick, "If there's anything you want, just ask for it, old sport."

Patterning: Follow the Zebra Stripes

How finely detailed is the party scene? Follow the zebra stripes, which form a line running through the scene's entirety. A clutch of pinstripe-suited men leap through the mansion's front doors, sporting white, red, and multicolored lines. Nick wears a striped bowtie. The torso-less woman's zebra-striped tights complement the zebra pool-toys and similarly striped floats. Helping to form the large circle of dancers, a red-haired man, wearing a red and white pinstriped jacket, gesticulates in the foreground. Late in the revelry the party's few Black women congregate at the pool's lower edge, and one dances with a red-and-black-striped,

1.5 Follow the zebra stripes.

enormous plush boa. Earlier, another had worn a similar one—and these two fashion moments secure a sort of closure. As Nick climbs to encounter Gatsby, stripes return with a vengeance. Several men in red-striped suits suddenly encase him. Do patches of stripes, black and white, provide an image with the means to accommodate a wider range of color and finer detail?[29] Jagged shaped stripes may shift register, foreshadowing the sharp turns and zigzag gestures that crowds, and most particularly Jordan, make. These complement the larger circular patterns (fig. 1.5).

Foley Sounds and Postproduction Effects

In the main hall a "swish" sounds on the fourth beat and then makes its way to the downbeat, thereby contributing to the scene's sense of revving acceleration. This sound's indeterminate source may be glitter poured from the feathered woman's enormous blown-up champagne bottle.

Suggestive of an antiquated camera mechanism, the "swish" triggers shifts among Nick's series of characters. There's also a sound like a blade against a knife sharpener that conjoins with Gatsby's ring in close-up before we meet him. A sense of regular rhythmic sound effects returns when revelers take dives into the pool. Crowd sounds run nearly continuously through the scene. Through Fergie's "A Little Party Never Killed Nobody" in particular, crowd sounds build in waves.

Scherzinger's utterance of "Bang" gradually becomes thinner and more mechanical, perhaps signifying young, wealthy women's robotic qualities, or an embrace of the modern. With Fergie's "You're Either Mine or You're Not," the song pans hard right and then left, with the volume brought up and down, to accentuate the crowd's surges. Through an intermedial blurring, revelers seem to toss music among one another. Small phrases of overlapping bands can also be heard (Will.i.am's patter subtly rises in the mix when Jordan talks to Nick).

Sound effects are often disjunct from their sources, creating a jarring, often disorienting effect. Yet the repetition of some sound effects establishes a pulse, providing a momentary sense of a ground. Sound effects often intimate a sense of the mechanical.

Actors, Gesture, and Movement: Crowds, Groups, and Individuals

Luhrmann's parents were competitive ballroom dancers, and he may have drawn on these experiences when choreographing actors and crowds. *Moulin Rouge!* (2001) has a spectacular can-can sequence; equal care would likely have been taken for *Gatsby*'s party sequence, especially since, as Fitzgerald's novel notes, it was Gatsby's means of luring Daisy.

How Luhrmann achieved his choreography has not yet been documented. Most likely he began with full-color drawings; blocked his costumed extras as avatars in pre-vis 3D software; gave performers eyelines to match, marks to hit, and simple gestures to perform in rehearsal; and then rearticulated performers' bodies in postproduction (it is now technically possible to move figures in space—after filming—to tug an arm this way or that, or turn a head further to one side or another). Luhrmann's crowds look different from the elaborate CGI-enhanced sequences we see in today's films, or of crowds in photographs and films from the Prohibition era. As mentioned, rivulets of subgroups cut through larger bodies of people; people cross in multilayered patterns behind key performers; heads turn in alternating directions for heightened intensity. Stills reveal how the extras in *Gatsby* depart from what we see in other films: faces suggest a blend of the *Sgt. Pepper's* cover and German expressionist painting. Each is intricately rendered and, in relation to one another, impossibly in focus.

Considering individual key figures, Luhrmann moves them around as if they were dancers, even in the most ordinary scenes. (Later in the film, Gatsby, readying for his rendezvous with Daisy at Nick's house, turns 360 degrees before stepping up to Nick's porch—a superfluous but poetic gesture.) In the party sequence's library scene, Jordan and Owl Eyes carry on a conversation while "dancing"—Jordan, stagily flicking lights on and off while flaring out her arms and fingertips, and Owl Eyes rhythmically wobbling. In the party sequence, Luhrmann moves larger groups of figures in surprising ways. In the grand hallway, performers pour forth like lava. Men in striped suits cut a faster rivulet (a sudden line of white pearls and flowers in women's hair form a second pattern). For contrast, "bang!" a glowing chandelier fills the frame, intercut with a winged, pedestalled goddess—the lava-like crowd combusts. On the patio, as the MC announces "a jazz history of the world," the crowd bursts forth.

Now there are crowds and their dance-influenced choreography: in the stairwell two women kiss one another twice, and one raises her palm in a salute. Oddly gestured, the couple's movements may have been choreographed as patterning to lead into the second Cab Calloway dance number. As the Calloway figure starts dancing, two men behind him toss their arms skyward, leaping in the air and then turning in pursuit of a woman to their right. A second row of men, two rows back, follow suit. These gestures help trigger the dance movements in the foreground, almost like a shudder. And again, this time from an unknown trigger, a shuddering movement ripples through the crowd: a sea of hats turns, beginning from the foreground and then sweeping toward the back, most likely to pick up the soundtrack's staccato "bang-bump bump." The bandleader and his dancers also rotate their heads in subtle jerking motions (possibly resembling birds).[30] In sped-up motion, near Gatsby at the scene's close, two flapper women run nervously past him as if guests had finally morphed into birds.

Again there's a concerted pattern at the pool, when revelers alternate diving in: first, in plunges a fully dressed diver, then another from the side. The third holds her handstand through the showy athletic event, then leaps backward, feet first, into the water. The timing of the dives must have been rehearsed.

Choreographer Doris Humphrey has claimed that a dancer's gestures can etch phrased visual lines in space.[31] As Nick dances at the pool, counting off each beat, he twirls like a top while using his foot as a break. It's not a pattern a dancer might choose, unless it's for the camera.[32] While the line of musicians in red hats step forward, hold still, and then bob together on the beat, one couple whirls through the crowd from the frame's left to its right. They're close enough to the pool's edge to put themselves at risk; it's not something dancers might deploy at a party in the absence of judges to impress. Almost unseen, it's a beautiful visual effect. The subtle play between moving line and staccato articulation shows off much of the music, but the patterning is so subtle it feels almost below the level of conscious perception. Overall, the scene's carefully choreographed dance gestures create a sense of fascination.

Individual Figures

Crowds sort from smallest to largest. The party scene foregrounds performers resembling figures from 1920s magazines, like *Vogue* and *The Atlantic* (note the man who holds a sleek cigarette-holder, and the pale pink–turbaned woman on the patio when Jordan and Nick first meet), as well as movie-star lookalikes of Lady Gaga, John Waters, Catherine Zeta-Jones, Christina Ricci, Matt Damon, Jar Jar Binks, and even Luhrmann himself. These momentary appearances of faux star performers, as Laura Mulvey has noted about entrances of Hollywood celebrities in cinema, seem to momentarily fix the moment, imbuing it with a sense of celestial transfixion.[33]

Small Groups

Patterns in crowds also develop because people cluster. Groups include 1) the bird-hatted white women, 2) the gold-and-black-dressed white women who step onto the dance floor from the frame's lower left, 3) the clutch of bathing-suited white men, and 4) the Black women who party together by the pool. Like the individuals, the moment of recognition of a group produces a sense of frisson.

Costumes

As with the music, the costume's historical deformations contribute to the viewer's sense of disequilibrium and delirium. *Gatsby*'s necklines plunge lower and the shoes are narrower than those of the 1920s; the fabulous hats would only have been worn on fashion runways. Costuming also provides some of the "arcadian" scene's greatest charms, as well as contributing to an image of democracy (every human performer counts). Each outfit is beautifully shaped for its wearer, as if she had chosen how she might wish to be represented; each clothing ensemble (dress, hat, shoes, jewelry, and accessories) works as a unique voice, within a small group, and as part of the whole. The scene's real stars may be the costumes.[34]

Nineteen basic techniques pull the viewer affectively and proprioceptively in different directions: 1) the periodic white-outs of confetti and tinsel induce a momentary blindness, even a brief amnesia; 2) tableaux elicit a sense of enchantment but dissolve quickly; 3) the mise-en-scène's deformations of scale (from the miniature to the monumental) provide excessive demands on the viewer's attention; 4) spatial layout is indeterminate, and the camera's exploration of it further obscures vision; 5) the camera's high angles and sudden drops, and the music's peaks and dips, induce a state of vertigo; 6) the camera's gaze often feels distracted and sometimes obsessive, even as edits are rapid and the framing is mobile, moments of tighter sync occur unpredictably; 7) the music refuses to provide a sense of ground; 8) sound effects provide a pulse that roots the viewer in the blizzard-like detail, but their uncertain sources produce disorientation; 9) the flow of crowds and the sudden emergence of shared dance-gestures create the sense of being pulled along; 10) the scene's color arc encourages the viewer to grasp at spots of color; 11) the zebra stripes provide direction, like a train track, but they quickly fall apart to reappear at different scales and in other domains; 12) miniature people, rendered as if in a dollhouse, invite the viewer's focus; 13) faux-celebrities and small groups produce shocks of recognition and excitement; 14) narrative trajectories involve foci dispersing a viewer's attention; 15) dialogue bleeds into music and sound effects as much as it advances story; 16) contagion, foreshadowing, underscoring, and patterning contribute to cross-medial smoothing, but also indistinct boundaries; 17) a viewer's eye drifts as we sort figures into individuals; 18) likewise, a viewer's eye drifts while sorting groups and crowds; and 19) costumes fix attention.

How do all of these effects work together? It's hard to say, because simultaneous unfoldings of processes become so densely layered that few produce particularized sensations. Their importance can only be understood hypothetically and in retrospect. A viewer can sometimes identify techniques combining and pulling together. In the grand hallway, the pinstripes of the zebras become more multicolored before they merge into the phoenix-like, variously hued, pedestalled woman. A viewer can feel riveted by the complicated deployment of a crowd (suddenly disposed like a painting) while still sensing other processes already underway, soon to become emergent, and to recede before they can be identified (like the corresponding soundtrack's disco swoops). A viewer's attention might shift rapidly among various effects—an extra with a striking costume, a crowd formation, a dab of color, a sound effect, a juxtaposition of musical samples, a moment crystallizing into a tableau—though the relative weight of these elements are difficult to ascertain. Postclassical cinematic aesthetics have been described as media intensified across every single parameter.[35] This sequence feels post-postclassical.

This scene showcases transmedia aesthetics. Luhrmann's background in music production, music video, commercials, theatre, opera and department-store window design shape this scene.[36] Luhrmann's signature style seems to project past his own craftsman-like touches to those of his many collaborators. This scene conveys a vision of information and power flowing across social structures; the film takes place in the 1920s, but it feels like 2013. As in today's media swirl, highly individualized figures in crowds attempt to project themselves. Ideas coalesce around small groups and ripple or shudder across the whole. Each participant stands three degrees from everyone else.[37] Celebrities and small groups function like magnets. Global capital seems both everywhere and invisible.[38] Ultimately, however, old money seems to run the show, and the billionaire is the face for us all.

Even though this film's budget is less than half that of most Hollywood tent-pole productions, the resources expended—glitter, champagne, fireworks, an enormous cast of extras—might feel obscene, a wasted bubble of dreams. Further reflection may help us see how much the scene offers a prescient image of new subjects (and consumers) in an era when wealth and global capital have run out of control. I'm haunted by the care with which Luhrmann documents the tear-down of the scene, as if the spectacle's destruction is integral to its momentary emergence. But for now, we might try to make good on Richard Dyer's suggestion that the musical can give us what utopia feels like. Now that we can experience a variegated and capacious world more clearly, let's go out and realize it.

2

Shattered Pleasures:
Michael Bay's *Transformers: Age of Extinction*

THE *TRANSFORMERS* FRANCHISE showcases what blockbusters can do. This chapter provides the book's strongest example of awe with razzle-dazzle. As a big object, *Transformers: Age of Extinction* (*T4*) from 2014 pairs with *The Great Gatsby*'s party scene. Their directors, Michael Bay and Baz Luhrmann, both transmedia artists who place their auteurist stamps across many forms, share commonalities. Luhrmann's productions include commercials, music videos, albums, operas, indie films, streaming series, film franchises, and department store windows. Bay's encompass roughly as much, but he's designed an amusement park ride to boot. Perhaps Bay has been able to work with many media because, as Mark Kerins notes, any Bay product is first an advertisement for Bay.[1] Are grand projects usually conservative? Bordwell says yes. It takes money to fund big Hollywood films, and to secure those resources, their content must reaffirm the status quo.[2] *The Great Gatsby*'s and *T4*'s politics could be said to be reactionary. Both create sharp divisions between powerful men, structural forces, and the little people below. Individuals can't do much without the benevolent figures at the top. These films are different from the music videos discussed in chapters 8–11. These videos, by Beyoncé, Kendrick Lamar, Anderson .Paak, and Janelle Monáe, are characterized by intimacy, shared history, and a call for community. Here, social justice seems like something we can achieve together. These tensions between elite and populist, conservative and progressive, high and low budget, help draw the map of the media swirl's contents (fig. 2.1).

Michael Bay is the second-highest-grossing director, after Steven Spielberg, and it's not surprising that critics and connoisseurs love to take him down. But neither supporters nor detractors have been able to say

2.1 Bay's personal style.

exactly what he does. Is he just good at making Hollywood blockbuster films, using standard techniques with a few twists? The most thoughtful attempts to define his style tend to culminate in highly ambivalent pronouncements, typically using traditional auteurist language. Manohla Dargis claims that Bay's "signature adorns every image in his movies . . . he's a perverse genius," while her colleague A. O. Scott suggests that "although they may look like soulless corporate studio product, [Bay's films] are really examples of personal cinema, expressions of the will and imagination of their director."[3] What could make this director of soulless corporate studio product a genius, let alone perverse? How can his films be so strongly personal if they don't actually look like it?

I'll focus here on what *T4* looks like—and sounds like—in order to characterize the kinds of experience it can create. Working through my own ambivalence, I've come to understand this director's style in terms of drive, energy, musicality, humor, intensity, even *jouissance*—an overload of pleasure and pain to the point of unbearability.[4] Bay pushes toward a moment when things can't be assimilated. But he stages these moments so we don't see them coming—and we may not have caught up with them before they pass. I'll show that virtually every parameter of these films becomes stripped down, heightened, transformed, and placed in the spotlight. These elements become pliant in service of musicality and speed. This pliancy, I'll demonstrate, allows Bay's films to go to some odd places. Robots, human characters, landscapes, editing, and color overlap and combine to form a tissue or web; everything is bound together.

Bay's films excel in what Richard Dyer calls the intangibles: movement, sound, line.[5] Consider his favored color palette: a sherbet blend of neon pinks, lime greens, and baby blues. Nor would most directors be so skilled with fast, disjunctive cutting, varied settings, and quick shifts of tone, like a move from dainty lights and streamers, very "girl party," to jet-black demons smashing it all up. Like Henri Matisse's mega-pink odalisques, Bay's sensibility isn't one everyone will appreciate. It's true that *T4*'s price of admission can be high: the film fits advice columnist Dan Savage's definition of relationships that you must accept some intolerables to be admitted into the game.[6]

Bay's stereotypes can distance viewers. *T4* begins cloyingly. on a small farm in Texas, with Bud Light and cornfields, and it ends with aluminum rice pots, old ladies, and red lanterns in China. But in between there's an embrace of the world of things. Even in the smashing of it, Bay's world is alive. I'd like to place my discomfort with the teen's short-shorts, the grownups' silly rants, and additional cringeworthy depictions, against other pleasures, such as vibrant images, and my reactions, moment by moment, which include real awe, joy, fear, and tenderness.

This chapter is broken into two sections. First, there is a consideration of *T4*'s shifting parameters: 1) geography, landscape and settings, and scale in the service of large-scale form; 2) characters, costumes, props, and dialogue; 3) tone, music, and sound; and 4) issues of identity. The second section analyzes two segments to show how *T4* creates long audiovisual (and musical) phrases with beginnings, middles, and ends. I'll close with a suggestion about why we might take Bay's films seriously.

Synopsis

Like the rest of the franchise, *T4* concerns friendly and hostile robots, but its questions of good and evil are more nuanced. While several reviewers have complained *T4*'s narrative is incomprehensible, I'd say it's just convoluted. Its many plot points and long run time of 165 minutes foreclose an easy description, but let me nevertheless attempt a recap.

T4 begins when small-time Texas inventor Cade (Mark Wahlberg) and his daughter Tessa (Nicola Peltz) discover and hide an Autobot Transformer, Optimus Prime, in their barn. In the Chicago war's aftermath, Harold Attinger (Kelsey Grammer), head of the CIA, mandates that Decepticons and Autobots should be eradicated. The CIA ferrets out Autobot Optimus, and Cade, Optimus, Tessa, and her boyfriend Shane (Jack Reynor) go on the lam. The team decides to infiltrate KSI, a corporation where a CEO inventor, Joshua Joyce (Stanley Tucci), is melting down Decepticons and Autobots for Transformium, a substance that can shapeshift into nearly any form, including KSI's new race of robot. The Asset (an evil alien robot), Attinger, and Joyce plan to exchange the Seed, a catalyst to make more Transformium, for Optimus Prime. Transformium's dangerous: the creators detonated Seeds during Earth's ice age, causing the Great Extinction and transforming some of the dinosaurs into the substance. Joyce has built a new superrobot, Galvatron, alongside an army of lesser robots, but he doesn't know that his progeny are tainted with Decepticon Megatron's evil DNA. A battle initiated by Joyce between Galvatron and Optimus Prime leaves Optimus wounded and Tessa trapped on an alien spaceship. Unhappy with Galvatron's poor performance, Joyce shifts KSI operations to his China facilities. Once Tessa and Optimus Prime are rescued from the spaceship, our protagonists follow after. In China, the Autobots, outmanned by a new race of robots, call forth robot-fighting dragons to fight them. The alien spaceship sucks up and drops metals in apocalyptic fury, but in the battle good prevails—at least for the moment. Tessa gets to go to her high school graduation.

Brief Description of *The Transformers* Franchise

The *Transformers* films derive from a 1984 toy whose individual parts can be manipulated to form a vehicle, device, animal, or robot action-figure (tagline: "Robots in Disguise"). Comic books, video games, and fan conferences followed. In 2007, to reengage older fans and introduce children to the brand, Hasbro, the manufacturer, produced *Transformers: The Movie*. All *Transformers* films are based on the premise that Cybertronic Decepticons and Autobots, after fighting on their planet, have come to ours to continue their battle.

By *T4* Bay had already made three blockbusters for the franchise and at that point, he wished to back away, but after witnessing a two-hour line for a Transformers amusement park ride, he decided he couldn't give his opus to another director. He negotiated a reboot, with an enormous budget, new cast, redesigned robots, and more adult themes. Critics have groused that *T4* is really about global capitalism and the digital era.[7] Filmic elements are interchangeable and human characters are expendable (previous stars have been subbed in by Mark Wahlberg and Nicola Peltz). And it's true that much has been refashioned on the modular level. In *T4* Optimus Prime resembles a figure from a mannerist painting;

his chest is enormously widened (befitting the clothes of the late sixteenth century), but he also wears lounge-lizard bell-bottoms. Bumblebee is more mature. *T4*'s backers hope the new look will sustain several future Transformers films, with or without Bay.

Recasting the Materials of Film

Figures, Landscape, and Form

If I were to condense *Transformers: Age of Extinction* into one synoptic GIF, it might be a slightly transformed emblematic one that *doesn't* appear in the film: we never see Optimus morph from his dirty, unpainted self to his shiny self. Along with this transformation I'd include Cade, with his toothy dragon helmet; a roiling landscape that's constantly transforming, stretching from Texas all the way to the Wulong Karst National Park in southern China; as well as the tall buildings, strips of greenery, and bay of Hong Kong. But that's the charm of *Transformers 4*—it's too mega-opus-like to hold all of it in one's imagination (fig. 2.2).

We might start with those robots. Bay has been accused of making only testosterone-driven films (and I'd love for him to make a woman's weepy), but I can see why they appeal to women. The robots look like jewel boxes—pretty, like Optimus's face. As they transmute their lines are flexible, graceful, elegant. And they're good creatures. Every Autobot would rescue a kitten from a tree.

2.2 *T4*'s landscape as Mobius strip.

Distorted Sets and Prismatic Terrain

One of the new digital cinema's pleasures is a geography that allows us to traverse an impossibly varied landscape. The question becomes: Can we take it all in? Bay's manipulation of sets and locations into strange configurations creates what I'd call a "prismatic landscape." KSI's headquarters are lovingly realized with an interior glass boardroom set off by a moat; a revolving entrance doorway that confusingly mirrors the lobby counter (out or in?); and a futuristic 1950s showroom. The offices are dotted with white orchids, turning the space into a grotto-like lair. By way of contrast, there's the worn, midcentury modern UN office, slightly musty and oily. Cade's barn, a homemade temple to technology, is tall enough to be a church and sanctified by the many amber lights that honey it up. Like other aspects of Bay's films, these sets "pop"—they're aggressive and prominent. Close viewing reveals greater strangeness: within and without Cade's barn, signage of flags, stars, and warnings of borders and crossings cover many surfaces. Together these create a sense of confinement but also an incitement to risk. The way we move among these settings plays a role. As the film unfolds, the locations get bigger and bigger. We also can't always be sure how trains, cars, or spaceships conveyed us there.

Scale

Lockdown, 'The Asset," is one of the first robots to appear. In IMAX 3D he emerges, twenty stories high, out of murk and shipping detritus. We don't even breach his shins. But by the end of *T4*, the monsters seem even bigger. Spaces and places do, too. How does the film do it? One way is through miniaturization. There's the tiny, slave-laborer Autobot Brains in his miniature aquarium prison, with Tom Thumb-sized bed and pillow. Near the end of the film, the flying dinobots hitting the glass skyscrapers resemble gemstone-studded brooches; and the shattered glass silver confetti and tinsel. The pieces of metal vacuumed up by the spaceship seem enormous, even the noodle factory's cutlery. So when we see the enormous heads of robots close-up for the first time, they seem more monumental than ever.

Buildings and their interiors also cheat scales. From the outside, a mini gas station looks so small it might only hold a urinal and a cash register, but on the inside it's more decked out than a spacious mid-1950s pub. We might assume that our hero's hideout is a modest brick church, but inside it's as big as Notre Dame. But that's music video training for you (Bay got his start in music videos and commercials, where directors have been cheating scale since the 1980s). Why would Bay stage the enormous Hong Kong battles in Detroit, so viewers can see the midcentury American art deco stone office buildings peeking out from behind the Asian portals and gates? Green screen would have been cheaper. Nevertheless, something oddly charming is gained here with scale.

Editing Geography: Match Cuts

T4 presents a sense of fluid time and space. Since the late 1980s, film directors have been using subtitles to help viewers follow quick shifts among locations. But Bay gave that up long ago. He just *goes*. From the dinosaurs to present-day Antarctica; from the middle of Texas to a DC State Department building; from the Southwest plains to an NSA flight; from a CIA meeting on an alien spaceship to LA, Chicago, Hong Kong, and mainland China. Match cuts, fluid camerawork, and Godardian sound-splicing get us there. At the film's opening, primordial Transformium goo kicks up, and oddly freezes, as the dinos flee. Perhaps the images of motionless ice and Antarctic snow appear to create a strong graphic match. Tessa slams her screen door, and there's an immediate cut to television footage of the Chicago war, but no television is on—we go straight to Attinger's plotting with the CIA. The recording devices of the homestead's mailboxes rationalize this.

Building Scenes

Bay builds scenes with sharp beginnings, middles, and ends. When Steve Jablonsky's thrumming soundtrack resounds from a helicopter, we know a scene is about to start. On city streets we should expect delays—and Bay is careful to terrace these: 1) the difficulty of buying a motorcycle when you don't speak the language; 2) wiping out on a bike; 3) missing the elevator; 4) catching your breath on the roof, 5) sipping a stolen yogurt drink, as a giant spaceship starts to cast its shadow over you. Sometimes beginnings and endings occur simultaneously: Cade fires up a torch to repair Optimus Prime alongside the abruptness of the lively Imagine Dragons song "Battle Cry"; Optimus asks Cade why he's willing to help, and Cade replies with both closure and possibility, "Because you trust me too?" In scene after scene there are strongly etched shapes, even when styles and lengths vary.

Shape

Circular and linear patterns repeated over large stretches of film also contribute to coherence and speed. The orbiting alien ships are ringed with chevron lights. Similarly, at the Texas homestead, the SWAT team advances in wavelike concentric patterns and the race cars then circle around the pond. In KSI's circular showroom, cameras, cars, robots, staff, models, and inventors maintain circles but also twitch and turn. On the alien mothership, multiple spirals interlock. Lines project form too. Trains and train tracks occur repeatedly, robots run up escalators, cars speed down roads, and high wires stretch from building to spaceship. The dinobots gambol along Hong Kong's long strips of greenery.

Large-Scale Form

T4 is essentially a chase film. The protagonists run after robots and the robots run after them. It's 1) lose your friend and home, 2) infiltrate the enemy to gain information, 3) rescue team members, and 4) battle the enemy. But the film shows more complexity. It's not always clear who began the conflict and who is good and evil. *T4* intimates that a godless mechanical universe is run by creators who force all to do their bidding. As Lockdown intones, "The problem with loyalty to the cause is that the cause will always betray you. We all work for somebody" (capitalism infiltrates everything). Does *T4* also retell the biblical story of Job, but with the corporation and robots vying for the role of God? At *T4*'s end, billionaire-entrepreneur Joyce benevolently makes good on Cade's trials, and Optimus Prime deflects basic questions, like who we are and why we are here—they're not our concern.

T4's explorations of scale are thrilling. Enormous robots, tiny people. What can the robots do—and do they want to eat us? (Joyce and Lucas wonder about this.) The fear of consumption emerges against a backdrop of historical and temporal stress. A war has just ended, and the world may soon suffer near-total annihilation. Cade and Tessa have narrowed romantic and economic options. As Kristen Whissel points out, digital morphs like the Transformer robots appear at cultural junctures. They suggest terror but also hope tied to new social formation.[8]

Signposts appear reassuringly at important nodes in the film—near its beginning, middle, and end, or some combination thereof. Simple lines help create form: Tessa says to Cade, "Perhaps some things should never be built"; Joyce says to Optimus Prime, "You cannot stop technology . . .

The world will approve"; Cade and the dinobot say to Joyce, "Perhaps he's saying some things should never be built" (and the dinobot roars in approval). At the film's beginning, Tessa can't go to the prom or have a boyfriend, and Cade loses his home and employee. At the end, Cade approves of his daughter's graduation and boyfriend, and Joyce agrees to rebuild Cade's fortune. Lucas's complaint that Cade and the government haven't properly compensated him resolves when Su Yueming, as she mounts the motorcycle toward the film's end, defiantly demands, "I need a raise!" A boat appears at the film's beginning and end. Tunnels appear three times: during Darcy's corporate check-in in Antarctica; Attinger and Joyce's quarrel about the Seed at KSI; and Su Yueming and Joyce's motorcycle ride in Hong Kong.

Dreamscapes

T4 is a dreamscape. Characters, places, and props reappear but change into new shapes, much like our dreams produce reconfigurations of the day and the past. The small-town movie theater owner resembles the cigar-smoking yahoo robot; the surly Irish robot Crosshairs chimes with Shane. The doe-eyed Drift mirrors the Chinese population. Tessa must rhyme with the imprisoned vagina dentata robot jailed in the alien's ship ("Bitch," the Autobot Hound calls her). Other touches encourage us to make these gendered connections. Tessa's sprint to her bedroom as she's chased by Prime's stray missile becomes restaged as her run down the alien spaceship's hallways; her snippy robot-dog morphs into the deadly hunting dogs that chase her. At the barn, Tessa says, "No lasers, Dad!" and then, of course, the alien ship is dense with lasers. Later, a shot of the Great Wall of China twins with the Monument Valley landscape, and the bay of Hong Kong becomes a larger instance of the Texas farm's pond.

Aural and Visual Motifs

Postclassical digital cinema offers new forms and viewing experiences. In action films large set pieces, busy with inflated CGI and bombastic soundtracks, can momentarily dip, allowing a space for a striking gesture, image, or line of dialogue to come forward. With so much activity, these moments acquire a different kind of weight: across the film, they can function as a string of motifs. These chains resemble those found often in pop music and music video, when audiovisual or aural moments come forward, recede, and then reemerge. Working as rhymes, no single moment in the string gains permanent ascendancy.[9] In *T4*, many references deal with death: Attinger, for example, calls his CIA ops project "Cemetery Wind." The Seed is a tactical nuke, branded with a skull and crossbones. The film is aptly titled *Age of Extinction*.

Some more deathly instances below:

- After the highway battle between Optimus and Galvatron, Cade, Shane, and Tessa hover at the roadside. A twenty-story-high faceless black robot suddenly emerges from the alien spaceship's maw. Repeated booming sounds emanate from the robot, along with the spaceship's high-pitched whirring. Falling sheets of black soot stain the air (notice the tree behind that looks like a gallows' frame).
- A run for the humans, this time from an exploding factory. Lucas, the slowest, is swallowed up in the encroaching river of fire. He becomes charred midstream, as if cast in Pompeian lava, and we see his carcass of ash and soot twisted into a lone statue in an empty field, missing a limb and wearing a clown's face's rictus.
- Once caged, now free, a mini-Autobot, forced to toil like the workers of Auschwitz who stripped corpses of teeth and hair, now stands in a daisy field, saying, "Not my problem anymore! I'm walking!"
- In KSI's corporate glass citadel, projected images of jellyfish float past Joyce and Attinger. A shot of the earth momentarily drifts in, resembling the blue-marbled orb; next a bonsai with red flowers; and then a white halo-like embryo, resembling Joyce's personal ball. Flummoxed, Joyce says, "I need a beat" (fig. 2.3).

2.3 *T4*'s audiovisual threads—orbs.

- The dinobots, freed by Optimus Prime, perhaps the now soon-to-be sole inhabitants of the Anthropocene, gracefully lope up strips of greenery past Hong Kong skyscrapers.

Motifs 2

Scholars have noted that new digital technologies make possible a painterly approach to cinema. I've claimed that cinematic form changes as well. Films like *The Bourne Ultimatum, Eternal Sunshine of the Spotless Mind, Moulin Rouge!,* and *T4* present a new paradigm where all levels of a film are altered from large-scale formal schemes to the surface style. Some theorists conceive of these films as historical-continuity-with-a-twist camp, like David Bordwell.[10] Camerawork and editing, such as shifting lens-lengths, a reliance on close shots, wide-ranging camera movements, and rapid editing, define this new "surface" style. Eleftheria Thanouli claims, from the other side, that broader changes have taken place: today's plots slacken and stories divide into intertwined subplots. These multigeneric films adopt a self-conscious stance, and realism becomes hypermediated.[11] Steve Shaviro, in the postclassical camp, states we are in a new era of "post-continuity."[12]

T4's digital postclassical devices may move us most strongly through the linking of these brief moments over the film's three-hour time span. *T4*'s strongest image of an individual's death—Lucas, the film's sacrificed surfer—crosses with the larger theme of annihilation just described. Let's zoom in closer at Lucas's thread: it's useful to look at how Bay excises a character from his films (fig. 2.4).

2.4 Lucas's mark of Cain.

- Cade's lowbrow, misogynistic employee, Lucas, first appears driving his Mini Cooper into town while singing some crass working-class white rock, "I'm a nasty woman! Gonna make you cry." He reports he's out of surfable waves and cash.
- Failing to catch Cade's football while standing in an aisle of a decrepit movie theater, Lucas falls back onto a pile of film canisters so high it might be a wave. The soot-blackened wall behind him appears ominous. This is his first "wipeout."
- Reclining on an old couch in Cade's barn, Lucas encourages a beer-delivering robot to bring him a cool one. The robot's markings contrasts with the blue smiley-faced and exuberant white silo the teenage girls drive past while they sing their school's-out song.
- In the barn, Lucas faces off against Cade and his transformers' truck (aka Optimus Prime). Optimus's front grill has a desaturated black and white center, and Lucas wears clothing to mirror it. His T-shirt features a swirl of brown and black specks with a black silhouette of a surfer at its center.
- Lucas hands Optimus Prime over for a bounty. In the process he gets clonked on the head again, and a red welt appears on his forehead, as if he'd received the mark of Cain. He complains of aortal contortions, and, when he drives up, his surfboard only shows the black of the yin-yang symbol. In a getaway car, he obsesses on the scariness of it all, closing by thanking the "stranger from the cornfields."
- The chase and the abandoned factory sets the scene for Lucas's awful wipeout and death. But Shane's leap onto a curved platform resembles his surfable wave. Tessa makes matters clear about a character who perhaps uncomfortably straddled too many roles—uncle, housemate, employee, coworker, lender, watchdog, friend: "Lucas is dead and my life is over."

Characters and Performance

Acting

T4's characters project quickly and sharply—which is essential, considering that *T4*'s dialogue is typically brief. CGI-intensive frames run hundreds of thousands of dollars apiece; with so much money to be recouped, every frame is under pressure to beguile us instantly. Bay is known for shooting his monumental images more quickly than other directors do; he achieves this partly by barking through a megaphone. This, too, forces a distillation of character.

To keep the film's energy going, the actors' performances are highly stylized and filled with business. Some examples of odd gestures and strange manipulations of props include the ways Joshua Joyce repeatedly points his index fingers, palms downward, toward his penis, sometimes following with a nice hand flourish upward. Both Cade and Lucas walk side-lopingly. Tessa often places her arms stiffly forward, hair adrift, while serving as sentinel. Cade repeatedly takes on or off his glasses at heightened moments (a mysterious prop, the thick-rimmed opticals wind up in Attinger's and Joyce's hands, too). These gestures help create emotional beats.

Characters

Against so much fast-paced activity, roles are quickly sketched but finely nuanced. The villain Attinger, a Rumsfeld type, however crazed, still possesses a recognizable worldview. Entrepeneur Joyce may be in it for the babes, self-aggrandizement, love of technology, *and* to make the world a better place. Tessa possesses some range: as a willful teenager she'll pout, but she still kicks ass when needed. Cade's character will sometimes pause in reflection. He'll glance out the window of his truck as he's driving into town, or look out at the stars and give thanks for his wife and daughter. This signals he has the most interiority of *T4*'s characters.

The film's last third overreaches with its assertions of Cade's masculinity. Cade shows he can drive into KSI and shoot that laser gun. Joyce has to tell him "You're good with a gun. You should have it," and Cade goes hand-to-hand with Attinger. Cade lets his future son-in-law drive the car through the alien spaceship's attack, but only after they've well-coordinated on a pilfered enemy flightcraft.

Props

Capitalizing on action film tropes, Bay repurposes things found at hand. During the CIA's black-ops takedown of the farm Cade grabs a small flying drone, hummingbird-sized, which becomes one of the film's main props. In Monument Valley, Cade uses the drone to project one of the Autobots' wrongful deaths on a rock face; later he uses it to hack into an ATM, and then to scan and fake photo ID cards in order to break into KSI. When

Tessa is pushed to the ground by the CIA's SWAT team she falls over her little red rider wagon, which throws its contents across the grass; the wagon had helped her lug repair junk home. In another scene, Tessa flips off and on the Christmas lights found in an abandoned mini gas station, as if trying to ignite a spark between her father and her boyfriend.

The Embedding of Props

Many of *T4*'s props and other film elements carry an affective wallop because they're embedded in the mise-en-scène before they take prominence. Our eye or ear registers them, and we're primed to read them as salient. A triptych of monumental photos of Joyce holding his white orb hangs in KSI's glass boardroom. Joyce will later float his orb for Darcy in a long, narrow hallway. Joyce's "sound secretaries," with their long legs and high-heeled shoes, appear once again while Joyce melts down over Galvatron. Their dainty legs wink out from behind the robot. Both consciously and not, viewers catch details and become more attuned to environments.

And then these props move into delirium. On the spaceship an enormous revolving orb floats near the spaceship's ceiling, which then might be imagined as the same orb, miniaturized again, as it drifts onto a screen in the Chinese corporate headquarters' glass office. Glass boxes recurrently pose problems for characters. While Joyce may have felt comfortable in his glass-centric KSI office building, in Hong Kong he says, "Great! I'm in the midst of a war and in a glass box!"

Dialogue

A director's ways of working with dialogue and intonation shape the film's texture. Jacques Tourneur spoke softly into an actor's ear, and told him to deliver his lines to the camera as if he were sharing a secret. John Ford would strip whole pages from a script until it was bare bones, not one extra word. Howard Hawks, on the other hand, would take the script and say, "Well, that's a start. Let's have some fun with it," and the actors and he would improvise on the morning of the shoot. Bay's up for improvising, and might sometimes shout through a megaphone to an actor very rapidly, "Give me a funny line!" "And another!" "And another!" It doesn't matter who's acting, most often the lines are driven, direct, and clipped. "His name is Shane and he drives, Dad!" is Tessa's. "They walk. They talk. We're dead. Kill them all," says Attinger. Perhaps this hyperaccentuated speech—surely heightened during looping—creates a counterpoint against the Transformers' mechanically modulated voices and sound effects as the robots coalesce and fracture. Because the robots' sound effects and voices are so musical—a pattern might sound like "Kuhng!" "Puhng!" "Twawk-twawk," and a high-pitched "bwee-bwee-twee-whipple-whir-whir"—human words become musical as well. They're kindred stuff.

Robots and People

Music video directors, including Bay, tend to display a range of activities in the frame. This speaks to the various rhythmic strata in a song. In *Transformers* "The Asset" is one of the slowest-moving and deathly, and the miniature imprisoned robot, Brains, the most nervous. Of the actors, Attinger is the most rigid and staid, Shane the most voluble.

As in music video, links between the inanimate and animate heighten the sense of musicality.[13] In *T4* humans take on the attributes of robots, and robots behave like humans. Attinger barely moves at all, and Darcy's walk is comically robotic. Cade dons a helmet emblazoned with a dragon robot face and detonates a missile in front of his groin, much like Galvatron. He later throws Shane's bottle of green mouthwash across the room; the robots often spit up green gooey "shizzle." Early on, Cade and Lucas shake the theater owner's grandson's hand and it waves strangely like a robot. Tessa, needing to move with robot-like precision, has "the best hands in the business." And of course the robots are very like people. I always feel sad when Optimus Prime gently whimpers, and I soften when Bumblebee looks up like a puppy.

Robot and Human Ids Run Wild

T4 concerns the struggle between good and evil, but when you're not looking, the two cavort. Evil Lockdown is the king of his "own personal prison," but in Cade's barn (his "temple to technology") Cade taunts potential buyers about corpses buried in the backyard. He threatens to crack their skulls and the "purple people eater" with a baseball bat—a foreshadowing of his deployment of the alien's laser gun. The alien ship's pretty glass domes also dot the city's skyline, including the tower Cade perches on. Inextricably, both Cade's farm and the ship have cricket sounds. Momentarily the alien prison ship looks nearly identical to the cityscape. Modern capitalism is our prison house.

Robot-Human Alliances

Transformers scenarios may also beguile because they tap into near-religious structures. Like the squabbling Greek gods who dallied among humans, these robots have overinflated ids. *Transformers* also has a bit of the golem story, a Jewish folktale in which townspeople shape mud into a large animate humanoid that ultimately returns to dead matter. *T4* may reimagine eighteenth- and nineteenth-century automata, like Jacques de Vaucanson's gilded copper duck that ate, quacked, splashed water, and appeared to defecate its food like a live bird. *T4*'s robots have terrific entrances: an evil one climbing up on the water tower and then scaling apartment buildings in Hong Kong, or Megatron calling the swarms to get going from inside KSI's factory. Then there's also the battle between Galvatron and Optimus Prime. I love when the good robots bust into KSI's lobby and then bound up forty steps with each leap along the escalators, tossing people off like handkerchiefs.

Sound

The sounds of robots disassembling and reforming is where *Transformers'* charm and soul reside. As with the soundtrack's other elements, these sounds feel engaged, enthusiastic, and noble. I could happily listen to the soundtrack alone. It's worth attending carefully, because we can never be sure what any sound-object connects to until sound and image coalesce on screen. *T4*'s world is enchanted.

Some of the sound design is odd. The sounds for the high-wires scene (threads running from alien spaceship to skyscraper) don't belong to high-altitude air with a terrible drop below. Instead the often lushly reverberant clunks and clangs sound like the clutch of a pirate ship, or the dankness of a prison's underground graveyard. Some effects sound as if they're underwater. Are they sonic overflow from the spaceship? Bay's soundtracks often build sequentially. Alt-indie rock music accompanies Optimus Prime (compressed as a truck) on Monument Valley's open highway. As he transforms from an old into a shiny new truck Chinese taiko drums overlay on top, to then be filled in by the Transformers brass-led anthem (very Wagnerian).

With the new digital cinema, distant sonic relations can be brought close. Joyce makes much of his KSI lobby sounds ("thung"), which chimes with Darcy's oddly muted voice in Joyce's glass boardroom (echoing Jacques Tati's *Playtime*, 1967). A linked series of sounds rising from the lobby's "thung" connects with an electroshocked Brains' feverish stutters of "Buh buh buh buh." KSI's Chinese corporate doors make a "thung," just like Joyce's LA ones, linking KSI globally.

Music

Four kinds of scoring shape *T4*: Jablonsky's run-and-gun pulsating drone-based material for chases, Skrillex's techno-cold sound collages, Imagine Dragons' indie-folk-pop tune, and traditional heroic horn theme. These are reworked and collaged in the film's final fight scene, where Skrillex's robot sounds cross-cut with the Imagine Dragons' tune. When Joyce "needs a beat," a few bars from the sonic world of elegiac British composer John Taverner appears. The film closes with a riff from the *Bourne Ultimatum* (2007). Spanish guitar appears more than once. Props and objects "sing," as when the drone's "zzz" becomes a melody as it tries to hack an ATM machine. Concrete sounds are woven into the nondiegetic scoring.

Music helps structure scenes. The Imagine Dragons tune begins with humming, wordless singing as it accompanies Cade's group while they plan to infiltrate KSI. Once the real fighting begins, we'll better understand this earlier audiovisual passage with its reflective, slightly mournful past-tenseness. Together, preparation and action sequence are long—fifteen minutes in total. Not only can digital audiovisual aesthetics direct moment-by-moment shifts and make connections among distant moments, it can also bind together sustained sections of film.

Bay's Musicality

This section pays additional attention to the soundtrack and describes a battle.

Musical Phrasing

Bay understands beginnings, peaks, and lulls. A close reading of the next two sequences show the ways *T4* parses action into musical phrases. Varied phrase lengths contribute to the larger sculpted whole. Clear beginnings are important. They are often established through people running energetically, music kicking in, or a Transformer driving through a passageway. Internally the sequences have peaks of emotional intensity, when characters start saying odd things like, "It was me, it was me, it was me!" Then there's a lull, and the film ratchets up again. Other directors might use some of these elements but skip the lull. In *T4* a character might look down; there might be a spot of humor; or a bass line might drop ominously even lower. These quieter moments help establish pace.[14]

Galvatron and Optimus Battle (1:14–1:18)

Three times a vehicle's long side flies toward us, almost to impact us straight on. Each time, the intensity rises—Galvatron, Optimus, and then an enormous 18-wheeler truck of lumber that breaches all the highway's lanes. On first viewing this scene seems to have cars rushing inexplicably back and forth, and in truth the scene's opening seems designed to disorient us. Galvatron twice exits the KSI garage. On the road, the camera films a red Camaro and him first from one side, then the other. But after that spatial relations quiet down a bit, though the pace doesn't slacken. Subtle cues help make shifts in screen direction sensible.

In the first large turn, many cars veer off onto the grass to clear the way for Galvatron. It's a wide and graceful shot, as if *T4* were a Western and the cars were readying to corral the herd. In the far distance, a green truck changes screen direction for all cars. Joyce and the control room staff also view a large projected diagram that should suggest where players are positioned, though I think it works more as a joke on critics. Galvatron jumping the road divider is confusing, because he disintegrates and reforms. What forms can he adopt, and where did he go? He drives straight into opposing oncoming traffic, while the camera crosses from one to the other side of his visage. Interlaced throughout this scene are some delicate bishop-moves that trouble spatial relations and help to shift screen direction.

The second time Galvatron disintegrates, he breaks into a star-shaped pattern like his flying bogies. The shot is stunning not only for the glory of Galvatron reconfiguring but also for Bumblebee's emergence. In an earlier shot, a side of Bumblebee's face edges the right eighth-quadrant of the frame. Then he appears as a little robot by the overhead pass in the far distance. Now Bumblebee materializes into a form we recognize—incrementally shifting from a mask into a face, with his voice finally coming into focus. When Bumblebee asks of Galvatron, "What was that?" we're in a state of wonder, too—about both Bumblebee and Galvatron. How many viewers followed both robots' metamorphoses?

The closing set piece also evokes wonder. Optimus Prime and others hurtle through the air on the long horizontal so that Optimus is streamlined like a swimmer. Everything seems extremely slow: the sound effects include an elongated, reverberant scream. The moment resembles the archetypical instant of extreme danger when your life flashes before you, focus is sharp, and time seems to crawl. It's a gorgeous audiovisual moment, with grace, line, and flight, but it also inspires terror. The robots are tossing humans back and forth like juggling balls, from elbows to knees to fists (fig. 2.5).

T4 loses momentum and becomes more convoluted at its close. Arriving in Hong Kong, the group resolves its Oedipal conflicts, leaving little to go on. Bay sometimes brings *T4* to moments of *jouissance*, but often it seems to bear a just-below-the-surface hysteria. The robots may lose it a lot, but they're just expressing the nuclear family's sentiments. Young boys' screams are often mixed in with the robots' sounds; the film gains power from the mirroring of humans and robots. *T4*'s last section drives instead toward what Lesley Brill shows us about crowds: rising and dropping objects combined with accruing groups of people suggest a multitude.[15]

A. O. Scott claims that *Transformers* reflects "the glorious uselessness of [Bay's] own imagination."[16] But the film possesses a moral dimension. Many of us attempt to capitalize on our time as we attempt to succeed at work-status and relationship-speedup. Time means much for *T4*'s characters, too. Among the explosions and CGI, they must demonstrate their mastery. It's awful that Lucas gets killed, but as Cade, Tessa, and Sean are leaving, there's an honest minute of mourning. Remarkably, it seems like enough. In a beat, too, Shane and Tessa declare their love in the midst of the final battles. Quick instances earlier, like the couple's momentary cud-

2.5 As the scene speeds up, the frames' contents slow down (elongation).

dle during the alien spaceship's flight over the Great Wall of China, help us trust in the couple's vitality. Joyce needs but a beat to do the right thing. In these heightened moments the film encourages us to ask whether, as individuals and as a collective, we too would act rightly.

T4's final sections—on the alien ship and in Hong Kong—are too long. But Bay and his collaborators may want to bury the film's annihilation motifs so viewers can reenter their daily lives unencumbered. Many of these threats draw on Holocaust imagery, some overtly and others refracted through popular culture. Optimus stowed beneath the barn's floor would be understood by young people more through Quentin Tarantino's *Inglourious Basterds* (2009) than from a historical understanding of the horror of the Nazis. Something still lingers, however. *T4* helps us experience danger in our bones, but not to a point where we can't function. Bay may also be inserting some distance between his rough depictions along lines of race, class, gender, nationality, and disability. He has been called out for these, but I suspect he keeps them in because they work as rapid affective triggers, which assist with his rises and builds—for example, a Black manager enters the robot showroom and Bumblebee starts rapping MC Hammer's "You Can't Touch This." *T4* is also "personal cinema," and toward the film's end, after the viewer may be worn-down and overwhelmed, compositions get crazy. Fire, flesh, and robots are on the bottom, and water is on the top; then all is inverted. Some of these moments are among cinema's most vertiginous.

T4 is too long, and I can't quite stretch my brain around it. But it encourages me to watch it again. What can I say about this overwhelming opus? I'm up for it again. I'm game. Count me in.

II Music Video and the Art-Video Border

3

Beyoncé's Overwhelming Opus; or, the Past and Future of Music Video

NO ONE HAS SOUGHT TO TRACE the history of music video's influence on audiovisual style and aesthetics—especially as it has changed over forty years, and as it has contended with cinema, commercials, and popular music.[1] While chronicling this history is beyond this book's compass, this chapter provides an overview that gives a sense of how music video's style has changed decade by decade. I'll propose a working definition for the genre; discuss its past, present, and future; and attend to some of the technological, social, and economic influences impinging on it. I'd like to show how one might analyze a music video with the genre's history in mind. Turning finally to Beyoncé, I'll suggest that we can gain a sense of the genre's history by analyzing recent videos that engage that history. Beyoncé is now the genre's fulcrum and its formal innovator and historical guardian. Her self-titled "visual album" *Beyoncé* (2013) and her audiovisual film *Lemonade* (2016) draw on music video's past, and suggest new possibilities for the form's future. This chapter gives us streamlined ways of thinking about music video and audiovisual relations. This established common ground will help us explore a variety of media and platforms (fig. 3.1).

Why should we care about music video? There are four reasons, I think. First is its cultural centrality today: it's one of our most popular forms of moving media. ("Baby Shark" has 10 billion hits and Luis Fonsi's "Despacito" has 7.8 billion, numbers approaching a mathematical sublime.) It's also the most viewed content on YouTube, with studies showing that music videos are the most common way for audiences to consume popular music.[2] Second, its aesthetics have seeped into nearly everything moving and visual, from *Transformers* and *Hunger Games* to Bollywood, and television shows like *Game of Thrones*. Third, it's a genre with its own

3.1 Beyoncé's *Lemonade*.

conventions, ways of carrying a narrative and eliciting emotions; deploying performers, settings, and props; and conveying space and time. I've written that YouTube can be thought of as a whoopee cushion, and post-classical cinema as a form that puzzles and pummels the viewer.³ Music video's specialty lies in conveying a brief state of bliss. It's dependent on ephemeralities of color, movement, and sound. Like popular music, music video possesses motifs, rhythms, grain, and fine details that carry weight. It resides somewhere between advertising and art. Fourth, it's a genre to think with. Music video, as delimited by MTV's initial launch, is but forty years old, but it has shape-shifted in response to dramatic technological, aesthetic, institutional, and audience pressures.

In MTV's first twenty years, viewers seemed to need little help determining what music videos were. The clips emerged from collaborations between record companies, musicians, and directors. The visual track was designed to sell the song. Several scholars noted that they seemed uncanny. Then, as now, they were brief and had to accomplish many things: highlight the star, showcase performances, draw attention to the lyrics, and underscore the music. To teach listeners what's memorable about a song the image might emphasize the movement from verse to chorus, or highlight an unusual timbre, melodic contour, or striking rhythm. The visual track might point to one or two musical features at a time, like a tour guide—for while music envelops us, visual features more often momentarily focus our attention, especially if they're working in the service of the song.

Lady Gaga's "Bad Romance" (2009) is a music video in the classic mode. Like director Francis Lawrence's other clips, it does a lot to show off the song. The melody resides primarily in a mid- and low range, and its sonic material is heavily reverberant, and we have a low-ceilinged space with a long sweep to the back. Historically the harpsichord has been associated with the affluent and cultivated, and there they are. The song's minor key has a flat sixth chord, along with an open fifth that sounds antique; perhaps this harmonic language sparked the idea of the Euro female slave-auction. Gaga's "ra-ras" and the snare drum sound like chants for ominous swarms of trolls, and we have the crown-capped gremlins. The deedle-dweedle sound effect suggests hard surfaces, which connects with the room's paneling. The song undertakes a sinuous, careful build toward the chorus, so the searchlights take their time checking the space out, and performers emerge slowly from their caskets. The chorus is big, and that's when the phalanxes of dancers appear. The music video also achieves novel effects: while each chorus foregrounds the big communal hook "I want a bad romance," it also subtly pushes forward the narrative. In a later chorus, for example, Gaga will be slipped an elixir and wrapped in a burlap sheet. Puzzles and conundrums—How much autonomy does Gaga possess? Should she have torched her buyer?—encourage repeat viewings (fig. 3.2).

Classically styled videos continue to appear on YouTube, such as Taylor Swift's "Blank Space" (2014), for example. But now YouTube's generic boundaries are so fluid that one might feel an urge to abandon the term altogether: cinema's musical excerpts, corporate adverts, amateur remixes, and found footage with incongruous soundtracks all look like music videos. In "Auto-Tune the News," newscasters' voices processed through Auto-Tune "sing" their stories accompanied by Fruity Loops tracks. Is

3.2 Lady Gaga's "Bad Romance": image diligently reflects music and lyrics.

it a music video? Why not then include "The Llama Song" and "Haha Baby?"[4] Today, indicators of production, reception, and intent often go missing. New forms both of musicality and audiovisuality emerge in many contexts. Perhaps all we can say about music video is it's a relationship between music and image we recognize as such.[5]

Music Video's Liminal Status

Experiencing music video today, fans and makers seem to possess a sense of rupture and perplexity. It's not clear whether we're ready to evaluate the genre's present and past, or gauge where it might go. Its history is poorly chronicled. Does the genre deserve or possess a canon? Beyoncé's *Beyoncé* visual album (2013) calls the videos "mini-films," rather than music videos, even though the clips are more reflective of music video history than nearly anything else circulating recently. Bands like Pomplamoose opt for new terms, like "video song," and Beyoncé's *Lemonade* (2016) is marketed as a visual album. Why erase the past? In order to discuss Beyoncé's recent long-play multimedia works, it's important to consider music video's past, present, and future. This is partly because younger fans don't know what she's talking about. Through attending to a clip from each decade, I'll provide a quick historical overview. While moving through them I'll highlight some of the genre's specificities, including its peculiar ways of forging audiovisual relations and handling performers.

Music Video's History: A Rewind and Fast Forward

Many know the first music video aired on MTV's first broadcast, "Video Killed the Radio Star" (1979) by the Buggles, but most subsequent clips have been forgotten. The second, Ph.D.'s "Little Susie's on the Up" (1981), is stronger than the first, and better addresses issues facing that era's relation to audiovisual sync. Pop music had recently changed—the 1970s featured lush, highly detailed arrangements with real musicians: think Earth, Wind & Fire, Steely Dan, P Funk. The 1980s were taken up by British bands like Flock of Seagulls, Human League, Duran Duran, and arrangements built up with synths and drum machines. The turn may also have been driven by a backlash against Black music, gay subcultures, urban settings, and dance; some have suggested it also embraced an expanding neoliberalism.[6] Perhaps also the new fashions and sounds were just so novel that everyone paid attention. (It has been suggested that Black musicians were excluded from the now visually whiter aesthetics because the bigger, teased and blow-dried hairstyles couldn't be well replicated by them.) The 1980s drum-machines and synths nested nicely with music video's fledgling style; the visual track was assembled cheaply and quickly, and was often produced in vacant TV studio late night shoots with musicians who didn't know how to move with playback singing. The performers often seemed shot up with elephant tranquilizer.

You can see this in "Little Susie's on the Up." The video underscores musically the simplest of things: the four-on-the-floor drums, the pounding booms of the synth, and the tail-end upsweep of the melody's contour. "On the up" the singer intones and performers look up. A waltz is suggested, so we have swaying against the blockier pumping. Already we can see one of the oddest features of the genre: the background figures (follow that man with the eyepatch!). Pop songs often relay utopian hopes, but only one singer articulates them, except perhaps for some confirmation by the backing vocalists. To depict these communal desires, the video needs to be populated by figures. They lack text, however, so we often see interstitial, mute stand-ins, like service workers, 2D dancers, models, dolls. Oddly, these figures provide musical gains. The background figures, along with a frisky star, help express a range of rhythmic strata from stillness to intense activity, thereby drawing attention to a song's heterogeneous, layered arrangement. In what follows, I'll demonstrate the ways the background characters become more nuanced over time.

In the 1990s video budgets rose to over several million, videos were shot on 35 millimeter, and director's names appeared underneath song titles. With this, as Roger Beebe has noted, came auteurism.[7] Many fans recognized the directorial styles of Hype Williams, Dave Meyers, Matt Mahurin, and Mark Romanek. These names alone could be counted on to encourage viewing and drive CD sales. BET, VH1, and other stations provided a wide range of programming, with specialized shows like *Alternative Nation*, *Midnight Love*, MTV *Raps*, and *120 Minutes*. Two genres—alternative and hip-hop—seemed to emerge as oppositional modes, almost always raced as white against Black. Each possessed its own iconography with distinct depictions of props, color, settings, and space.

One wouldn't swap the visuals from these two alternative and hip-hop clips, for example: Nirvana's "Smells Like Teen Spirit" (1991) and Notorious B.I.G.'s "Big Poppa" (1995). "Smells Like Teen Spirit" exhibits textural details that might be called both coarse- and more finely grained. The raucous guitar, bruised voice, and the stripped-down chords reiterate unchangingly across the verse and chorus. This approach works nicely against the malevolent, smoky, overexposed image. Butch Vig, Nirvana's producer, expertly collaged many of the band's raw takes in Pro Tools and then added much processing and ambient sound. Director Samuel Bayer deployed much smoke, as well as rougher textures. Sweaty high school kids, invited to a free late-night performance, were encouraged to trash the gym. The video's song and visuals both seem grainy and in the clip's delirium it seems to create a new amalgam of sound and image. We might imagine a transmutation, with the elements mimicking the properties of water. The guitar's brief, isolated, ringing motif sounds like a poison arrow that, as it drops into a pond, expands ringlets outward that could tip the kids off their bleachers; an increasing growl might destabilize things, and force an added pump by those anarchist cheerleaders; the chorus's "I feel stupid and contagious" builds to a tsunami that could wash away the ground locked, dunce-capped janitor. Here's another of music video's oddities: best is to have a set of inscrutable characters and props placed in relation without clear causes. In such a fragile ecosystem, the music might become the primary agent and suddenly push everything in a new direction. Or, just as likely, a shamanistic janitor might appear to be the primary cause (fig. 3.3).

The antipode of "Teen Spirit" would be Notorious B.I.G.'s "Big Poppa." Like many hip-hop videos, it is weighted low in the arrangement and in the frame: the dancers drop to their knees, the camera sits near the car's hubcaps. Cuts fall unpredictably, yet the editing maintains a relaxed feel. Languid attractions wink in and out amidst a golden-tinted, mellow communality. We might or might not like to follow that thin, bobbing synth in the high register. At the time of this video Black director Hype Williams was celebrated for his sensitivity to people and places, and New York–based Notorious B.I.G. was appreciated for his loose, easy flow (fig. 3.4).

Then, in the early 2000s, downloading hit, the record industry lost revenue, and music video budgets were slashed. MTV found it cheaper to program its own teen-reality sitcoms, which advertisers preferred. It's not necessarily what viewers wanted.[8] There was a dearth of high-quality clips on the internet, and finding them wasn't easy. OK Go's "Here it Goes Again" (2006), with band members doing choreographed routines on treadmills, was one of the first to assert music video's regained cultural relevance. With its single concept and stripped-down means, it celebrated the new austerity (fig. 3.5).

Today, several factors contribute to music video's centrality. In 2009, three of the major record labels banded together and launched Vevo, a music video website. In 2013 Billboard started including YouTube views

3.3 Dreamlike music/image relations in Nirvana's "Smells Like Teen Spirit": multiple indeterminate causes return us to the music.

3.4 Notorious B.I.G.'s relaxed and communal "Big Poppa": the image attends to the upper-register synth melody.

3.5 OK Go's "Here it Goes Again,": music video in the age of austerity.

in their pop charts, which gave corporations measures by which to judge music video's currency. Pre-roll ads and product placement within clips generate revenue. Budgets often remain low, however, because with an enormous pool of cheap talent, companies can depress wages.[9] Even though budgets have dropped, directors and production houses can sometimes still afford to make clips, because production costs like cameras, tape, and software packages have also dropped. Media agencies also want to hire music video directors, because their clips, posted on a company's website, attract clients. Performers who appear in commercials like working with music video directors, because these directors have sophisticated and up-to-date pop-culture sensibilities.

Katy Perry's "This Is How We Do" (2013) bears traces of today's economic, social, and technological constraints. It's shot on green screen, which is faster, cheaper, and easier to work with than location shooting. The wan colors seem like a product of the economic downturn. "This Is How We Do" sounds like an older generation's pop music, and the video acknowledges this with desultory old-school costumes. But there's a twist. The Swedish pop songwriters Martin and Ahlund structured this song according to "the soar." "The soar" famously relies on a simple structure: a tiered chorus, which draws on principles of layering and textural "builds," long a staple of electronic dance music. The song begins with a relatively sparse texture, then repeats a second time with added layers, along with a propulsive dance beat. A two-part chorus drives to a rapidly building textural crescendo. The verse scales back before the beginning of the pre-chorus, so it can make the buildup of the chorus even more dramatic. Many musicologists don't like the soar; they feel listeners are hectored into the chorus' ecstatic high. But in a music video this songwriting technique offers new possibilities. Against the song's regimented structure, color can adopt a contrapuntal voice; visual motifs like Perry's watermelon can also separate from others and skate with and apart from the music.

Music Video and Media Genres

So now let's zoom out and ask some broader questions. Do music videos follow other genres' arcs, such as, for example, that of the Western in American cinema? With the Western, formal devices shift through time: first there's a schematic beginning with a few prescient outliers, then a drive toward stylistic crystallization, a colonization by competing genres, and finally a highly self-critical stance. With music video, signs point in so many directions I honestly can't answer this. Perhaps a more manageable question is: Which era, the 1980s, 1990s, or today, seems most experimental, vibrant, rich? And how do a period's technologies and production practices both enable and limit possibilities? In the 1980s, videos were often shot on 1-inch tape and edited on U-matic decks that slipped frames. Fine sync was unachievable; the technology was cheap but cumbersome. If you pressed the wrong button, your control track broke. Your work-tapes dropped generations, either when you made duplicates during the editing process or included postproduction graphic effects. Your image's color scheme could only be changed globally: you might highlight some orangey-red from a fireplace and a cigarette tip, and then wash the image teal blue, but red was a difficult color anyway.

The music had similar resistances. The sounds were crude and bulky. But something aesthetically interesting emerged from these intransigencies. Music video may first be about the song's and image's relation, and what that meeting point conveys. Perhaps these function as an emblem of human relations. In George Michaels's "Father Figure" (1988) a taxi driver haunts an elusive fashion model, and their struggles seem class-based. A haze coating the image heightens the distance the characters must breach. Today this is all too easy. Compare Michaels's "Father Figure" with Beyoncé's "1+1" (2011). Beyoncé's face seems impossibly malleable; colors and textures ripple off it. The music is equally subject to manipulation, as are the relations between music and image. But that lack of friction may suggest that nothing counts. Why not change it all up again? Could I go back and capture some of that 1980s aesthetics by shooting on videotape and fooling around with antiquated synthesizers and drum machines? No—because ways of knowing and feeling have changed too (figs. 3.6 and 3.7).

Animation may provide some account of stylistic shifts apart from technological changes. In the last thirty five years approaches to 2D effects may have remained more constant than has live action. INXS's (1985) "What You Need" is sophisticated, but Rihanna's (2009) "Rude Boy" is more so. Comparing these illustrates one of music video's contributions to today's visual language: a freeing up of the frame. Unlike "What You Need's," "Rude Boy's" figures and objects reside on the angle. Planes of activity are more richly developed. In the background upper quadrant, a black stain seeps down while much unfolds in the foreground. The black stain is where the action is.

But by pulling select examples, I may not be providing a fair picture of the genre. To understand music video we'd want to look at a vast quantity of clips, year by year. If we considered dispositions of characters and

3.6 George Michaels's "Father Figure."

3.7 Beyoncé's "1 + 1": audiovisual relations offer a metaphor for human relations.

props, and their audiovisual kinospheres, we might also glean a bit of what it felt like to be a person in each era. In our process of discovery, we'd also likely find the datedness of some clips amusing. Kim Carnes's (1981) "Bette Davis Eyes" offers a compendium of the era's tropes. It looks low budget, as if it were shot on a soundstage after hours. Cut outs over the lights help direct Venetian slashes on the walls; these complement projected silhouettes. A wind machine blows hair and gauzy fabric. The large blocks probably belonged to the studio's everyday prop collection. What's the video all about? Beats me. Surely clips with short expiry dates are produced as often today; perhaps Katy Perry's "This Is How We Do" will seem equally goofy in the future. Twenty years from now we'll know which of today's videos dated most quickly, and these videos will tell us what means to be embedded within a time.

Music Video's Present and Future

Because there are more streaming venues, less censorship, and fewer constraints on product-placement or length, new forms and genres of music videos are emerging. I'd like to describe these new configurations through four categories: corporate, independent, interactive, and formal.

Taylor Swift's "Blank Space" from 2014 is a corporate product as glossy and richly budgeted as those of the 1990s. Back then, when directors were as famous as court painters, stars would collect them as if they were commissioning artists for their estate portraits (I want a Matt Mahurin; I must have my Mark Romanek). Perhaps we're again seeing these directors' clips because sentimental young rock stars remember them as tweens. Or probably more likely, with the returning budgets comes a conservatism (David Bordwell has noted that today's Hollywood cinema remains formally static due to high production costs).[10] Funding for these pricier clips often comes from product placement: cell phones, designer glasses, and liquor. In the past, MTV didn't allow advertising in clips. Shakira's "La La La" (2014) in partnership with Activia Yogurt works as a music video, a fundraiser, and an ad. Viewed half a billion times, the clip's closing encourages viewers to click through to donate to alleviate world hunger. Dannon, the corporate head, has tracked the clip's effectiveness for increasing yogurt sales.

Which directors to hire, how to meet pop music's and music videos' quick release dates, where to place ads, where to post clips, and how much support to throw behind these are all concerns for corporations now. Companies are investing in invasive technologies like EEG, facial recognition, fMRI, eye tracking, galvanic skin response, and large surveys crunched by algorithms to help answer these questions. They've lost revenue as they've watched their clientele migrate from film and television to online content, and they feel adrift and anxious. Is there some magic formula to predict whether a clip will go viral? Directors will soon surely be pressured to conform their big budget videos to perceived experiential schemas.

Another new genre is comprised of interactive clips, some of which feel akin to video games while others resemble video performance art. Arcade Fire's "Reflektor" (2013) lets you "dance" with your cellphone and computer monitor. A quick-loading clip of Bob Dylan's reissue of "Like a Rolling Stone" (2013) lets the viewer, as if wielding a television remote, access and edit footage with a mouse click. With Bjork's "Stonemilker" (2015) a viewer can pan the image 360 degrees in all directions, its framing led by the mouse's trace. In the future, immersive, interactive approaches may reduce the need for moving media to carry a narrative, allowing the sensual intensities of sound and image to take over.

There are also indie artists' low-budget videos, and clips for bigger artists who have lost their label's support. These clips often foreground technological gimmicks and devices, like kaleidoscopes. They're attentive to music video history and frequently sardonic. Once these low-budget clips might have aired on MTV's midnight programming; now music video and pop music connoisseurs scour the web searching for blogs that post them. Close audiovisual relations may not be as important in these clips (concert tickets or a logo T-shirt might be a video's end goal, rather than mp3 sales). My students, especially, seek out these thousand-hit videos as a way of showing off their indie cred.

There's also what I'd like to call the new, unfunded creative class. It's now possible for a band, with no manager, no record contract, and no tangible media, to at least partially make a living through YouTube and iTunes streaming revenue. The band Pomplamoose bought their house this way. They created a patronage system (Patreon) which supports talented artists and musicians.

Finally, there are new formal configurations. Music videos can now showcase long intros and endings, breaks in the middle of songs, and song medleys—devices MTV and other satellite services previously disallowed. Depictions of violence and sexuality are more graphic. These, among many other devices and trends, make possible novel forms like The Weeknd's "In the Night" (2015), Kanye's *Runaway* (2010), Frank Ocean's *Endless* (2016), and Beyoncé's *Beyoncé* (2013) and *Lemonade* (2016).

A Detour: Music Video's Place in Media History

Before I turn to the final section of this chapter on Beyoncé's self-titled "visual album" and *Lemonade*, let me describe the ways music video may have contributed to contemporary media. This description will also help articulate the ways Beyoncé's album departs from others before it, and the video album, may well shape moving media's future. To make this case, I'll need to quickly shuttle back and forth through music video history again, this time with a focus on digital technologies. I'll start with today, return to the genre's beginning, and head out toward the future.

Today, we're in a period of what I'd like to call intensified audiovisuality. In cinema, both sound and image have been dramatically reconfigured. The soundtrack has become "musicalized": sound effects and dialogue are now shaped alongside composed music into musical phrases. Sound effects and other sonic features can also adopt leading roles, driving the film forward; or sound can mediate, enabling individual film parameters to come forward. The image too acquires a sense of speed and flexibility: its contents can seem as if they had been poured from one shot into the next. Cutting, too, can bestow an almost percussive rhythmic drive. The image in the new digital cinema often avoids a ground, because the sound wafts it along. Only by being so sound-centric can the image detach itself from a codified, shot-bound format; images released by sound can be filled in by it.

European art cinema, Hong Kong action films, American experimental filmmaking, Hollywood musicals, and horror film soundtracks have assuredly had a strong impact on this audiovisual style. So too have iPod culture and the musicalization of public space, and technologies like Dolby, 10.1 surround sound, light digital cameras, and Avid editing systems. This is work for media historians. What is music video's role in this shift? I'd claim it's central. Craig Marks and Rob Tannenbaum's *I Want My MTV: The Uncensored Story of the Music Video Revolution* features excerpts from over four hundred interviews with bands and industry personnel about MTV's first decade. It gives a sense of each brief zeitgeist. Says Chuck D of Public Enemy: "These days, everybody has a hi-def camcorder, 'Okay, so what?' But back then, it was a main event"; Nancy Wilson of Heart recalls that "Everybody wanted their MTV so bad. I remember *craving* it like crazy"; and Lenny Kravitz says, "I was watching music video 24/7. On vacation, holed up in a hotel room, my parents asked 'what's the matter with you?'"[11] My sense about music video's relevance also derives from my youthful experiences. In the 1970s and 1980s, filmmakers and I watched foreign cinema through film schools, late-night repertory theaters, and VHS rental houses. But how formative were these encounters? Unfortunately, they tended to occur relatively infrequently. Repertory theaters like the Hollywood's Nuart screened a narrow, often middle-brow playlist—*King of Hearts* and *Harold and Maude*. The foreign film collections of most VHS rental houses were limited. In the 1980s, you'd see music video programming almost everywhere: friends' houses, in beauty salons, hotels, gyms, and bars. A common party icebreaker was to share wonder over a new clip or the anticipation of an upcoming release.

Beginning filmmakers found music videos attractive because the genre provided one of the most direct ways to break into the industry—one could build a showreel and land a film gig. Making music video was also a training ground in its own right: a director could be responsible for all phases of production, including conception, props, and editing. You could pitch an odd treatment, head out to an obscure location, and shoot a ton of footage—and no one would know what you were doing. With commercials, the treatment was usually written by an ad-agency, and shooting and editing were supervised by industry reps.

In the 1980s music video was the laboratory: an editor might try anything (turn the image on its head and stain it blue). Music video used cheap, reusable technology in the service of quick deadlines (make it fast and creatively). In the 1990s music video-directors streamed into cinema, helping drive the new, audiovisually intensified postclassical film. A second wave then emigrated as funding dried up in the 2000s. Music video directors like Michael Bay, David Fincher, Spike Jonze, Francis Lawrence, and Mark Romanek have flourished because they're attuned to new technologies and new audiovisual relations.

One might have sped up Godard and placed pop music against it, or taken a Hollywood musical and intensified both the film's soundtrack and its images, but this would never have gotten us to the audiovisual aesthetics we have today. It has a peculiar configuration based on historical events. And something's at stake.

If schools, museums, and libraries paid more attention to "minor arts" like pop music and music video, we might interpret our contemporary mediascape differently, and we might be more attuned to the ways in which audiovisual ideas flow through today's media swirl. I'm troubled by the documentary "Side By Side" (2012), narrated by Keanu Reeves, with interviews from directors David Lynch to Danny Boyle. The film describes the digital turn as a silent one—lighter cameras, postproduction techniques like color timing. We need to keep the audio in.[12]

Or we might put aside our desire claim historical precedent and just say intensified audiovisual aesthetics are often music video aesthetics. Multitracked, heavily worked popular music and music video provided the model for what is today a mixing-board approach. Imagine it this way: new digital technologies allow a filmmaker to redraw an image of a house every time it occurs in a film. She can change its color in each iteration, and modify other parameters, like the texture of the forest behind it, or the sounds of crows sitting on its roof. The soundtrack can be modulated to work with the scape of the image, and then the image can be modulated once again. This is different from working on one of the first *Star Wars* films and having to send your assistant to the vault to locate two reels of film to splice together. I've worked with audiotape and interviewed sound designers about their professional experiences, and we agree that sound editing against picture editing in the analog period was like banging rocks together.

Beyoncé's *Beyoncé* and *Lemonade*

On December 13, 2013, Beyoncé surprise-dropped an entire album of seventeen videos on iTunes. The media immediately blissed out. The *New York Times* called it "perhaps one of the most important pop events of all time."[13] Katy Perry tweeted, "Don't talk to me about anything but Beyoncé today."[14] The iTunes servers crashed. Within this media onslaught, Beyoncé and her team shaped the flow of information. The press release's opening line was, "Music is now seen." Released all at once and only purchasable through iTunes, the album could only be experienced as a whole. Fans felt compelled to buy the collection, and many went into a binge mode of viewing/listening as they tried to assimilate the album's sweep. Every few weeks individual videos and mini-documentaries were released on YouTube, keeping fans engaged for much longer than typical with an album's release. Such a coup would be impossible without Beyoncé's financial and staffing resources, and her artistic vision. The project would also be unimaginable without the new audiovisual digital technologies.

It's hard to describe quickly how the works form a whole. The album is remarkable, partly because it's heavily rooted in the star's life experiences, from having parents who fought racial injustice in the South and became successful businesspeople in Houston, to her childhood training in pageants and pop groups. This autobiographical dimension makes her work different from that of other divas like Madonna, Lady Gaga, and Rihanna. The varieties of a woman's experience help bind the *Beyoncé* album's clips.

The first half explores heterosexual monogamy, and then the album heads elsewhere. High-water marks include three fanfare-like songs, at the beginning, middle, and end. Clips dovetail, either through continuities of time, color palette, visual references, or story. Though the videos might at first seem unrelated, cohesion is provided by the many characters close to Beyoncé—family, including her husband and daughter, friends and dancers. Places—the roller rinks and streets of Houston, the palaces of Vienna, the apartments of New York, the beach—also recur. Color and textural schemes—black and white, pop pastels or deeply saturated more earth-like hues, grain or static—also return, providing continuity. The collection showcases sound's ephemerality, the way sounds attack and diminish through time.

Let me return to my story about the crows, trees, and house: Beyoncé's album would be impossible without the new audiovisual technologies. The singer recorded over three hundred fully arranged songs before winnowing down the album to seventeen. The computational resources to keep track of the materials must have been significant. The singer filmed the music videos while she was on tour in over eight cities and four continents, including São Paulo, Houston, Miami, New York, and Paris. One of the main production hubs was Australia. The soundtrack and visuals are lush. But the clips could be realized within a day's shooting, partly because they emphasize site-specific settings. The project's codename was Lily, and almost no one knew, including the video directors, about the album's scope or release date. Keeping files secure and directing an international workflow must have been daunting. Beyoncé is an auteur—performer, songwriter, director, businesswoman—and her team are the most talented in the field. The album draws on directors Beyoncé has collaborated with for over the last fifteen years: Jonas Åkerlund, Jake Nava, and Hype Williams, as well as up and coming ones. Through these choices, the album as a whole can look both backward and forward. Several of the clips pay homage to videos by Madonna and Janet Jackson; others are influenced by YouTube and new media. This album also jumpstarts the process of analyzing music video's history and argues for its place in the future. "Haunted" gestures toward Madonna's 1993's "Justify My Love." Hype Williams's "Drunk in Love" signifies on Herb Ritts's video for Madonna's 1989 "Cherish." Melina Matsoukas's "Pretty Hurts" draws on Madonna's "Like a Prayer" (1988). Hype Williams "Blow" echoes Klymaxx's 1984's "The Men All Pause," and so on. In this section I'll describe five contrasting clips to acquaint readers with Beyoncé's *Beyoncé*: "Blow," "Pretty Hurts," "Jealous," "Haunted," and "Flawless."

"Blow" (Track 5)

"Blow" homages high-class roller-disco hits like Earth, Wind, and Fire's "Boogie Wonderland." Many late 1970s through 1980s songwriting styles receive gentle nods: a bit of Prince in the guitar playing; the close vocal overdubbing of Chaka Khan; the rapping over panting by the girl-group Klymaxx; some of Sheila E's percussion playing. The syndrum sound (a little swoop) and the four-on-the-floor rhythm are also disco signifiers. The setting is a roller rink Beyoncé knew as a kid growing up in Houston. A Bootsy Collins lookalike takes us back as well.

Hype Williams draws attention to the song's fine touches, including its close vocal harmonies, interesting drum fills, and quiet beatboxing. Williams's models rap their knuckles on the roller rink's lockers to match the snare; musicians appear when catchy licks come forward in the mix; and Beyoncé is shown in close-up as she performs vocal melismas.

The video seems inspired by the literal meaning of the lyrics, rather than their sexual implications: "Can you lick my skittles" is taken as a color cue, not a provocation. The video is coated with a haze of rainbow-like candy hues. The skaters adopt various poses—freezing, twirling, pumping, and gliding—helping us think of the ways sound attacks, grows, and diminishes, "That sugar babe, it melts away." In the clip's opening, Beyoncé's close-ups are followed with blinking lights and rotating disco balls, as if to extend the resonance of her voice before the sweetness fades. The video, like the song, seems to want to "keep us going, keep us humming."

For this kind of close-reading, Michel Chion's and Nicholas Cook's approaches to audiovisual analysis are helpful. Chion's concept of synchresis, for example, the irrevocable meld that happens when image and sound are placed in relation, and Cook's models of conformance, complement, and contest as well as gap-making, provide ways of describing sync. Cook also draws attention to new metaphorical relations that can emerge from the meeting of sound and image, and that many types of relation can occur on different hierarchical levels simultaneously. Like Chion, Cook, and Philip Tagg, I practice analysis through various modes: for example, listening to the music and watching the image alone, attempting to hear, view, or experience in a purely material, non–culturally influenced way, and then the obverse.[15]

Music/image relations can seem quite fantastical, as if sound and image might express the desire to influence one another, or to overcome, assist, or repress what the other hopes to bring forward. In "Blow," males seem more vulnerable than the women—they're covered with lipstick kisses and cower in the back of the frame. While music videos have traditionally oversexualized Black women, here white women are the most objectified. Cross-cut against Beyoncé twerking is a companion image of Beyoncé, her sister Solange, and another woman patrolling on their mini low-rider post–tricycle bikes, while wearing giant capes of fur. Cross-cut also are images of Beyoncé phallically playing an imaginary electric guitar, slung from the hips, with audiovisual echoes of 1980s videos like Klymaxx's "The Men All Pause." Here Beyoncé takes over all roles. The car is also a magic car that seems at her beckoning, like something out of the Powerpuff Girls: it exudes steam rather than smoke, as if to ride off into the sky (the video's theme of locomotion is jacked-up here).

This setting also underscores the song's final section's arrangement. The bass line is now bigger, and the arrangement fills out into a denser texture. It's good to go outside and find a new location away from the rink. Beyoncé's crimped hair suggests one character among many, and she claims her sexual expectations: "I can't wait until I get home and you can turn that cherry out." The males' cat-calling responses don't faze her. Her Chaka Khan-like overdubbing recalls Khan's authority, as in "I'm every woman." The clip also contains a subliminal homosocial or lesbian element. The ways Beyoncé gyrates with the women in her band suggests that that's what's most satisfying. A viewer senses Hype Williams's and Beyoncé's bid for preeminence within a long history of audiovisual and musical production.

"Pretty Hurts" (Track 1)

Melina Matsoukas's "Pretty Hurts" shares techniques with the best of 1980s and 1990s videos, including Madonna's "Express Yourself" and "Like a Prayer." A common technique of music videos is to begin with close sync between music and image as a means to suture the viewer into the clip. As an opening of the whole album, "Pretty Hurts" foregrounds tight audiovisual relations: it carefully guides the viewer through the clips process from images of failure to success.

To establish a sense of flow, music videos employ more match cuts—where two unrelated images are juxtaposed to show their graphical similarities—than narrative films. Blue award ribbons are arrayed in Beyoncé's apartment in the same pattern as the pageant's curtains. Repetition of objects like wigs help create a sense of continuity, as do the colors: Beyoncé standing tall, with a yellow streak in her hair, against the glittering blue curtain; the blue gloves entering the frame in the bridge; Beyoncé's lipstick and hair matching the woman who wins the trophy. The teardrop lampshade (weeping) and the porcelain tchotchkes help tell the story. Beyoncé is tied to a decorative crouched cat and the winner is identified with a tiger figure (peeking out from behind a sofa in one of the last shots). A subtle match cut: Beyoncé's streak of blonde hair is prepared for by her porcelain cat that perches above her head on a television set. The high points of the chorus are set with her standing tall, arms spread, or brandishing trophies.

A lot of empty space shadows the vocals; the multitracked vocals provide a sense of haltingness, they make you wait. But Beyoncé is almost always in multiples, harmonizing with herself or doubling her lead vocals. Marvin Gaye often surrounded his lead vocal with closely overdubbed vocal tracks, especially when he was speaking about community. (Here Beyoncé is singing for and about a community of women.) The rhythm tracks are supersaturated. Every single sixteenth-note is articulated. The music and image also work together to convey the story: the lilting melody seems to offer the characters some comfort, even as the rhythm arrangement encourages them on.

In pop songs the verse's lyrics often narrate the story, while the chorus crystallizes the theme. The same goes for their videos, especially "Pretty Hurts." In the first verse, Matsoukas shows the models preparing for the pageant. She takes us to the stage by drawing attention to musical landmarks. As the prechorus begins Beyoncé steps onto the scale, and dancers toward the back of the rehearsal space reach tall, twirl, and step forward to help carry her along to the chorus. The song's chorus is grand and so are the visuals: the stage has Greek columns, rows of beautiful women, and blue sparkling curtains. (Beyoncé marks the pumping-heartbeat rhythm with her forearms.) The second verse's arrangement thickens, with the voice more multitracked. The section becomes more active: Beyoncé bicycles and presses weights, and the camera pans more. The song stops, as if recoiling from the lyrics "fall down, down, down." As Beyoncé searches to answer the MC's question of what she seeks most in life, she plunges into water. The song's bridge offers the most scathing critique of the fashion industry. Most often in music videos and pop songs, the bridge suggests possibility, an alternate reality. In the bridge in "Pretty Hurts" Matsoukas and Beyoncé tie us more firmly to the fashion industry's exploitation of women. Choruses, too, become more punitive. By the out-chorus, Beyoncé finds an escape; the song closes with the message that happiness comes not from winning beauty pageants, but from seeking ways to be at home with oneself.

"Jealous" (Track 9)

In "Jealous," both song and image work to convey the song title's emotion. Audiovisual sync loosens and patterns are delayed or staggered, as if to convey the unhappy star's desires remain tantalizingly beyond her reach. The song's title appears red, scribbled on a wall at a distance from Beyoncé, as she walks regally (if sullenly) down the stairs. Objects in the frame—falling grapes, burning candles, broken crystal, a painting of thorns—further underscore Beyoncé's darkened mood. When she sings "Just one shot left of this drink, in this glass. Don't make me break it," the world goes either too fast or too slow: clouds stream quickly, cars barrel down streets. Now slow, Beyoncé wears a black lace collar and dress with a train as she grimly paces and dissolutely strokes marble heads. She switches from this outfit into a deeper red lipstick and a reddish-purple, film-noirish trenchcoat as she heads for the streets. The bridge's one respite—Beyoncé's imagined night on the town with another man—feels unachievable, part of another era. The camera moves slowly and heavily. Beyoncé sings in the low register, with some grit. The rock guitar carries its traditional feeling of angry intensity. I hear the singer's opening screams as sonic darts: the reverberant echoes peel off from the voice and guitar, projecting Beyoncé's uncomfortable feelings outward, even as chorused voices counsel restraint ("If you're keeping your promises, I'm keeping mine").

"Haunted" (Track 3)

Jonas Åkerlund's "Haunted" works more elliptically, asking us to puzzle out its audiovisual relations. This approach makes sense for a video that draws on the horror film: to find that ghost or curse, what taunts us from the periphery. What is that weird long-toothed monster on the TV screen? Why does the fire surge behind three chairs and a glass speculum? How could Beyoncé's reflection appear in a painting before she arrives before it? And what does Madonna's famously censored "Justify My Love" have to do with any of this? Fine audiovisual details suggest answers: a "slap" coupled with a man unfurling wing-like devices, which later seems taken up by Beyoncé when she says "Slap me" while the camera rapidly crosscuts among her dancers. Sounds of gears shifting suggest rotating hips but also larger clusters of flagrantly posed bodies. Cries and moans might belong to the elderly or the young, the possessed, or those simply seeking succor. What generates these sounds is ambiguous—the fan man, Beyoncé's commands ("Slap me"), the music, or Madonna's ghost? The functions of the location remain uncertain: perhaps we're inside an asylum, where patients seek sexual healing through nonnormative means. More visual details encourage us to keep seeking an explanation: dots and splotches of red blood, bathtub handles that resemble miniature skulls. Two metal heating pad lids placed on a bed seem to pay homage to Hitchcock.[16] Accompanied by nearby bells, the heating pan lids in "Haunted" seem ominous.

"Flawless" (Track 13)

"Flawless" takes place in what looks like an abandoned warehouse. Beyoncé's dancers mosh. Her costume—a Pendleton plaid shirt, bulky metal jewelry, and thick eyeliner—suggests alliances outside of heteronormativity. She jumps up and punches the air like a competitive boxer, and then falls into a spastic, trance-like dance as if she were plucked out of Jacques Tourneur's *I Walked with a Zombie*.

Strange and ambitious, the video opens with a sped-up sample, "I'm from H-town, coming down." Beyoncé's main vocal melody flows and it resides in strong contrast to the rhythm arrangement's brittle percussion. A synth sound becomes the vehicle for an edgy eight-bit melodic hook with a sinister lowered second. This percussion-heavy texture, with the snare on every beat and sped-up rattling drum-fills, situates the song as electronic dance music. The keyboard pad provides some harmonic support, but the surprisingly lyrical melody is mostly on its own—especially because the lyrics conflict with it ("Don't say I'm just his little wife"). Then, suddenly, a disembodied, heavily reverbed, classically operatic voice enters along with someone speaking, and a harpsichord-like synthesizer sounds. Then all the elements return together, and a subsidiary hook ("I'm flawless, my rock") begins. The dance gestures show off what's hard to embody in the music, like the swoops for "My dia-mond, my rock."

Stomping boots and moshing dancers articulate the song's fast tempo of 140 beats per minute, while the slow-motion footage of Beyoncé's leaps above the crowd projects a more leisurely 70 beats per minute. (The song can be heard either fast or slow.) The closing trancelike dancing, vocal swoops, and general revving-up seems to drive toward a new rhythm, and the hope of transcendence (fig. 3.8).

3.8 "Flawless": a strange and ambitious song and video suggest alliances beyond heteronormativity.

New Subjectivities, Post-Fordist Economies, and *Beyoncé*

The magisterial achievements of Beyoncé's *Beyoncé* come partly from the album's responsiveness to our cultural moment. The video album speaks to anxieties about fluid capital, neoliberalism, work speedup, the demand for affective labor and flexible skills, and identities. Steve Shaviro's *Digital Music Videos* convincingly shows how today's music videos capture affective states (like anxiety and uncertainty) we're unable to access, because to do so would risk paralysis. Shaviro's clips, like those in Beyoncé's *Beyoncé*, tap into these affective states through exploiting properties basic to music video.[17]

I've described five of Beyoncé's seventeen videos, each projecting a different persona with a unique role and state of mind. All cover a broad range: Beyoncé as the loyal, sexual, married partner; the faithful, doting mother; the businesswoman; and others that reside outside of heteronormativity. We might wonder what's driving her: Is it true there are problems within the confines of marriage (she's jealous), or work (that trail of broken trophies)? Or maybe marriage and children are the most pleasurable and satisfying ("Rocket" or "Blue"), and the rest is about play? That's what's remarkable about music video (including long-play ones like *Beyoncé*). When we watch, we're asked to attend to all elements—music, image, and lyrics. The work shimmers, suggesting multiple possibilities. In Hollywood film closings, possibilities tend to become limited and hierarchized. But in a music video, strings of images can attach to various musical materials that come to the fore and recede, with none being annihilated.

Besides mirroring today's demand for fluid identities, Beyoncé's *Beyoncé* speaks to our sense of spatiotemporal compression, multitemporality, and especially accelerating, evaporating time. Audiovisually intensified moving media often reflect the fleeting qualities of sound—the ways that, as Chion has emphasized, there's first an attack, and then decay. In *Beyoncé*, the singer and her supporting performers adopt multiple, shifting roles, and the objects and settings around her participate in time's passing: much is already past tense, and other materials mark the ways things fade—while others emerge. Performers transform into zombies in "Flawless" and "Haunted," freedom fighters in "Superpower," and beauty-pageant winners in "Pretty Hurts." Elements from nature break apart and reform: water, mist, smoke, fire. Multitemporality is also captured through sped-up and slowed-down footage, flickering, and glowing and glimmering electric lights, as well as footage that's distressed (mottled with television grain or other distortion). The clips' collection catches the new landscape's multitemporality—the ways things run fast, slow, medium-paced, all simultaneously veering off in different directions. The ultra-slow tempo of "Superpower" feels as if someone were dragging the tone arm against an LP rotating near zero rpm; crisp rhythms in "Ghost" are fast enough to sprint against a day-temp programmer meeting a start-up's deadline. Jagged, layered, cross-cut rhythms run across clips such as "Jealous" and "Flawless." Beyoncé's prescient opus wows because it taps into our anxious relationship with time.

Beyoncé's spatial locations are compressed and collaged. She and her performers move fluidly across locations (the clips themselves resemble sections of music videos). Many sites are open to people from all economic strata, but a few privilege the 1 percent, to which Beyoncé belongs. Again, because a music-centered soundtrack can support multiple perspectives and places without hierarchy, the album holds together despite its brusque spatiotemporal juxtapositions. In "Haunted," Beyoncé visits a seaside mansion where she can dream about practicing other sexualities, as she herself gets older; in "Flawless" and "Superpower," she can participate in militant subcultures. "Yoncé" and "Partition" show her as hypersexualized in a limo, on the street, and on the catwalk. In "Heaven" and "XO" she can hang out with a friend or mingle among crowds. She can be with her husband and daughter, relatively alone on a separate continent ("Blue"), or muse about her childhood, or shepherd a bevy of children ("Grown Woman"). She can even take a distanced gaze on it all in places outside of any location ("Mine," "Ghost"). The album closes with her being apotheosized, as if she might be an Egyptian goddess with several children on her knee.

We might feel critical toward Beyoncé's social mobility, especially since she nods so frequently to experiences unavailable to the rest of us. But we might instead embrace Stanley Cavell's argument about the wealthy young couples of the 1930s screwball comedies, who, not having to worry about money, can more fully explore the possibilities of romantic and professional relationships.[18] As with *Lemonade*, *Beyoncé*'s range of movement allows for contemplation of extremes: she can criticize the sexual dependency of heterosexual monogamy and the pressures of marriage, even as she also valorizes marriage. (In "Jealous," Beyoncé angrily recites, "I cooked for you naked," but also earlier sings, "all I'm really asking for is you.") Beyoncé's performances are multivalent. Does she twerk for her own pleasure, or to hold Jay-Z's (and our) interest?

Though criticized by scholars as reactionary, *Beyoncé* stretches equally toward progressive ends.[19] By including Chimamanda Ngozi Adichie's sampled quote in "Flawless," Beyoncé can ask, "Why do we teach boys to be sexual but not girls?" "Ghost" targets late-modern capital. Beyoncé wonders, "All the people on the planet, working 9–5—how come?" Her running in place as she tries to keep up with the electronic dance track captures the desperation of trying to gain a ballast in uncertain economic, familial, romantic, and work worlds. Modern anonymity is captured, too, in "Mine." While the clip celebrates relationships, it also intimates a partner is someone chosen blindly from a range of goods: capitalism penetrates to the most private spaces. The diva's album draws from traditionally Black genres like R&B, gospel, and soul, but "Mine," structured around EDM, begins early in the clips' rotation. Is it there because of Beyoncé's engagements, or to cultivate young, white audiences? Or perhaps the choice of EDM, as a register of post-Fordist neoliberalism, as Robin James has argued, immediately hails us all.[20]

Beyoncé's *Lemonade*

Beyoncé's *Lemonade* is, like *Beyoncé*, a magnum opus. Her skills have been honed over several decades. At a young age, Beyoncé's father coached her in singing, performance, and dance. Her mother designed her costumes, and Beyoncé also competed in beauty pageants. Later, Beyoncé cultivated skills in songwriting, music production, acting, film directing, and business management. From when she was young, both parents shared with her their commitment to social activism. All these experiences, as well as an army of supporting artisans, most likely contributed to *Lemonade*. Most striking is the way *Lemonade*'s soundtrack lacks the strong profile of almost all successful pop songs, including those on *Beyoncé*. Most surely a deliberate choice, the recessive soundtrack supports a strongly integrated audiovisual work. Only Beyoncé's oeurvre has directed such a unified, extended work, while comprised almost entirely of music video-like clips.

Many scholars believe that influential aesthetic innovations are triggered by multiple influences—cultural, technical, socioeconomic. Today's long-play music videos like Beyoncé's last two albums (and Kanye's *Famous* and Frank Ocean's *Endless*) may be emergent now because of new economic structures. Online streaming music services like Apple and Tidal fronted the money for these audiovisually intensified films to lure new subscribers. Tie-ins provided additional venues and revenue streams. But surely some of the reasons for these new forms are idiosyncratic. Megastars like Kanye and Beyoncé, drawing on their long experience in the entertainment business, create new forms partly for artistic self-realization. Additionally, much as today's mega-directors (Michael Bay, Baz Luhrmann, Francis Lawrence et al.) adopt multiple roles, including producers for film and television, and content-makers for multiple formats, just to keep their stable of their favored artisans employed and sharp, Beyoncé most likely produced these long-play music videos to maintain relations with long-term director-collaborators, as well as to embark on new ones.

I've expressed an interest in this chronology because I wonder about Beyoncé's role in relation to what I'm boldly calling the fourth phase of film history. The first (as identified by Tom Gunning) was a cinema of attractions; the second (as detailed by David Bordwell) was Hollywood's classical period; and the third (as described by Thomas Elsaesser and Warren Buckland) was the postclassical era, with films like *Memento* and *Eternal Sunshine of the Spotless Mind*, which foregrounded busy surfaces with fast editing and convoluted narratives.[21]

I'll call the present, fourth phase a post-postclassical moment. Directors have figured out ways to unify disparate cinematic techniques and smooth out discontinuities; a dense, fast-changing audiovisual surface can coexist with more traditional storytelling. As in a music video, multiple, contradictory subjectivities can be presented relatively seamlessly. Individual moments can come forward and recede, counterbalancing larger sections, without any gaining primacy. The serial or multiverse blockbuster has taken over most of the cultural space, but we can still see the emergent trend. Partly through a densely worked soundtrack, for example, in Baz Luhrmann's *The Great Gatsby*, Daisy's all-over emotionality suddenly shifts to a cold evaluation of Tom Buchanan, and it's game over for Jay, but her affective modes are never put in relation. In *The Hunger Games: Catching Fire* spaces and environments are collaged without hierarchy: a train suited up in nineteenth-century décor barrels through a barren landscape and a futuristic city. Architecture drawn from Auschwitz, Italian fascism, and sci-fi dovetail together, and it all works fairly well.

I can't predict where we're going, but doesn't this seem to fit our moment? Beyoncé's *Beyoncé* and *Lemonade* are remarkable and innovative works. *Beyoncé* demonstrates this new style: seventeen pieces, all different, all revealing multiple temperaments and modes of address, but improbably reflecting one person. This is not *Memento* or *Eternal Sunshine of the Spotless Mind*; *Lemonade* is the first fifty-minute music video-film, with minimal interstitial text. It has no precursors. Technique, technology, finances, and the moment have coalesced. *Beyoncé* arrives just in time for our post-Fordist society.[22] And who knows? We may once again turn to music video as the driver of it all.

4

Avant-Gardists and the Lure of Pop Music

THIS BOOK AIMS TO HELP readers develop interpretive skills. As chapter 1's analysis of *The Great Gatsby* suggests, much can be gained from exploring audiovisual aesthetics that depart from the mainstream or straddle genres. This chapter focuses on avant-garde audiovisual pieces that incorporate pop music. Experimental and avant-garde directors most often strive to avoid or radically critique mainstream media's practices; they seek to create works that speak differently. Not surprisingly, analytic techniques must bend to this new subject matter. This chapter proposes new approaches that I came to believe also apply to the mainstream objects analyzed elsewhere in this book (see chapters 10–12).

Avant-garde and experimental film- and videomakers do not often incorporate pop music. When they do, scholars tend not to write about the results. Readers may be surprised by my first claim. In the post–rock 'n' roll era, both experimental and popular artists are thought to flaunt conventions and to identify as countercultural; one might expect they would collaborate. This chapter considers the institutional, formal, and cultural reasons why such collaborations tend not to happen. It posits that the reasons for not collaborating also color these artists' audiovisual relations. Pressing further, this chapter presents close readings of some celebrated works and a model for thinking about this subgenre.

I will claim that avant-garde films and videos with pop soundtracks tend to emphasize unique kinds of audiovisual relation.[1] While sound-image connections within narrative films, television trailers, commercials, YouTube clips, and music videos often reveal a family resemblance, those of the avant-garde/pop strain tend to exist at a further remove. Considering this subgenre helps us not only chart the possibilities for sound and image; it expands our knowledge of audiovisual relations more broadly.[2]

What is an experimental artist? What counts as pop music? For purposes of this chapter, an avant-gardist's primary focus resides with experimental media and exhibitions in galleries, independent film-screenings, the arthouse circuit, and museum shows. By pop, I mean pieces intended for American and British mainstream consumption.

Kenneth Anger's *Scorpio Rising* (1963) and Andy Warhol's *Vinyl* (1965) may be the best-known examples I discuss. (They stand in contrast to work by experimental filmmakers like Hollis Frampton, Maya Deren, and Stan Brakhage, who distanced themselves from popular music). As queer artists, Warhol and Anger may have been more willing to break boundaries through engaging with pop and representing nonheteronormative sexuality—an issue I explore later.[3] Following Anger and Warhol, however, things get murky. There is no canon of experimental films or videos that foregrounds Anglo-American pop music. One thinks of figures like Derek Jarman, Pipilotti Rist, Laurie Anderson, and Bruce Conner, but their work, their core audiences, and the larger archive of experimental film and video demonstrate little engagement with pop songs.

The paucity of exchange between experimental videomakers and pop musicians may be because the crossing is hazardous. Simon Frith has emphasized the ways that pop songs are infused with sentiment; they seek to immerse a listener in an emotional experience.[4] But as P. Adams Sitney and Akira Lippit have argued, avant-gardists aim to reveal a system (formal or institutional) and critique it. According to this view, a director should not risk becoming subsumed by a commercial genre or medium, nor facilitate a viewer's seduction by a soundtrack's siren call.[5]

Access and resources are also factors. Directors might want to work with up-and-coming pop musicians, but nurturing such alliances might prove difficult, as would timing a project's release in tandem with a song breaking onto the charts. And by the time a song has sold copies it has accrued many associations, making its meanings more difficult to shape. Avant-gardists tend to possess meagre resources. Purchasing usage rights can be expensive. As Joanna Demers has written in connection with sampling, creative decisions have increasingly become economic ones.[6] Musicians and companies who grant reproduction rights might feel more suspicious of avant-gardists than of commercial artists.

Pop songs also tend to have strongly articulated forms that may be resistant to an avant-gardist's intentions. The song possesses a grid. It has a pattern, a sense of time, and a voice; few artists want to be "slaves to the rhythm."[7] An avant-gardist is expected to show that she can impose a distinctive persona upon whatever material she uses. Interviews with music video directors reveal a surprising respect for the pop songs they set. More than one director has said that "the song has all the answers."[8] This kind of receptiveness to commercial culture is rarely an avant-garde trait.

Success at combining pop music and strong visuals might require training in both music and the visual arts, which is rare. There is exciting work by musicians like David Bowie and Flying Lotus, who have had some traditional art training (often from the university) and find innovative visual artists to collaborate with, such as Floria Sigismondi and Mark Romanek, but their videos are not normally tagged as "experimental."

My topic needs a well-chronicled history that has not yet been written. Sitney, a key theorist of avant-garde film, places the director and folklorist Harry Smith at the beginning of the story I am seeking to tell here.[9] In the 1940s, Smith put jazz to his films and screened them in San Francisco's clubs.[10] Sitney reports that Smith remembered proclaiming in the 1930s that all sound-image relations work beautifully; the brain enjoys forging meanings between media.[11] According to Sitney, the early experimental filmmakers' commitment to purity and disdain for pop lyrics' banality may have limited crossings over (until 1947, for instance, Maya Deren screened her films silent).[12] Sitney notes that several later central works have richer stories of cross cultural influence, if not always direct incorporation. Another chapter might explore the trajectories of Jack Smith's *Flaming Creatures* (1963), Bruce Baillie's *All My Life* (1966), Stan Brakhage's *Christ Mass Sex Dance* (1991), and Bruce Conner's *Cosmic Light Ray* (1961). Martin Scorsese, for example, after having seen Anger's *Scorpio Rising*, chose to foreground a pop song in *Mean Streets* (1973); this gesture inspired a new generation of auteurist directors to include pop songs in films.[13]

The institutional, formal, and cultural barriers I have sketched limit the degree of engagement between avant-gardists and pop music. These fraught relations can be seen and heard in the work itself. Audiovisual relations can seem troubled, even estranged. Their makers express similar ambivalence. This experimental film and video subgenre reveals odd patterns: many of the field's biggest directors chart their success through their distance from pop music; some who clearly love pop music still treat it cavalierly; and others dally with pop songs once or twice before quickly returning to their home practices. But the work they produce often possesses interesting moments.

To conceptualize a corpus of pop music within experimental media, I will describe five characteristic approaches: 1) the use of a whole or nearly whole pop song, incorporated late in the process; these examples are most often resolute, with little direct sync; 2) a musical number within a larger work; these pieces showcase audiovisual relations that are more often distributed and relaxed; 3) examples that use fragments of pop music as one among several sorts of source material, sometimes in a collage, or in a reduced arrangement; the image is most often fragmented or eroded; 4) music videos directed by avant-gardists; these are often one-offs, an experimental filmmaker making a single foray into the genre, and tending not to compete with the genre's best, these clips often possess a striking tone and memorable moments (successfully or unsuccessfully); and 5) pieces that offer meta-discourses about pop songs and the institutions in which they exist; these often sardonic works extend beyond film and video to a variety of platforms and venues.

When these approaches work well, it may be because they reflect the ways material can be worked—whole, part of a whole, composite, meta-, and neighboring genre. When these approaches fail, it may be because they are insufficiently historicized, prone to engendering overlap, or too blunt. This chapter's close readings seek to show the ways these works cluster ideologically and reflect particular subjectivities. This analysis also aims to capture something about how these pieces feel audiovisually, how they work within socioeconomic and historical contexts, and how they present audiovisual relations different from those of mainstream media.

Pop Songs, Added Late in a Film's Production

This category became most prevalent in the 1970s and 1980s, when experimentalism's relevance still needed to be asserted. Film and video technologies were more primitive than now—achieving fine sync was harder—and the makers' skills with audiovisual technologies were typically less than stellar. Several clips I discuss—excerpts from *Scorpio Rising*, *Rose Hobart*, and *Vinyl*—present un-empathetic and resolute audiovisual relations; more than a multitude of relations come forward. Since these relations are the most difficult to describe from my examples, this will be the chapter's longest section.[14]

Kenneth Anger's *Scorpio Rising*

Kenneth Anger's *Scorpio Rising* from 1963 features an army of gay Nazi bikers who experience pain and pleasure, while sexual and sadistic symbols are intercut—or so says the film website Rotten Tomatoes.[15] Though this synopsis captures the film's tone, it neglects basic facts. Anger claims his film's documentary subjects comprised a small group of straight male motorcycle-club members who worked in the Brooklyn shipyards. Proud of their cycles and somewhat vain, they enjoyed being filmed. After returning from an eight-year hiatus in Europe, Anger was drawn to America's new pop music. Eschewing dialogue, he built his soundtrack from thirteen contemporary songs strung together consecutively.[16] The film is famous partly because it was seized by Los Angeles police during a screening; the case, tried before the California Supreme Court, became a landmark in the fight against censorship. *Scorpio Rising* remains slippery and enigmatic; I am not sure of its greatness, but I will attest to its opacity (figs. 4.1–4.3).

The section I am considering is remarkably bare. A man works with tools and then polishes his motorcycle between glances in the mirror. Another man dons a leather jacket. A third lies on a bed, wearing leather chaps. These three sequences, connected by the Angels' "My Boyfriend's Back" (1963), are a bit inscrutable.

Philip Brophy claims that *Scorpio Rising*'s "music is unnaturally laid onto film . . . its soundtrack is ontologically Other."[17] Traditional methods for audiovisual analysis get us no closer to the film.[18] *Scorpio Rising* has been described by Jeremy Carr as "pre-music video," but there are few real affinities.[19] I have claimed elsewhere that music video image aims to draw our attention to aspects of a song.[20] Analyzing a clip, I tend to consider visual, lyrical, and sonic parameters in isolation—color, harmony, props, a hook, a timbre—and then see how each connects with another feature within a corresponding medium (music to lyrics, lyrics to image, image to arrangement, and so on). Connections happen on many levels. In the process of discovering these connections, the viewer can carry herself through the video as if dancing along with the song—soaring above it, anticipating a peak, collaborating in a slowdown. But this approach is not helpful for *Scorpio Rising*. As with the work of several other avant-gardists in this category, audiovisual relations seem too tenuous. They seem to function on a different register—though one feels there must be some important connections.

Scorpio Rising encourages an analytical approach I shall employ based on schematics, mixings and matchings with the help of YouTube and After Effects. A form of "What if?," this approach functions as an audiovisual equivalent to the ways that academics respond to colleagues' talks or publications. Counterexamples work in service of reducing or expanding claims, tightening or extending boundaries. Philip Tagg has long

4.1–4.3 The enigmatic audiovisual relations in three settings of Kenneth Anger's *Scorpio Rising* (1963) suggest resoluteness—a man works on a motorcycle in a garage; yearning—the man unbuttoning his pants; approachability—the recumbent male.

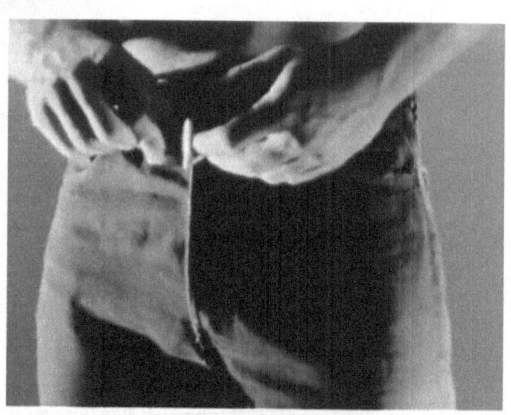

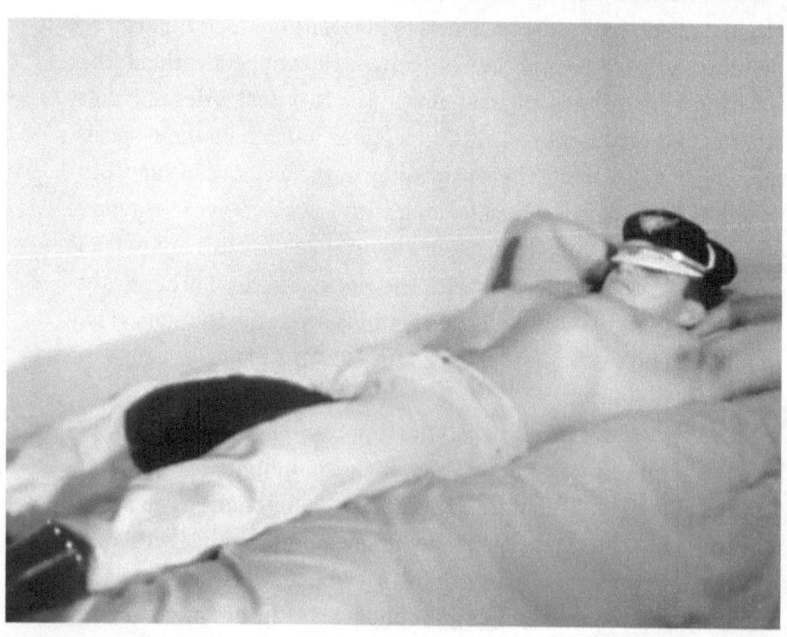

incorporated some aspects of this approach.[21] Drawing on recent platforms and software, anyone can quickly explore how a work's mise-en-scène, camera, editing, lyrics, and arrangement contribute to the shaping of time and an intermedial conversation; I hope this approach becomes more common.

With *Scorpio Rising* (and later with *Rose Hobart* and *Vinyl*) I opened two YouTube windows, keeping the original image in one and streaming a variety of soundtracks in the other. I then reversed the process (maintaining the soundtrack as a constant and running different imagery in the second window). I also stripped down and built up footage and audio in After Effects and ran comparisons again. I chose a range of materials, sorted by what I judged as proximate and increasingly distant from the original source. With each trial, one question remained constant: What does the combination of this soundtrack and this image bring to the fore or suppress?[22]

Here are the results of a few trials with the *Scorpio Rising* clip. I first stripped the image down to a mnemonic (a reduction of its most general features) and ran complementary materials against it.[23] Imagine the man and his motorcycle as a statue of a man, this time holding a sword lovingly in his outstretched arm (as in Jacques-Louis David's *Oath of the Horatii*, 1784), or, even more reduced—both man and machine as one obelisk (like the Washington Monument). Then I reduced the camera movement. Mostly, the authoritative camera slowly tilts up. This gesture could be said to resemble a knife on a whittling stick, or the petting of a cat's fur in the wrong direction. What musical accompaniment might work best, reasonably well, and worst with these two schematized visual parameters? Let us begin with the worst. Joni Mitchell's "California" (1971), with its widely leaping, flowing melody and jaunty, light rhythmic approach, was among the least successful possibilities. The Rolling Stones' "Sympathy for the Devil" (1968) seemed like a strong choice, but the test revealed its music as too raucous and uncontrolled. Led Zeppelin's "When the Levee Breaks" (1971) also seemed like a viable choice, but it was not right (too dispersed?). After trying many more songs, I judged the image track as less empowered and less pliant than I had originally imagined.[24]

What is it about the 1960s girl groups that works so nicely? To my surprise, similar songs of the same moment, like the Marvelettes' "Please, Mister Postman" (1961) and the Shirelles' "Will You Still Love Me Tomorrow?" (1961), among others, do not work either. Thinking about the music against Anger's depictions, the not so thinly veiled aggression in the Angels' "My Boyfriend's Back" may be its most compelling feature. The song pushes into the space of *Scorpio Rising*, but not deeply. It bounces back against the viewer. The braggadocio seems directed at us. This is partly because of the musical arrangement. The song has been recorded in mono in the style of producer Phil Spector's "wall of sound." Instruments and voices are often recorded two or three to a part, and much reverb is added.[25] Along with the song's many sharp entrances (accented attacks in the voice, guitar and drums), call-and-response, and coarse, shouted lyrics, this sound creates the sense of contained force. The sense of containment derives also from the setting (a narrow, deep, nondescript garage the song does not seem to fully penetrate). The camera, too, comes near, but steadfastly holds its own, straying neither too far nor too close. The camera and image, with the music, remain disjunct, contributing to the video's ultra-charged affect.

How might we strip down "My Boyfriend's Back?." Perhaps we should drop most of what makes the song music, instead subbing in a girl nastily saying, "My boyfriend's back and you better back off," with a nasal, brash voice. Now what is transpiring seems clearer. All the clip's elements exist in suspension. The man, motorcycle, and camera remain unengaged; man and motorcycle seem so desirous of one another, but must keep their distance. The camera sidles up against them (blindly and harshly), but never gets close enough. The song seems to observe but refuses to acknowledge what it perceives, instead demanding the viewer remain at an even further remove from the scene. With other songs subbed in for the *Scorpio Rising* soundtrack, though audiovisual relations are attractive, the film flows more quickly and easily into the next sequence. "My Boyfriend's Back" creates a special charge because the music, image, and camera claim the monumental. They stand unwaveringly in the immediate present. Other music adds a sense of forward motion.

The trials with the Marvelettes sequence encourage me to more freely assert claims about audiovisual relations. The next sequence in *Scorpio Rising* incorporates Bobby Vinton's "Blue Velvet" (1963). A man dresses. The song makes his thighs, hips, and jeans seem more rounded and fleshy than if the image were accompanied by another song. Visually and audibly, events unfolding during "Blue Velvet" feel languorous. Vinton sings the undulating melody with glissandi; when he stops, the background singers seamlessly pick it up. The performers' open vowels, "blu-u-e vellll-vehht," "oh, oh, oh," "blu-u-u-u-ehr thahn," create a sense of spreading. For the receptive viewer, audiovisual relations can sometimes create odd synesthetic illusions. Here, the song seems to spread itself like oil over the male subject. It may be a mild shock to see him, in a subsequent shot, thintorsoed and blonde, tugging on his shirt. The lyrics' fetishism (perhaps never making it past the fabric, "she wore blue velvet") and undetermined object of desire make the scene more freighted, as does the hovering sexuality in "My Boyfriend's Back."[26] The image takes up a few of the song's details. The walking bass line seems to direct the camera's slow pan up the legs, for instance.

Music videos typically present a multitude of connections. This sequence of *Scorpio Rising* brings forward only a few strong sync points. The "My Boyfriend's Back" sequence also only has one or two moments of tight sync. That sequence momentarily becomes euphoric when the camera pans past the cycle's crowning skeleton puppet and the puppet suddenly seems to joyfully second the "nah nah nah" of the background singers. That moment is prepared for by another sync point: the loosely bent arms of the cyclist suddenly doubling the shape of his handlebars, with the singer's now victorious "Yeah, my boyfriend's back" (this third time, the camera sidles up to him). Two strong sync points also occur here—too few for a music video.

Thus far we have experienced two sequences with impenetrable images. One projects free-floating hostility and the other shows unrequited desire, so it is wonderful to see, intercut with this second setup, a shirtless recumbent man on the bed. He smiles at us. Thus far, features of the recordings have created the illusion that the song has not penetrated the space, only dusted or smeared over it. Suddenly the music seems to roll over this recumbent man (the moment works cross-modally, transferring scene 1's stroking camera movement to the music's running across the man). Of special note are the man's chaps and his cap (always fetishistic things, especially on top).

My situatedness fails to capture other viewers' experiences. A second perspective, from gay pornographer Paul Morris, contributes to a richer interpretation. For Morris, *Scorpio Rising* is saturated with irony and mired in a fetishistic engagement with distanced, linear, heterosexual time. Anger's tortured ironicism reveals itself through several signs:

> "My Boyfriend's Back" means my boyfriend's ass or backside; the distance between "Anger" and the female voices in that song is the same bitter distance the viewer is posited from the imagery and from Anger himself; the director's quoting of Puck—"What fools these mortals be!"—aligns with that distance as well; and the distance between blue velvet and blue denim, the same.[27]

Like me, Morris values running tests. For him, a comparison between the *Scorpio Rising* clip and a YouTube clip from Chicago's Circuit Club in the late 1970s (a gay dance venue and haven of the disco era) reveals Anger's ambivalence toward homosexuality. The director "presents a complex system of forefronting but also suppressing the male body, particularly genitalia." Better, advises Morris, to embrace more liberating media like *Bijou* (1972) by Wakefield Poole, or Michelangelo Caravaggio's *Amor Vincit Omnia* (1602) that offer "utopic, orgasmic, extended segments of time."[28]

Joseph Cornell's *Rose Hobart*

My second example of works emphasizing a lack of sync is Joseph Cornell's *Rose Hobart* (1936). The director made *Rose Hobart* after buying a copy of Universal's *East of Borneo* (George Melford, 1931) from a junk store; Hobart is the film's leading actress. Cornell added a few documentary scenes from an eclipse and reedited the ninety-minute film down to nineteen minutes. For later screenings he also removed the original soundtrack and substituted two songs from Nestor Amaral's *Holiday in Brazil* (1957). Cornell projected the film through blue glass and slowed the projection speed to that of silent film. Stan Brakhage claimed that *Rose Hobart* was the most loving tribute to a Hollywood film star ever made.[29]

Holly Rogers claims that *Rose Hobart*'s sound and image fail to connect: the song heads one way, the image another.[30] This seems right to me, but I would like to take her analysis further. It is doubtful that no close audiovisual relations emerge, not only because we habituate to the relations between the music and image, but also because, as Michel Chion claims, viewers desire a connection between the two.[31] What holds *Rose Hobart* together? Perhaps it is the cultural associations of its ambiance. The music has a Latin sound and the setting is the South Pacific; Latin America and the South Pacific are not the same. (Shot on a Hollywood lot, the film plays fast and loose. The extras and buildings are not accurate, nor are the alligators.) For casual listeners, everything from the Global South belongs together. Still, less comes forward than we might assume. Why? Rogers is right that Hobart barely moves, and the background's settings remain remarkably still as well.

With so few strong rhythmic gestures in the image, it is hard for the soundtrack to forge connections. Substituting one passage of music for another, or a different visual track that is within the same family—the same strategies of substitution adopted for *Scorpio Rising*—tells us something about the film and Hobart the actress. Instead of Hobart's expressivity, we might sub in Greta Garbo's—say, the moment in *Grand Hotel* (1932) when she cries, "I want to be alone."[32] With this attempt Amaral's songs seem to pick up, reflect, and even grant Garbo a stronger sense of character. She has extreme gestures, strong physiognomy, and intensity of mood. The music now flutters around her, providing additional touches, helping to more clearly etch her movements. We might now take the famous first song from Heitor Villa-Lobos's *Bachianas Brasileiras No. 5* (1938–1945) and run it against the *Grand Hotel* scene, as well as one from *Rose Hobart*. With Garbo, it is not very flattering; it colors her as histrionic. But with Hobart, the music seems to pick up visual details and put qualities into her, a sensitivity and interiority we would never grasp about Hobart without the music. Might we now assume that *Rose Hobart* possesses facile music and a not very expressive actress? (Villa-Lobos's music against *Rose Hobart* works exceptionally well.) In *Rose Hobart*, is Hobart a callow figure who fails to project a strong interiority; is the music frothy Muzak? Perhaps both are a little stupid, in an understated way (figs. 4.4–4.5).

But let us put this aside for a moment and run a few more experiments on *Rose Hobart*. Trying variations in color can be useful. Cornell's blue-purple is so distant from the environment's natural landscape that we could be watching sci-fi. Green would animate things. If the image were crisper and in its original black and white, the music might sync more tightly. Or better, if we took different shades—blue, green, pink, red—varying them by sequence or shot, might we get a sense of progression the music could play against? Or if we shifted the music backward or forward a touch, or reframed the image slightly, shifting it slightly closer and to the left? Did Cornell deliberately seek moments of nonsync? I think so.

I have argued elsewhere that audiovisually intensified works remain incomplete.[33] The music points but does not name its objects. Lyrics tend to be elliptical; image stands at a remove from us. In a music video or other nonnarrative audiovisual work, we vaguely sense a desired object, an attitude, or a feeling, but less than one might assume. Is Cornell intent on keeping his material occult? My schematics and substitutions have only shown so much. It might matter to the film that Hobart advocated for better working conditions in Hollywood. Tossed in among alligators and monkeys and in front of the camera seventeen hours a day, when shooting *East of Borneo*, she felt angry and exhausted: "This isn't acting," she claimed.[34] Perhaps her mood had a different tenor than the frothy pop songs Cornell chose. Cornell's lavender tint, slowed-down footage, and

4.4–4.5 Audiovisual relations in Joseph Cornell's *Rose Hobart* (1936): evaluating Greta Garbo's performance in *Grand Hotel* and *Rose Hobart*'s performance in relation to pieces by Heitor Villa-Lobos and Nestor Amaral.

absence of movement may help bring to the fore what Hobart was really feeling, though in a way that keeps this knowledge obscure.

Andy Warhol's *Vinyl*

My last example of resistant sync, this time more deliberately casual, is *Vinyl*, a 1965 black-and-white experimental film directed by Warhol at the Factory. *Vinyl* adapts Anthony Burgess's novel *A Clockwork Orange* (1962). The unrehearsed actors read their scripts for the camera and flub their lines, and action was squeezed into one corner of a room and recorded in three static takes.

One sequence features Martha and the Vandellas' "Nowhere to Run" (1965). On first viewing this segment might suggest some Factory's denizens hanging out, listening to records. The actors form a group but they are isolated, or in pairs or small clusters. Why then the horror-movie laugh emanating from a man in the midground? Often I have wondered whether fine audiovisual relations are required for a music video or a musical number; perhaps, if an image is rich enough, a viewer will find enough to keep watching, no matter the soundtrack. This seems true of *Vinyl*: on its own, the frame seems engaging. A man in white pants, at the far back, whose thighs divide the frame down the middle, helps buckle the image into clusters of people and planes of activity that press forward or back. The man dancing in the foreground (whom we have to steal glances past), is a violent he-man. In the far left recesses, two men flirt or plan an assignation. Before them, serving as a barrier, are two black-suited seated men, one of whom laughs maniacally (are they CIA?). Center and frame right is the enigmatic Edie Sedgwick, her body broken in half, dancing with mermaid-like arm movements. Activity picks up; not only the he-man's gestures but also Sedgwick's swimming become increasingly aggressive. The white-panted man is wrapping a man's head in thick plastic, the latter seemingly being tortured or submitting to bondage; his head drops forward and the body goes limp. Is this consensual? Does it contribute to our pleasure or give the image depth? How complicit are the rest of *Vinyl*'s participants? How does the song play into this? Neither of *Scorpio Rising*'s songs, "My Boyfriend's Back" or "Blue Velvet," work here, but many other songs substitute well, even the community-oriented Martha Reeves and the Vandellas' "Dancing in the Street" (1964). The clip celebrates togetherness more than I had assumed. These young people seek a bracing beat. The beat allows them to hold their own while still participating in a felt rather than acknowledged experience of the group.

Penny Woolcock's *From the Sea to the Land Beyond*

Not all clips belonging within this first category showcase resolute or detached audiovisual relations. Penny Woolcock's *From the Sea to the Land Beyond: Britain's Coast on Film* (2012) differs from my other examples partly because of its materials and their treatment, but also because of its era. Digital technologies afford finer sync. Woolcock's documentary comprises archival footage of Britons working and playing in and by the ocean over the course of a century. Its soundtrack includes complete songs by British Sea Power. Avant-garde cred comes from the way these images are present but hauntingly inscrutable: these people were alive back then, we are now. How are the figures in the frame like or not like us? Do they do the same things, do they take the same pleasures? The soundtrack does not demand attention, even as it contributes a sentimental sheen. (As Kevin Donnelly points out, British Sea Power's guitar-oriented songs are "strongly melody-led and insistently memorable, accompanied often by quite basic and disciplined arrangements and little in the way of musical pyrotechnics.")[35] The image's content—swimming, dancing, rowing, promenading—would sync with nearly any regular pulse, and today's digital technologies can improve on this, offering nearly invisible fine-tweaks. The aurally receptive image can be further finessed—an oar periodically dipping into water, waves cresting into foamy tips, a waitress's skirt apron getting swept up by the wind, or people proudly strutting single-file before the camera.

Audiovisual relations in the first three clips I have discussed could be characterized as anempathetic; the autonomy of the songs and images come forward, more than a multitude of relations. I have argued elsewhere that audiovisual relations can resemble human relations.[36] When sound and image refuse to relate, this metaphor seems even more apt. These media can resemble a long-term couple who seek a therapist but resist change. The ways the arrangement, image, camera, and lyrics chart out psychic territory, claim physical space, and project a tone make them seem like agents.[37]

Pop Music as Part of a Larger Film

Experimental directors sometimes include prerecorded pop songs in feature-length films. Compared to the rest of these films, the song sequences are more open-ended: they do not need to seek or hold a particular audience, nor function on their own. As clips on YouTube, these sequences function differently, but in their original contexts they offer a respite, some novelty, or a place to stretch out. The distinction between avant-garde and Hollywood directors here can be hard to gauge. David Lynch's practice continues to be linked to the avant-garde, while Tsai Ming-Liang and Chantal Ackerman provocatively use threadbare settings to revalorize and defamiliarize musical numbers. Mainstream Hollywood has many experimental moments in musical numbers as well.[38]

David Lynch's *Blue Velvet*

Ben (Dean Stockwell) lip-syncing Roy Orbison's "In Dreams" (1963) to Frank (Dennis Hopper) and others in an apartment in *Blue Velvet* (1986) may be one of the most beautiful and subversive moments in the history of audiovisual aesthetics. It possesses the same spirited transgressiveness as Luis Buñuel's and Salvador Dalí's *Un Chien Andalou* (1929). In this sequence the characters' dispositions and movements describe the song, but in a temporally unfolding, spatially distributed way. Everything seems to emanate from Dean Stockwell's performance. As he sings he appears to glide above the music, much as the song's vocal line coasts on its arrangement. He is more delicate and restrained than the vocal recording; regardless of how ominous he appears, his performance makes room for Orbison's voice. Stockwell's appearance functions like Charlie Chaplin's, as a mixture of signs: for James Naremore's Chaplin, a bowler hat, cane, tattered shoes, baggy pants, and curly mustache are a mix of ostentatious signaling that points to everything from hobo to patrician, mime artist to dandy.[39] Similarly, Stockwell's attire and presentation are a combo pack. His shirt and jacket are so ornamented and frilled that they are beyond anything one would see in a funeral parlor, Las Vegas, or a high school prom. Suddenly he reveals a long feminine cigarette holder, while in his other hand he holds a more butch gaffer's searchlight. His curled, manicured hairdo and white-painted face resembles Joel Grey's in *Cabaret* (1972). A sconce next to Stockwell resembles a woman's bustier. Frank, on the other hand, is reduced: tight and primly groomed, with three sharply tipped triangles embossed on his shirt and neck tie. Stretched behind Frank, like the mirrors at the end of *Citizen Kane* (1941), are three arch-like awnings—his subconscious (fig. 4.6).

Frank takes to the music too late (he is a person out of sequence). His slow-to-rise lip curl suggests extreme pleasure and a repressed sneer. Besides Stockwell's weightless glide (the vocal line) and Frank's rigid, poorly modulated witnessing, other elements pick up aspects of the

4.6 Audiovisual aesthetics in David Lynch's *Blue Velvet* (1986): musical elements are distributed across a temporally unfolding, spatially intensified image. Dean Stockwell functions as catalyst.

music. Breaks in Orbison's voice, and its increased tautness as it reaches the higher register, seem matched by Frank's strong desire and the snake dancer's voluptuous rising swirls in the back. The three figures disposed as one clump of a chorus might reflect the song's inner voices, here as horror, bemusement, and pleasure. Then Dorothy Vallens (Isabella Rossellini) promenades through the back door, followed by a second visitor, picking up the bass line as it accrues energy. The music also has a sense of stasis, which suggests we shall never leave this place; the rest of the figures, propped on couches in the background, look like pottery or gargoyles. I wonder if Lynch was thinking about Warhol's *Vinyl*. Lynch's S&M activity in the background, with characters disposed in a tiny space, euphoric music and everyone listening ecstatically, seems like a remake. And the scene is painterly, also like *Vinyl*. The strangely tinted walls and stilted paintings—a nudie who looks just like Dorothy—do not seem much different from the characters themselves.

Pop Music as Collaged Material

In most of the work in this category—including pieces by Bruce Conner and Pipilotti Rist—fragments join to form a disparate but whole work. Questions of causality, authority, and production come to the surface. The fragmented music and image provide an opportunity to critique institutional structures that appear monumental and entire—patriarchy and the military-industrial complex. In the late 1980s and the 1990s, audiovisual works designed for the gallery were often composed of fragments like these; the videos seemed particularly well suited to installations.[40]

Bruce Conner's *America Is Waiting*

One of the avant-garde's most influential videos, Conner's *America Is Waiting* (1981), has become nearly unobtainable, even on the web. Its soundtrack seems like a pop song, but it is a borderline case. A collaboration by Brian Eno and David Byrne from their LP *My Life in the Bush of Ghosts* (1981), it includes a rhythm section of drums, electric bass, and electric guitar, but what comes most to the fore are mechanical sources that resemble the sounds of machines made of metal and rubber, chopping and banging, squishing and exhaling. Instead of a singing voice, two male voices intone. One flatly claims, "America is waiting for a message of some sort or another," and the second, sounding almost hysterical, calls in rising inflections, "Takin' it again, again, again, takin' it again, well now, no, no, now." Contextual knowledge helps deflate some of the voices' mystery: both were bootlegged from the radio, the first from a late-night talk-show host, the second from an auctioneer. But even for a listener who knows these facts, the voices remain powerful and surreal. The two appear to be trying to spook one another. There follows a dreamy, twangy, solo guitar lick, then we are back to the men's repartee.[41] This should not sound like a pop song, but it does. The voices and guitar almost comprise verse, chorus, and bridge. Together the song's disparate elements feel unified, even while the song pulls in multiple directions.

The images, too, are multisourced and mysterious, comprising military and commercial found footage from the 1940s and 1950s. Like the soundtrack, the visuals are composite. Paired satellite trackers scan the sky, but they get quickly turned back by a jump cut, flash-frames, or mechanical sonic punctuations. A subsequent rhyming image of a needle, as it tries to creep up a dial, soon gets tugged back as well. There are plenty of war-oriented images: atomic bombs detonating, men running into bunkers. Also appearing are images of 1950s domesticity, such as that carefully disposed nuclear family in front of the TV set and a classroom with students and teacher. Two young boys, shot with split-screen, play war games; wearing oversized helmets and speaking through walkie-talkies, they run out of the brush with huge bazookas (the clip looks like it's been repurposed from a toy commercial). All of this suggests recoil and strike, an air of paranoia (figs. 4.7–4.8).

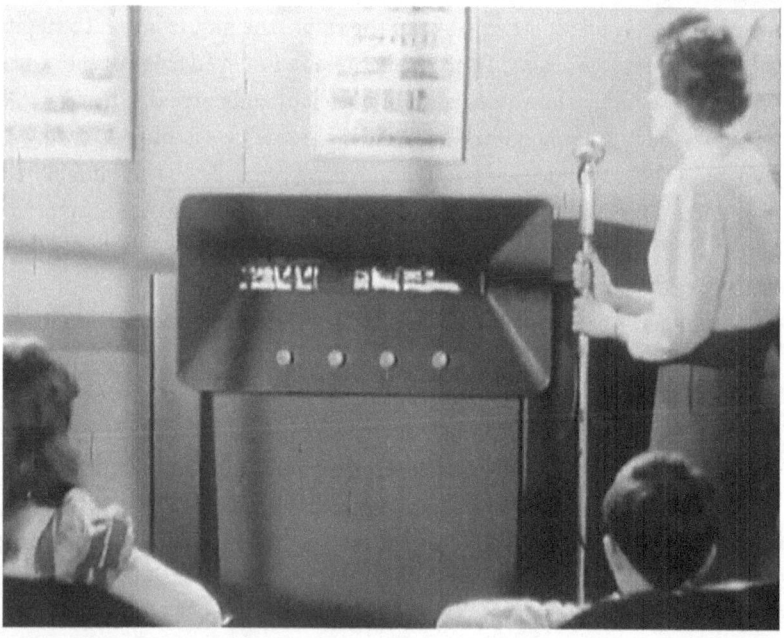

4.7–4.8 Bruce Conner's *America Is Waiting* (1981): song and image pull in several directions. The video asks, "Is America on the verge?"

What is driving it all? Is it the song's mechanical sounds that seem to trigger the periodic multiplication of images, like the question marks that hover over a recumbent hospitalized man, while a male voice pronounces "no will whatsoever"? Is it the subterranean connections among machines depicted in the images? A white-coated man walks up to a bank of first-generation computers and pushes a button. Next, refrigerators and ovens start parading along an assembly line before an early pop band; the commodities look like people. Or perhaps the video's tone is fueled by sentiment, an affective, frozen edginess produced as a byproduct of Cold War surveillance. Or is this simply something about America that we always knew was on the verge? In relation to previous music and images, a late shot of Mount Rushmore feels like the monument is on alert (waiting for something, again and again).

Pipilotti Rist's *I'm Not the Girl Who Misses Much*

Like *America Is Waiting*, Rist's *I'm Not the Girl Who Misses Much* (1986) is a composited although simple work. Wearing a low-cut little black dress and clunky, high-heeled shoes, Rist repeatedly sings the first line from the Beatles' "Happiness Is a Warm Gun" (1968) in a barren studio. The lo-fi video image shifts frequently, but it is almost all extremely blurry. Sometimes the image is played too fast, sometimes too slow. Slow parts have a bit of red tinting, and a deliberate analogue glitch rips from one side of the frame to the other, two-thirds into the piece.

The work begins with Rist close to the camera, so we can make out her luridly red lips. She then backs away and starts dancing as the tape speeds up. Her vocals (already sped up) jump up a perfect fifth, then another major third, to span a major seventh (seemingly reminiscent of teens' games at inhaling helium balloons to become giddy and mimic Alvin and the Chipmunks). Further transpositions alongside the tape's speeding up and slowing down feel frequent and sporadic.

In the video's most striking moment, the recording slows and drops two octaves as the video assumes a red hue and Rist's body—arms outstretched like a crucifix—sinks slowly through the bottom of the frame (this is the one point at which John Lennon's sampled voice sounds directly borrowed). For those familiar with the song's aggressive lyrics (which Rist doesn't sing)—"I need a fix 'cause I'm going down . . . / Mother Superior jump the gun"—Rist may seem like a target. Suddenly exhumed from a possible underworld, Rist next reanimates (in fact, she claims that "the use of different speeds is for her an exorcistic dance . . . things in slow motion . . . that's 'reality'").⁴² As her voice jumps again into higher registers, the melody starts fracturing and parts we did not notice come forward. Some pitches sound like pants and dog barks. The melody's opening seems absurdly obnoxious, like a whining kid; the middle becomes a birdsong with well-defined contours, while the closing "doo la loo la loop" devolves into a tweedling warble. As she dances, she flays her arms at 45-degree angles, tipping this way and that, to comical effect. She might capsize. As the dancing speeds up, we hear a graceful but nonrhetorical tapping (unnoticeable at regular speed).⁴³

The clip is eerie. Rist looks ridiculous, but we know she put herself here. She celebrates an auto-eroticism resembling children's repetitive twirls. As the clip slows, she melts to the bottom of the frame and then lunges forward and starts again like a caged animal. At certain points her arms push back and forth away from the camera, and sped up, the action seems aggressive and forceful, as if she could catapult herself out of the clip. Which actions drive the clip? Who knows? We are watching some new imaginary cyborg-like creature: frightening, archetypal, humorous, and threatening. Fragmented visually and sonically, she really is not the girl you think she is.

Sadie Benning's *Me and Rubyfruit*

Although Sadie Benning's short video clip from 1990 *Me and Rubyfruit* is also a composite, it feels whole. It therefore stands out from the other works in this category. Benning takes fragments from Prince's "Darling Nikki" (1984) and Aretha Franklin's "(You Make Me Feel Like) A Natural Woman" (1967) and gives the sense that the song's entirety surrounds it: we can admire the knowledge and ear required for her to choose that just-right bit. The image is extremely lo-fi, shot on a Fisher Price toy camera. This brings the songs to the fore. Close-ups of eyes, mouths, miniature unscrolling hand-drawn text on paper, a part of a cat—which Laura Marks might call "haptic" images—throw additional weight onto the soundtrack.⁴⁴ The warmth and immediacy of Benning's work makes it stand out against Conner's and Rist's.

Once we notice individual works clustering within a category, we can make claims about the ways they share strategies. Beginning with musical and visual fragments, Christian Marclay's much-lauded *Video Quartet* (2002) and Mark Leckey's *Fiorucci Made Me Hardcore* (1999) are both structured through strongly imposed rhythms. Marclay draws on a 4/4 rhythm, with antecedent and consequent phrases and periodic builds to peaks. The video asks viewers to imagine a community of musicians that might coalesce into a "family of man," or should not.⁴⁵ Ryan Trecartin has recently reenergized the form, working with even smaller cells: bits of phrases, music, lurid colors, and pop-culture detritus that also establish a brisk, repetitive rhythm. He fashions something anew that is meant to critique what seems to be monumental, whether straight culture or the media as an all-encompassing world.

Experimental Directors Making Music Videos

A significant number of avant-gardists have directed one or two music videos: New Order, for instance, worked with several avant-gardists and independent directors, including Robert Longo, Will Wegman, Kathryn Bigelow, and Robert Frank. But this work remains underanalyzed. Most of the crossings between the avant-garde and music video occurred in the 1980s, when the medium was incompletely defined and still had cultural cachet. In the 1990s MTV mostly screened 35 millimeter, large-budget clips by well-known directors, and participation by experimental artists dropped to nearly zero. An uptick has recently occurred: now that music videos reside on the internet and are not subject to MTV's censorship, expanding genre boundaries and easier dissemination make music videos attractive again. Andrew Thomas Haung and Björk's "Mutual Core" (2013) and David Lynch and Chrysta Bell's "Bird of Flames" (2012) are examples of this experimental reemergence.⁴⁶ Why did so many of these directors make one or two videos? As burgeoning artists, were they simply experimenting with every medium and genre they could realistically get their hands on? If they did not continue to make music videos, did their experiences enrich their artistic practices in other media? I have selected four examples to show how these works showcase striking moments and push toward the genre's margins.

Videos by Damien Hirst, Derek Jarman, Tony Oursler, and Chris Marker

Two music videos directed by avant-gardists jar us just the way we might expect them to. Tony Kaye's "See the Light" (The Hours, 2008), with art direction by Damien Hirst, depicts a woman in a hospital gown running amok in a shopping mall, squeezing herself in among displays and curling up within a coffin-sized Plexiglas showcase for shoes.⁴⁷ She slaps bloodstained handprints next to giant animal carcasses, a Hirstian touch. For the clip's moments of relative quiet she is ferried on a gurney into an MRI machine, lasers etching patterns on her face; this lowering of intensity is a music video convention. The song is undistinguished indie rock. The clip's audiovisual abrasiveness creates the distancing we have come to expect from the avant-garde—but is this enough to get the work into the art gallery, or to disqualify it from MTV?

Derek Jarman's compilation of three videos for The Smith's 1986 album *The Queen Is Dead* breaks conventions through its larger scope. Willfully nonchalant, the title track is awash with messy chroma-key. Even more than "See the Light," it is frenzied, giving it an experimental edge. The tender second video, "There Is a Light that Never Goes Out," has a simple construct. Against a field of fluttering gold and red vertical streaks (which appear to have fire as their source material), a blue-tinged, nearly still image of an almost undressed, reclining boy is panned and shifted through the frame. Superimposed elements also appear, mostly of a silhouetted burning car driving along the z-axis. Why do I find this clip so intensely moving? The video encourages a viewer to work hard to find a whole. Might Morrissey's keening voice express a hope for love, a loss of it, or a moment-of-now, when all is swept away but this boy, an arcadian model of beauty? Do we want our loved objects to remain still, to coalesce into something we fully possess (hence the boy's passivity and his tinted funereal blue)? The boy is beautiful, the fire is dangerous, Morrissey's voice is mournful. But the affective characters of these elements begin to cross and blur (fig. 4.9).

Like *Scorpio Rising*, *Rose Hobart*, and *Vinyl*, Jarman's "There Is a Light that Never Goes Out" seems resolute. Though the boy and the flames bind together, neither consumes the other. They are held in an intimate but polarized relation. We viewers, and Morrissey's voice, remain distant from this compound image; even the burning truck barreling into the boy fails to pierce us. This clip has sync. Subtly, the camera's panning across the boy often tracks Morrissey's voice (as if the boy might be listening); when Morrissey's voice swells, the boy moves toward us. When the chorus intensifies, an embracing couple appears, later to be mirror-imaged (as the boy will be). The rippling patterns of the yellow-orange field pick up the strings' vibrato, and the jaunty, perhaps ironic flute melody momentarily lifts the mood at phrases' ends (so we might begin again with more unrequited yearning). Perhaps each medium's sense of unreality contributes to this video's distancing effect. The static image of the boy occasionally blinks, rendering his status uncertain. The field of fire is most likely tinted rippling water, first shot on the horizontal, then inverted. The strings that

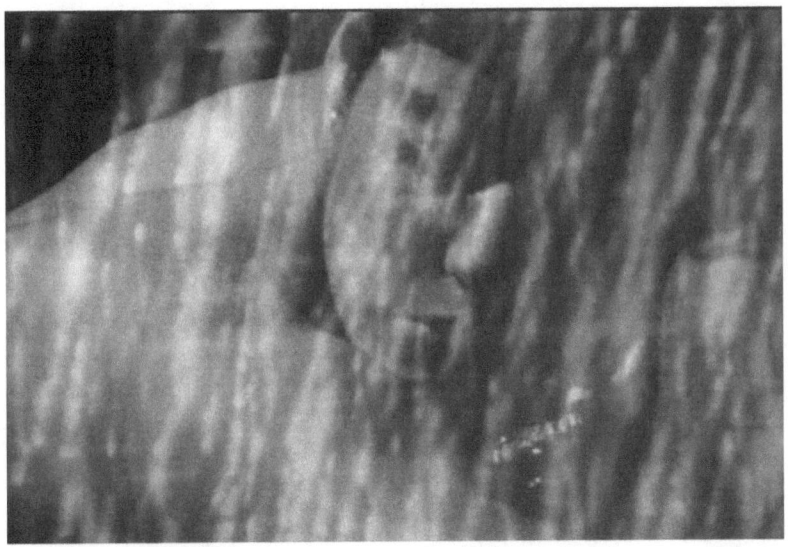

4.9 Derek Jarman's "There Is a Light That Never Goes Out" (1986): audiovisual relations suggest loss, intimacy, and aloofness.

were originally meant to be lush are digital (the band lacked the budget for real strings). I hear Morrissey's momentary hums as the song's most intimate feature.

Tony Oursler's video for Sonic Youth's "Tunic (Song for Karen)" (1990) feels both confusingly wonderful and embarrassingly amateurish, perhaps even proudly stupid. It flaunts its nonexistent budget. The band appears in one of those boxy, anonymous 1980s television studios, with no lighting except for a few blunt Fresnel lenses, directed flatly at the band. The video begins with each band member running out, carrying an enormous foam letter to help spell out the song's title. Then, periodically, the female singer Kim Gordon lies on a divan, garlanded with large, garish paper flowers or plush toy animals. Not very promising, but quirky things transpire. At various distances from the foreground, the band members point their fingers at her from the frame's four corners. Video noise periodically fills the frame; some rough animation of the band, cruder than MTV's *Beavis and Butthead*, also gets time. Is Oursler making a meta-video with some of music video's most unhappy features? Other aspects suggest so. The lead singer's dress changes frequently. And things happen in a way typical for music video. The director's trademark stylistic approach appears more assertively—close-ups of a skeleton and a doll's head superimpose on the lead singer's face. Big heads with even larger lips and miniature bodies appear. Finally, there is a puppet show. Like experimental director Will Wegman's video for New Order's "Blue Monday '88" (1988), Oursler ensures his signature appears often.

Further research into the song complicates our reading. One of the most successful avant-garde rock groups, Sonic Youth experimented with unusual forms, unorthodox guitar tunings, and prepared guitars that strangely altered their timbres. Lead singer and bassist Gordon wrote the song's lyrics, which she claims share her sympathy with Karen Carpenter's terminal anorexia; Gordon imagines the late star finally happy in heaven—her body growing smaller and her voice growing bigger.[48] But Gordon's singing is so deadpan and drowned out by the other musicians that this is nearly impossible to make out. This backstory gives the video an elegiac character.

In Chris Marker's video for Electronics' "Getting Away with It" (1989), a caped woman resembling a pre-Raphaelite subject (like Dante Gabriel Rossetti's 1870 *Beata Beatrix*) wanders in the woods, occasionally wearing headphones, sometimes gently lip-syncing. There's an uncanny connection between her and the animals she encounters—a peacock and a wallaby. The bird's long legs rhyme with her skirt and the marsupial's hop connects with her leaning forward to push branches aside. The clip seems simple and emotionally freighted. Drab, the image's color and grain have been stripped. The song seems amenable but also forgettable. A clever gambit joins the woodland walk with the band performing in the studio (leaves start falling on the musicians). The clip is saturated with a melancholy tone that feels authorial. It is hard to say how, but like the other clips I have described, it leaves a strong aftertaste. All the clips I have here detailed reveal a subtle, odd audiovisual turn that sets them apart from most mainstream videos.

Videos That Offer Meta-Discourses About Pop Songs and Art Institutions

Reflecting on the ways these avant-gardists have incorporated pop music into their work, my response is mixed. Their atypical and heterogeneous audiovisual relations reveal experimental traits. This experimental attitude manifests itself in explorations of form, critical distance from mainstream media, playfulness, and a sardonic tone. But I am also dismayed by the paucity of examples. I have not discussed the few directors who composed both music and image, like Laurie Anderson and Robert Ashley. These could be folded into an additional fifth category, that of meta-discourses about pop songs and the institutions within which they reside. Anderson's and Ashley's work, as well as more purely extra-musical conceptual projects like Banksy's recent guerilla swapping of his own remixes within the packaging of Paris Hilton's, creates new possibilities.[49] Now that out-of-the-box video and audio software are available more widely than ever before, these practices might extend beyond film and video to a variety of platforms and venues, spur new configurations, and be adopted on a larger scale.

This chapter yearns for a world in which pop artists and experimental filmmakers collaborate and cross borders. I would like to celebrate the work of some high-art-trained music video directors whose work would adapt well to the gallery—Floria Sigismondi, Mark Romanek, Kevin Kerslake, Hiro Murai, Yoann Lemoine, Chris Cunningham, and Michel Gondry, among others—but who have not received the appropriate commissions.[50] I might add the already mentioned musicians who collaborate with these directors (Bowie, Björk, Flying Lotus) and do stunning work. I have tried to capture ways of experiencing audiovisuality, pop, and experimental media in the hope that we might start fresh and build a new canon. What are the most provocative, sublime, beautiful, or politically engaged dance clips, movie scenes, vaporwave videos, DIY clips, music videos, and interactive installations? What would happen if we placed them against the body of work I have just discussed? What new histories might we chart?[51] I hope for some new social, economic, and political configurations.

5   Carol Vernallis, Lisa Perrott, and Holly Rogers

Beyoncé's *Lemonade*: She Dreams in Both Worlds

BEYONCÉ CALLS *LEMONADE* (2016) a "visual album." Since its release there's been a buzz about the image of Beyoncé smashing up cars, and a lot of talk about the lyrics' autobiographical themes (lines like "better call Becky with the good hair" have been getting attention for the way they call out Jay-Z's mistress). But this 65-minute film's songs, text, and sound design haven't been talked about in relation to its images. *Lemonade*'s unusual form—a long-play music video—gives it the capacity to draw connections between the personal pain of infidelity and America's terrible history of racism.

Lemonade's twelve video clips are linked by brief passages comprising poetry, visual tableaux, and sound collage. These interludes lean toward avant-garde aesthetics. One thing avant-garde aesthetics and music video share is the capacity to hold several vantage points in suspension. In *Lemonade* this capacity allows the work to embody opposites: love and hate, engagement and alienation, forgiveness and revenge.

Lemonade's mixing of avant-garde aesthetics and pop music and culture allows it to cross from high to low with grace (as does The Carter's "APESHIT," discussed in chapter 6). At the same time, it departs from *The Media Swirl*'s earlier film segments, which, like many of the big Marvel blockbusters, project shock and awe. Both *The Great Gatsby*'s party sequence and *Transformers 4* present us as little people facing an unchanging status quo. Beyoncé's work differs. With *Lemonade* there's a sense that we can draw on our communities, those outside our present context, and even spirits or ghosts. Many people and forces are summoned, including us. We can connect, and we can find a right way forward. One goal for this chapter is to put forward a dialogue in order to sharpen readers' commitment to participating in the commons.[1]

Lisa   I'm from New Zealand, Holly's from England, and Carol's from America, and we're white. Though we'd like to contribute some audiovisual analysis, I feel hesitant. In New Zealand, my interpreting Maori culture would raise concern.

Holly   Yes, but we might still do our best. There aren't yet many scholars who provide close readings of sound and image. Considering *Lemonade*'s audiovisuality leads us to different readings from our fellow academics, even, to our surprise, our mutually revered bell hooks, who finds the film violent, apolitical, and overly invested in showcasing beautiful Black female bodies.

Lisa   Let's first address some of hooks's concerns about Beyoncé's "fantasy feminism," then discuss *Lemonade*'s special avant-garde/music video aesthetics, and finally consider the ways the film negotiates infidelity and America's racism. Hopefully we'll answer critics like Adam Szetela, who claims *Lemonade* is "boutique activism of the Left."

The ways *Lemonade* politically incorporates Black men is first subtle, and it's addressed to the ear. The many instances of the film's plaintive, empathetic singing performed by men, often in the role of chorus and/or call and response (The Weeknd, James Blake, Kendrick Lamar, Jack White, and early field recordings of male, Black prisoners) is one example (fig. 5.1).

Carol   It's important to say that editing and camera also suggest a space beyond the fourth wall (as do the songs, sound design, and lyrics). Beyoncé's first addressee often seems to be Jay-Z

5.1 Incorporating men: James Blake sings "Forward" while a young girl holds a photo (of a deceased relative?).

("You're the love of my life," she claims, directly addressing the camera; "If you try this shit again/You gon lose your wife," hurling her wedding ring at the camera). A girl holding a photo of one of the murdered Black men, dressed in a Native American Mardi Gras costume, also circles a table with empty place-settings. As she approaches the lens, the scene mirror flips. I love the moment when a girl puts her foot on her father's and they spin together around an implied center, again playing with the two sides of the frame—an open, evolving space for better relations. This moment (Beyoncé sings "woo hoo") begins our journey through a sequence that celebrates community. That offscreen space is a live space, for any gender.

Holly A second aural example: during passages between songs, Beyoncé's voice is so close-miked we might feel we're eavesdropping on her thoughts. This interiorized self references listening and silence ("pray I catch you whispering, I pray you catch me listening"). A moment later, as the "Pray You Can't Catch Me" song splits in two to make a space for a more avant garde–influenced, poetic, interstitial section, she asks "Where do you go when you go quiet?" Later, a drummer sits at her instrument, silent and motionless; later still, Beyoncé laments "we can't hear them [the orchestra]." These evocations of seeking to utter and straining to hear suggests a facility at both guiding and responding to an offscreen auditor. Beyoncé's intense attentiveness, a musicianly approach, might also be read as a mark of oppression—people with power don't need to pay close attention (fig. 5.2).

Carol There are also visual moments when young men prepare to turn away from patriarchy: the adolescent driver who meets the president, the prepubescent boy who kisses a horse.

Lemonade's shifts between moments of audiovisual sync and nonsync also provide an opening. Sometimes we're asked to turn away from what we're experiencing to construct histories and futures. When the young man speaks about meeting the president, the lack of sync initiates a confusing temporal play that continues when we see this man again in (anachronistic) Super-8 home-movie footage. Sonic connections deepen this temporal confusion: the Super-8 footage appears alongside sounds of rain and thunder, and later, in the song "Freedom," Beyoncé sings "tryna rain, tryna rain on the thunder."

5.2 Beyoncé wonders, "Where do you go when you go quiet?"; her overdubbed voice is dislocated from her body.

We're also asked to turn back. The previous sequence emphasizes a matriarchal line of descent: young girls play in a Southern manor with Beyoncé's voice-over ("You look nothing like your mother. You look everything like your mother. How to wear your mother's lipstick"). Then there's a closing shot of a smiling, seated elderly woman; Beyoncé says, "Your mother is a woman. And women like her cannot be contained." Might we bridge time and see her (and the young girls) envisioning a grandson? What happens when? This section, with its striking sonic and visual disjunctions, encourages viewers to make connections.

Avant-garde and music video aesthetics have also been known for eliciting a mix of embodied participation and critical distance. Often, when moments of ambiguity and nonsync appear, we're also held in suspension to then be ferried or carried across to a moment of communal sync (much like the young daughter in "Daddy Lessons" who is lifted up, kissed, and then carried on her father's back in a series of intermittent shots). Near *Lemonade*'s beginning, Beyoncé appears kneeling before a red-curtained stage, singing as if in prayer. Her voice, layered on itself, is strong and unified, but dislocated from her body. Later, in a section devoted to images of community, we see archival footage of a New Orleans jazz band playing in the street. While their performance seems plausible, we hear nondiegetic music (the trumpeter fingers a different tune; the camera shifts perspective while the mic's point of audition remains constant; no one is clapping). In moments like these, we're thrown. How might we align ourselves with these instances? But following these are often moments when we're swept back in—Beyoncé enunciating the word "Texas"; the girl wearing the Mardi Gras costume shaking her tambourine, and James Blake intoning "oh death"; Beyoncé exclaiming "magic" before an infant appears; or declaiming "freedom!" from the stage. Surely many viewers might wish to bond with others during these communal, political moments. I agree that *Lemonade*'s hybrid form moves us affectively and encourages critical reflection. bell hooks might claim that a viewer would not perceive these moments on first viewings, but music videos are intended to be watched many, many times.

Lisa In *Lemonade*, demonstratively performed physical gestures sutured to heightened moments in the soundtrack also momentarily pop. Music videos and *Lemonade*'s clips often showcase what we might fancifully call audiovisual koans strung together like an archipelago. Throughout "Anger," Beyoncé's gesturing body directly addresses the camera, as though unleashing her anger upon all men who have ever been unfaithful. Arm, hand and finger gesticulations, head rolls, lunging and strutting all serve to parody many gangster rappers' expressions of masculine power (note her later "suck on my balls"). By reperforming these overtly masculine power-gestures as a strong woman oozing with femininity, Beyoncé challenges the predominance of these gestures in popular music video, and thus engages in an act of detournement (fig. 5.3).

"Apathy" and "Sorry" are also rich with gestural signification. From painted faces (inspired by Yoruban rituals and designed by Nigerian-born, Brooklyn-based Laolu Senbanjo), swaying bodies and heads nodding in unison, to provocative twerking, and then playful switching between the pointing finger, the "peace" fingers and the "middle finger up" to denote disrespect breeding disrespect, audiovisual moments shift teasingly from close sync and non. "Bye, bye, bye, boy" and "middle finger up" could be addressed to a younger person; it's underscored by late-1980s, low-fi, quick-decay, bell-like synth sounds.

5.3 Physical gestures suture to heightened moments in the soundtrack. Beyoncé directly addresses the camera.

Holly   *Lemonade* claims that painful emotions like anger, so close to love, can be transmuted to grace—and activism. Images that evoke political activism follow Beyoncé's "Sorry." Women stand in military attention around a graffitied van; multiple Beyoncés, or she and many others like her, march upward through grass—an audiovisual nod to Beyoncé's overlaid vocal tracks, and the long swatches of marching in the film's second half. "Sorry"'s closing bell-sounds, melded with the music box playing *Swan Lake*, could be heard as gamelan, music nearly always performed collectively. The music box's tune, first appearing in a minor key and a-rhythmic while Beyoncé drives a monster truck over parked cars, jars against the previous "Hold up" (sung in a major key with Jamaican rhythms as Beyoncé laughingly dances). The music box's tune has now been incorporated, even if its mood remains mournful. This is the first, perhaps unsuccessful, attempt at collective political action. (I interpret the gamelan-like sounds as a hearing of and calling out to other women.)

Carol   The next, more politically successful audiovisual sequence draws on a viewer's memory and *Lemonade*'s mirrored, dreamlike arch structure (ABCBA), in which songs in the first half point to the second. First Jack White traces Beyoncé in "Don't Hurt Yourself." Later, James Blake's heartbreaking falsetto at a home piano, seconded by Beyoncé's voice, sounds against images of women holding pictures of lost male family members. Soon we hear the song "Freedom," a meld of a 1960s Caribbean psychedelic group, field recordings of imprisoned Black men, Kendrick Lamar's political rap, and Beyoncé's raw voice (gospel-influenced, distorted as if through a megaphone), while she performs on a late-nineteenth-century stage before a rapt audience. Engaged viewers may find themselves turning back to "Don't Hurt Yourself": its musical arrangement, lyrics, voice-over, images, and onscreen text ("Motivate your ass, call me Malcolm X," "The most disrespected person in America is the Black woman" [Malcolm X], and "Love God herself").

We should say something about how *Lemonade* draws on music video's poetics—its form, length, and use of interstitial passages are unusual, but all its sections, even the interludes, do the kinds of things we tend to see in music video. It's true the *Lemonade*'s songs and experimental audiovisual passages feature atypical forms and unpredictable lengths. These unusual forms and lengths can also keep viewers watching. The video clips don't follow traditional treatments. (In a typical music video the verse might show the singer walking and singing, and the chorus will shift to several people dancing in formation.) Here, songs with audiovisual inserts group together into larger, more filmic sections. Despite, or probably because of, these formal distortions, *Lemonade* elicits a strong sense of beginnings, middles, and ends—much as music videos do.

Moments of emergence are especially crucial because of *Lemonade*'s dark themes: Beyoncé moves from a suffocating underwater bedroom to a Kubrickian opening of city hall doors and floodgate of waters. We soon hear low hums, sputters, and other David Lynch–like sounds that morph into musicianly drumming. She calls forth "I am the dragon breathing fire." Out of a dark vaginal hallway, Beyoncé steps up in search of pesos. Later, a young girl plays a tambourine and calls up the spirits around a table with empty place-settings. Then Beyoncé and her crew suddenly call "magic": we see an infant on the bed and we hear a celebratory Hammond organ. Beyoncé climbs up from the underground through a slit (fig. 5.4).

Sections with long, tracking camera movements or figures continually in motion also appear as beginnings, middles, and

5.4 Moments of beginning and emergence: Beyoncé opens the city hall's doors.

ends; but they're primarily in middles, as a way of creating continuity. Some examples include the monster truck driving along tops of cars; the camera's traversal of a red, darkly lit hallway; the young girls' running to a fence in the distance; and Beyoncé's extended lope through streets in "Hold Up."

Endings are very clear, often characterized by extreme quiet: the drummer who listens; the music emptying out and Beyoncé calling "come back" at the end of "6-Inch"; Beyoncé saying "we can't hear it" after a string quartet stops playing.

Music flows in time, and music video imagery changes to show off the music. A core music video technique is the deployment of varied visual speeds to highlight the many levels of rhythmic articulation in the music. At mid-tempo, *Lemonade*'s figures move in imaginative ways. Beyoncé rides horseback alongside a moving car; she lopes past cars and a fire hydrant, striking at them with a bat; she sings on a stage with a ballerina dancing before her; she and a group of women walk through water. Stationary or slow-moving military trucks and vans present a different kind of movement (fig. 5.5). Fires, smoke, candlelight, noisy film-footage, wind, circling dabs of light, leaves fluttering, and other representations of motion connect with faster musical articulations. Complementing these forms of movement are images of near and perfect stillness—the periodic appearances of bounded stages (Beyoncé's squared rim

5.5 Visual speeds highlight the song's varied rhythms: at mid-tempo, figures move in imaginative ways.

of fire, the glass performance box nested in a white house's facade). These images, too, create strong formal demarcations.

Lisa Yes, and besides very active bodies are the still figures, sometimes ghostly, sometimes like dolls or mannequins, or posed as living photographs. The latter provide links between music videos and the interstitial poetic sections which are more like tableaux. The motionless figures also highlight the music's slowest rhythms, like MeLo-X's long, heavily reverberant electronic bass lines.

Carol And there are many other details one might draw attention to, like the way songs in the film's second half mirror the first. "Hold On" and "All Night" connect via Jamaican ska (both have reverby guitar on the off-beats and heavy bass on the strong beats). "Sorrow" and "Love Drought" foreground glistening synths (reminiscent of DX7s of the 1980s) and light, busy percussion pads in the high register. *Lemonade*'s songs and sonic materials sometimes transition smoothly into one another. James Blake's "Forward" fluidly emerges out of "Sandcastles." "Sorrow"'s bell-like synth slowly thickens to become what Holly has described as a gamelan figure. The rhythmic pattern that momentarily comes to the fore as Beyoncé sings "better call Becky with the good hair" threads through the album. Might *Lemonade*'s atypical forms and unpredictable song-lengths showcase Beyoncé's fluid phrasing and unusual rhythmic delivery?

Holly   All right, we're moving to our close! We've said that the sound design in the experimental-avant-garde-interstitial sections works with a variety of types of audiovisual sync, from close to striking ruptures, encouraging a viewer to pay close attention and to consider questions about futurity, presence, and memory. The three-dimensional sonic space also complicates the visual space. *Lemonade*'s songs come from a range of genres—dubstep, hip-hop, country, reggae, indie rock. These bridges are comprised of three elements: visual tableaux, either moving, relatively static, or still (reminiscent of Andre Tarkovsky and Ingmar Bergman); poetic, intensely personal spoken-word poetry (by Somali-British poet Warsan Shire); and rich sound design (breaths, machinic hums, water dripping, all recorded with microscopic focus).

Sound takes us inside and out in many ways. The audiovisual bridges often evoke horror or noir tropes. Internalized sounds are often strange, even nightmarish. During the "Denial" passage the noises are strangulated, distant, and not immediately identifiable in the image, although they speak to a similar aesthetic. Sometimes sound does not belong directly to the world depicted, but rather to memory, thought, emotion, or something momentarily alluded to in the song's lyrics. As spoken passages draw to a close they frequently morph, sonically as well as visually, into the beat and timbre of the next song. The ambient, abstract sounds of the underground carpark that pulse like Lynch's famous room-tone slowly coalesce into an intermittent drum beat; this beat becomes the driving force of the raw, low-fi "Don't Hurt Yourself," featuring Jack White. The heightened sounds that refer to nothing onscreen—footsteps, sighs, and less-identifiable noises—crescendo upward as we travel up the Kubrickian red until releasing into "6 Inch," with its low, gravelly voice and lush vocal texture. The distorted sounds that stretch beneath the voice-over and that move into James Blake's tantalizingly brief "Forward"—the only song that foregrounds a voice other than Beyoncé's—quickly falls away again into a real-world noise tableau. The movement from noise into music ensures that the long-form and shadow story of *Lemonade* holds together, and that the songs speak to one another despite their sonic differences.

Carol We can now talk about the ways that *Lemonade* shimmers between depictions of infidelity and a history of racial oppression—the murdering of Blacks, from the Middle Passage and lynching, to the floods of Hurricane Katrina and police shootings Much has been written about *Lemonade*'s focus on infidelity, which is clear on the surface ("You can taste the dishonesty/It's all over your breath as you pass it off so cavalier . . . my lonely ear"). But there's been little on the film's broader themes. Perhaps the sound in the interstitial passages, as Holly has described it, connects to the shadow story for *Lemonade*. What if *Lemonade*'s first brick edifice resembles a slave ship or warehouse? (Fort Macomb, a pre–Civil War structure outside New Orleans, bears a striking resemblance to the abductees' cells in Ghana's and Nigeria's castle-like prisons.) Or if Beyoncé were on the lam? If her crime of arson burnt down the massa's house (as in Quentin Tarantino's *Django Unchained*), and the river and bayou enabled her second flight? If the too-heavy fruit of her mother's neck were the same as Nina Simone's version of "Strange Fruit?" If the women standing and seated in the tree branches, with others keeping witness on the ground, were a memory or reenactment of lynchings? Also worth considering are *Lemonade*'s ghostly figures: Beyoncé's first white-fleshed and white-haired guises, and the painted-white female dancers in the night-lockers, necks snapped back and then forward, as if they had been cut loose from the hangman's rope. Later, when an immobile Beyoncé intones "Freedom" from a stage, the dangling lights behind her resemble nooses. In "Formation," her bobbing head and grasping hands alongside a "doing-doing-doing" sample might suggest a shadow memory of a hanging. Other details, too, take us back to the era of slavery and later structures of oppression: the antebellum kerchiefs worn by Beyoncé and young girls, and dangling iron chains; a woman with a scar; old photographs scattered among grass and metal. Beyoncé's threat of "your worst nightmare" may be this. As she sings in "Formation," under these circumstances, "Always stay gracious, best revenge is your paper."

Lemonade's cluster of dark imagery is complemented by other, more redemptive images. Music videos can develop several visual and aural threads, each containing symbols and meanings. Because each is connected to separate musical motifs, timbres, and/or song's sections, none needs to win out or be annihilated.

Sometimes a motivic strand has a strong affect that shifts between positive and negative valences. In one of the interstitial passages Beyoncé says "plugged up my menses with pages of the holy book," and in another "Tills the blood in and out of uterus. Wakes up smelling of zinc." It's frightening and profane. Later, the camera tracks down a terrifyingly red, Kubrickian hallway. But then she says "are the hips that cracked the deep velvet of your mother and her mother and her mother?" It's a moment of reconciliation (this section is called "Forgiveness"): we see Beyoncé's feet as she walks toward the camera, in a domestic setting that seems clearly like "home." We then move up through a birth canal of brick and candles (the first- and second-born daughter) to the march of a drum and heartbeat. This sequence is bounded by James Blake's "Moving On," with images of mothers holding pictures of their murdered children and then Beyoncé's "Freedom" (figs. 5.6 and 5.7). Even as Beyoncé's gown turns white, by the film's end the birds have become blood red. Bird songs carry through the video. Contra bell hooks, we find this strand highly political: the vaginal imagery leads directly to a revolutionary call for freedom.

Images of race become more inclusive; depictions of whiteness could also be said to become more generous. First linked to ghost corpses, whiteness is posed in relation to Blackness and vice versa. As the film progresses, we see a young girl who is possibly albino; a woman who might be first identified as transracial (she has vitiligo); a young girl, most likely multiracial but also able to pass as white (with braids and fairer skin); and then in "Freedom," some characters we've seen earlier whose skin is now painted lighter or darker. These depictions raise questions about the tendency to link identity with skin tone. In "All Night," couples of many ethnicities, with a variety of gender affiliations, embrace.

Suggesting redemption, skyward lights are seen from an underwater bed, or from the ground to a parking-lot roof, or a street lamp. They become horizontal (the cut-out square in the hallway), to rise up again and become part of a thunder

5.6–5.7 A mother grieves the murder of her son; a shadow memory of a lynching.

cloud during the day, and then as a burst of light like a star at dusk (Hattie's birthday party, the sun behind Beyoncé for "All Night").

A series of beautiful Black women with long oval faces evoke Madonna figures: one with a scar and a tattoo saying "dream big"; two, one as a medium close-up, one in long-shot standing on a street; one as a sculptural head on a side table; one an image of Nina Simone on an LP cover.

What is the relation between the themes we've been discussing—fraught heterosexual relations; the painful history of violence against Blacks, and an acknowledgment that the oppression continues; and calls for receptive listening and collective action? At certain moments Beyoncé's and other women's words suggest that rechoosing a relationship is the right choice: "I'll trade your broken wings for mine; I've seen your scars and kissed your crime"; "We're going to heal"; "L-O-V-E the Lord." We assume that the principles that have enabled a people's survival have become a sacred mode of life ("Grandmother, the alchemist. You spun gold out of this hard life. Found healing where it did not live. You passed these instructions down to your daughter. Who then passed it down to her daughter").

Lisa: In *Lemonade*, and in many music videos, the sheer complexity of the relations between music, image, text, and lyrics can seem overwhelming. Correspondences between music, lyrics, and image can range from the strictest to the most subtle or enigmatic—the most fragile can suddenly seem to carry the most weight or become the most engaging. We haven't even gotten to the music videos proper! Or the beautiful ways gesture is choreographed to the music. There are six credited choreographers, even though we don't see much conventional dance.

Holly: The dance, art, and film allusions Lisa, Carol, and I point to—Pina Bausch, Stanley Kubrick, Pipilotti Rist, Andre Tarkovsky, and Jacques Tourneur—differ from references that others have found (like Terrence Malick and Julie Dash). *Lemonade*'s allusions create crossings among visual and aural threads. The second instance of Yoruban face painting (after "Love Drought") took me first to experimental-film director James Broughton (so I'm suddenly carried back to the 1960s countercultural, largely gay San Francisco renaissance; the corresponding synthesizer sounds now possess greater resonance), but the face painting also points back to "Sorry," and its allusions to Nigeria (many of *Lemonade*'s characters are of Nigerian descent). There's much more watching, listening, and thinking to be done.

Lisa: Fans and critics have already commented on the enormous range of contributors to sources for and influences on this film—129 credited musicians, producers, and composers (including Boots, Diplo, Diana "Wynter" Gordon, Led Zeppelin, Burt Bacharach)—and on its many references to Africa and the African diaspora (Akan clothing, Nefertiti's cap-crown,

Oshun's yellow dress, Venus figurines). Half a dozen music video directors contributed to the project: Jonas Åkerlund, Kahlil Joseph, Melina Matsoukas, Dikayl Rimmasch, Mark Romanek, and Todd Tourso. Knowing something about who and what shaped this work deepens my respect for it.

Carol: Beyoncé says she "sleeps in both worlds." I turn back—a music video's ending often encourages a return to its beginning, and a sense that everything is present simultaneously. *Lemonade* closes with Hurricane Katrina; at the beginning Beyoncé could be said to dive into its waters from the ledge of a tall building. Jon Brion, who did the music for *Eternal Sunshine of the Spotless Mind*, composed *Lemonade*'s music for strings; MeLo-X was also responsible for the soundtrack's often concrete score, its backward voices, record clicks, helicopter sound effects, noises of breathing, and reverberant electronic tones. *Eternal Sunshine*'s score returns its protagonist back to his strongest memories. Together, Brion and MeLo-X help carry viewers back to collectively repressed memories in *Lemonade*. Beyoncé, too, drives back hard to them. She takes a monster truck over parked cars and *Swan Lake*'s music (with its myth of a beautiful but cursed princess), then follows three women into an underground passage, coming upon the ghostly women in an abandoned locker room. We may go back before antebellum times, to older religious and cultural practices ("Her teeth as confetti. Her scalp, a cap. Her sternum, my bedazzled cane"). I shuttle forward across the film. The waters of "reconciliation" remind me of the Middle Passage—Beyoncé's shrouded body, shipwrecked. Beyoncé, in white paint, is ministered to by women again. Later, a woman clad in gold warrior's costume, standing in a crumbling brick basement, reminds me of the Underground Railroad. Thunderclouds against a brightly lit sky reenact the struggle ("Tryna rain on the thunder").

In *Lemonade*, a bus appears behind a suburban street parade (a spooky moment: I hear a train, though none seems present). It reappears in "Sorry" as a conveyance to the afterlife, then becomes a revolutionary, military vehicle. There are threads we haven't yet considered—lineages of families, the shots of New Orleans today that look like the 1970s (gold tones and Super-8 footage). "Formation" makes the connection clearest, with its imagery of local stores, Walmart, and American cars

5.8 A sonic and spatial struggle? A fight for air, a fight to breathe?

once built in union-run auto plants like Detroit. Clocks embedded in the imagery and soundtrack raise questions about time. So many eras accessible at once, sonically and visually.

I shuttle again to *Lemonade*'s beginning with Beyoncé and Jack White: "When you hurt me, you hurt yourself. Don't try to hurt yourself." I think of Trump, with his schemes of excluding Latinos and Muslims, creating huge numbers of broken families. Helicopter sounds on *Lemonade*'s soundtrack remind us how our world can feel like a police state. Is this an audiovisual, spatial, sonic struggle? A fight for air, a call to breathe, to gather information, to get "in formation"? (fig. 5.8).

6

Tracing the Carters through the Galleries: "APES**T/APESHIT" and the Louvre

THE CARTERS' "APES**T" (2018) is a music video featuring Beyoncé, Jay-Z, the Mona Lisa, and dancers in the Louvre. It's a strong example of the ways a music video can move past its generic boundaries to embrace other art forms. The clip combines high-art aesthetics with pop culture, and European and African American art and history. (Chapters 4 and 5, on avant-garde aesthetics and Beyoncé's *Lemonade*, are good preparation for this one.) Perhaps even more than chapter 7, on Lady Gaga's "Paparazzi," this chapter encourages us to flex our skills with audiovisuality and politics. This chapter asks how this video is and isn't progressive.[1]

Beyoncé is part of our cultural imagery, partly thanks to her music videos. Music videos could also be more richly theorized.[2] The genre's aesthetics are shared with many other forms of moving media, including commercials, YouTube videos, trailers, political ads, and audiovisually intensified segments of postclassical cinema. Beyoncé is important to us for many reasons, including how her work speaks about performance, race, gender, sexuality, autonomy, politics, and ways of being in the world. But studies devoted to her are only now getting started.[3]

This piece was part of a colloquy I formed that provided perhaps the first multiperspective, in-depth look at a music video. The paucity of music video scholarship is not only due to the fact that, as Ann Kaplan has observed, music videos straddle a border between advertising and art, but that the analyst must also feel comfortable with addressing the music, the image (including the moving bodies, cinematography, and editing), the lyrics, and the relation among them.[4] (This might include looking at a dance gesture against a harmonic shift and an edit, and asking how these might relate to one another.) Probably the best way to understand a clip and the genre, a collective approach also adds some benefits. Music videos are open forms, and as each analyst charts his or her path through the video, we can get a sense of a personal perspective (and readers can then more carefully track their own trajectories as well). I hope our tack will inspire a confederated approach, where art historians, dance scholars, media experts, and those who work on poetry and rap lyrics, costuming, and architecture would write alongside us.

My analysis in this chapter reflects both support for and discomfort with "APES**T." Are the Carters and the Louvre first promoting one another's prestige? "APESH**T" might be most like a Tarantino project, an imaginative game (like *Django Unchained* or *Inglourious Basterds*) that deliberately confuses our notions of history. Or might we experience the video in a more positive light, in that it helps broaden our sense of what counts as art and shifts our anchor points for what matters most? We now can experience art as more inclusive, with special place of pride for people of color and others who have been marginalized. The museum may now feel *more for us*. Is it possible, I wonder, that all these aspects might be true simultaneously?

My questions include the following. Can mass art be radical? Both the Louvre and the Carters, at different moments, celebrate wealth and commodities—is there something special about the Carters' relationship to wealth? How does race overlap with economic justice? If we could see wealth, would this change our relationship to it? Will we then ask that the 1 percent share more of their resources with the rest of us, or will we feel the present distribution is fine? And how might artists from other races, gender affiliations, and sexualities work against a dominant art practice? How might "APES**T" have been realized differently?

Some readers may wonder whether this much attention to a brief clip is productive. But today's audiovisually rich content seems to wield great influence—from sequences in tent-pole blockbuster films, YouTube clips and music videos, commercials, political advertising, and broadcast news clips (for Fox and MSNBC are highly aestheticized). Together, watching/listening closely, we may learn more how these works speak to us. From here there might be possibilities for opening the discussion, for sharing experiences of our world.

Some readers may feel more aligned with Beyoncé and Jay-Z and their work than others. Why? Is this connected to our core identity, values, and beliefs? This may sound a bit starry-eyed, but I hope that if we can get in touch with, come to understand, and then share with one another our perspectives of the media objects we care about (music, film, literature), perhaps we'll be able to open a conversation and more richly understand one another.

This reading provides a sequential analysis of "APES**T." I'll also show how the clip makes political claims. As we cathect to sonic and visual moments, we cut paths through them. I'm in the Beyhive, a booster for music video, and a lover of museums, so my reading is thus positioned. Almost entirely, "APES**T"'s artwork is ethnically white, and its performers, ethnically Black (for brevity, I won't identify each appearance, but rather mention race when it's most useful for my argument) (fig. 6.1).[5]

The Silence of Artworks and a Rap Video

John Berger claimed that paintings convey a quality of silence. They project an aura: the painter's brushstrokes and the paint's materiality bring the viewer back to an originary moment. When reproduced, however, paintings become indistinguishable from advertisements, stripped of their political content and immediacy.[6] One might thus expect that Beyoncé's "APES**T" would denature the Louvre's artworks. This is especially so because the paintings often function as backdrops for performers, or appear in partial views—for Berger, fragments of paintings become no more than simple statements, like "a woman with her hands over her head" or "the eye of a horse."[7]

6.1 The Carters at the Louvre.

But I'll take a more optimistic view. With its sharp gestures, rhythmic and timbral vibrancy, and varied voices, the song awakens the paintings; they appear to vibrate. At some level, audiovisual aesthetics are about relations between the image and the soundtrack; "APES**T"'s relations, though often kept at a distance, still project contentious, high stakes. These relations reflect *this* song's attributes. (Some YouTube experiments make this clear. Play "APES**T," and then something soporific, like Yanni, against the Louvre visitors' slideshows of the galleries, documented through still images or shaky footage.) "APES**T" snaps the artworks into life, almost as if their figures might emerge from their contexts— as if their faces begin to move. If we crystallize these relations into one moment, we might judge that "APES**T" shares qualities with Eugène Delacroix's painting *Tiger and Snake*.

In "APES**T" the paintings become animate, and the totemic figures take on the residual stillness. It seems as if the two might be trying to talk to one another, but we can't determine what they're saying. Images also cluster into suggestive groups, but we can't be sure how. "APES**T"— like other music videos—may leave us with a vague sense of something ephemeral, a haunting, a museum tinged with a new resonance.

The video's force and vibrancy derive partly from its instrumentation. Its high-hat could be considered a horizontal reconfiguration of cymbals. Like "APES**T"'s snare, cymbals have a long history in military music (cymbals became prominent in eighteenth-century Turkish marches, during the same period as "APES**T"'s Jacques-Louis David paintings). The berimbau, an Afro-Brazilian instrument, is traditionally used in capoeira, where it can be understood as a weapon disguised as an instrument. The song's high-pitched reiterating tone might be imagined as a targeting device, like an infrared scope. Along with this instrumentation the song's many voices—those of Beyoncé, Jay-Z, Migos, perhaps Pharrell, and shouts from other exuberant males—seem to press into the Louvre's galleries, skimming past paintings to seek out depths. The camera sometimes comes in on a diagonal (as with Beyoncé, Jay-Z, and the *Mona Lisa*), as if to veil the music's force.

The video could also be seen as haunted. Some examples include 1) the angel on the museum's steps; 2) the shifting lights passing over the ceiling; 3) the fragmentary images of the Madonna and a beseeching elderly man oriented toward supplication but not meeting; 4) the whooshes and roars that seem to wake the dead; 5) the camera's heading alone down a hallway; 6) the slave ship bathed in red light; 7) the unseen male voices, and images of the Middle Passage (and perhaps the youths dancing with

Beyoncé by the Great Sphinx); 8) Beyoncé and Jay-Z with their various statues, especially before the *Venus de Milo*;[8] 9) the song's sudden starts and stops, with music's indeterminate causal role; 10) the figures on pedestals in the darkness who slowly become animate; 11) Beyoncé and Jay-Z before the sphinx as a summons; 12) Beyoncé's and her dancers' pause before the *Coronation of Napoleon*, as if their animacy is not yet decided; 13) Beyoncé looking a bit ghostly when her skin is fairer and her hair is blonder; 14) the montage sequences, like the narration of a Black male's death as well as the composite of male and female dancers, sculptures, and paintings that break free from the fetters of ropes; and 15) the poured wine (or blood) that calls forth figures in the painting and reminiscent marks on the basement ceiling.

Music videos can help us understand "APESH**T"'s sense of hauntedness. The first writers on music video argued for the genre's uncanny qualities—they saw elements of dreams and schizophrenia.[9] I've argued that this uncanniness is mostly a function of heightened audiovisual relations.[10] In our world, sounds trail objects, but in music video's metaphysics it's the other way around. With music playback on set, sound puts everything into motion: physical gestures, the camera, and material and immaterial elements such as props, wind, and light. Pop songs structure time in a way that densifies it and seems to turn it into a grid; with software like Logic, Pro Tools, and Ableton Live, this spatialization of sound is reflected in the interface. Music video image can intensify this sense of space and time: the distance between figures can feel palpable, like an ether. Our visual fields encourage us to seek a focal point, while sound and music envelop us. But the image in music video often mimics sounds' attributes in an attempt to draw our attention to the music. At the same time, music video image can have a "mute" quality because of the genre's brevity and lack of dialogue. The terms I'll be using throughout this analysis—"multitemporality," "heterogeneity," "undetermined cause and effects," "animation," and "haunting"—are linked phenomena that derive from these uncanny audiovisual relations.

"APESH**T" is so rich with overlaps, cross-fades, processes, and hierarchies that it can be difficult to parse. The visual, musical, and lyrical threads encourage the viewer to adopt different modes of attention. When might we experience "APES**T" linearly, in segments, teleologically, or as isolated instances? Let me provide a sequential reading, and then turn briefly to others that present equal validity, including those that embrace attention to instances, continuities, and sections.

A Sequential Reading of "APES**T"

Music videos keep options open; no audiovisual moment annihilates the others.[11] Videos can open themselves to multiple paths and a variety of readings. "APES**T," however, is unusual in that it could be said to commit to a forward-driving story. This is partly because the music can be experienced as continuous. (Harmonically, the song lingers on an incomplete minor tonic chord, momentarily shifting to a bII or bVII.) Its media are also atypical. The Louvre's paintings can project the times when they were painted; if they were staged reenactments we might not be able to leap centuries, since the image would be infused with a sense of now-ness.[12]

The video opens with a contrast between the celestial/spiritual (the angel-boy crouched on the museum steps) and the haunted/supernatural (unattributable colored lights seep across the painted ceiling alongside ethereal held tones and acousmatic footsteps). Next, fragments from paintings suggest a contrast between supplication and beseeching—the figures' gazes and hands don't meet. This opening raises questions about authority and gender: Whose footsteps echo? Are they Beyoncé's heels? Why would she inhabit this space while Jay-Z explores the museum proper?

A whoosh—we shift to a different time.

The berimbau, exclamations of "yeh yeh yeh," and the trailing male voices in the hall of the *Mona Lisa* suggest a testing and claiming of space (fig. 6.2). The sounds might connect to a viewer's phantom image of a shaman's feet, bent knees, and stick tapping the floor for treasure—water, blood, or oil—and with other haunting touches, like an earlier painted image of a limb swaddled in fiery red and orange cloth. Why does the camera track toward Jay-Z and Beyoncé on an angle? Jay-Z's white sneakers pop from a distance. As the video unfolds, this patch of whiteness rises through the frame, emerging as a thread. The harmony brightens as it switches to a major chord (bVII). This accentuates the regal air of Jay-Z, Beyoncé, and the *Mona Lisa* as the camera tracks back.

Another heightening: the imperial Beyoncé and Jay-Z stand at the top of the staircase before Nike, the *Winged Victory of Samothrace*. Then a third intensification. The song's suddenly thicker arrangement—snare, bass, and high-pitched tone—animates inert bodies. (And there are other mysterious forces: who beckoned their Pure Barre "V" roll-ups?) Standing on pedestals along the gallery's walls, shadowy figures make tiny stomps;

6.2 The soundtrack tests and claims space; Jay-Z's white sneakers.

later they flutter their fingertips. In another emergent thread, these bodies and others may be released from their bonds.

The camera arcs past David's *The Oath of the Horatii*. Who has the highest authority here? The camera? The couple? The music? Our eye may light on the painted figures' outstretched arms and a sword. (These, as well as Beyoncé's and Jay-Z's subjects, with their spiked arms and legs, may form another thread, culminating in the swords near the video's end.)

Seated with Jay-Z on the divan, Beyoncé seems aware of their vibrancy as a couple (she sings "I can't believe we made it"). But they haven't yet pierced the museum's space. There's room for progression—camera, music, and lighting will more fully inhabit the galleries by the end of the clip. Through a subtle audiovisual transfer, the ring of tiny lights at the base of the divan relate to the song's reiterating high-pitched tones. These lights become a node in an emergent thread leading us to Marie-Guillemine Benoist's *Portrait d'une Négresse* and beyond.[13] I take seriously the song's repeated allusions to building a spaceship. The divan is part of this construction (why else those lights?), and a future, potential escape.

The camera tracks down a vacant mahogany hallway. Again, the music sounds out its environment and seeks objects with which to pair; it's a disembodied force, a haunting.[14]

Beyoncé, Jay-Z, and the Great Sphinx in front of a large, illuminated arch heighten the hallway's yonic qualities. Beyoncé wears the uniform of a colonizer, a World War II beret and cloak, but with a leopard pattern. Must the video's protagonists adopt colonizers' roles if they are to return to and claim what belongs to a people and a culture? Beyoncé's outfit has touches that extend images of emancipation: her boots are crossed with shiny black strips and tiny wattles dangle from her cloak (perhaps to help carry forward her flapping wings).

The staircase with recumbent figures appears again, but this time its sides are bathed in red light. Might this be a slave ship (fig. 6.3)? Red and the history of oppression become threads too.

Beyoncé before the *Nike* is a striking image: its sculpture features a ship's prow with a headless maiden for its mast, yet Beyoncé is our maiden-queen, seated below. She and the statue might yet shift roles; folds of fabric merge with the statue's attributes (fig. 6.4). The sharp gestures of Beyoncé's hand and forearm and her rhythmically tighter exclamations (like "pay me in equity") feel like summary, though we're not yet sure of their context. The sculpture's base, a boat's prow, will be carried forth thematically. We'll see kneeling NFL players, the I. M. Pei pyramid, and Jay-Z approaching and receding from the camera on a diagonal, and then inhabiting the foreground with his hands steepled in prayer. This moment feels potent.

Beyoncé and her dancers, in formation before David's *The Coronation of Napoleon*, valorize the couple (fig. 6.5). Beyoncé, with her hair in a bun, has been crowned before Josephine. The song thickens with Beyoncé's voice, autotuned and multitracked against the full rhythm arrangement. One might guess that this sonic configuration will repeat, but it doesn't, giving this moment, in retrospect, a special prominence. To Beyoncé's left there are the painting's folds of white fabric (a node in a thread contributing to the headdress of the woman in *Portrait d'une Négresse*). The dancers' line, fluid with serpentine-like motions (like the z-access phalanx of dancers' dropping heads and torsos before the *Nike*), seems nearly effortless but for their sharp chin-tucks and turns. Stillness is summoned before movement.[15]

David's painting *The Intervention of the Sabine Women* chronicles the tale of women who, to end a war, intercede with their men and prevent them from murdering their rapists. "APES**T" takes the painting's formal properties rather than its message: one woman's bent arms are doubled by Beyoncé's, and another kneeling woman's and child's golden hair is echoed by Beyoncé's headdress (another node in the video's gold-white thread).

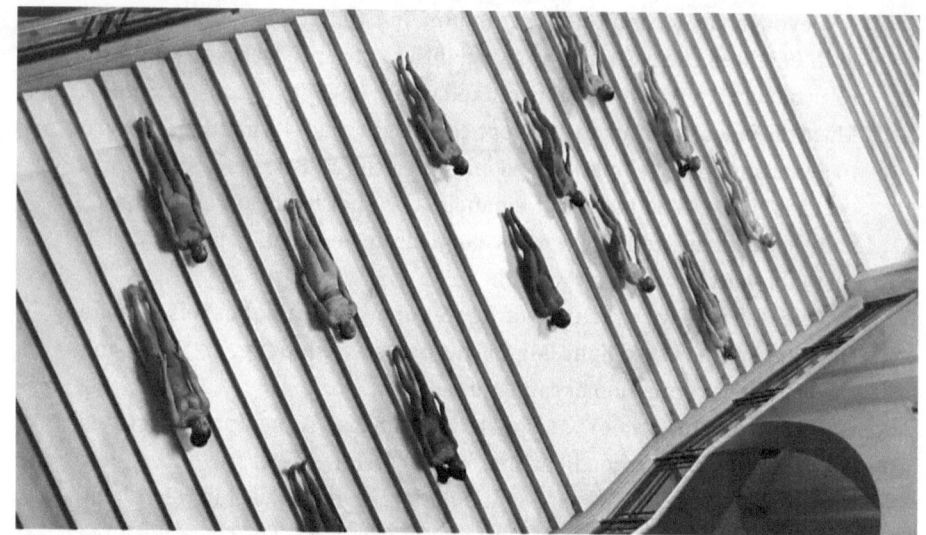

6.3 The slave ship.

6.4 Beyoncé and the *Winged Victory of Samothrace* might yet shift roles.

6.5 David's *Coronation of Napoleon:* Beyoncé is crowned before Josephine.

Beyoncé refuses *The Sabine Women*'s ameliorative stance, gesturing wildly while throwing off her cap. (Her "Get off my dick" seconds her refusal.)

The dancers' rippling wave of falling heads and torsos suggests both flow and stasis. The rhythm arrangement, too, changes tack—dropping out to leave spongy synths and Beyoncé's singing, increasingly fuller. The synths and Beyoncé's autotuned voice can be aligned with the mechanical, and perhaps the regularization of the dancers' gestures also suggests a machine (might we be building the spaceship?).[16] This section feels somewhat apart from the video's texture.

The museum gains authority. Two women seated in front of David's *Portrait of de Madame Recamier* suggest an additional piece of furniture, or the Madame's slaves. The musical arrangement reduces to bare, held tones. The bells seem to weigh on the shadowy dancers.[17] But the museum's sonic and visual control will not hold. In the basement, a worker (or athlete) with blood-red shoes stomps angrily; a skull dangles from a colleague's necklace. We hear the berimbau and voices through the ceiling (as if the youths are also in the slave ship's hold). A whoosh transports us to a historical painting of a wounded man embraced by a female lover; we cut next to a couple in a similar embrace. (Has something happened to the young man with the red shoes? The subsequent painting with the blackface Jesus figure might suggest so.) Two boys seem to bless the couples.

The sequence ends, maintaining its silver-colored thread as a means to bind it together. A lost moment.

"Roar!" "Stack my money fast." The opening's reappearance suggests a new trial. Beyoncé, on Jay-Z's arm, might seem to present herself as mixed race (her hair and skin have become lightened). The white thread continues with a close-up on an African man's raised hand holding a handkerchief, a fragment drawn from near the top of Théodore Géricault's *Raft of Medusa*. The painting narrates a terrible story (the French allowed 140 people to die).[18] Then there's a white flash-frame. The video's engagement with whiteness comes briefly to a halt, as if rescue and passing are no longer options. The video turns to poorly illuminated images. Perhaps Jay-Z's gesture, which breaks the frame as if to say, "What a painting," really asks, "What the hell?"

The protagonists adopt more self-determined and militant approaches. The video draws on Eisensteinian montage: a collision between shots edited together produces a new concept. (Film director Sergei Eisenstein believed this technique most effectively mobilized the proletariat.)[19] We might instead chart its origins from what Tricia Rose calls "the cut" in rap.[20] This sequence begins with a partial view of Paolo Veronese's *The Wedding at Cana* (of party-goers and waiters with hats), and then the sword and horse's eye from Géricault's *The Charging Chasseur*, the man standing on the horse, and then a motorcade. At this last instant the bass kicks in. Together these elements suggest gathering forces to be reckoned with. (To strengthen these claims, Jay-Z's rapping intensifies, adopting a rising, quickening arpeggio.)

Jay-Z's rapping is fast and aggressive, emphasizing plosives. A triangular formation of kneeling men, perhaps of the NFL, now in formation, appears likely to spring. Jay-Z riffs, "You need me/I don't need you."[21]

"Stack my money fast, fast." For the third time a long section with the song's most characteristic materials reappears. Beyoncé and Jay-Z stand before the *Venus de Milo*, the setting tinted dark blue. Beyoncé's bodysuit, shadowed with darker areas (note her hips and breasts), links her to the earliest, voluptuous Venus figurines (marking art's beginnings forty thousand years ago, rather than with Greek sculpture). From this first start (with support from "APESH**T"'s earlier yonic imagery) the video develops a new line, a new way of going forward (fig. 6.6).

Alongside Beyoncé's rapping, the second Eisensteinian montage in "APESH**T" is grander: an armless sculpture; a Venus sculpture with shortened upper arms; a Black male dancer with arms pulled back; an image of Beyoncé with arms overhead; perhaps Black male and female

6.6 Art's history begins with the earliest, voluptuous Venus figure.

dancers' hands in ropes; fragments from Géricault's *Raft of Medusa* with ropes, and the cross-cut breaking free of ropes; a Black female dancer vigorously dancing; the same dancer in full flexion with her hair thrown back.

Jay-Z's rap set piece is virtuosic, but something about Beyoncé's takes one's breath away—she's remarkably stern, fleet, and low-pitched. Her narration focuses on a party with wine and drugs; but again, we might take her narration as a call for political action. Images, sounds, and lyrics start swirling and becoming compressed. *The Wedding at Cana* suggests partying with the poured wines, but quickly we shift to imprisoned Black figures. (We also see rave-like dancing around the sphinx, and hear the reiterating high-pitched tone and various pulses.) Beyoncé references wealth, perhaps obscenely so ("250 for the Richard Mille"), but the lyrics also tie to negative depictions of Blacks (jigga, gorilla, coupe). Might her rap be an attempt to mix everything up, so that perceptions of race lose their fixed positions? Jay-Z's rapping connects to the rimshot (like sabre-rattling) and becomes machine-gun volleys. Nodding, Beyoncé counts off her subjects: we'll take those swords (including a fragment from *The Intervention of the Sabine Women*, the NFL team with arms raised, and a sudden brightening to the bVII). Beyoncé cradles her hand to her chin, forming a sword. She raps, "Wanna see the stars," and "I'm a Martian, they wishin' they equal." A profusion of small visual details such as spots of light, pearls, and painted circles alongside larger, more slow-moving shapes (the performers' stilled bodies) direct our attention to the song's multiple tempi. A wider range of imagery reoccurs near the joins of song sections (Beyoncé and Jay-Z before the *Mona Lisa*, the Pei pyramid, and the blue-scaped *Venus de Milo*, alongside Beyoncé's quickened rapping; shorter bridge-like material of the spongy synths and "take a top shift"; and the predominant section, "stack my money fast and go"). This gives the illusion that we traverse song sections. A detail stands out, connecting with the space-ship theme: in a blue-tinted scape, behind Beyoncé, is her entourage of women, wearing metallic-shoulder-padded 1970s-like costumes—imagery associated with Afrocentric sci-fi.[22] A warrior, perhaps released from a painting, cuts through the dancing crowds.

The video closes with more inclusive gestures. With each reappearance, the single line of dancers before the *Nike* comes closer to the camera. The video culminates in a close-up of a Black woman grooming a Black man's hair. We also see the couple before the *Mona Lisa*, and we might imagine an exit (the spaceship). There's a sequence of gentle, loving, and quiet hands, with a variety of skin tones; their gestures recall the *Mona Lisa*'s hands (fig. 6.7).

The ending of "APES**T" might work as a spell, deploying technologies for magical purposes.[23] One could use Pei's pyramid to gather light, sounds, the camera's drive, and the gestures of the figures and direct them past the embracing, waltzing couple (as if through a prism); Benoist's

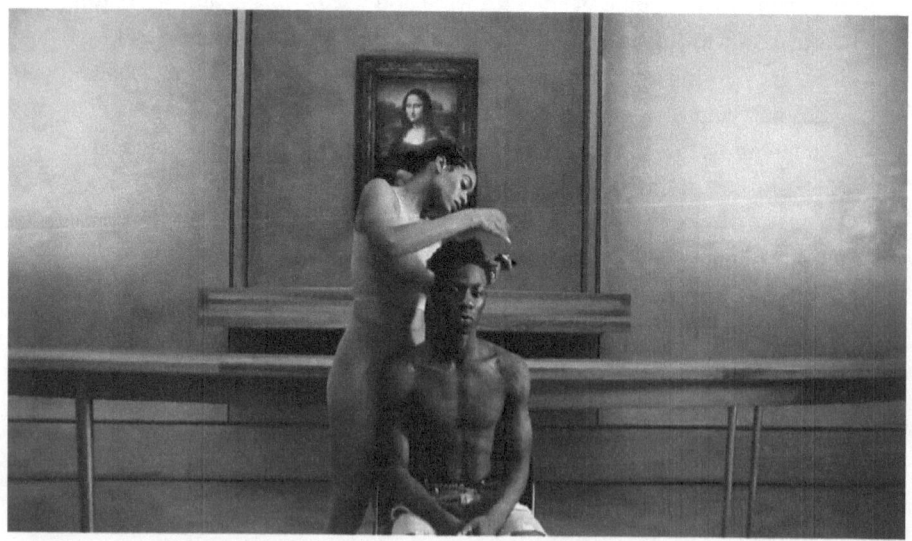

6.7 Reconciliation.

Portrait d'une Négresse; the camera arc over to the ceiling; Beyoncé's and Jay-Z's tilt; and the *Mona Lisa*; to where we might want to go.

Music Video's Peculiarities and "APES**T"'s Potential for Political Change

"APES**T" supports three modes of attention. The video's multiplicity supports a variety of interpretations.

First, listening as a line: in some ways the song seems to glide forward, unchanging. The harmony hovers around a tonic-minor stasis. "APES**T" could be said to reflect neoliberal experience—we never get the relief that earlier song-structures can provide.[24] The music's constant drive seems to fit well with the Louvre's long, narrow galleries (substitute shallow ones against this song instead). Since at one level the song embodies continuity (as if spanning a long, flat horizon or desert), details across distances may link more easily (the sword-inspired shapes and Beyoncé and Jay-Z's regal appearances as bookends, for example).

But the song can also be experienced as highly segmented. Each set of four- or eight-bar measures showcases a new effect: the high hat, the spongy synthesizers, and the moments when the arrangement foregrounds an addition, subtraction, or oscillation of material, like the reiterated high-pitched tones. There's also Beyoncé's and Jay-Z's flow and the men's responses. With this kind of listening, sharp visual contrasts become more apparent, such as the Eisensteinian montages, and the "militant" section juxtaposed with more peaceful imagery toward the end.

The song and the video also seem to brighten and intensify overall, thereby suggesting a teleology. The deployment of the Louvre's artworks appears to support this, because while there's back-and-forth among the sculptures, the paintings progress historically and finally give way to Pei's modernist pyramid. Jay-Z's and Beyoncé's late-appearing, virtuosic rap set pieces can be experienced as a heightening. The high-pitched tones start oscillating. Jay-Z's rap traces a rising arpeggio. Production touches strengthen a sense of teleology. Beyoncé's "I can't believe we made it" takes its most ebullient turn, and then gets reiterated on the vocoder (an instrument associated with Afrofuturism). The signoff rapping is not "yeh yeh yeh" but "yip yip yip," a brighter vowel (and there's also "honky honky honky").

Complicating all of this are the visual, musical, and lyrical threads that cross and encourage viewers to shift their modes of attention. One can trace the unfoldings of the white, the red, the green, the swords, the hands, the fabric, the sculptural forms, the paintings, the imagery tied to slavery, the Afro-futurist imagery, the dance gestures, and so on. One might be following the snare, and then suddenly Beyoncé's rap takes on a heightened character. (Why now? Has she been listening to the rhythm arrangement all along?) Throughout the video, we're encouraged not to engage in Mickey-Mouse listening, but at the end we suddenly have several opportunities. The dancer's body and hair unfurl against a "roar"; Beyoncé faces the camera and exclaims, "Uh"; Jay-Z pantomimes advancing machine gun fire against sonic sabre-rattling; and a blown-bottle sound pairs with a dancing male figure. What kind of weight might we give these moments of sync? Is it only through political action that we can really be-in-time? Are the tiny white lights and the oscillating high pitch a linear or rising function?

Perhaps "APES**T"'s audiovisual relations feel difficult to determine, and its threads more interwoven than many music videos, because the video must somehow span the distance between paintings, sculptures, and live figures. It's common for music videos to distort a figure's identity, offering doppelgangers, replacements, substitutions, models, mannequins, statuary, and appendages instead. This device reflects popular music's heterogeneity and promiscuity: musical motifs, timbres, and rhythms often adopt one another's characteristics. The moving image, too, can reflect music's varied speeds, from slowest to fastest. "APES**T" does all these things in a slightly different way. Is the museum entranceway's angel the same as the lover on the bed, or the blonde boy?

Who are "APES**T"'s background figures, and how much should they matter to us? Music videos tend to work in the service of a song, showing off its most attractive features; only one or two characters get to sing, and everyone else becomes relegated to the background. Bodies are deployed in the service of form. In "APESH**T" the dark-green scapes with shadowy figures are used near the ends of sections to help slow them down. Techniques like these have haunted the genre since its inception and can raise concerns about audiovisual relations' politics.

The claim that the collaboration of Beyoncé, Jay-Z, and the Louvre stems from an attempt to enhance one another's prestige and capital has grip. Many of the eighteenth-century paintings celebrate plunder, and were gathered through colonization. And the lyrics for "APES**T" play with similar, over-the-top descriptions of commodities. But the video and the collaboration have progressive aspects; encountering a museum, "APES**T"'s viewers might be able to more deeply inhabit its space. I might adopt "APES**T"'s approach, choosing a few paintings I felt affinity for, seeking out isolated elements within these, and then moving out from there.

But of course this isn't enough for anyone who's desperate for something better—when the corporations and the rich seize most of our wealth, with Donald Trump and other despots, and the earth's precarity. The video's progressive nature is hard to claim, in part, because a music video's experiences can be so fleeting. But perhaps the intensity of "APES**T" derives from the video's awareness of this fact: the makers pitch their hopes on our ability to access the past and present as we face our uncertain future.

7

Storytelling on the Ledge: Lady Gaga and Jonas Åkerlund's "Paparazzi"

WHAT CAN MUSIC VIDEO DO, and what are its limits? Much has changed since MTV's first broadcast—platforms, technologies, social configurations, and economic structures, as well as the genre's ripening and (possible) maturation. Makers' and viewers' shared knowledge about forms and conventions has also caused shifts. Most strikingly the arrival of YouTube, prosumer work, and the end of censorship—more sex, drugs, and product placement—seem to make it all so different.

My book *Experiencing Music Video* makes claims about the limits of music video's ability to narrate.[1] To some extent these arguments still hold: music video is a short form that tends to draw attention to a song's features. It has limited resources—just lyrics, no dialogue—and it bears a responsibility to foreground the artist. But in the last few years my students and I have gone back and forth on music video's narrativity. One music video director has long confounded us—Jonas Åkerlund. His clips, including Lady Gaga's "Paparazzi" and "Telephone" (both released in 2009), were among the first that seemed to call out for new approaches to narrative. Both suggest something about the nature and possibilities of the genre. In this opening section of the chapter I'll argue for and against music video's ability to present a narrative, taking "Paparazzi" as a case study. This clip, I'll show, mobilizes both traditional Hollywood narrative and musical forms. I'll close with the claim that the style that emerges produces transgressive images of personhood that allow Gaga's persona to hover uncomfortably between murderer and victim. These rapid shifts of valence are something that Gaga is suited for, but they may produce an ambivalence in the viewer that neither song nor plot can resolve. Through overlapping and often conflicting patterns, the song, image, and audiovisual relations of "Paparazzi" encourage me to support a revenge killing. The video's ability to push unpalatable values makes it a good choice for analysis in *The Media Swirl*. Later we'll move toward readings of political ads and news programming outside of our affiliations, as well as work that may strike as immediately or latently problematic. A reading of Gaga's "Paparazzi" shows that while narrative structure is important, musical form and local audiovisual flourishes are ways a piece's affects and meanings are generated.

A Scuffle

What do I actually know about the more traditional, Hollywood-like narrative plot of "Paparazzi"? Lady Gaga becomes disabled after a fall off a balcony (though I don't learn whether her lover intentionally pushed her off, or if in the struggle she was accidentally shoved). Toward the video's end, she poisons her boyfriend. But even then this poisoner may not *really* be the same Gaga—this is an *evil* Gaga, who's been overcome by some sort of Mickey Mouse–like avatar. ("Telephone" shares similar narrative conceits: Gaga is released from prison, and at the clip's end she poisons a fleet of customers at a diner—here, however, I'm more certain I'm following a consistent character—a recidivist jailbird, her wardrobe hangs together more.) Both "Telephone" and "Paparazzi" share much funny stuff in the middle, such as Gaga's dressing up in a half-tutu in "Paparazzi," or wearing a phone on her head in "Telephone." And why is Beyoncé dressed up like she's a member of the Beatles' *Sergeant Pepper's Lonely Hearts Club Band*, and why do the bandits' closing costumes resemble Aubrey Beardsley–wear in "Telephone"? Beats me. It's all up for grabs. So maybe I'm not watching a narrative. Actions I understand as sensible or coherent begin well before the song's opening, or the first substantial break before leading into the song proper. The closing incidents occur as I'm heading into the out chorus. In the middle I'm somewhere else. I might claim instead that I'm watching something like a musical, with one nonnarrative music video–like number embedded in it.

Readers may say I've overstated the case. Admittedly I'm starting with a definition of narrative that has tight constraints, though it's applicable to almost all feature films. This characterization of narrative derives from David Bordwell's *Classical Hollywood Cinema*, which requires the following elements for a story: that all of the events we see and hear, plus those we infer or assume to have occurred, can be arranged according to their presumed causal relations, chronological order, duration, frequency, and spatial locations. Bordwell draws upon an Aristotelian understanding of narrative: it ought to contain characters with defined personality traits, goals, and a sense of agency who encounter obstacles and are changed by them.[2] I'd claim that Åkerlund's characters are too unfathomable and unreliable and the ways they encounter and respond to obstacles too mysterious for me to get a bead on things.

One counterargument is that I *can* impose a narrative on these videos. A five-act structure for "Paparazzi" might look like the one shown in fig. 7.1. I can move through these five turning points while tracing emotional rises and falls. But, playing devil's advocate again, I may find a plot here only because this is familiar shadow of a narrative—not because of patterns inherent to the music video itself. The music video remains agnostic and offers many trajectories. *I* force an understanding on the clip; I adopt this trajectory, but I could just as easily take another.

So let's chart a more narrative-driven path first through "Paparazzi." The first task of a Hollywood film's narrative is to elicit the viewer's support for the protagonist, through either a display of the protagonist's admirable qualities or deft handling of a hurdle. "Paparazzi" opens on a manicured lawn, and then in the bedroom, of a grand villa. A powerful Gaga, engaged in foreplay with her boyfriend, commands him to kiss her and declare his love. He carries her from the bed sheets to the balcony's ledge, where I assume a furtive photographer captures celebrity pics. It's unclear whether Gaga panics and the lover, reacting too quickly, throws her over, or, perhaps intent on financial gain, deliberately shoves her over. Having nearly died, Gaga returns home in a limo. With much pomp—and vogueing—her wait-staff carry her into a wheelchair and then push her forward; she, with their continued encouragement, stumbles down her foyer's carpet on silvery crutches. The video draws here on familiar tropes of the fighter's great rehabilitation: nursing old wounds, she pushes her body forward against nearly intractable odds. Intercut are sexual activities among Gaga and three young, androgynous characters on the couch (dressed like *Blade Runner*'s Pris or rag-dolls with mop heads and suspenders) who too seem to bestow health and vigor upon her. (Gaga becomes increasingly more sexual and mobile through their embraces.) Also intercut are a number of murdered dead women, presumably her staff—in the bushes, in the bathtub, by the pool. Since Gaga is recouping and has gained my sympathy, I don't implicate her in these deaths, even though her hand forms a cocked gun that points at these women out of frame.

In the second chorus, Gaga nimbly runs out into the villa's main hallway with back-up dancers (supporters?) in tow. I interpret her costume—tights, half-skirt, half-collar, earrings made up of upside-down crosses—as

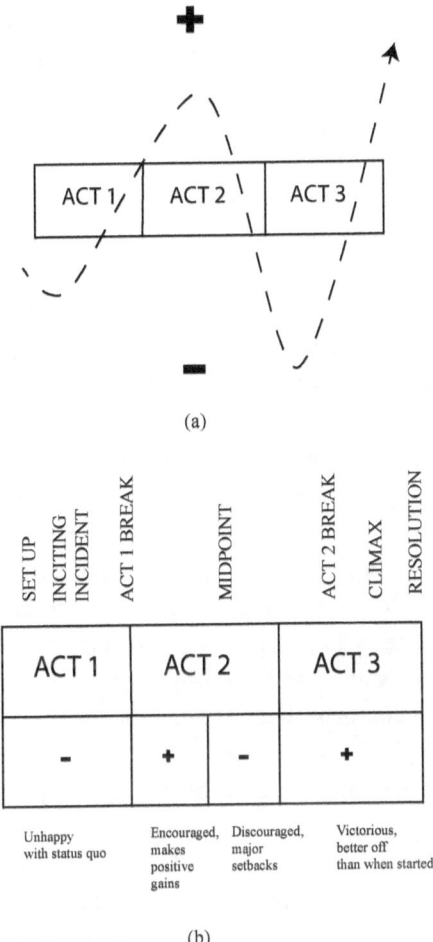

7.1 Traditional narrative Hollywood film form.

a sign that she's partially recovered from her injuries; her background dancers' Pierrot-like headgear (which she had worn previously when she was in crutches) and her tightly cinched, high-heeled shoes (linking to the concerted close-ups on feet in the previous scene), reminds me of her history of severe impairment. Unlike the previous scenes focused on striving, Gaga's Pierrot-dance has a melancholy, vulnerable feel to it.

And now she hits a nadir at the song's bridge, though I suspect Gaga's low point is due only to my projection as a viewer; such a turn fits snugly within a narrative curve, and when a darkest hour in a music video *might* come. The video offers few immediate signs to help me read it this way. The section opens with another dead female staff person, limbs unnaturally twisted, but this time on the bed. As any female viewer might suspect, punishment, sexual behavior, and women are linked. There's another dead woman in ivy and one who has possibly hanged herself, feet dangling with (again) dainty shoes. The music sounds dark, and color has been drained to black and white. Gaga wears spools of film in an odd headdress (the death of celluloid and the new reign of the digital?). There's one lone Dalmatian and a simple (cheap?) wooden wall. Gaga sings of libertine behavior: too much partying. There's also one crotch shot (like with the lovers on the couch). But still the scene is so undersketched (a medium close-up against a bare wall) that this section may only suggest waiting, emptiness, and passage. The rest are my viewer's contributions.

I cut now to the final chorus. Once again there's a conjugal scene with Gaga and boyfriend, now both seated on a living room couch, while her maid, in the foreground, prepares drinks. The maid resembles a woman who has been murdered, causing confusion about the video's earlier deaths. Gaga and the maid seem to be in the know; as Mary Ann Doane has pointed out, a woman wearing glasses (as this maid does) can suggest both vision and power, especially in women's melodramas.[3] A dropped newspaper telegraphs Gaga's ascendance as "The New It Girl." Perhaps Gaga's maid conspires with Gaga and helps prep her poison. Tasting the toxin in her black Mickey Mouse outfit, with her heavy black makeup and black glasses, Gaga seems like someone from the underworld. She seats herself upon the couch as her boyfriend drinks her concoction, stages a moment of recognition of the evil deed, and slumps dead. Here the music video truly moves out of joint, though I don't yet realize it. I've invested in the protagonist, and I support her vengeance. I want her to succeed but she's enjoying her payback too much. I'm surprised by the flatness of her 911 call: "I've just killed my boyfriend." After Gaga's exoneration, as her limo travels through public space with her fans visible outside her car window, she seems spacy. When she poses for a mug shot she looks so white-trashy that she might indeed have been the perpetrator of the crimes. This new counterevidence almost, but not quite, shakes my support for the star.

Moving Toward a Close Audiovisual Reading

The tale in "Paparazzi" could be read as a strong departure from traditional narrative. Gaga might seem unstable and incoherent, perhaps even posthuman. More than Michael Jackson's "Thriller," "Paparazzi" presents a protagonist who is equal parts lovable and hostile, and goes further by pushing this ambiguity in the clip, and it doesn't trade in zombies or werewolves. Jonas Åkerlund's radical presentation of identity is in sync with understandings drawn from contemporary cultural studies and psychoanalysis of people as composed of multiple forces that are shaped and constrained by social frameworks. Such depictions of persons, however, can be threatening and hard to assimilate; the myth of complete identities can be reassuring, providing a surer sense of self and others, as well as a sense of control. If people are multiple, I will be unable to predict behavior. Everyone, under the right circumstances, may be floozies, murderous, vain, vulnerable, sexually precocious, frozen, communally directed, melancholic, romantic, desolate, striving, endearing, frightened. The myth of complete identities gives me a surer sense of myself and others. In "Paparazzi" the character's dark sides emerge suddenly, but in a way that feels right. In this fiction I am able to support Gaga as a killer. Perhaps I cheer her on because her character has experienced great wrongs. She's able to gather power by aligning with the destructive proclivities of large institutions (Disney, the United States). Her supporters, fellow dancers, and friends accept her behavior. Subtle signs suggest she's a special kind of human, a demigod. She has an inhuman appetite. She's immune to poison. She gnashes her teeth. She makes eye signals showing she has special communicative powers. And she becomes increasingly robotic, frozen, allegorical.

To achieve such transgressive depictions, Åkerlund draws support from visually-based narratives, as well as musical and audiovisual forms. All of these structures depart from the ways life normally works: life may rarely follow the traditional five-act narrative structure, nor the logic of musical or audiovisual forms. Typical pop song structures can suggest telling a tale (verse), reflecting on it (chorus), and finding a moment outside it (bridge), but their rhythms only sometimes map onto lived experience. Audiovisual moments can unpredictably break from the texture, connecting to others farther away. A music video that interweaves narrative, musical, and audiovisual teleologies may be able to achieve something quite radical. Thus far I've shown how "Paparazzi" reflect narrative forms, and in what follows, I'll illustrate the ways "Paparrazzi" overlays and showcases musical and audiovisual ones. What's remarkable about music, as Nicholas Cook and Levi Strauss have argued, is that it's able to resolve difference or myth.[4] A musical composition can present one element, attribute, or state, embodied as musical material, and another that goes a different way and makes them meld, mingle, or resolve. If images are tied to musical elements and follow the music's trajectories, all sorts of differences can be worked out. Visual materials and audiovisual moments bound to the music of a pop song might drive us toward conclusions we might otherwise not accept.

Let's return to my initial question. For me, in "Paparazzi," Gaga seems like a good woman who's been treated badly by her boyfriend and fights to make a comeback. How does she turn murderous, while at the same time garnering my support? I've trusted Gaga and I've invested myself in her project. When she kills her boyfriend I find myself thinking "go girl!" But I don't understand how I've come to such a position—so shocking! Can looking closely at "Paparazzi" help me understand myself and contemporary artmaking?

The Audiovisual Contract

I've argued that music videos show off features of songs so that they can "sell" them. The image teaches the viewer memorable aspects of the song so she'll wish to return to it. In music videos we can sometimes even sense the image reaching to forge a connection with the music. Conversely, Bernard Herrmann quipped that film music seeks out elements in the image.[5] This linking, exchanging, and imparting create a range of relations among image, music, and text. But it's important to note also that music and image can be polygamous. One particular connection may be engaging, but many others will do. The music might work just as well with another set of images. It's helpful to consider what Jonas Åkerlund heard in "Paparazzi" that might have encouraged him to choose particular images, and it's useful to ask what we as viewers pick out in the relations between music, image, and text. We should keep in mind that different viewers will make different connections. Still: What in "Paparazzi" makes song and image seem to belong to one another? A fine skein of connections leads the listener (and viewer) to the boyfriend's death. These overlapping patterns suture us into the video and lead toward an outcome that feels increasingly inexorable as the video unfolds.

Arrangement and Song Sections

The song sections and musical arrangement of "Paparazzi" are the two most forceful structuring elements in service of its story. The song's high-register synthesizer sounds a bit like a theremin. The theremin has been associated with Gothic and horror films and can set the stage for multiple killings in the mansion, and more broadly, the clip's more macabre tones. When this synth-sound breaks away from the voice and hovers in the musical texture, it might also relate to aspects of the setting: the villa's high ceilings, for example. The song proper begins with a tonic minor seventh chord, but the root immediately drops out, leaving a major chord built on the third scale-degree: this unsettles any sense of harmonic centerdness, and this uncertainty may open up space for seeing Lady Gaga as damaged goods. Simultaneously, the song's opening "da-da" rhythm suggests a big arrival, hence the limo, glam clothing, and waiting staff (fig. 7.2). A dirty sounding synth in the middle register sounds a bit 1980s, perhaps enough to suggest high shoulder pads and the rhinestone-studded retro look. A second, soon appearing squeaky-squishy synth timbre might correspond to the vinyl strips Gaga wears. Overall the verse is reiterative and spare, with much empty space around each carefully produced sound element: percussive hits, especially, are finely crafted. This might suggest why Lady Gaga doesn't go far in the verses; she remains in her foyer, or on the couch. Her voice is dissonant with the synths underneath her, and this too might encourage the video's sense of trauma as Gaga stumbles. Sounds are ping-ponged in the stereo field, which creates a sense of enclosed spaces. The men hover around Lady Gaga tightly. She's irised in the couch. She's hemmed in by bandages or her metal outfit. Her hands make bounded, circular shapes in front of her face.

7.2 Music and image support Gaga's grand entrance.

The choruses are more luscious than the verses: they are where we as viewers want to be. The chorus is the good object. Its harmonic rhythm speeds up to one chord per measure, and gains a cycling quality. (This differs from the verse, which stays primarily on the tonic.) The voices are multitracked with reverb, creating a wash of sound. While the verse's percussion is brittle and harsh, the chorus's percussion become progressively warmer, taking on increasingly human-like qualities, to eventually sound like domesticated hand claps. This is partly why the choruses feel hospitable, like home.

Gaga's straight and gradually raised arm at the close of the verse also conveys us into the chorus. "Paparazzi"'s first chorus departs from traditional forms of music video, because it stays rooted in the same environment as the verse. Nevertheless, the two sections are different. In the first verse Gaga hobbles on her crutches, but the chorus adds a sense of movement and flow through the appearance of her waiting staff, who, in two lines, encourage her onward with flowing fringe. After much lying on the couch in verse two, in the second chorus Gaga runs into the large hallway and dances with broad frontal gestures with her supporting performers. And in the third chorus she comes forward off the couch and heads for murder. All this movement from the back to the front of the frame suggests greater mobility and freedom than in the verses, and I applaud her progress in the third chorus (fig. 7.3).

7.3 Gaga and her dancers own the choruses.

The contrast between the sparsely arranged verses and the thickly orchestrated chorus may be enough to align me with Gaga as she commits murder. The breaks, however, solidify these relations. They are even sparser and more repetitive than the verses—they're stripped down to almost nothing. In the first break, Gaga's waiting staff strut off, almost as if they might leave her. In the second she's backed into a corner, and she's dressed in black and white with celluloid spooled on her head. The flash-frames make it difficult to see, but she seems to be in bondage. At one point her head turns away from her body, like a possessed Regan in *The Exorcist*, with her hands spread like talons. It's a frightening image. Gaga drops in the frame against an adjacent shot of the dog's foot with its sharp nails; the dogs might attack her. All this moves too fast to take in, except subliminally. But I may experience palpable fear that Gaga may become one of the dead women. In addition, the music foregrounds the sound effect of a fuse being lit, and Gaga's wrapped in celluloid. If a match is struck she'll go up in flames. In the third chorus, as the flashing light transfers its rhythmic pattern to the repetitive synth in the conjugal scene with the boyfriend, I may feel a sense of relief. Gaga's out of danger; she's not like the dead women. I can trust the music to carry me out of a dangerous situation. I align myself with it. I support Gaga's mixing of the poison. Better him dead than my heroine.

The chorus's flow, with its rejuvenating possibilities, supports Gaga in what may first look like a loyal act of mixing a drink for her partner. It's only at the sprinkling of the powder that we see there's been a turn. The choruses have brought us here. The first two possess harpsichord-like sounds that oscillate quickly and are reminiscent of Baroque music. Since the location is a grand villa from the Baroque period, the orchestral touches might suggest that Gaga and her dancers possess both a knowledge and history tied to this place. Its moneyed surfaces and high style belong to her, not the maids or the men. In the third chorus, the arrangement drops out, and all that's left is the women's voices and a reiterating synth figure, which I hear as, "This is your moment!," "Do it now!," "Take the stage!"

Performers

My description thus far might sound grim or dour, but the video isn't. It stays cheery by capitalizing on the nature of performers in music video. The dead women are models who function as mannequins. Mannequins are meant to be more an absence than a presence: they display clothes, so these high-fashion dead women's business is to trade in absence and stillness. Music videos are not good at dealing with real death, or even stillness, however. Nor do they have true villains. No musical or audiovisual element can ever be completely vanquished or extinguished in a pop song or music video. In music video, music washes over the whole surface, animating everything. Almost nothing is really inanimate.

In music video clips, supporting characters often function as odd, mute, inanimate symbols, and they appear only in interstitial sections. They possess a blankness that's almost deathly. (Such depictions started early: the second clip screened on MTV's first broadcast, Ph.D.'s "Little Susie's on the Up," contains a background figure lurking around like a silent executioner.) Jonas Åkerlund extends the depictions of the background character much further than their initial and historical uses, suggesting something new and uncanny. The functions of the mannequin-like characters in "Paparazzi" are impossible to determine. The video's inability to suggest cessation or death is revealed by the music's pause after the poisoning. Two uncanny doctors are needed, both with glasses, one with blue skulls and another with green, to keep the body down. Real, depicted death tends to be rare in music videos. (Sometimes in a hip-hop video a member of the posse might toss a handkerchief at a camera, whose lens peers skyward from the bottom of a grave. A body in a casket might appear, as in Jay-Z's "99 Problems," but the corpses tend to like to open their eyes. Even Guns N' Roses' "November Rain" was unable to bury its corpse.)

So perhaps "Paparazzi" is cheerier and more life-affirming. The clip exploits the ambiguity between one real death and many supplementary ones, or one real death and many who are just ornamental symbols of something else, like the death drive of fandom. It's unclear. The video is also chipper because, though some of the material in the verses might be bleak, the choruses are opulent. Gaga's singing here is prettiest, when she hits the highest pitches on "until that boy is mine." Here, the voice is colored with a bit of sadomasochistic teasing. Gaga is able to suggest something vulnerable and lethal at the same time: perhaps she's offering death through orgasm. And even if this video suggests death, the handsome materials of gold, fur, marble, diamonds, orchids, and glitter gild the video. Vibrant pinks, purples, greens, reds, blues, and oranges also brighten it. The model's bodies are also strewn like Easter eggs. They seem more like clues or hieroglyphs, text to be read, than real dead bodies. The video hovers between the real and the unreal.

But the most surprising depiction of performers occurs in the third chorus. Here, as mentioned, the thick arrangement of the first two choruses fails to appear. Only a pulsing synthesizer fills its place. This encouraging synth along with a bevy of multitracked voices feels trustworthy, like home. Lady Gaga rides this wave and struts forward to commit murder. I, too, come forward, and am implicated in this gesture. When her glasses are removed, I see her face. She's an Olympia, a puppet doll! She's become like the mannequins, and perhaps even more so. Is she the queen of the dead?

Flow

Many subtle sonic and visual features work together to suture the viewer into the video and lead her, as an active witness, to the third chorus's murder. Visual motifs, for example, reappear in tandem with other processes like shifts in color or rhythmic patterns to form wavelike builds that carry the viewer into the third chorus. The mop-like straight hair of Gaga in chorus two (the sad Pierrot section) initially appeared less prominent (when she was in her wheelchair and her lovers were on the couch). Flounces adorn the edges of the skirts of women's dresses as the women form two supportive lines ushering in Gaga's rolling wheelchair and then her march down the foyer. Gaga also wears a short flounce on her couch in the first two verses and choruses, and then her clothes become extremely flouncy by chorus two. The line of the waiting staff in the first chorus also showcase long strips that ripple, and then a single strip trails the female maid's dress as she turns to mix the poison, almost like a path, or something unspooled (Gaga had spools of celluloid on her head in the bridge). Cross-hatching appears on Gaga's dress both in the first verse and the chorus. In the bridge, where she's stripped down, in black and white, in an S&M scenario, the cross-hatching becomes more extreme. These shapes: flounce, coil, ribbons, crosshatching appear and reappear based on song section, gathering greater intensity, and, as decorative patterns, flow. Every image also possesses a spiral and something that juts out. Consider Gaga falling through space, hands and arms at odd angles, before the twirling "vertigo" wheel. A larger alternating pattern of flow and stasis established across shots also extends through the video.

Color

Color takes on form and meaning in "Paparazzi." In the final chorus, when Gaga poisons her boyfriend, her bright yellow jumpsuit appears as an eruption. The pinks, purples, and greens also return from the opening; nature has been brought back in an orchid-like environment. Notice, too, the green from the cobra candelabras and phone, as well as the purple of the candlesticks, teacup, and boyfriend's socks. In the clip's center, the blue of the sky seems to flow down to the dancers in the second chorus, and to the pool with the dead girl at its edge, as well as the blue plastic tarp (a second pool?) on which a dead mannequin model rests. Red lipstick and pink mouths and tongue and red and blue jewelry erupt almost as moments of unleashed sexuality. The dark green and black of the Dalmatian and dead woman with ivy, and the fiery puddle of gold pooling from the maid's mouth, are nadirs. Several functions—patterns of color, costume, lyrics, and gesture—provide enough momentum to carry me like a wave into the murderous chorus. Each alone is sparse, perhaps inconsequential, but as an additive effect they get me there.

Lyrics

As in most music videos, the lyrics establish a range of connections between the music and the image, from direct to remote.[6] One obvious connection is Gaga saying "got my lashes" followed by a cut to the eyes of a stunning, green-eyed woman. The "ta-da" of the song's opening suggests a big arrival, hence such heavy makeup. Mascara is worked overtime in the video. Colors are suggested in the lyrics: "yellow dance," "purple teardrops," "cherry pie." Similar big splashes of color pop out against a white, blue, and gold background. The lyrics "cigarettes / shadow is burnt" is also underscored. A flayed-out dead maid sprawls at the bottom of a spiral staircase, with a vomitous puddle of fiery goo pooling from around her mouth. Earlier, on the couch, Gaga had made rapid-fire gestures as if she were puffing. In the bridge there's the sound of a fuse being lit, or the flicker of a lighter. These establish the sense of smoking (and the bloodshot Great Danes seem to corroborate this). As is often the case with music video (as I've claimed elsewhere), lyrics head off in another direction from where the imagery suggests.[7] The line "until that boy is mine" is opaque. Is it possible Gaga takes her boyfriend's life to make him hers? The ambiguity establishes a tantalizing distance between music, image, and lyrics.

Ambitus

The song's range from high to low extends from the Theremin-like synthesizer to the highly compressed bass drum. Åkerlund reflects this space visually with the clip's highest point: a woman's feet dangling from the ceiling as if she's hung herself with a rope. It's almost as if this is the point from which everything will descend. Height is sustained through Gaga's tall, punk-mohawk black-and-white headdress during the bridge, and her beehive extravaganza, postmurder, as she's driven through town. The video's lowest point is the dead maid in the ivy: Gaga seemingly drops toward that depth, almost falling off her couch in the second verse, and, in the bridge, sliding downward off frame in response to the threatening Great Danes.

Gesture

"Paparazzi"'s patterning traces the metaphor of Gaga as a young bird breaking out of its shell. Actions overlap, repeatedly returning to earlier stages in this process; across the clip, I seemingly find myself at various junctures of Gaga's attempt to break out of her confines. When Lady Gaga comes out of the limousine, she's encased in a neck and chest guard with her waitstaff angularly vogueing around her, giving her no greater space than the narrow boundary of her wheelchair. On the couch Gaga is enframed by a black iris, and she's dressed in black crosshatched veneer bands. She repeatedly makes pointed gestures with outstretched fingers as if to pierce a boundary and break out from the space. When kissing her lovers, Gaga's and their tongues meet, almost like hungry young birds. The wait staff's fluttering fingers and flowing fringe seem an encouragement to propel oneself forward, even to fly (the waitstaff looked to me a bit like 1950s airline stewardesses). In the Pierrot section (second chorus) the dancers make full arching clock-like shapes with their arms, as if they were claiming a larger sphere. Their leotards are smooth, as if Gaga and her dancers had been newly born, and the ruffles on their costumes resemble remnants of a struggle to break loose, but their gestures ape the postures of the mannequin's dead bodies, suggesting the impossibility of departing from the past. In the bridge, Gaga's tall head-gear of piled up celluloid and feathers resembles a cockatoo's, and the two Great Danes adjacent to her lend her an animal-like quality. Gaga propels her head forward in aggressive birdlike gestures. All of this imagery of emergence, of an attempt to get out, encourages me to cheer her on as she walks forward to mix a poisonous elixir to kill her boyfriend.

Close Relations

As mentioned, song sections and musical arrangement are the clearest means by which the viewer becomes implicated—but many other functions contribute as well. One is simply sewing the moment-by-moment flow of the music and the image together in a way that naturalizes them. Åkerlund adopts a range of approaches to highlight local features in the music. Some of the gestures are so grand and obvious that they could be read as Mickey-Mousing. Near the opening of the first verse, Gaga's waitstaff ferry her from her limo to her wheelchair. One Black chauffer pats Gaga's shoulder on the beat, and then two of the men freeze on a synthesizer hit. At the end of this first melodic phrase a dirty-sounding 1980s synth comes forward, and Gaga and her waitstaff repetitively cross their palms straight out before them, as if to catch the funny quality of the timbre. Toward the end of the verse there's a sudden harmonic shift, and Gaga's melodic line finally opens up into something more song-like. Here, she starts pulling off her long stocking-like gloves. Her movements, established across shots, suggest an opening out that responds to the harmonic movement. Gaga then stumbles forward on crutches, first on one knee and hip and then on the other, emphasizing each downbeat measure while her staff strut, passing her by.

There are other subtle touches. At melodic high-points, performers showcase the brighter features of the voice through raised arm gestures. Note the chauffer's hands high above his head directly behind Gaga's wheelchair at "we'd be so fantastical." Gaga also raises her arms above her at "promise I'll be kind." Also, through the thicket of gestures, the waiting staff trace shapes across edits. As Gaga is lifted out of the car, a sense of line is created by the waiting staff's demonstrative pat on Gaga's shoulder, followed by the waitstaff's swirling gestures around Gaga, to finally resolve on a shot of Gaga's feet. As Gaga is rolled down the carpet, a dancer traces a complicated swirling gesture against her left arm, as if to extend the melody's resonance. On beat four of each measure, a waitperson's hand makes a funny gesture, something fluttery, or suggestive of a "halt." The first times Gaga appears on the couch, glistening postproduction effects are added to the fabric to make these phrases pop.

Verse two distinguishes itself from verse one through less moment-by-moment underscoring. Groups of images are phrased together to suggest melodic lines. Gaga swoons off her couch, and then the dead woman's torso and outstretched arms, revealed through rapid editing, form a larger pattern. One of the song's prominent rhythmic articulations is a triplet. The triplet-like shots of dead women, each slightly offset from the other, are punctuated as if the shots were recollecting this pattern. Gaga, too, just once, on her couch, bounces up and down like a mechanical doll, three times, as if responding to the rhythm. Toward the end of verse two the sync becomes looser, providing a moment of respite or openness before a strong contrast: the crisp, demonstrative articulations of the dancers in the Pierrot section (chorus two).

The Detail That Juts Out

A plethora of eccentric details supports the murder in "Paparazzi." Different visual marks or musical moments might stick out for different viewers. Those I find most prominent function similarly to what Slavoj Žižek calls "quilting points," Hitchcockian details that poke a hole in the film's fabric.[8] In "Paparazzi" these include the following: a sudden cross-hatch that appears on Lady Gaga's cheek in one shot of the first chorus; blue, not black, finger marks that are imprinted into the dead woman's neck at the bottom of a red-tiled bathtub; an odd crown of spikes worn by one of the women who's been killed; the flaw in a beautiful woman's green eye; the drooping of one of Gaga's half-shut eyes, and the fact that her eye-shadow seems to change from thick black to silver and black, and back again across the first verse. The Great Dane's eyes are dirty red. The camera's light that illuminates the mug shot's snaps at the video's end is as dirty as a mottled egg. The dead women's bodies are twisted into odd shapes like thrown-down Barbie dolls; they're also wrapped in their original plastic (like Rosenquist's paintings). The sound of a fly's buzz pops in for only a moment against one pink rose at the video's opening. In the second chorus Gaga wears fragments of clothing as she runs out as a Pierrot figure, and her cross-shaped earrings, dangling upside down, sway.

In "Paparazzi" these odd details become predictable. This sets the stage for the out-chorus's closing scene in which Gaga commits murder. It takes place in a Victorian death room, unaccountably embedded with a wide array of odd protruding, disruptive details: the snake candle (which appeared as two long standing candle sticks in the first verse at the end of the foyer); a scary coffin-like hooded Victorian seat; a black jacket hanging on a chair; a weird tchotchke perched on the table that looks like something belonging to one's great grandmother; a replacement of the photograph in the boyfriend's newspaper from Africa to two ominous figures, one draped in yellow, the other in black; and last an old pea-green rotary phone hovering on a background table. Like the other green in the room, the phone's a sudden eruption of nature. (Green has been downplayed so far.) So when Gaga steps forward in the last chorus, with her odd suit peppered with faces, her strange goggled glasses, and blackly etched faces on her fingernails, she is only one more odd detail against a larger scape of death. Her glasses, the faces on her outfit, and her fingernails with faces all stare back at me (a triple staring-back) without seeing me.

Final Kill

I may accept the scene in which Lady Gaga murders her boyfriend for two additional reasons. Åkerlund here draws together many elements I've previously seen, and their recapitulation gives a sense of closure and rightness to the act. I may also be so busy trying to track the connections among these elements that I don't properly attend to the murder Gaga is about to commit.

Here are some of the strands that get taken up in the third, deadly chorus. The pink rose with its green leaves at the opening could be said to return, now fractured. The color of the green leafery suddenly appears in the cover art of the magazine that is thrown down, as stark text "She's back!," and the cobra candles and pea green telephone. The pink of the rose suddenly reappears as the poison Gaga mixes and pours into a pink flowery tea cup. There are also the red bottles that are reminiscent of the blood and lipstick of the previous murders. And, as with each chorus, Gaga starts at the back of the frame and gradually brings herself forward. When I see her in this last chorus on the couch, as she steps forth, recapitulating material appears in proximity immediately around her. Her glasses suddenly have the same diamond studding she wore in the first verse. Her ring has spikes that recall the dead woman on the staircase with her crown of spikes, and the spiked gloves Gaga wore on the couch. The poison Gaga sprinkles from her ring glistens, much like the sparkles we saw on the couch's upholstery. (The powder also flows like the streaming detritus of the petals and dust from earlier sections.) These last items appear first, on the left side of the frame then on the right, then on the left, then on the right, pulling me back and forth, perhaps reminding me of the aural ping-ponging so predominant in the verses. I may also be primed for this moment by a transmedial exchange between the flash-frames of white light in the bridge and the synth pulse in this third chorus. Gaga brings a spoon to her mouth that reminds me of her penitent, robo-android silver cap, bodysuit, and crutches in the first verse, as she made her promenade down her foyer (fig. 7.4).

I've claimed that "Paparazzi" superimposes classic Hollywood narrative structures on musical form: the music video's allure stems from the way that both forms unfold simultaneously. I can't get a fix on which one deserves preeminence, so I can't decide what's transpired. The narrative suggests

7.4 Poisoning.

a classic character arc in which Gaga starts out as a woman who's been wronged and who eventually decides to take revenge, but the music and audiovisual relations tell a different story. Pop songs often focus on recurring musical events, and they often possess an air of inevitability. Gaga moves between the abandonment of the breaks, the inhospitality of the verses, and the lush choruses, which seem connected with women's voices. She aligns with the chorus's multitracked voices, which we might decide belong to the women strewn around the villa. The melodramatic opening piano accompaniment too might be associated with turn-of-the-century stage plays and old black-and-white films, both showcasing strong villains and victims. I surmise that someone will be rescued and someone must pay. The music that accompanies Gaga as she lies injured on the sidewalk suggests she's aligned with strong forces. She is owed something. Even though the visual scapes of the choruses and the verses change, Gaga acts with determination, moving briskly or gazing fixedly as if on a mission. If I take these moments seriously, I might assume she was set to kill from the beginning. Psychologists have noted that when we interact with people we experience two separate streams of information, visual and aural. People often dissimulate, cloaking their true intentions and desires. We are better interpreters of our interlocutors' intent when we attend to the voice than when we focus on visual gestures. A jury might not convict Gaga, seeing her as a victim of abuse, but I might, against my better judgment. The jury might vaguely sense that the song's bridge places Gaga at risk,

7.5 Though a jury might not convict Gaga, I might.

and it's either her or the boyfriend. But I've been attending to the song and its relations with the image. Gaga's determined comportment at the openings of song sections, and the siren song of the lush choruses, lure me to follow her as she prepares the poisonous drink. This seems like premeditation, but I bet Gaga will get off scot-free. For me, Jonas Åkerlund and Gaga get away with murder (fig. 7.5).

III Music Video's Late Late Style

How to Analyze Music Videos: Beyoncé and Melina Matsoukas's "Pretty Hurts"

MUSIC VIDEOS LEND THEMSELVES to analysis: they're rich, evocative, and short. Repeated viewings bring new aspects to light. But there aren't many analytical models to draw upon.

To build media-reading skills, this chapter takes a hands-on approach to analysis in real time. Over the last twenty years I've taught courses on music video, and I've sought ways to help students write up their analysis. The close readings I appreciate attempt to account for both the soundtrack and the image, but a student needn't have musical training to explore audiovisual relations. Characterizing a song's elements in everyday terms (buzzy, bell-like) rather than specifically musical ones can be helpful, as can drawing on liner notes and reviews, and suggestions from musically trained friends. I've provided a webpage, https://themediaswirl.com, with tip sheets on how to begin an analysis, and links to models. In this chapter I'll take "Pretty Hurts," a clip directed by Melina Matsoukas from Beyoncé's self-titled video album (2014), and see where it leads.

When I begin working with a music video I often ask: "Why do I like it?" or "Why does it puzzle me?" I hold this question in reserve with the hope that answers will emerge later. In "Pretty Hurts," the *Beyoncé* album's first clip, the singer competes in a beauty pageant. The video seems to both celebrate and critique the fashion industry: it considers professionalism and authenticity, and what might enable collaboration and personal happiness. I'm particularly drawn to a moment in the song's chorus when Beyoncé waves from the podium amidst the rows of women (3:12), and I'll pay special attention to the question of how and why this moment moves me (fig. 8.1).

Beginning an analysis, I watch the clip many times. I'll listen to the song alone, I'll watch the images silently, I'll read the lyrics apart from

8.1 Beyoncé waves from the podium (3:12).

both, and I'll run the clip in my imagination. I'll take a single visual or aural parameter and follow it through the clip's entirety: tracking the song sections, counting out the rhythm, tracing the melody, attending to the musical arrangement, following the figures in the frame, studying the editing, and so on. Sometimes I feel I'm in a conversation with the video, querying it. "What about that odd spot of color?" "What about that chorus?" All the while I take copious notes. As I start learning the music and image I'll note key moments of audiovisual synchronization, and my attention will follow predictable paths through the video—almost as if the video and I are dancing together. I'll follow these paths, but I'll also direct my attention in other ways. In this analysis I'll track a process in which insights emerge gradually and unpredictably. Readers might periodically refer to the clip. My goal here is to help others have a richer experience of a music video, to see and hear more, and to want to watch it many times.

The video for "Pretty Hurts" has a moment when Beyoncé waves while standing on stage with the other contestants. This happens at (3:11) in the song's first chorus. I wonder why this moment stirs me. So why not begin with the choruses? Music videos, like feature films, use many devices to achieve their ends, and leave other techniques aside. Since each video leans on certain techniques, and it's the chorus that draws me in, I might begin by asking whether the video breaks into strongly demarcated song sections. To follow this further I might ask: How much does this video highlight song sections? (Lyric sheets and tablature transcriptions can be useful for determining sections even when a student doesn't have musical training.) Often, especially in classic, commercial music videos, visual and song sections parallel one another. This is true of "Pretty Hurts." For the first two choruses, Beyoncé is on the podium. In the third chorus (following the bridge) she and the models appear on the stage again, but then the image shifts to their self-inflicted harm. In the verses Beyoncé preps for her competition, and while someone or something twirls or circles, she tends to take one step up. Most of the painful techniques demanded by the beauty industry occur in the bridge, and Beyoncé looks frustrated and angry here. And that tells me something. In a pop song, the verses often discuss the everyday, while the bridges provide another way of seeing things. The choruses often crystallize an idea—a view that can seem more timeless—and reflect a communal wish. That Beyoncé can't transcend her situation during the bridge suggests that hers is a real struggle. The third chorus's shift in focus intrigues me (4:38). Continuing to work on this, I'll make greater sense of the last chorus. But I don't know this yet. What question might we consider next? To analyze this video, let's consider its various parameters in turn.

The Use of Color and Texture to Convey Music and Story

The color scheme emphasizes browns and golds. The warmth of the home's wood paneling, shag carpet, and silky outfits suggests a cave or burrow. I hear the song as exceptionally warm, and I think the mellow colors and textures draw our attention to the song's capaciousness (fig. 8.2). There are also isolated spots of blue. Blue latex-covered hands intrude in the frame, looking uncanny (5:10). There's also a violating syringe and the models swallowing cotton and vomiting. (Afterward, when Beyoncé emerges from the toilet, her earrings have sharp edges, as if they'd assimilated the women's self-injurious routines. At the video's triumphant end the earrings will form full, large circles, mimicking Beyoncé's own richer sense of self.) Alongside the warmth of Beyoncé's voice and the often lullaby-like-rocking supporting vocals and the percussion, I ask: Is there anything in the music that has a little sharpness?

I turn to the musical arrangement. Halfway into the first verse, the hard and brittle sound of the drum slaps on beats 2 and 4 (what's known as the "backbeat," here possibly a processed hand clap with an enhanced snare) could be seen to press Beyoncé onward (2:25). Earlier we had spied on the women pushing and shoving her, then turning away, perhaps setting her in motion (Beyoncé is very much alone in this video). Perhaps this timbral/rhythmic detail carries weight. John Mowitt reminds us that drumming is a form of beating.[1] There's also a bit of a protrusion or rushing

8.2 Warm, cozy settings (5:52).

in the second verse's melody when Beyoncé sings "is all that matters . . . bigger is better" (3:22; 3:28). These stand out from the smoother, constantly articulating rhythm arrangement, overdubbed voices, and reverberant synthesizer. These melodic touches, the sharp accents on beats 2 and 4, Beyoncé's concluding full-throated singing of "When you find yourself alone," and the fragmented, speechifying "pretty hurts," may support Beyoncé's trashing of her trophies. (Envision the video without these musical touches, and the close is harder to imagine.) Aural and visual protrusions don't necessarily need to simultaneously match what we see and hear, I believe. If the visual or aural motif is catchy enough, it can still forge a connection from a temporal distance.

As I continue to analyze "Pretty Hurts" I'll discover more about color, but for now, let's turn to another parameter. When analyzing a video I'll often work on one parameter until I catch an idea, then turn to a second, or to several, to then return to parameters I've already considered. I sometimes find myself posing questions to the video several times, and I don't always get an answer. I simply wait.

The Implied Geography of the Video

I'm interested in the gorgeous images of Beyoncé, so I ask about the implications of setting and space: how do the figures move and where are they placed in the frame? The longest and steepest trajectories move from

Beyoncé on the podium to her drop into water, and from the podium to her lying, belly-up, on the carpet. She also seems to step up toward and away from these locations. These points help to chart her struggle to achieve beauty and win the pageant. But they might also describe formal distances within the song, such as how it moves from section to section (fig 8.3). Against this, I notice the stage's columns appear to suspend space and objects in attractive proportions, as do the podium's tiered steps that firmly and generously support the women. The song's spare opening also reflects a sense of balance and stasis. Against this, I might want to consider internal movement: the women's cat-fighting for hair dryers, their brisk pushings aside and graceful balletic moves, and then the more archetypally womanly flowing gestures Beyoncé adopts. Sometimes, but not always, the contours of the melodies and bass line can be reflected by the placement of objects and movement of figures in a frame.

So far this feels like what I would call a classic music video. It's attentive to the song and committed to showing off its musical features in a balanced way, especially since its song sections are so carefully articulated. Individual phrases are also clearly shown: when the melody dips or a phrase ends, Beyoncé often glances down. At melodic high points, a woman's enormously tall hairdo or a suspended hair dryer crests the top of the frame. In the opening, one woman buttoning a dress and another pinching flesh from her sides might reflect the isolated chords of the accompaniment. A camera's pan or a figure tapping in the background elucidate the ways in which the sounds trail off. I see and hear these shapes, but I don't expect other viewers and listeners to necessarily hear and see this as I do.

The Role of Lyrics

The lyrics begin like this: "Mama said, 'You're a pretty girl. What's in your head, it doesn't matter.'" For me these lines are so emotionally resonant that they hover over the clip. We might consider how the mother's advice shapes the video's iconography. Beyoncé's furniture looks like it belongs to an older generation. She may still live with her parents.

How might the line "When you find yourself alone" also shape the video? The moment when Beyoncé stalls for time, as she seeks an answer to the question: "What is your aspiration in life?" feels jarring (4:03). As she falls into water, the microphone comes up from silence and starts buzzing reverberantly and words, too, become garbled (fig. 8.4). Some of the sounds seem as if they had emanated from the sustain and pedal of

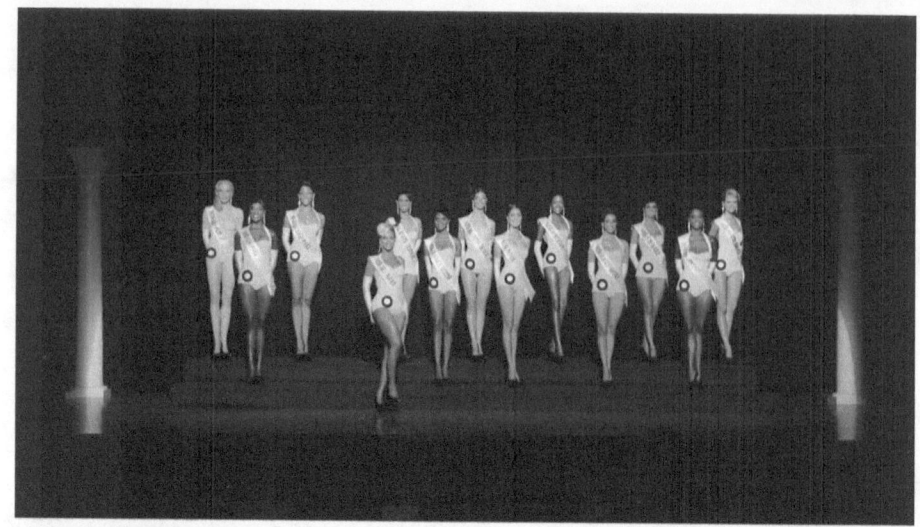

8.3 Long, steep trajectories from the podium to the water (4:12).

8.4 Beyoncé falls into the water.

the opening chords, which also begins to warble and merge into microphone feedback. Earlier, in the song's arrangement proper, every eighth note had been filled in with insistent percussion fills, sometimes using tiny bell-like sounds. Song sections frequently end with buzzy distortion, and the choruses open with a high-pitched breathy-like whistle (probably filtered white noise). At this point it's worth noting the musical arrangement sometimes functions here as an *unhelpful* partner—its noisy internal chatter or a buzz of activity keeps Beyoncé apart from herself. The isolation and silence of the water provide Beyoncé with an opportunity to ask questions and for the pageant's horrors to emerge.

In general, the song's overdubbed backing vocals support Beyoncé's lead voice, but Beyoncé's fellow models do not. So does "Pretty Hurts" suggest another, more receptive audience? In verse 1 especially, Beyoncé's overdubs of "Pretty Hurts" move forward dramatically to the front of the mix, claiming our attention. At the song's end, the rejoining "Pretty Hurts" becomes increasingly emphatic. Does Beyoncé improve upon her parents' and colleagues' advice, counseling us on ways to nurture ourselves? Are we her intended audience?

The Influence of Rhythm on Narrative Flow

I first listen to the song alone. There's the hand-clap snare on the backbeat, and small articulations that might sound like flamenco steps—possibly played by a güiro (a gourd instrument with ridges, stroked with a stick)[2] or snare with brushes—taking up every eighth note. The bass drum is syncopated. In the choruses, the bass drum articulates a four-on-the-floor (every quarter note is articulated), the backbeat drops out, and a thick synthesizer pad fills things in (this kind of synthesizer pad is often used in the chorus, in the recently popular songwriting technique of "the soar").[3] The chorus's arrangement is highly unusual. Perhaps the producer and arrangers (Ammo, Rob Sucheki, Derek Dixie, and Stuart White) wanted an insistent and dramatic shift without change of scale between the verse and chorus. I count off the measures as the video progresses. In the verses, I notice Beyoncé tapping the carpet with her fingertips (Beyoncé's hands before her crotch seem either vulnerable or powerful—it's hard to determine what her posture might signify). The opening's editing is slightly irregular against the pulse and becomes smoother as the video progresses, as if Beyoncé and the pageant have become more coordinated. Beyoncé's cycling and walking also establish a pulse. In the chorus, when the rhythm becomes a straight four-on-the-floor, Beyoncé becomes less mobile. Does the pulse then become internalized as something more subjective, like a heartbeat? This would support other aspects of "Pretty Hurts"—like Beyoncé's drop into water—that seem more like an allegory, dreamscape, or memory than a documentary of a recent event.

The Foregrounding of Continuity

Because music video images often aim to keep pace with and draw attention to the song's flow, they tend to draw on several devices to establish continuity from shot to shot. Match cuts are unusually common. In "Pretty Hurts" the stage's blue spangled curtains draw back and Beyoncé's blue award ribbons tacked on the den's wall etch the same pattern. She stands against a wall next to a hanging spangled beige dress that frames her as much as the curtains do. (The camera before her bathroom stall reveals one extra wall-as-frame as well.) During the song's break (4:11), the camera cross-cuts between Beyoncé submerged underwater and the contestants preparing in the green room. A large bunched-up green duffel bag matches, via shape and placement, Beyoncé's submerged body.[4] There's also a preponderance of repetitive material to create flow. Wigs and hair curlers, for example, dot the video. Extra crowns surface, too. It's also worth following the video's images of feet, especially those gangsta socks and the way one foot delicately articulates the beat (2:10). There's an absence of feet in general, except when Beyoncé steps on the scale, or her foot trembles in the bridge. When Beyoncé is submerged in water, rows of shoes seem to upbraid her. But that's one of the tricky parts of analyzing a music video: such a heterogeneous unfolding of material competes for attention. One can be pulled away.

Melina Matsoukas's Style

Watching a director's other work can help us to tease out themes that thread through her oeuvre. Matsoukas's other clips reveal an engagement with a neglected and worn-down 1950s America. She also likes muted colors. The visual language of "Pretty Hurts" suggests that the pageant is regional, small, and working-class: on the podium and in the green room, for example, sashes say "Miss Jersey Shore," "Miss South Bronx," and "Miss Jamaica Queens." Is the winner's title of "Miss Shaolin"[5] a sign of otherness, I wonder? How might these visual touches help to create sentiment, even nostalgia? And do these touches make the video's primary message more palatable? The video wants us to recognize the damage inflicted by women competing against one another as well as the fashion industry's harmful practices.

In another of Matsoukas's videos, Beyoncé's "Why Don't You Love Me," an American flag projected onto Beyoncé is so prominent it feels like a personal statement, so I look for similar symbols in "Pretty Hurts." Sure enough, when Beyoncé sings a cappella before the judges, she wears black stars against a white field, with blue spangles behind her, although we're missing red. The video seems from this moment on to seek its missing red element: it's smeared here and dotted there within the images, only finding its real weight at the video's close, when the MC's assistant, in a luridly red-sequined gown, hands off the crown to Beyoncé's competitor while our diva-heroine looks on.

The Use of Props

Matsoukas states that with "Pretty Hurts," she attempted to freshly capture unplanned moments.[6] Beyoncé's vomiting wasn't scripted. But I believe there must have been a great deal of preparation before shooting occurred. In the music video's well-budgeted heyday of the 1980s and 1990s, directors and their crews often arrived at a shoot with several truckloads of props. Laid out on set would be rows of shoes, earrings, plates, and underthings. Several alternatives might be filmed on the spot. The outfits and accessories in "Pretty Hurts" adopt an "arc" that seems more determined than spontaneously chosen, however. The jewelry alone suggests a path from beginning to end, from the gold bands around Beyoncé's ankles (like a ball and chain) to the earrings that become whole at the video's close. The appearance of porcelain animals and human figurines throughout also seem too concerted to be last-minute fortuitous decisions, especially since they appear to accrue meaning as the video unfolds. Most intriguing is a white porcelain figurine of two seated women, one embracing the other, on the coffee table in front of Beyoncé. Traditionally, this would be a pair of heterosexual lovers. Yet a close look reveals two women wearing dresses, embracing, with one holding up what one might assume to be a pageant sash. At the video's close Beyoncé molds herself into the shape of the supporting porcelain figure, as if providing strength and support for the woman who wins the award. The visually choreographed doubling of statuary and live performers could be understood as pro-feminist, homosocial, or homosexual. (Foreshadowing this, in the intro at 0:33, against the tender but stoic chords, a woman's hand momentarily reaches into the frame and gently strokes Beyoncé's shoulder as she stands among the women.⁷) The white porcelain cat also gains meaning. Early on the cat is placed over Beyoncé's head, doubling her blonde-waved hair. At the video's end Beyoncé crawls on all fours, stalking forward to the camera, as if a cat-like alter-ego had emerged from inside her, and now, as female aggressor, she's readying to pounce on that oily MC (6:36). The fierce porcelain tiger peering from behind the top of the couch resembles the beauty pageant winner, Ms. Shaolin (their faces and expressions are similar) (6:09). Both figures seem to shadow or haunt Beyoncé. On the shelves of the exercise room, there's also a jeweled crown and a zebra. (Note that items seem to have been carefully chosen and edited into the video; there's a match cut between a pageant woman's yellow dress and the yellow magazines stacked in a shelf's corner.) It's hard for me to decide on the zebra's role (3:20). I might imagine that with the predatory environment of the video (including that fierce porcelain tiger), the zebra suggests Beyoncé's vulnerability. But I could also imagine that the animal was chosen because it rhymes with the striping on Beyoncé's gym clothes. Matsoukas, too, may be like the music video and film director Francis Lawrence, who says he always adds a lot of flora and fauna to enrich his videos.⁸ I'm also tempted to wonder—but this may be too much of a stretch—whether this and other "Pretty Hurts" images might be linked to Africa or African American culture: the antique lamp has a black figure holding it up; the gold anklets might resemble shackles. Again, perhaps this is a stretch, but at this point I'm taking it seriously. The white cat has one single blue eye (6:35)—less stereotypically Anglo-Saxon-looking models often opt to wear contacts to lighten their appearance.

The Beginning and End

Just as in film, a music video's opening often foreshadows its end. I notice the deep jade-green and spangles returning (0:10; 6:22–6:44), and then I catch that Beyoncé's blue and silver shorts match the MC's silver jacket and blue curtains. There's even some dusting of silver over the periodically reappearing white porcelain cat (2:07). This video is both color-coordinated and patterned. Horizontal lines traverse the frame, including the bands of light on the shiny gold drapery.

What about the song as a whole? Music videos often close with ambiguous double endings that encourage a viewer to watch the clip again. Michael Jackson's "Thriller" famously does so, and "Pretty Hurts" does so as well. I count four ways of reading the end of the video. First, Beyoncé triumphs. Yes, she loses this pageant, but she's reflecting upon or fantasizing about moments when she competed as a child, so she's in many ways already a winner. We're aware that she's more beautiful than any of the other pageant contestants and "should" win. We viewers recognize her as the "real" Beyoncé, who has already achieved a top position in pop-music history, so we can feel she's already risen above the event. A second way to interpret the ending is that Beyoncé is angry about the pageant. She breaks trophies, encourages women to rebel, and threatens her MC. A match cut shows him fixing his bow tie followed by Beyoncé stalking forward on all fours as if she's going straight for his jugular—good for her! A third reading is that she's made peace with herself and with the pageant; fourth, she absents the event and has encouraged the women to do so as well. (The "Pretty Hurts" sash remains slung across the chair.)

Gestures That Cross Media

I suspect that some of this video's actors heard the song so often during filming that their mannerisms picked up aspects of the song's musical materials. This gestural exchange among media gives music videos a certain density. Toward the second chorus the MC seems to pause and share an empathetic moment with Beyoncé, saying, "You've done a great job in the competition," but then he abruptly turns and exclaims, as if repressing his sentiment, "as have all our ladies!" The judges attentively listen, enraptured by Beyoncé's singing, but then look down quickly to note their scores. The models seem to be listening to Beyoncé, but then swiftly turn their backs. Beyoncé gingerly gazes up at her trainer, and then he brusquely shoos her away. The song proper does this too. Gentle "aha, ahas" suddenly become drowned out by the verse's very busy musical arrangement.

The Use of Costuming to Underscore Music and Story

Bea Åkerlund, the designer, chose the wire Playboy-bunny ears because they lent Beyoncé a quality of innocence.[9] I seek other touches. The gangsta socks quickly suggest a different set of alliances and history. There's also the strange designer jumpsuit and white plastic shoes that suggest the 1980s. The jeweled blouse and white mink fur that Beyoncé wears for her Botox session contrasts with her other outfits. (Note the way this scene's star-studded, high-heeled sandals chime with her opening black-starred dress.) Matsoukas reports that Beyoncé wears a strait jacket beneath her mink, but even though I can see some of her straps, the outfit doesn't really resonate with me.[10] My knowledge of this detail, however, may help me to notice that the MC's accessories are ominously black. Instead of the traditional white or pink carnation, he wears a brittle black spiky brooch that resembles a sea urchin. It projects potential to harm—especially Beyoncé. She wears earrings with dangling, diamond-studded crosses (3:41–3:46).

The MC's black accessories (establishing a villain), along with Beyoncé's range of hairstyles, costumes, bodily dispositions, and expressions, help to establish "Miss Third Ward" as a densely textured character. I think the numbers attached near the hips of the models' pageant dresses reduce the women to packaged wind-up dolls or graphic logos from a Fernand Leger painting. I also think the opening mirrored dress Beyoncé wears resembles her outfit for "Partition," another clip from her *Beyoncé* video album. Many types of hairstyles, lipstick colors, and earrings come forward, looking chosen by Åkerlund and Matsoukas. Beyoncé's lipstick becomes the color of her competitor's gown, as if she bequeathed some of herself to her. Additional audiovisual rhyming and promiscuous cross-media sharing include Beyoncé's home's teardrop-shaped lampshade that resembles her waved hairdo (that of Harvey Keitel, who has a cameo as the pageant's host, is similarly waved—do these shapes intimate weeping?). The models' pageant dresses are chosen to create match cuts across shots. One woman's shiny black and gold striped dress presages the living-room's design scheme. The living room's gold modernist mirror (its beveled glass pieces resembling a sash) rhymes with the room's furniture and Beyoncé's gold earrings and anklets. Even the mirrors down the den's hallway remind me of Beyoncé's "Partition" dress. Beyoncé's earrings sway and the models wave their numbered paper sheets back and forth, all marking the rhythm. Standing at the end of the rehearsal line-up, a woman dressed in baby blue and pink doubles for Beyoncé's tyrannical coach.

The Role of Harmony

A pop song's chord changes can often be found through a Google search using the song's title and the word "tab" (for guitar chords tablature). Sheet music is also often available for purchase. The chord changes on "Pretty Hurts" are simple—(I–ii–vi–V–I)—with the verse, bridge, and choruses all using the same chord progression. (The bridge, however, begins its progression on ii, as if the system had encountered a slight hitch. It also has one chord that's new for this song—a bvii chord.) The song's harmonic scheme suits the video's theme of a largely repetitive cycle.

Depictions of Race, Class, Gender, and Sexuality

The güiro and syncopated rhythm of flamenco footsteps have Latin associations. (Glenn McDonald, principle engineer for Spotify and Echo's Nest, has said he was surprised to discover how much of Beyoncé's music can be categorized as Latin pop.[11]) These musical choices may provide grounds for the video's many contestants of color. Although one might argue that the regional setting has mostly a documentary value—it's not the kind of beauty pageant most people saw in the 1970s—this location may have been specifically chosen to speak to the music. The pageant's professionals—the MC, judges, plastic surgeon, and beautician—are predominantly white or male. The meanest contestants are white. The coach is albino, although he may be seen as lower in status, and therefore closer to the women. These race relations accurately represent the current state of the culture industries in Hollywood and beyond.[12] But, analytically, I'm not getting a lot here yet. I'll just have to keep watching and listening (fig. 8.5).

There comes a point in most analytical work when I feel I'm not making progress. I've wondered how much a successful music video needs strong audiovisual relations. Is a visually acute, flashy director enough? Some videos seem driven by intimate audiovisual engagement, and such relationships can serve dramatic ends. "Pretty Hurts" both heightens our identification with and critiques the fashion industry. How can I be sure exactly how close these relations are? I can't. Relations that emerge in the

8.5 Beyoncé is placed between women of different skin tones (2:48).

process of analysis tend to feel apt, and it makes sense in this case that the director would use close relations to elicit the viewer's empathy and antipathy. I also intuit that the video shares features with classic videos like Madonna's "Like a Prayer" (1985). Both "Pretty Hurts" and "Like a Prayer" have close sound and image relations: images and music that respect strongly demarcated song sections, with each section telling a different story; explorations of race and of musical performance, and a variety of vocal styles; the podium as a separate realm; and an interplay between models and characters.

I have not seen any studies that show whether viewers tend to perceive what I am describing. The reader might simply check if the description seems true for them. The most popular and critically admired clips seem, I've found, to hold up well to this kind of close viewing. With YouTube, music video's generic borders have become blurry, so that many types of audiovisual relations seem to count as music videos. But well-funded commercial videos function much as they always have. They still tend to emerge from collaborations between record companies, musicians, and directors (as with "Pretty Hurts"). The visual track is designed to sell the song—and, as the first clip on the album, "Pretty Hurts" may have been especially bound to do so. Commercial videos tend to be short, and often can seem uncanny. They need to accomplish many things: highlight the star, showcase performances, draw attention to the lyrics, and underscore the music. To sell a song—to teach listeners what's memorable about it—the image might emphasize the movement from verse to chorus, or highlight an unusual timbre, melodic contour, or striking rhythm. The visual track might point to one or two musical features at a time, like a tour guide. For while the music envelops us, visual features more often momentarily focus our attention, especially if they're working in service of the song.

Suturing the Image to the Music

I discover verse 1 of "Pretty Hurts" has many moment-to-moment instances of audiovisual synchronization:

- The melody's contour rises while strips of light playing on gold surfaces behind Beyoncé gradually rise in the frame—even though she gazes down and looks away from us (0:08–1:03; 2:02–2:21).
- A güiro or snare with brushes makes a scratchy sound. Simultaneously, Beyoncé rips off the hair-removal strip adhering to her

face. Soon, one of the models pulls something off the back of a competitor's dress, and I assume the gesture elicits the same sound (2:17; 2:23).
- The vocals arrangement presents a gentle "aha," and Beyoncé delicately pats her sinuses in the mirror. Soon she'll lean forward, and her bunny ears will bounce softly against another "aha." The next melodic phrase begins a step higher, and Beyoncé will step up to the weighing scale. The song now seems brighter and she stands a step closer to us (2:04; 2:05).
- A ballerina in the back of the rehearsal space stretches upward, and another dancer pirouettes. These gestures help to carry Beyoncé and us into the first chorus. (Without them we wouldn't have such a graceful sense of movement to convey us into the next song section) (2:26–2:38).
- A brush drags across a cymbal, giving a voice to the curtains as they swing open (2:41).
- The camera pans on an open vowel in the lyrics, like "hair" or "stage." In general the camera pans gently, perhaps aligning itself more with the vocals than the rhythm arrangement (3:14–3:18; 3:31).

The images for verse 2 possess a stronger sense of movement and flow than verse 1, and the song has a more foregrounded synth pad. The stationary bicycle's wheels spin. Beyoncé pumps her arms up and down. The needle on the scale oscillates without settling. Again, Beyoncé steps up as the melody rises (3:15–3:45). In verse 2 the women turn around together on stage. Rotations have been performed before (including by a ballerina, and the women who turn away from Beyoncé). Finally, it seems these gestures of isolation or hostility have been harnessed into a coordinated structure. We might suddenly admire the competition and its models for qualities of discipline and grace (3:20–3:22).

In the song's break, simple piano chords reappear and the camera and the figures in the frame gently seek connection with them through contour—up one whole step, down a third, a glance up or a look down (4:10–4:40). Beyoncé heaves forward to vomit. We hear the chorus's main hook ("pretty hurts!"). Does this moment suggest some suddenly emergent latent content? Beyoncé's singing often seems immediately generous and expressive. I wonder if she must sometimes deliver a performance that feels internally forced; Beyoncé is such a consummate performer, we'll never know (4:54).

In the bridge, many of the images are horizontal. A doctor's hand enters the frame, straight across. Beyoncé spreads her arms directly out, and the tanning spray and the beautician's arm also project parallel to the ground. The voices overdubbed closely together seem to form a thick, flat, horizontal band above the song's rhythm arrangement (5:09–5:39).

Watching for synchronization leads me to follow subtle touches that jut out from the video, seemingly untethered to the music. There's the nauseating orange juice next to a red candle. I note Beyoncé's logo-stamped tracksuit; perhaps she has been sponsored by a corporation. One of the judges has striped glasses, with blue light making him look ominous. I focus on the alternating beige and purple carpeting of Beyoncé's den. (It's so real, just like the bad carpeting I saw growing up.) Beyoncé, with arms spread, momentarily resembles the circulating post–Super Bowl internet pictures her rep requested be taken down (5:42).[13]

Returning to Form

Perhaps considering song sections in light of narrative will help. I've mentioned that the MC's question to Beyoncé, and her watery plunge, grant her an instant of reflection and an internal reset. The third chorus can now reveal the models' most painful preparations, like the self-harm of swallowing cotton balls and vomiting in toilets (4:51–4:55). This chorus's revelation, along with the bridge's new focus on the fashion industry's mercenary practices, may provide enough insight for Beyoncé to choose to leave, hopefully along with her fellow competitors.

So perhaps I have a story, but it feels hypothetical. I wonder if turning to Beyoncé's singing and the song's musical arrangement will reveal more of where character change takes place. Perhaps the video's mystery and charm stem partly from the fact that the music of "Pretty Hurts," more than the video's image, accomplishes much. The opening singing of "aha" is tentative and traditionally feminine. At the song's outro, Beyoncé is belting out the question, almost as if it is a call to arms: "When you're alone all by yourself . . . Are you happy with yourself?," and the overdubbed voices behind her concur, fragmentedly declaring "Pretty hurts. Pretty hurts." The voice in particular seems to guide us from failure to success, from the dressing room to the stage, from the verse to the chorus. Empty spaces shadow the vocals, giving a sense of haltingness: they make you wait. But Beyoncé is also almost always heard as multiple, either harmonizing with herself or doubling her lead vocal. Marvin Gaye often surrounded his lead vocal with closely overdubbed vocal tracks, especially when he was singing about community. Here Beyoncé draws on 1970s soul practices, singing about and for a community of women. The rhythm tracks are supersaturated: every sixteenth note is articulated. While the lilting melody seems to offer the characters some comfort, the rhythm arrangement encourages them on.

Musical moments lead us and cue what's important: the timpani rolls that open the bridge overshadow the cymbals that accompany the curtains drawing back, for example. Beyoncé's opening fanfare suggests that her angry and bluesy singing should carry weight. Verse 2 has a greater sense of flow and more of the synth than verse 1. The voice, however, sometimes appears singly, or in multiples. Here Beyoncé works to pull herself together, but at this moment we're still picking up the song's momentum. As the video progresses her soloing and overdubs become increasingly florid and emphatic, until finally, at the clip's end, we might imagine that she has convinced her confederates to leave the pageant. Beyoncé's chair is empty, with only her "Pretty Hurts" sash (not "Miss Third Ward") crossing it. We didn't see or hear all this activity unfolding, but somehow, mysteriously, the change has taken place. Now we must watch the video again to see how it has happened.

Returning to Gender, Sexuality, Race, and Class

Matsoukas has noted that Beyoncé requested the winner of the pageant be albino.[14] This woman will most likely strike viewers as attractive, but no match for Beyoncé. The competition's models are also more racially diverse than we might expect from the era depicted in the clip. In the first chorus, shots reveal women with the same bone structure and facial features, looking nearly identical except for skin tone. When Beyoncé preps in the dressing room, she sits between one woman with very dark skin and another who is very pale: the video seems to suggest that beauty pageants oppress many races. These choices of skin color might also be said to shift the video away from the mode of documentary realism to a broader discussion about how we think about beauty. Perhaps they also reflect a personal dreamscape, allegory, or wish.

Returning to Rhythm

The song is in 4/4. As in much funk, soul, and R&B, the "1" is dominant. Beat 3, coming up from behind, supports beat 1. Beats 2 and 4, the backbeats, maintain the pulse, or, more often than the others, allow some slack. For the first two verses and choruses, Beyoncé is often highlighted on beat 3, as if she's a racehorse making a break for the lead. (Count the beats: you'll see her face or body appear there.) In the bridge, when the beauty industry obliterates the self, Beyoncé falls away from the beat. But in the last chorus and the out-chorus, she begins to take command of the rhythm. On beat 1, she crawls forward on all fours toward the camera; she also destroys her trophies on the downbeat. The winner of the pageant accepts her award on beat 3, while Beyoncé watches. Although the competitor has won first prize for "Miss Pretty USA," she's not a real winner. She has simply adopted Beyoncé's role as a struggler in a larger power structure. The last shot reveals a single close-up of Beyoncé that stretches across almost all four beats, as if she's broadened herself to fill in almost everything.

I listen again to the production of the backbeat. I had described the articulations on 2 and 4 as beating, possibly pushing, Beyoncé on. Toward the end of the song, the backbeat's timbre changes, assimilating what sounds like a punch. (With her trophy slung over her shoulder, I could imagine Beyoncé decking her MC.)

Returning to Timbre

The vocals are nasal and forward in the bridge—more aggressive. One could hear this nasality transposed down to the lowest vocal register in the out-chorus. Here, sonically, power and aggression come from below. Similarly, in the video, the floor is where the focus is. Count off every beat: even when Beyoncé lies on the carpet, she appears strong (fig. 8.6). We can feel her and the other contestants weighted to the ground. Even though Beyoncé gives away the crown, she's poised.

Beyoncé has commented that the *Beyoncé* album embraces imperfection: not everything has to be prettified. In the third chorus, a harsh, striking vocal fragment twice comes forward (an "Eeaow" at 5:58–5:59). It falls in the midst of moments when Beyoncé spreads out her arms and legs, looking ferocious or aggressively crawling forward. These moments wouldn't work as synergistically if Beyoncé wasn't someone to be reckoned with, and if the fragment wasn't so raw.[15]

Returning to Shots, Camera, and Editing

I'm surprised that the average shot length of "Pretty Hurts" is low for a music video. (This is a stately clip!) Then I see it, part of the reason I'm drawn to the chorus: the color sweeps through the video, from the verses

8.6 The carpeted floor is where power resides (6:17).

to these sections, from dull greens and tannish golds to a more viscerally vibrant setting containing bright lemon-yellow bathing suits, Beyoncé's shock of blonde hair, and a more saturated, deep sky blue, sequined curtain. Later there will be glistening, primary-hued, multicolored dresses. So a color arc builds, cycling through song sections to more heightened experiences in the choruses. The women are also more tightly organized and multiple in the chorus, a (potential) collective rather than the earlier isolated and scattered configurations. Of course the chorus is going to punch! These sections remind me of Spike Lee's *Bamboozled*. In Lee's film, the quotidian struggles of network producers and talent were shot on low-res video, and the television show proper—an objectionable valorization of minstrelsy—was filmed on gorgeous 35 millimeter. The minstrel numbers, which return cyclically like choruses, should evoke a sense of revulsion, but a viewer's response may be more mixed, because the image looks so strong. The Black actors perform their roles with such wit, musicality, physical dexterity, and grace, one cannot help but admire them. "Pretty Hurts" works similarly.

Reflections on the Analytic Discoveries

I think "Pretty Hurts" sets a hard task for itself—a task at which it succeeds. Perhaps its closest kin is Martin Scorsese's *Raging Bull* (1980), which aims at a critique of boxing's misogynistic, racist, and homophobic culture but still moves many viewers as much with its stunning cinematography, editing, and sound. Some of Matsoukas's techniques make the pageant strikingly attractive, especially through the selection of beautiful women with their synchronized movements (like hand-waving), the warm textures and colors, and the sweeps that lead us from section to section. But many devices also work to critique the pageant, including the deployment of props and color, and the close attention to vocal performance, musical arrangement, and song structure.

"Pretty Hurts" starts in a traditionally feminine way and ends with a call to arms and a sense of community. For me, this is the video's most striking feature. Many details support this broad shift: the changes in Beyoncé's vocal style and the song's use of her overdubbed voice; the break's recasting of the rhythm arrangement as distraction; Beyoncé's big statement that indicts the beauty industry, heralded by the bridge's opening timpani roll; the singer's slow advance toward and eventual seizure of the downbeat; the role of props and costumes as markers of change—those earrings, of course! But I'm drawn to the white cat that enables Beyoncé's alter-ego to come forward. The video might even suggest a shadowy revenge narrative—Beyoncé, like Irena in *Cat People*, attacks and kills her MC. But at the same time, "Pretty Hurts" possesses a yearning and nostalgia for the fashion industry. Its historical turn and old-school musical touches are reassuring, including the Marvin Gaye vocal overdubs, the soft, cozy fabrics and the muted browns and golds. The video, shot at a high school, has a miniature quality. (These spaces are often scaled for adolescents.) Everything plays a role, including the smallest details: they work through contagion, substitution, expulsion, and reincorporation. Beyoncé shares her lipstick with the winner, who adopts Beyoncé's position on beat 3. Beyoncé's closing vocal fragment breaks into pieces and dissolves into the arrangement. It's a transmedia object linked to striking images of bulimia and anorexia. How well might the video work without these small details? I think they contribute much. The similarity between the production of Matsoukas, Beyoncé, and Åkerlund and the contestant's preparations is worth considering. Fine visual choices lend the video a beautiful sheen with some dark touches. The contestants also produce themselves: Beyoncé applying Vaseline to her teeth for a bit more glisten—that's new to me.

"Pretty Hurts" and Madonna's "Like a Prayer" could be said to draw on the "backstage musical." We see not only the big stage productions, but also their behind-the-scenes preparation. We follow someone who, through talent and hard work, becomes a star.[16] Madonna's "Like a

Prayer" puns off the star's name (Madonna plays a Madonna to Christ and closes out the show). Our protagonist in "Pretty Hurts" also draws on her star status outside the video. Our knowledge of Beyoncé's diligence and attention to detail inform our experience of Houston's Miss "Third Ward."

Now I've done the work of gathering together analytical material, which normally might be primarily notes at this point, and started putting it in an order. Next I'd sketch an outline, draft paragraphs, and reorder. I won't do that now. Rather than a finished interpretation, I've opted instead to show the slow, unpredictable, and repetitive path music video analysis can take. Posing questions and taking notes can demand patience, but it can yield sudden insights. (When I'm successful, I feel like I've caught a fish!) It's an odd practice, one not everyone does.

I like to think of analysis as but one part of the film- and media-making process. Color timers, sound mixers, and postproduction artists most likely engage with the work last, often adding touches that highlight or de-emphasize elements, thereby etching more deeply a particular path through the work. Although the critic doesn't alter the work directly, their insights suggest an affective stance that a viewer might take toward it (curious, affectionate, sardonic); by drawing attention to some features and not others, the critic, too, can direct a viewer's unfolding experience.

I've enjoyed writing this chapter. If I hadn't tried to document what I thought of as I engaged with the video, I wouldn't have seen as much. You may not see things as I do, but maybe you'll now find other things. Directors who know viewers are thinking about their work often become excited and push harder. Together we might build a shared cultural literacy and analytical practice.

There's an important reason to consider music video based on its relation to the larger culture and other media. Audiovisual aesthetics—the ways in which sound, image, and lyrics can be placed in relation—remains relatively unexplored. Short-form genres also remain underexamined, and they contain their own aesthetics. We participate in an audiovisually intensified media landscape, and skills gained through interpreting music videos can help citizens become more discerning about Cambridge Analytica advertisements, Instagram teasers, blockbuster-film trailers, and Fox News segments. "Pretty Hurts" is a tale of empowerment, and we might take the lessons we've learned, partly through the bodily experiences we've gathered as we've encountered the video, to leave—like the characters in the clip—a more familiar space for a hopefully richer relationship with our communities.

Dave Meyers's Moments of Audiovisual Bliss

RESPONDING TO *THE MEDIA SWIRL*'S GOAL of building media literacy and helping readers develop skills with interpreting media, this chapter showcases an auteurist director's style and how it has shifted over the years. It strives to sensitize us to the voice of a videomaker.

Many of today's transmedia directors have developed techniques and approaches from working across music videos, commercials, and films. Capturing what influenced them and how their styles have changed across several decades feels challenging. This chapter focuses on director Dave Meyers, whom I interviewed and wrote about in 2008. Then as now, he was a preeminent music video and commercial director. I'll focus on two of his recent videos, Kendrick Lamar's "All the Stars" (2018) and Maroon 5's "Wait" (2018), with glances at earlier projects. I'll characterize what has changed and make suppositions about the director's influences. In the 1990s and early 2000s I was able to interview several members of his cohort—up-and-coming music video directors who've since become even more successful (including Francis Lawrence, Jonas Åkerlund, Floria Sigismondi, Marcus Nispel, and David Fincher). Looking at their work now shows that some of these directors have blossomed while others have maintained a consistent voice. I'm surprised that it's Meyers's work that moves me; I think of it as the very best in the music video canon.

Meyers's "All the Stars" (a music video for the film *Black Panther*) possesses a beauty that comes from its audiovisual relations, the ways its sound and image work together. Describing the clip's audiovisual aesthetics may seem a bit ephemeral. As abstract as these phenomena may sound, their traces can still be shown. I'll begin with the ways sound permeates performers, objects, settings, and spaces, because these are some of the most structurally important features of "All the Stars." First, I'd like

9.1 Sound permeates the image's ether.

to claim that the song, at the far distance, penetrates the image's ether. Second, it envelops the human figures, giving the air a different weight. And third, it resonates within bodies, its musical features felt (fig. 9.1).

In the clip's first shot Kendrick Lamar stands as the skiff's guide, ferried by a sea of waving hands that forms rivulet-patterns. As his craft zigzags toward us, we see, in the distance, lightning bolts breaking through dark clouds seemingly triggering synths in the high register. Thunder and lightning make good subject matter for music videos, because they raise questions about cause and effect. Thunder and lightning happen simultaneously, but while we say "thunder" first, light travels more quickly to us than does sound. Perhaps there's an uncertainty for us, for why would our language confuse these phenomena? In "All the Stars," the synths appear after the lightning bolts within a long enough interval to make us unsure about whether we should link these events (and thus we're not sure how we might begin to forge connections between sound and image). Some other playful cognitive challenges that "All the Stars" presents include the following: Lamar, later, gazing from a rooftop, raises his arm toward fireworks resembling bursts of dark dust clouds, synchronized by what we might hear as sonic pops (why dustclouds in the sky?). Images of stars, and the camera, too, will circle singer SZA as she emerges from a pinpoint, materializing within a studio space depicting galaxies (her emergence is accompanied by a loud whoosh). SZA will reach forward and grab a phantom (or is it a real?) star, and Lamar, as he walks toward us, will suddenly produce a cigar interlaced among his fingertips.

The above gestures form a rhyming structure about reaching. They could all be described as holes in the video's audiovisual fabric. The sudden materialization and animacy of sounds and images is a favored technique of Meyers's, but here they take on a higher function—they could be called auratic. Drawing on the same techniques (where sounds and images pierce spaces) the director used for "All the Stars," Maroon 5's "Wait" shows unspooling strings passing through the video's environs and, later, meteors falling while trails of fire arc back up toward the sky. Here again, there's the forging of audiovisual sync (the former, linked with a reiterating 16th-note rim shot, and the latter, rising synth glissandi). These show off the ways sounds trail and fade away.

It's more difficult to show how sounds envelop figures. Listeners tend to bind a song's musical elements to objects within a clip's frames.[1] Even more, we start projecting audiovisual trajectories for both figures and sound. This video's characters walk, turn, and twirl, and as their limbs gracefully glance along the sides of their bodies we sense the air and sound pressing in on them, carrying them aloft (fig. 9.2).

"All the Stars" also resonates within bodies. The clip's foregrounded dancers press deeply into the ground, with their heels stamping out the song's rhythms so vigorously we might guess the song's pulse resounds within the performers (fig. 9.3). Each performer seemingly nurtures a

9.2 Sound envelops singer SZA.

9.3 Sound resonates within performers.

private trajectory that traces a unique feature of the song. And another example about sounds within bodies, one drawn from the director's favored techniques. Even in his earliest videos Meyers often placed children at their beginnings. I took this as a means for enhancing charm or reassuring viewers about music video's often fraught representations; they'd then intuit that the clip unfolded within a privileged space. But now, raising a child, I'm aware that Meyers's engagements might reflect something different (he too is a family person and now has a changed relation to children). A child's consciousness differs in some marked way from an adult's; children take in the world differently. A child offers a connection to a song apart from the video's other characters.

The ways sound permeates all aspects of "All the Stars" may be its most significant feature, but many other aspects contribute to the video's beauty as well. The clip's opening shot resembles a kōan, a poetic metaphor for the song and image in their entirety. Like Lamar, we're ferried by (as the video's titling notes) "Meyers and his homies," as if we and they were on a journey, buoyed by the sea of waving hands; even when the song's tempo or direction appears to shift, we can count on this not-quite-locatable but continuous progression. I'd like to say that this forward gesture offers an uncanny sense of movement resembling an airport's moving walkway. Lamar and we seem to search without a clear goal. Is he a kind of Moses? Who are the totemic figures? Are they connected with Biblical figures?

The video comprises patterned layers of sound and image that cross edits; each layer, like the video's performers, possesses its own trajectory. One can think of these swathes of aural and visual material as tectonic plates, sliding over one another, and, as they extend across shots and musical phrases, at least one plate, even as it drifts forward or reveals a gap, still offers a sense of ground. How is this effect achieved? The song's high-register synth pad has an insistent tremolo that might suggest a bath in which other materials can slide. The bass line, doubled at the octave with harmonically inflected pitches schematically filled in, suggests big chunky sonorous chords, like heavy moving objects. The heavily processed bass drum and hand-clap sounds suggest forward motion as well as depth. The rhythm arrangement has a lot of detail, like a reverbed, flanged click that immediately precedes the bass drum's articulations. The rich, bass-heavy rhythm arrangement thickens our relation to the song.

The image also foregrounds features that suggest change within an unceasing flow. When SZA dances within a galaxy of stars she first performs big gestures, with her arms thrust out and her body twirling. Later, her gestures become miniaturized, her hands placed before her face: she pantomimes something resembling windows and doors opening and closing (fig. 9.4). Here, musical material can be carried forth across domains. A shock of recognition may thrum later, when SZA, perched higher in the frame, overlooks her dancers circling with great assertiveness. The

9.4 SZA carries material into new contexts.

performers seem to carry forth the deep-blue gestural weight of the previous section, as if they'd heard what unfolded and could carry it forward into new contexts.

All the video's characters seem to have their own arcs. Lamar sometimes seems sadder, slower, and more introspective than the visual and musical elements surrounding him. (In the song he comes across as angrier, at least in his verses.) The image is generous in the ways that some of its fastest rhythms (the dancers with bent knees and kicked out feet), and some of its slowest (the planes of water, boat, and Lamar drifting upon it) provide an expansive upper and lower limit, which cradles the song. And in fact, for all of the lyrics' anger, the song also presents a rocking figure.

Over time, Meyers has learned to free himself from the ground, and to deploy complex spatial configurations. In "All the Stars," buildings, people, and telephone poles tilt. The horizontal plane through which SZA and the other dancers move shifts periodically from higher to lower in the frame. Perhaps this helps to highlight the distance between Lamar's and SZA's vocal registers, as when the melody vollies up while SZA sings "all of the stars." The voices' cresting helps to underscore the lyrics "All the stars are closer." The frame's placement of performers and objects also dovetails with other visual materials: for example, Lamar's reaching toward the dust-firework bursting patterns in the sky that echoes and helps to chart a distance from the earlier, ferrying hands that form a kind of sea (figs. 9.5 and 9.6).

"All the Stars" showcases other spatial deformations. We don't expect Lamar to turn away or drop his gaze from and then once again reconnect with us at such surprising moments, or for SZA's dancing to play so much at the frame's edges, with sudden sweeps toward and away from the camera. The video's totemic figures are also distorted. A giant goddess appears near the clip's beginning; while her head has dimensionality, her chest seems rendered in 2D, forming a kind of paper cutout of a tent (fig. 9.7). The goddesses at the clip's end whom Lamar looks up to seem both elongated and gigantic. All of Africa, rendered as points of light, is framed within SZA's hair.

Maroon 5's "Wait" has similar deformations. Lead singer Adam Levine twists his head and shoulders back and forth as he seeks his lover at several hallways' juncture from the ground floor of a modernist glass house. The lover, who comes in and out through various stairways, hallways, and an atrium, encourages Levine's continual pivot, and the space seems as complicated as an Escher drawing. Part of our confusion derives from a piling

9.5–9.6 Dancers shift from low to high in the frame.

9.7 The video's totemic figures are distorted.

up of visual rhymes, now realized in the black paisley-patterns on Levine's white shirt. (Earlier, his mother-in-law had worn a black, lacey butterfly-like pop-up accessory off her shoulder, and Levine had dropped a similarly shaped black scorpion onto his girlfriend as she lay in her wake's coffin.) The reiterations of the patterns on Levine's shirt is too subtle to be unpacked on first viewings, yet its piling up, along with other audiovisual materials, carries weight (figs. 9.8 and 9.9). This sense of accrued detail is made good on later. Levine will soon be immersed underwater, surrounded by hundreds of iterations of his girlfriend, at first glance looking mermaid-tailed. He'll then be trapped within his car underwater, and next, as the car door opens, he and water unspools into an oil field (a birthing image) with his girlfriend seated, waiting for him on an abandoned mattress. "Wait" shows a puzzling and impressive trajectory of settings. What, we might wonder, does the working-class bungalow in front of which Levine's girlfriend and what most likely are previous girlfriends, all in solidarity, wielding baseball bats and bottles at him have to do with that earlier modernist home? Is this Levine's return to earlier relationships or to childhood memories? And other threads make matters denser. Some are tied to questions of vision. Realistic blinking suggest Levine's or our occluded vision. Levine also wears thick glasses at one point, and his girlfriend sometimes flickers in and out, and at other times is visible behind a gossamer veil. There are also the unspooling strings, falling meteors, and rising lines of fireworks to make sense of.

All of this is wonderful, but perhaps not an unexpected shift in technique and style. Meyers has long specialized in fantastical imagery. Limp Bizkit's "Boiler" (2000) had a delirious sequence with pod-women succubuses, for example. So if not this, what has changed? Perhaps it's that in Meyers's earlier videos the musicians seemed to be consciously assuming the mantle of performers inserted into music video scenarios, and they often seemed somewhat bemused by their situation. Now they are actor/performers who don't need to be singing or playing instruments, and they belong to their environments. They hold backstories and futures that we have less access to. They belong here, and what happens matters; we have only a small window into their larger world.

It's not entirely clear where Meyers's new approach to characterization comes from. Fully inflected characters are rare in music video; videos are brief, lack dialogue, and have difficulty suggesting futures and pasts. My guess is that Meyers studied the handful of videos best able to depict characters and their worlds, such as Francis Lawrence's and Justin Timberlake's "Cry Me a River," and the videos of Mark Romanek. His

9.8–9.9 Visuals rhymes start piling up.

work in commercials has surely played a role. (His website posts recent work, and YouTube playlists can help give us a sense of his earlier oeuvre. It's not surprising that they're all fast-paced.) Meyers has an affinity for speed—he directed the dancing silhouettes for the iPod. In the last few years, however, the amount of time Meyers allotted to present a person seems to have telescoped to a third of a second. Meyers is a long-standing photographer—how to capture the sense of a person in an instant must have interested him. A good example of how the director engages with an instant occurs in Janet Jackson's "Made for Now" (2018). Note the gaze of a potential paramour in a kind of Virginia Reel line of dancers; the potential lover seems to intuit that he has less than a millisecond to kiss Janet Jackson's hand and project the intensity of his ardor. Meyers also wants to direct more Hollywood films. His film *The Hitcher* (2007) feels like a B-movie noir that a 1940s and 1950s studio would have been proud to have cranked out (and it's a remake of Ida Lupino's famous 1953 noir, *The Hitch-Hiker*). The script isn't compelling, but the villain is strong, and the directing—its visual scape and pacing are well done. I didn't notice a direct shift in style after Meyers made the film, but effects can be far-reaching. (As a side note, Michael Bay produced the film, perhaps as an attempt to build a stable of directors. In conversation, Meyers told me that he reached out for Bay's help only in the instances when it was really needed, which may also provide a glimpse into the film's production context.)

Commercials, music videos, and Hollywood film could have offered Meyers some new approaches. Documentary is also its own mode, and Meyers has made a wonderful short of Ice Cube showing off his favorite Los Angeles locations for the Getty.[2] Being able to separate how much narrative and documentary filmmaking has shaped Meyers's experience, as opposed to photography, commercials, music videos, and so on, would help present a richer picture. Like the other music video directors I've spoken with, I've gotten the sense that for-hire directing can be a growth experience, but not that rewarding. Meyers still wishes to make another film, one that is hopefully more personal. And this drive surely shapes his music video making and his commercials.

I also like to think that Meyers (like hopefully me) has grown up. He now has a family, and people and interpersonal relations may now matter even more deeply. He's long worked with remarkably talented artists, and in his interviews he's mentioned how inspirational collaborations with P!nk and Missy Elliott have been. Did the stars influence Meyers? Wanting to do well by so many people surely must have an effect.

Meyers is also working with songs within genres that he respects, and to which he feels in debt. I think he's aware that his relation to hip-hop is one that isn't seamless, but rather complicated. A white person who makes hip-hop videos has many responsibilities. It's probably intentional that many of the songs that he chooses are "woke," and I assume that his careful depictions are partly a way of expressing gratitude. This leads me to wonder about the rough-and-tumble stars Meyers used to work with (such as Ludacris and Kid Rock). Did they offer different affordances?

Keeping with this line of thought, here's another supposition about changes in Meyers's work: Do the songs today provide richer affordances? In other words, is there something more three dimensional, narratively inflected, and humanistic about recent songs? The cartoonish ornamental surfaces in which Britney Spears and P!nk move in "Lucky" (2000) and "Get the Party Started" (2001) seem to fit their songs well. Since Meyers has often worked with the same stars over a long period, we might be able to make some comparisons. One could argue that there's something deeper about Janet Jackson's "Made for Now," with its African edge and bouncy mix of Latin and Caribbean vibes, than there is with "All For You" (2001) and its breezy 1990s feel. Though "All for You" is a lovely song and a lovely video, it's hard to imagine what more one could do with it.

There are broader effects like the media swirl, and larger social contexts, as they rub against the development of the music video genre, which we should take account of as well. It's one thing to make a video in the 1980s and 1990s for a very young artist, with you as a well-known director, knowing that because of your reputation MTV will most likely play this video or another. It's another thing to make a video for a seasoned artist today who possesses a whole history of music video production behind her. Even if record companies helped boost viewership on YouTube, there must be a sense that you can't be sure an audience will be there for you. Now the media landscape is different, and competition may feel steep. The time and what people need from their media surely carries weight as well. Capitalist America has always been difficult, but somehow with Black Lives Matter, Me Too, Trump, enormous income disparities, work speed-up, the gig economy, affective labor, global warming, and so on, we may need something much more from our media, and some artists may be more sensitized to this fact than others.

I've claimed that the chance to work across various media has been crucial for transmedial directors today. Though I want to argue for the relevance of Meyers's practicing many forms and drawing on other directors who do the same, I also have the intuition that Meyers's receptivity to, knowledge about, and playfulness with popular music has also had shaping influences. Over time, Meyers has discovered new ways of drawing attention to a song's elements and to give them meaning in a visual context. The emotional weight in "All the Stars" comes partly from Meyers's underscoring moments within the vocal performance, as when SZA sings the first word in her sweeping melodic line "*maybe* the stars," or Lamar's opening rap, "*tell me*." There's a quality of a raw heartbreak at these moments, a tear (and I'd like to use "tear" in a doubly inflected sense, both as a painful injury and as weeping), and yet the singer and the rapper continue, following through with the phrase and making good on the line.

This sense of vulnerability and heart shows up visually in "All the Stars." The orange glow emerging from within the tent (at the outskirts of the city) resembles a cloaked but visible beating heart. A first goddess, with a hollowed-out chest, possibly made of paper, links to notions of the heart's intimacy and vulnerability. The solemn cluster of youths, wearing bright, soft red hats and traditional wax-dyed shirts who gather around Lamar in what we might guess is a spiritual context, do too. There's Lamar's constant look away, which is emotionally affecting (perhaps some thoughts are too private). Meyers once told me that he wished to make videos everyday people could relate to, which sometimes meant showing the star in a down position. In Maroon 5's "Wait," Adam Levine's girlfriend aggressively attacks him (she wields a bottle of booze as if it were her penis, pouring its liquid on him like urine; soon, we assume, she'll throw down a lit match; she also threatens him with a baseball bat), but

9.10 The viewer's identification splits—a field of glory.

her rage feels warranted. It's an inference that must be drawn from outside the video's diegesis, but a viewer who rearranges the images might assume that Levine was unable to stop her after a fight, which led to her death. I think we take seriously that the threads' unspooling becomes Levine's unraveling. And the fraught distance between the couple is set meticulously as roughly four inches between the couple's two faces, recurrently faced off and profiled. The song seems to foreground exactly that gap too. In the chorus, Levine sings and there's a pause—no music, "Wait" (fig. 9.10).

It would take a scholar's devotion (perhaps at the level of Tag Gallagher's monumental book on John Ford) to track moments of change as they unfold through Meyers's work—and some of the difficulties might derive from inventorying the director's work across various media. Here are two instances to be identified and followed. Directors like Meyers often become enamored with a motif, technique, or parameter, extending, reworking, and possibly denaturing it. Recently Meyers has been working closely with some admired choreographers to sharpen gesture, and dance is much richer in his recent videos than it was previously. Meyers has also had an interest in skies since his earliest videos (in the 1990s his skies were often lurid, with intense sherbet colored sunsets, and Britney Spears's "Lucky" was full of glittery stars and a moon). In "All the Stars" the depiction may have reverberated for Meyers in a way that he couldn't quite let go of. In Ariana Grande's "No Tears Left to Cry" (2018) she's nestled in a cocoon-like web of star-like lights, and in Camila Cabello's "Consequences" (2018), stars surround the ghostly characters like fireflies.

I once claimed that Meyers takes us on picaresque journeys: we travel from one wondrous tableau-like setting to another, as aural and visual motifs come forward and back. He was a song's devoted tracker and he found ways to direct attention to an often unloved portion of a song that other directors might have overlooked, perhaps a brief break, as in Missy Elliott's "Get Ur Freak On" (2001). And his attention to musical sound was striking—we couldn't help but notice that suddenly sounding luminous silvered trumpet! Now, however, Meyers brings forward sonic elements in a different way, so that they seem to drill more deeply into the video's space. It doesn't mean that the videos have necessarily become more narrative; it seems, however, that they carry more weight.

Let me show what I mean, returning again to "All the Stars." At first, we hear something in the low bass. Is it a heartbeat? What, we might wonder, at some not-quite-voiced level, is keeping everything flowing? We try to follow. This sense of being brought forward is underscored in one tableau as Lamar walks through an expanse of blackened tree trunks, with black panthers pacing before and behind him. Suddenly, one rushes forward as if pressed on by the rhythms of Lamar's rap, "tell me what you *do* for me," and we suddenly turn our attention for an instant to Lamar's poetry.[3] But what's unfolding doesn't make narrative sense. The panthers don't seem to be listening to Lamar's rapping. Once again, it's one of those weird events in a music video's cosmology: preconsciously the viewer may wonder, What encouraged the panther to rush at this moment? Is it the music? It almost surely can't be, but what else can we assume? As the clip draws to a close, and a male voice (Lamar's?) and SZA sing a duet, suddenly we're in a field of bronze-gold hanging African-designed motifs, layered over and spangled, from the fore to the background (against beautiful women stoically and perhaps hopefully posed in costumes of bronze and gold). It has a bit of a Gustav Klimt look to it. Kendrick drags himself through this field of glory, relatively unmoved. But for the first time, our experience may fork dramatically from his. We've been following along partly because of the sense of his heartbeat; at this moment, however, we may feel suddenly hopeful. If we continue and hold on to what we believe in, if we can raise our voices, being flexible enough to shift up or down as the video has done this far, to trust passage, and to participate in at least one line of the vocal duet, we can happen upon something as glorious as this. A similar technique tied to the accruing of meaning through audiovisual motifs occurs in "Wait." The song's rimshots "tick tick tick" gradually become slowly identified with the spool of unwinding twine, Levine's goldfish-like girlfriend's wiggling tails, and then finally Levine's unraveling. These come late in the video. These instances, across the course of the videos, show us that sound can be discovered and understood, especially if we're a bit more attentive than Levine or Lamar. We might even be able to rescue our own relationships through attention and care.

These powerful, fleeting moments pair with the videos' sense of contemplation. In "All the Stars" SZA spins and twirls, arms over head, perhaps on water or ice. She then forms the role of a female Auguste Rodin sculpture, and the next shot match cuts to Lamar also posed contemplatively. This sense of thoughtful stillness spreads out in "All the Stars" to the handsomely dressed high-cheeked woman in a West African green dress and later to what we might assume is her similarly regal male partner, dressed in blue, as well as the somber children. The tempo for these senses of contemplation start forming a continuum with other events, objects, and people expressing different types of awareness.

The setting in "All the Stars" is not a completely accurate mélange, but it still serves the video. There's housing possibly at the city's outskirts, with clay walls, imported tin roofs, and men dressed up as fancily as princes, yet the dancing is probably more American. The children most likely couldn't afford the shoes and starched shirts. In the bridge, SZA lies in a field of pink water surrounded by African designs cut out like puzzle pieces, but the pink feels, at least for American audiences, probably closer to Broadway or Las Vegas. Yet though this sounds jarring, this setting feels fully integrated. What does this mélange tell us? Is the clip partly aspirational? At this point, we might turn to recent and earlier videos and compare. What's the same and what's new? What I'd like to do is a slow process, and most helped by thoughts shared from the director, fellow practitioners, and audiences. To do this with many directors might tell us how we all find ourselves in a new moment.

Janelle Monáe's "You Make Me Feel" and Anderson .Paak with Kendrick Lamar's "Tints": Getting Up in My [Rearview] Mirror

THIS CHAPTER ANALYZES TWO VIDEOS that differently explore similar themes—privacy, autonomy, and community. Both track the musician/performer closely as he or she (or they) explore socially unsanctioned sexualities. Both are also well-crafted pieces. Janelle Monáe's performances of intimacy and elusiveness in "You Make Me Feel," as well as her dense allusions to communities and histories, including the LGBTQIA community and her mentors, both real and imagined, establish a warm, engaging clip that leaves a viewer hungry to participate in its tableaux. Anderson .Paak's and Kendrick Lamar's "Tints," however, is harder. .Paak performs as a Black man who escapes from the police and associates, as well as his veiled (multiple?) lives; he struggles to gain a variety of sexual, social, and financial pleasures. The speed, historicism, and complicated stereotyping within fraught, highly valent, zany tableaus in "Tints" make for a challenging clip. Both music videos are worth thinking about, together and apart.[1]

Janelle Monáe's "You Make Me Feel" (2018)

Released simultaneously as a music album and a forty-six-minute narrative "emotion picture" (to use Monáe's term), *Dirty Computer*—alongside other multimedia releases such as Beyoncé's *Lemonade* (2016)—raises intriguing questions about the extent to which its audio elements can be extracted from its visual components, and more broadly, about the nature of the album itself. In April 2018 Monáe released *Dirty Computer*, a group of eight music videos with interlaced material. An Afrofuturist forty-six-minute narrative shown mostly on YouTube, the work extends the story of Monáe's alter ego Cyndi Mayweather Metropolis, who had previously appeared on her albums *The ArchAndroid* (2010) and *The Electric Lady* (2013). Critical reception was enormously positive, including claims that *Dirty Computer* is "a milestone not just as a work of art . . . but as the perfect celebration of queerness, female power, and self-worth," an "extravaganza by a female black panther," and "more personal than the android dared."[2]

Concept video albums are a new phenomenon, enabled in part by technological and economic changes: streaming services, such as Apple Music and Tidal, have invested sizable budgets in music video-like "tentpole productions" to attract subscribers. Billboard's charting of YouTube's music video views has also contributed to increased revenue. Each of these long-form, music video-oriented works tends to foreground a new twist. Frank Ocean's *Endless* (2016) flaunts pop and avant-garde through a fluttering exploration of a single space, and Kanye West's *My Beautiful Dark Twisted Fantasy* (2010) combines highbrow aesthetics with hip-hop, but with a Matthew Barney verve. Beyoncé's *Beyoncé* (2013) and *Lemonade* (2016) are the most spectacular examples. Her audiovisual albums place large swathes of Black culture and history in relation to her marriage.

Smaller scaled than Beyoncé's works, *Dirty Computer* also spans larger social configurations and personal narrative. Its music videos explore editing, narrative, gesture, and timbre with a sureness about the genre's unique affordances. Its progressive edge, which derives in part from its celebration of pansexuality and the LGBTQIA community, also contributes to its allure. Three singles released before the album, "Make Me Feel," "Django Jane," and "Pynk," sparked curiosity among fans and critics. How might these be folded into a soon-to-be-released narrative?

It's worthwhile taking a moment to consider "You Make Me Feel" against some of *The Media Swirl*'s other objects, like *Transformers* and *The Great Gatsby*. Alan Ferguson's video is realized with minimal materials—a portion of a nightclub, a film studio's cyclorama or cyc wall, performers with carefully curated clothing, a few interesting pieces of furniture, and a lot of paint and gels. Yet while "You Make Me Feel" may have been shot in a day, it still suggests layered worlds. This density is formed through intimate, nested spaces (the latrina), and Monáe's exhortations to come close but maintain distance. This wouldn't be a COVID-19 video, unless everyone were sheltering-in-place, but there's a sense that this small group of participants is enough. This video, like those analyzed in chapters 8 and 9 offers models for progressive politics.

How would we describe the stylistic features that distinguish Monáe's video, "Make Me Feel"? Director Alan Ferguson is key. In collaboration with Monáe, he creates a look and feel that favors attention to sonic details. With an MFA from Howard and training in classical guitar, Ferguson likes to track songs closely. Elements like the song's main hook line, assertive electric guitar, close-miked tongue clicks and finger-to-cheek pops, and rubbery mid-range sound can encourage viewers' proprioceptive participation. These sounds also offer Ferguson a chance to foreground musical and visual details. Monáe and her girlfriend slowly glide into the club and then spy a white-gloved man seated at a distance at the bar who flips his oversized glasses at them. I feel something here—a sense of reaching toward him and getting snapped into place in the song's mix.[3]

A music video director often glosses on the music and lyrics. In "Make Me Feel," parameters like dancing, costumes, makeup, and props seem to interpolate us into the song and video. I sense the overturned deer-headed legs from the alcove's table; Monáe's shifting fingernail polish, hair color, eye shadow, and lipstick; the swiftly changing lighting effects; the off-the-beat sighs and whispers and darting synthesizer motive tell us about this song (fig. 10.1).

Here is an example of how a director and artist can help us hear a song. The tongue clicks and finger-to-cheek pops are striped across the track without changing much. They disappear during brief pauses, when much else in the mix gets pulled back as well, and change direction halfway through (from high-to-low to low-to-high). The colorful lighting effects and trying on of sexualities seem to reflect this switch. But for me as a viewer, their presence feels most strongly foregrounded at 3:00, when Monáe turns her feet while her backup dancers dip and sway. (Much within the frame has turned silvery, like Monáe's high-heeled boots, which may echo the white gloves.) These oral/aural sound effects come with a twist: like a revving truck, the electric guitar powers down and up through the mix; the bass drum enters, with a pattern like an excited heartbeat; and Monáe sings "I'm powerful with a little bit of tender" (fig. 10.2).

Contemporary pop music, it could be claimed, often instantiated on digital platforms like Logic and Pro Tools, is riven with repetitions and subtle alterations of material.[4] Directors often use these repetitions

10.1 Interpolating the viewer: detailed props.

10.2 Showing off the tongue-clicks and finger-to-cheek pops.

and variations in service of audiovisual rhymes, sometimes direct and sometimes freer. Some of Monáe's and Ferguson's audiovisual tracings are direct, such as when Monáe sings "pow" as she spreads her legs and when she reminisces about a "sexual bender" while her finger traces a wavy downward figure. More freely, Monáe's "pow" could be said to be picked up by her fluorescent water gun, her hand forming a gun, and the windmilling of her arm as it's montaged against her girlfriend's unraveling a fan. In music video, cause and effect can be multiple and mysterious. Does this string of audiovisual rhymes converge to form a phantasmagorical phallus? I should also call out the equally affirmatively resolute shapes suggestive of yonic forms, like the recesses formed by dancers and the urinal/alcove, and Monáe threading herself among her dancers' V-positioned legs. How might this content give energy to Monáe's exclamations of

10.3 One of several gestures highlights the "pow" in "powerful."

a role? Many factors contribute to this effect, like the song's now denser arrangement. A brighter rhythm guitar is now foregrounded, and Monáe's singing moves her toward a sound like Prince's spirited twin ("Good God!" Monáe holler-shouts, calling for a redirection). The mural's abstract design has been formed by a sudden compression of previously appearing larger and smaller squares, including the club's checkered floors, models with Mondrian-patterned chests, and larger blocks of colorful fluorescent lights. Even a visitor's hair is inked with colored squares and triangles. Perhaps the chevron's sharp edges are now underscored by the deep latex red of Monáe's dancers, the star's rose-patterned pants, and even her soon-appearing white dotted lips (from the milky white secretions of the snapped rose's stem and thorns, "mess me up," sings Monáe). Things have gotten edgier. We might reach toward Monáe, the video seems to say, if she says yes. A viewer can seek out favorite gestures in this new section—I like the way Tessa Thompson drops her coat and herself for Monáe (figs. 10.4 and 10.5).

The song ends suddenly, and so does the video. I'm curious now: Monáe describes herself as a "sexual bender," and celebrates the pleasures of another. Are there audiovisual moments that reflect this? Much has caught my eyes and ears (the video's turn toward silver, and a synthesizer that darts in and out), but now I find myself following the hot-pink dabs (especially a tuft of a visitor's hair crowning Monáe). I've embraced a few places in the clip. This is what is lovely about Ferguson's work: there is material for each of us to find our own paths through a clip, to perhaps discover new modes of embodied engagement (fig. 10.6).

10.4–10.5 A new space: roses and thorns then draw us in, but maintain distance.

10.6 Suddenly the video ends. How might we listen and watch again?

"Tints" music video (2018): Anderson .Paak and Kendrick Lamar, "Get Up in My Rearview Mirror"

I'd made a commitment to this music video right away, but it's taken me a while to gather insights into it. The song's hook line, "I need tints"/"(Windows tinted)," seems doubly inflected. Tinted glass windows are often valued by rappers and rock stars for style and anonymity, but "tints" also serves as a metaphor for what we wish to hide from others. Perhaps deliberately on the part of the director and artists, this sense of something cloaked or out of reach will stay with me throughout the analysis. I notice first that the car's donuts are echoed by the camera's carouseling among later peek-a-boo scenes with the physician, preacher, and college student. Spatial deformations in the girly show might prepare viewers for these larger formal patterns: note the clients' booths' curved seating and staggered placement.

The song unfurls. Its running vocal melodies are drawn out through .Paak's overdubbed singing in call-and-response, and then the extended melodic lines by the women's voices, high-register synth-pad, and plucked guitar. The synths also have a twang that could be heard as a "dee-yow-ow-ow" kind of sound. A viewer might forge audiovisual connections with these musical materials.

In the first verse .Paak stands in the middle of the street, bloodied and riddled from bullet holes (fig. 10.7). Distorted indentations ripple alongside the left side of his skull. This swerve is continued through the diner's morphing window, and the dancer-grifter with his wet mop. The line continues through the camera's winding path among the dead police, .Paak's rock back and forth with the puppy and the wave of sea-foam that fills the TV screen. Continuing on, the women in the strip show, .Paak, and Lamar kick their legs and swing their arms and shoulders like a car's internal motor, which, along with the spark of the cell phone, seems to power up the red, twirling Chevrolet. Later there will be the carousel of peep-show rooms, but also a finer level with elements fracturing—.Paak's drumming with refracted colors and smoke, the flying money and wetness on his face, and finally just dust motes in the air.

"Tints" is a great song and a striking video. But I can't get a bead on it, or even its most basic questions: Is it about one person, two blue-collar laborers crossing over into white-collar spheres, or five or six separate individuals?

Now I see it's *that* kind of video: "Tints" embraces a common technique wherein a varied gesture or topic returns at the same points in the

10.7 .Paak stands in the middle of the street, bloodied and riddled from bullet holes.

choruses or verses. In "Tints" and other videos this technique can complement the ways varied content within song-sections convey a story. Here something appears in the first chorus and comes back in the second and third, which creates a dreamlike quality. Near the beginnings of the first three verses, .Paak and Lamar embody stillness. The ends of verses are busier—.Paak scrubbing blood out, .Paak's and Lamar's arms circling, or .Paak playing drums.

Howard Hawks's films show that if you keep viewers interested, you don't need to always make sense. *The Big Sleep* contradicts itself and elides content in perplexing ways. Recently, Colin Tilley has adopted a similar approach. In Post Malone's "Circles" (2019) the singer begs to be released from a relationship, and it's just "the sex y'all," but then he rescues the maiden and rides off with her on horseback into the sunset. Halsey's "Without Me" shows a couple hitting one another; the male has done something terrible, but we neither discover their tipping point nor why she's first in handcuffs and free at the end. More than narrative films, music videos can foreground these aporias, because no moment can override another. A flute melody can't undercut an earlier bass line. An example of contradictory audiovisual moments occurs in Michael Jackson's "Thriller." Jackson adopts the mantle of various personae and creatures, from a supportive boyfriend to one who is less so, a zombie, and a werewolf. In "Tints" too the protagonist inhabits many scenarios, bridging white- and blue-collar experiences in somewhat realistic ways. .Paak performs much of the tight-knit arrangement, including the overdubbed singing and the drums. Since he plays these multiple musical roles, might he adopt multiple guises in the video? Are "Tints"'s varied personae plausible?

What roles can sound and image play, and how do they affect our sense of the video's plot? How do we as viewers respond to "Tints" as a realistic or dreamlike construction? Could .Paak have killed those guards and survived after receiving bullets in his chest? How do these occurrences relate to the moments when the NRA-card-carrying elderly couple stow him in their trunk, and bribe the police? Are they just taking a gagged and bound .Paak on a joyride for stealing from their diner? We don't know. And then the video shifts away from these incidences to a series of sexual escapades. Perhaps the video should be read backward, with the closing's punishments and retributions appearing at the opening? A closer look reveals more puzzling details. The doctor's office has Southern Law books on its shelves and the physician's badge is falling off. What's this about? The sexual encounters appear consensual, but look a little seamy. Men pay to view women's bodies, and that Christian cam-girl looks underage. Perhaps .Paak is the dominatrix's significant other, and he fronts for her as Lyft driver, painter, doctor, preacher, college student, and leader for a Narcotics Anonymous group. Many of the setting's other details suggest something has gone awry (figs. 10.8 and 10.9).

But this puzzling material has to be apprehended in conjunction (or disjunction) with .Paak's exhilarating performance and the openness of the song. Events turn this way and that: with so many brief, surprising, and recurring turns, we may be loath to condemn—or exonerate—the character.

This conjunction or disjunction raises questions about the work of close reading. Considered against the song as a while, the beginning and end of the video may feel too punitive (especially for the viewer and .Paak's girlfriend). Bracketing them off might seem like an odd interpretative move, but I can't move forward without doing so. It's challenging to construct .Paak's contexts, but I unquestionably feel that hiding information from his partner when she's asked to be included in his world isn't ethical. Who is he to decide for her? It's worth leaving these parts of the video behind for the moment. Here forward, I'm attending to four minutes and twenty-three seconds of song and image.

"Tints" has wonderfully exuberant moments, like when the protagonist plays drums, or dances while mopping a floor, or makes 360s with the car. Along with the swish-pans and wipes later on that shape the tableaux of

10.8–10.9 The sexual encounters appear consensual, but look a little seamy.

sexual encounters, these gentle the more freighted material. In one example, .Paak rocks back and forth with bloodstained hands while holding a puppy, who looks similarly perturbed. This moment is suddenly intimate and fragile. But does my sense of this shot draw on my own racism? How much does the puppy help me care?

A music video can extract and condense parts of a song's melodic contours, rhythmic gestures, and timbral features, and represent them visually. In the song .Paak sings "I need tints!," and these exclamations puncture the texture. The image shows this off through one-to-one correspondences (e.g., the painter's shoulder's bump against the apartment door), but also highlights .Paak's declamations through visual signposting at other moments, encouraging us to recall earlier moments in the song. As a father gesturing to his daughter, .Paak makes sharp, crossing hand and forearm movements. At the opening, the policeman's roving flashlight functions as a precursor, a smaller-scaled, similar gesture. .Paak often abruptly swivels his head to face the camera. There's also a second level of carefully choreographed gestures—a light tap by the dominatrix's hand, the fall of the policeman's head, the painter flicking his cigarette butt. These craggy audiovisual gestures function as their own threads.

Against these sharper audiovisual moments, the song foregrounds the vocal arrangement that forms long melodic lines crossing from low to high or high to low. These lines come forward more strongly because they're traced by synths an octave above. The camera supports these melodies through long tracking shots, as when the camera swerves forward over the path of dead security guards. These lines build across the song's phrase structure and the images' shots and edits. Even the camera's recurring left-to-right scanning reflects these whip-turns.

The song's sophisticated minor-mode harmony keeps the song in constant motion. It provides the bedding for a smoothly propulsive groove that feels brighter than the video's imagery. The chord's extensions through added fourths, sevenths, and ninths lends an urbane, jazzy feel, and the move from the verse's first to second chord feels bright. The synths and women's voices in the verse's second half soar away from the rhythm arrangement, reaching for the chorus and brightening things further. These moments especially keep us from getting too locked into the verses' first grim images—.Paak muzzled and tied in a car's trunk, or standing, bleeding from his chest, in the middle of a road. There's also Kendrick Lamar with an oxygen tank and the Grim Reaper behind him, and then there's .Paak as a doctor watching a girlie show on his laptop with his pants swaddled around his ankles. We're carried past these tableaux partly through the song's momentum and a viewer's curiosity about what will happen next, until we get to the chorus, which reaches a higher plateau with an even stronger feeling of exhilaration. These sections of the video have a wonderful sense of movement (the dancing while mopping the diner's floor, the 360s of the car, the carousel-like flipping rooms).

But the video returns to the verses' lonelier openings and ends with a deflated out-chorus; in showing respect for the song's form, Tilley opts for some grim restarts. At the end of the chorus, the line "I need tints!" starts to sound anxious, maybe suggesting a darker mood. The higher and lower voices in call-and-response, sharing some of the lyrics—"I need tints on my windows"—might reflect a repressed, anxious, or divided self. Halfway through the choruses Tilley tacks again, this time toward dimmer outcomes: the shooting up of security guards, followed by blood on the sink; .Paak hovering by a window (the orange T-shirt reminiscent of prison uniforms); the wary, duplicitous gaze of the Christian cam-girl.

Turning this way and that, rising to the ebullient chorus, then shifting down again to the verse's beginnings, the video engages attention. Which way will we go? Music videos like "Tints" often convey stories through their treatment of song sections. In this video song sections struggle for authority, and, for a moment, the chorus's joy takes the lead. By the third verse, the freer, celebratory, and longer sections of the chorus advance into the verse's body. Here .Paak jubilantly plays the drums, haloed by fractured red, green, and blue lights, and white dust—celestial. This mood helps buoy us into the last chorus's rapid twirling of rooms that feature sexual escapades (a play on the car's 360s in an earlier chorus). But we're misled about these more open possibilities. The video employs this exultant imagery only to drop us down harder. There's the NA meeting (kudos for our protagonist!), but then .Paak flames out. He shoots up heroin in a space that's half office building and half dark alley. But this out-chorus also connects to the opening like a dream. The heroin puts the burning car at a distance. The drugs numb his and possibly my pain, a state of mind I appreciate.

When I analyze a video, I consider musical and visual parameters separately—song sections, the rhythm, the arrangement, color, lyrics, and so on. While listening through headphones, with my attention directed to the song's arrangement, I notice a lot of fine percussion panned sharply right and left; this makes the chorus fuller and adds to its frenetic feel. Extending past the singing, the verses' running line of plucked guitar now sounds more metallic; there's a "sh-sh-sh" sound too. The voice and synths, placed closer to the center of the stereo field, suggest a heightened tunnel vision. Do they contribute to .Paak's sense of drive?

I've argued elsewhere that music videos' lyrics often function strangely. An individual word or phrase can be picked up by the image and hover apart from the clip as if it were a totem or lodestone. Lyrics are sometimes momentarily set off directly, but more often elliptically or as puns. "Paparazzi wanna shoot ya/ N****s dying for less here" seems somewhat direct, but the lyric "flash" might be picked up by the policeman's flashlight. We don't see much from a rearview mirror, but there is a "bad bitch in my whip." Lamar raps about "fishbowlin'," and the lyrics refer here to driving behind the wheel of an untinted car or lacking privacy, but the production design team decided to take the term literally. Via a large circular hole, the camera tracks in on Lamar seated in a room festooned with empty aquariums. Two of the rappers' visual takedowns play on the lyrics: "Presidential" has .Paak with his pants around his ankles, and "respect me from afar" has Lamar on breath support at a girly show.

We might cut Tilley and his collaborators some slack. Imagine you're setting this video. The lyrics for the less heavily arranged out chorus probably call for a visual realization: "I think I'm 'bout to black out/ . . . I got the goons up on the payroll." Driving in an open convertible in the Palisades probably won't cut it. In Colin's favor, he responds to the lyrics, which are about deriving pleasure, perhaps through illicit means and beyond others' views, and then losing that pleasure through discovery.

The color purple aligns strongly with the NRA-toting old folks in their car, as if they're local officials on parade. (Historically, purple was discovered late, and proved difficult to produce, so it was reserved for royalty and the elite.) This color reappears but never again with such force. Do the old folks rule the video? Notice purple's aftermath: a thread of pink and lavender from the painter's hair crosses to the Christian cam-girl, and then a montage-flashback appears at the song's end (color forms its own arc).

For me, the fine details of costumes and setting don't adhere to .Paak, but rather hover near him in the audiovisual mix (e.g., the doctor's peeling medical patch or our protagonist's varied hairstyles, six in all; does this imply six separate characters?). Is this because the producers placed many of the song's materials in isolation? The triangle has its own unique reverb, the cowbell and synth too. .Paak's voice, too, is mellow and rough (like good whiskey?), which contrasts with much of the song arrangement's smoothness. This haloed-separation extends to .Paak.

The Media Swirl advocates trying to read nearly everything. If a piece of media takes you aback, it may sometimes be better to come to an understanding of what beguiles you and pushes you away, rather than to leave it aside. Several of Tilley's recent pieces have moments that could be read as retrogressive or abject, but their music/image relations create something new. The music and image push to a new elsewhere, someplace beyond what we're experiencing now.

Jonathan Leal argues that "Tints" draws from the blues.[5] I wonder if "Tints" projects a more zany Lucille Ball-type mood.[6] Scholar Sianne Ngai's book cover for *Our Aesthetic Categories*, where Ball finds herself in a zany situation because mechanical or social processes have spiraled out of control, is an example. How might we reconcile these two readings? What do they tell us together? In chapter 4, I found myself in a conundrum as I tried to analyze a piece by experimental film director Kenneth Anger. Finally, I hit on a method of schematizing and mixing and matching music and images. On YouTube, I open two browser windows, mute the sound on one and minimize the image on the other, and play them both (this produces one audiovisual experience with a different image or soundtrack than its original). I also create stripped down, iconic versions of the image and run them against music or schematize the music and run them against the images. This tells me something.

Both sound and images for "Tints" have elements that feel laden and heavy (as noted earlier). With my audiovisual tests for "Tints," I found it most helpful to first conjure up a visual reduction for the images that expressed its laden and heavy qualities. I build up an image of the front pew of a church with a coffin, either open or closed. But the song's wacky features might also be visually set with a reduced context. So at the coffin's far end, peeking over its edge, I prop Punch and Judy puppets, perhaps dressed in Día de los Muertos skeleton costumes, along with their cloaks and more traditional wear, bopping one another. I use them advisedly, because of their imagery of spousal assault and battery, and their negative, historically accrued meanings. But I'm aware I still have a sentimental attachment to the puppets from my childhood.

And now I'm a little spooked that after running these experiments, I'm perhaps unconsciously channeling something. .Paak shares in an interview that he had a hard upbringing.[7] Both parents became addicted to drugs and served jail time. When .Paak was seven, his father came home and beat up his mother so seriously that his dad was taken away to jail. .Paak didn't see his father again until he was twenty, after which he soon died. .Paak has dabbled with drugs and crime. He learned to play drums through backing the choirs for Oxnard's Black churches.

With the still image of the coffin, church, and puppets, I play Earth, Wind and Fire's "Serpentine Fire." The song has similarities with "Tints"—both foreground dense, finely crafted arrangements—but "Serpentine Fire" feels more regal and controlled (.Paak has called Earth, Wind and Fire one of his childhood's most influential bands.) But on the other hand, "Tints," unlike "Serpentine Fire," has enough force and verve to catch hold of and unhinge these images—wafting them off-angle. The music's a bit wild and untamed. That odd detail, the puppets, is essential. "Tints"'s sound and image together create a new amalgam.

There's too much to digest in the image-track of the "Tints" video, and then we land briefly on a freer section—images of .Paak drumming, or the fast swaps across rooms, or driving 360s. Here are some examples of the images' heavy yet oddly tinted content:

- .Paak rocks back and forth and cowers after possible killings, but the poodle seems to be a better match for the song's affect.
- .Paak watches a girly show, probably of the religious webcam girl; his pants, however, are swaddled around his ankles, his medical badge across his chest has lost its stitching, and the room is a bit too bare and tawdry.
- Kendrick Lamar is kingly, but he's on a breathing machine—and the Grim Reaper may have the best pose.
- .Paak is tied up for S&M, but the bed is too large, and oversized curtain sashes and a horse's bit look goofy.
- .Paak is with three women who are wearing rhinestoned bras and undies. Straddled by one, his face is wet from water or urine.
- .Paak refuses a trans woman's solicitations, and his gestures read as disgust. But as he turns away he appears gleeful (his tongue's out to one side), suggesting he has enjoyed this encounter. I wish the video showed his sexual partner's amusement, too, through an exchanged glance or an over-the-shoulder two-shot. I don't find this moment progressive, but a later one when two men give one another a hug during the NA meeting might soften its effect.

But music video's audiovisual aesthetics can be complicated. The music and image seek corollaries to one another, and these tend to come to the fore. The audiovisual contract is so capacious, however, that sound and image can also relate elliptically or distantly. My analysis for Peter Gabriel's and Matt Mahurin's music video "Mercy Street" (1986) draws attention to this. The song sounds like a depressing murmuring of a lullaby, but the image is a full-on horror show, with suicide, electroshock therapy, and drowning (it's an homage to poet Anne Sexton, who committed suicide). The unresolved differences between music and image create a puzzle which the viewer can't resolve, thereby encouraging multiple viewings. Perhaps Tilley, Dr. Dre, Lamar, and .Paak wanted to convey something autobiographical and gleeful (the video has a 1970s feel).

Tilley suggests that he gets strong performances from his actors because he strives to build worlds for them through staging, props, costumes, and decor, and they just drop into it. I surmise he brings a quality of aliveness to the set, too. .Paak responds vibrantly to every situation. I feel I share some of his fury about being shot at the opening, and some of his enthusiasm for the various women (though I wish their contexts differed).

Perhaps the video's allure partly stems from the ways it conjures up contradictory states of mind. I'd have a hard time playing all of the video's roles, and that challenge extends me a bit (we really are different people in different contexts). I can imagine shooting the guards and musing about it afterward, tied up in the trunk. But it's harder for me to visualize being bound and gagged within a car trunk while reminiscing about dancing with a mop while I cleaned out the diner's cash register. I can imagine being a doctor and peeping at the Christian girl's webcam, but not maintaining a physician's mindset while eschewing a trans woman's solicitations. This may reflect my personal limitations—what's near and far in my web of experiences. It might not be yours.

.Paak describes ups and downs in his life.[8] His mother sold organic produce; when strawberry season was good, they were in a mansion, and when the rains were inhospitable, they returned to poorer housing. She ran into trouble with the IRS and gambling in Vegas, and was sentenced to fourteen years in prison. The performer's learned to embrace churn and shifting fortunes. I'd like to know how much of "Tints" directly or indirectly reflects lived experience.

Knowing more about the clip's context may help viewers. I still can't make sense of the fact that I feel relatively at home with the "Tints," but I'm concerned for other viewers. I worry they'll think the clip is a comedy, with a person of color as the butt of jokes. But who are these viewers? It's important to ask if historically negative representations of Blacks play into "Tints," and in what ways we should worry about this. I think of Marlon Riggs's documentary film *Color Adjustment* (1991). In it, actress Diahann Carrol shares that her parents wouldn't let her watch Stepin Fetchit or Amos 'n' Andy because the representations were so objectionable, but as she grew up she realized they were real artists—they were really funny. It may matter that Dr. Dre contributed much to "Tint"'s storyline. Katy Perry's "Last Friday Night" (2010) is another clip that shares the sense of self-deprecation and freedom in "Tints." In "LFT," an adolescent Perry invites high-school partiers over once her parents leave town, and experiences nontraditional sexual escapades. Yet Perry's strange prosthetics, makeup, and braces keep her character distanced from her star persona. This doesn't seem as true for .Paak. Could Post Malone or one of the Jonas

Brothers have played .Paak's role? Or Kendrick Lamar? And I wonder whether the qualities of self-deprecation and freedom contribute to something I like about the video—the character's courage—as he dares to cross racial barriers to participate in Latinx, European American, and queer communities, here adopting roles as lover, father, student, and physician.

When my students and I watched "Tints" I asked whether we might wish for narrow, uplifting representations of underrepresented groups. Representations of outsider groups still feel too few and too precious. When I consider the license I grant to other groups this doesn't feel right, but there may be times and places for work. Lady Gaga's "Paparazzi" (discussed in chapter 7) features vindictive women who murder men. Why would I more readily condone this representation but hesitate with "Tints," which features a protagonist who mostly dallies a bit?

It'd be nice to have different realizations of "Tints." The transgender character could take the lead, with punishments ameliorated or redirected. Or Lucille Ball. Or the French actress Isabelle Huppert, who plays a sexual voyeur and predator in Michael Haneke's *The Piano Teacher* (2001), though that film, too, was punitive. Perhaps "Tints" could also be performed by an older, less glamorous actor than Huppert.

Jeffrey Zacks is a neuroscientist who studies the ways that people's cognitive processes form boundaries within time spans (e.g., how we know when a scene ends or a shift in conversation occurs, and what we remember based on whether an incident happened in the beginning, middle, or end of an event). He has noted different experiences when a viewer participates with coarse-grained or close attention.[9] If one attends carefully to "Tints," most of it feels good, I think. Partly this is because situations constantly flip, and .Paak is so sympathetic. But when one just attends to the broad arc, it may not seem as progressive.

Catherine Clement argues that operas are rife with misogyny.[10] Many beloved operas often have their heroines die at the end—but for opera lovers the end is only one part of the experience; the opera begins again and the audience returns to beautiful, overwhelming moments. Both operas and music videos form their own amalgams. Like music alone, their moments of beauty or transcendence come upon us anew—we can be most in a present moment of glee, surprise, or freedom, and the sense of an ending can be far away.

"Tints" may narrate multiple protagonists' stories (note again the changes in hairstyles). If so, it doesn't provide enough detail to exonerate or condemn its characters. There's a sense that if we watch attentively we'll be able to piece out what's going on, but I've decided this isn't going to happen. Because of the music, movement, gestures, and facial expressions, however, we can surmise how we might feel in the characters' situations even without knowing much of their contexts. Trying on these feelings can be a positive good.

Pop music points toward something that can't be named (I feel proud of . . . joyful about . . . desirous of . . . what?). The lyrics and the image can suggest targets, but they're vague: Who's "my baby," or that performer in that odd set? Music videos first provide a mode of bodily comportment, an attitude, a feeling one might adopt in an already-abstracted situation. If the image, lyrics, and music are in the ballpark for us, we may be open to going along for the ride. If the beguiling qualities of the song hail us, and the drive of the camera directs us, we may feel invited to kinesthetically embody the characters—and we're willing to try on "Tints." Certain relations are more difficult. Lars von Trier's *The House That Jack Built* (2018) would be hard to bear with the "Tints"'s song as its soundtrack.

I'm engaged with almost all of the clip's moments. The strongest exception is .Paak throwing money at and being straddled by rhinestoned dancers, because another tableau doesn't give the scene a sudden twist—it doesn't have an engaging hinge to other settings. Even the Christian cam-girl appeals to me, because when she leaps and crashes into the splits on her bed, startling her preacher/father, who upends a wall hanging and his TV dinner, her Rube Goldberg chain-of-events is funny. I'm also engaged when Lamar watches the girly show, because the Grim Reaper is right behind him and the women, Lamar, and .Paak together form a G5 (a Gulfstream G500 business jet).

The song's lyrics focus on cars contributes to the images' machinic drive.

I stay with "Tints" because almost everything gets an extra turn. Questionable activities accrue, and at some point an internal censor says "Wait a minute! That's too much!" This censor kicks in right on cue for the deflationary out-chorus, matching the music, and constraining my pleasure. Perhaps the song's close is so deflationary because in some oblique way it resembles the Middle Passage or "the sunken place."[11]

I'm in favor of practitioners being given some latitude, all the while receiving feedback from scholars and other viewers. One can't predict where the work will land. I believe Tilley is committed to Black communities, and wishes to do what he can. We all need to try out intuitions. Sometimes a beloved project will come together well, and in another instance, reveal its seams and vulnerabilities. Right now I like "Tints." I think we all could make an assessment here. It's best that we're all in this together.

IV Audiovisual Aesthetics Online

Who Needs Music Documentaries When There's TikTok and *Carpool Karaoke*?

WHO NEEDS MUSIC DOCUMENTARIES when there's TikTok, *Vogue*'s *73 Questions*, and *Carpool Karaoke*? And, while we're at it, how much do we need pop stars? I'm glad to devote my time to TikTok prosumers' dance moves, lip-sync, and animations for song-snippets. The documentary *Jawline* (2019) shows how our experience of musical performance has changed. The film traces YouTube influencers' trajectories with their mega fan-bases: these young men (I don't think there are many women) tour the country and hold concert events just like mid-tier musicians. Onstage they dance and deejay a bit, but their main attraction is their physical beauty and fan-directed inspirational messages: "Keep with the positive," "You're beautiful," "Don't let anyone take you down." Between sets the fans do funny things with the stars, like drape them in toilet paper and whipped cream. These scenes resemble live concerts in documentaries, but with a difference.

Here's another example of the ways filmed musical performance has changed. I spend a lot of time watching music video, which draws me into pop culture's center. But of course most of these clips don't foreground completely live shows. And I don't think I'm watching them for their divas—it's more about aesthetic experiences of patterned sound against patterned image. I'll follow along with supplementary materials, perhaps Harry Styles on a late-night talk show (seemingly live on a stage apart from the interview set, but surely with a canned arrangement, if only the backing tracks), or Troye Sivan's videos on YouTube, talking about how he applies makeup. These clips are far from stadium concerts and traditional music documentaries.

What I'll call YouTube's ancillary depictions of musicians (like interviews, live performances, and so on, rather than music videos) have their own strong aesthetic. These clips are often revealed in almost seamless environments, with props and soundtracks that showcase their performers in surprising ways. These clips also form networks of intertextual relations. Many of us spend a lot of time on YouTube, and it's how our concepts of musical artists, directors, and actors become more shaded. The distance from Hollywood blockbusters to intimate, sometimes prosumer works help map the media swirl.

A little background: this chapter, in part, strives to show off both the near briefest of moving media's materials and the media swirl's updating-churn—quickly. I feel an obligation to capture this because of my book's title. But how? The topic seems vast. Fortunately I encountered a good turn: I was invited to give a keynote in Germany on music documentaries. As I researched the project I started thinking about how old-school, long-form music documentaries differ from what's on the web now. Just this framing device—platforms, genres, technologies, and socioeconomic changes in relation to musical performance—provided a window into our larger mediascape. Initially my talk for Germany felt daunting. Long-form musical docs add up to a large corpus, and though I'd seen many, from *Woodstock*, *Sympathy for the Devil*, to *Amy* and *Homecoming*, revisiting this content seemed challenging. Most run at lengths similar to features; I don't know about you, but I'm more inclined to devote my time to films and streaming series (like critics' best-of-the-year lists, including 2020's *Once Upon a Time in Hollywood*, *Gloria Bell*, *Parasite*, *Marriage Story*, and *Mindhunter*). I started tackling the challenge like any internet junkie would today, which is watching music documentary *trailers* and reading top-50 lists (*Vulture* has a nice one). Then another turn: in the middle of the project, with an unrealistic deadline, I discovered there was little scholarship on music documentaries—Phil Auslander, David Harvey, and Susan Fast, but that's about it. A wide, uncharted terrain with my keynote's hard deadline made me feel freer. I'd stay with my own experiences and insights, with a historical eye, but a focus on now.

I soon developed a theory for why I often find old-school music documentaries less than satisfying, though I'll also celebrate their merits. I find their inabilities to create diegesis (or opportunities for immersion) distancing. Elements are broken up, material is patchwork, and some of it is stronger than others. There might be musicians performing, then a glassy-eyed manager, sister, stepfather, or another well-known musician who admires the star, most often seated upright in a chair, head turned slightly to one side, and engaged elsewhere, since they're struggling to project a sincere reminiscence. Then we might see a road before us from what we'll come to surmise is a tour bus's front window, but with little sense where we might be going. Then back to images of the star in the green room or among her fans, or of newspaper clippings. Jagged! To provide structure, these films are often dependent on milestones and temporal markers: the divorce, the decline through drugs, the failed contract, the Grammy. Or a chronology: the first decade, second, and so on. We're forced to ask: How is this documentary departing from, but also hewing to the schematic we already know? At what moment will this documentary really kick in?

Today, two-hour music documentaries feel like a sideshow to Netflix's more popular fare—less generously budgeted or viewed, as well as aimed toward much older audiences. Recent documentaries about Billie Eilish (2021), Justin Bieber (2021), and Taylor Swift (2020), all arguably under Beyoncé's shadow and powered by competitiveness and financial resources, go for higher stakes. But still, I've continued to wonder whether devoted fans can gather something similar through clicking among Instagram, YouTube clips, and fan-originated blogs. These are patchwork, too, but they can be mentally stitched together into a composite.

I'll argue that while there are strengths to both the more traditional form and today's internet-driven experience, we should privilege today's model. Moment by moment, this new material possesses greater density and richer connections. It encompasses aesthetics, fandom, and artists' lives, to genres and platforms. Among other things, I'll explore the possibility that we don't need stars in the ways we used to. Of course the biggest stars' orbits are wide (Rihanna, Ariana Grande, Justin Bieber), but alongside them all kinds of configurations unfold. Many of these have shifted our sense of who counts as a musician-performer, and what's "musical." These shifts carry across genres, media, and platforms. Film stars and directors, in their brief YouTube clips, seem like musicians. Much YouTube content, from studio session recordings to the "Makings of Music Videos," feels musical. Sometimes musician-performers cross genres on YouTube and Instagram; pop star Dua Lipa (2020) released a five-minute 1960s-nostalgic sitcom (*Dua's World*), for example. There's a black-and-white clip of Justin Bieber talking about his tattoos. There are genres for stars to dip in and out of, from *Vogue*'s *73 Questions* to *Carpool Karaoke*. There have always been the talk shows, but they're more highly curated. Of course there are also the YouTube covers by unknown amateurs, most charmingly realized by pairs of school-aged teens, and the TikTok shows with "average folks" performing in their bathrooms, bedrooms, and stairwells. Second-by-second, these outpace most music documentaries.

Traditional, long-form music documentaries and YouTube's current ancillary material give me different depictions of lives, ones that can be compared with my own. I'm probably more likely to feel envious of successful pop musicians than most, though perhaps the reader will also recognize herself here. I'd been a musician, a composer, and a videomaker before becoming an academic, a shift I didn't fully embrace. Even now at some level I've assumed that a successful artist's life is best. To live within the realms of sentiment and gesture, and to externalize so much of oneself—I envisioned myself creating a circuit from my affects, movements, and imagination, to the world and back again in ways that seemed lovely. I've always been aware of the many limitations here. Why didn't the knowledge of these impracticalities take stronger root? I know that few people manage to maintain a professional music career past late middle age, and even fewer achieve success. Much of an artist's labor is devoted to a wordless state of repetition for long stretches of time. Would you rather hang out with a musician or an academic? I prefer academics. Considering music documentaries has helped me see the dampening effects envy as well as narrowed possibilities have had on my life, and to value my context more.

A worldview concerning a particular concept of personhood has also shaped this project. I believe that we're comprised of multiple selves, and we're called upon and shaped by the contexts we participate in. This multiplicity is highlighted in long-play music documentaries. The quotidian musician-self is often presented as someone like us; this depiction corroborates what I've experienced in my encounters with actors and directors. This self is the self who's hanging out as makeup is applied or is waiting for a phone call. There's then also a second self that's engaged with music-making. This second musician-performer often appears in a heightened state, infused with joy, focus, and flow. But there's often little overlap between that self and others. While depictions of the split self come forward most overtly in the most recent documentaries (like those for Taylor Swift and Justin Bieber), I prefer earlier ones that require more teasing out, like the documentaries about Amy Winehouse, Kurt Cobain, and Lady Gaga. In these the musician's performer-self doesn't seem capable of soothing other parts of the self. In *Five Foot Two* (2017) we see Lady Gaga standing on the lawn outside a studio, describing her wish for a boyfriend and her desire to become more mature. Here she doesn't seem particularly unique, insightful, or articulate. Then she enters the studio, gives a few people some hugs, walks up to the mic, leans back, and seemingly out of nowhere belts out a line full-blast: "Hey Girl!!" A viewer might feel tempted to wonder, "Where did *that* come from?" We'll soon see her stretched out in pain on the couch, or cornered in a kitchen complaining that she doesn't have a lover, while surrounded by handlers.

The Cobain documentary (*Kurt Cobain: Montage of Heck*, 2015) works similarly, but with a twist. Psychologists, musicologists, media theorists, and philosophers have all drawn attention to the ways a person's actions, or a moment in cinema, a song, or a novel, are shaped by a number of causes, from which a primary one can't readily be disentangled. There are hints at some possible causes for Cobain's distress: family members' rejections, depression, ADHD, stomach pain, or heroin. Then there's his music, which is such a beautiful wash, but which can't seem to envelop him (fig. 11.1). I believe some stars have it all, but that number is probably minute. Is it Beyoncé? Or Rihanna? Joe Caramanica suggests that Rihanna is living the best life.[1] This might also be true for Harry Styles. Many stars come from middle- and working-class backgrounds that might involve pasts they can't transcend, and which many people still experience. So perhaps some 3 percent of elite tastemakers are leading a clearly enviable life.

Viewers may take solace (or experience Schadenfreude) in the fact that a pop star has a lot to carry. Many of these documentaries, especially those about women, emphasize pain and injury. Untangling why we see so many artists depicted in pain is difficult: Gaga has fibromyalgia, and Ariana Grande has PTSD (from the bombing at her Manchester concert in

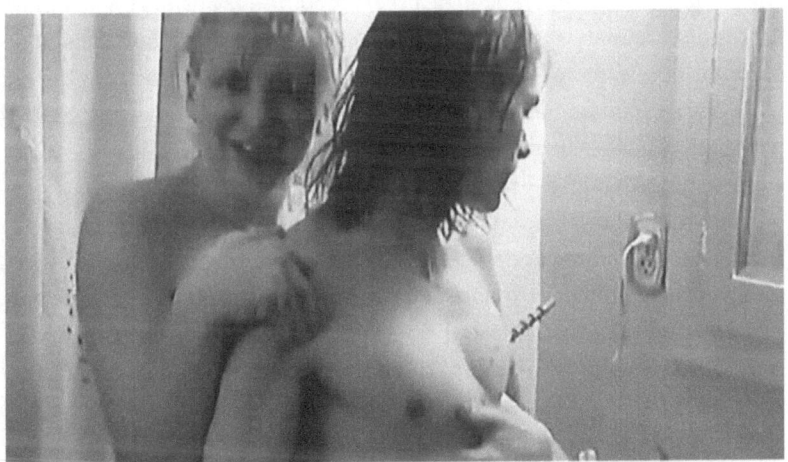

11.1 *Montage of Heck* suggests possible causes for Kurt Cobain's distress.

2017). Justin Bieber has Epstein-Barr and Lyme disease. Taylor Swift has an eating disorder. Beyoncé develops preeclampsia and must lose sixty-five pounds—she's hungry.[2] Cobain, Winehouse, Elton John, and Miles Davis all struggled with drugs. The levels of difficulty we as an average population face are unacceptably high. But that of the stars, as a demographic, seem higher. Every case, of course, seems legitimate.

Might pop stars be canaries in the coal mine? Stressors they experience from work and from the environment might resemble ours, but in a heightened fashion, and thus take higher tolls. Stars form a highly sensitized population. Skilled at feeling and responding more, they may have thinner skins (and the 2018 documentary *27: Gone Too Soon* makes a feature of this); one might expect them to be more vulnerable to illnesses. One stressor may be today's career intricacies. There are only a few top slots, and the only way to reach them is through tireless work, backed by an army of skilled assistants. Every PR move carries weight. Many performers want to feel close to fans; they feel responsible to them. As Swift notes in her *Miss Americana* documentary, they can easily cancel you. Nourishing the approval and love of fans must seem like an enormous pressure, especially in the era of the internet (the Bieber, Gaga, and Swift documentaries all devote time to fan maintenance).

Against this intensity may be dullness. Hanging out in green rooms with make-up artists, sycophants, and costume designers constantly appealing to and handling you doesn't seem like the best life (this happens a lot in Gaga's *Five Foot Two*). Is the dullness against the intensity particularly toxic? It's possible that long-form docs may exaggerate the gaps between pleasure, tedium, and ill health. Director Dave Meyers told me that his music videos always include the star momentarily in a down position, so that everyday people could empathize with her. Recent documentaries, including Swift's and Bieber's, may draw attention to these contrasts—the pleasures of pop performance, including its preparation, against the trials the artist must endure—in order to mitigate viewers' jealousy.

YouTube's short, audiovisually intensified clips, especially when curated by a star's production team, don't explore these stressors as extensively as do long-form documentaries. This is probably because the monumentality of the scale and emotions isn't conducive to brief forms. In favor of the long-form docs, I think this material's good to experience and reflect on.

What *can* be learned from more traditional long-form documentaries? The knowledge we gain from today's highly curated, brief web materials are nearly always present-tense-oriented, and highly controlled. For the patient viewer, on the other hand, something revealing can peek out with documentaries that adopt a long view, especially from the vantage point near the end of an artist's career. *Miles Davis: Birth of the Cool* (2019), for example, shows aspects of the trumpet player that aren't in the memoirs and biographies. A voiceover, alongside sounds and images, makes the content more affecting. *Birth of the Cool* can create a new sensitivity to the vulnerability of his sound. The curated concert footage shows how each of the band-members would improvise in turn, and then, at the set's close, Davis, having held back until then, suddenly plays a summative solo that threads individual performances together. I didn't know about some of Miles's more private affairs, like how he didn't leave any of his inheritance to two of his sons (it's assumed he felt they were too critical of him). Or perhaps it's just the way the documentary hovers at the doorways of an array of places he lived, in Malibu, New York, and Paris. We can imagine Davis in these buildings, place these images alongside the documentary's other materials, and assemble a greater sense of who he was (fig. 11.2).

There's something else to be applauded about long-form documentaries. Perhaps because most of them have devoted resources to depicting a single performer's life, each long-form work finds ways to tailor itself to its material. Each conveys a unique audiovisual aesthetic. In the Miles Davis film, interviewees' faces are shot like medallions, in profile, with the next scene's imagery crossfaded behind them. Their faces then dissolve over the scene: here these speakers serve as a kind of portal or gateway. In relation to Miles this is clever, because he himself was mysterious and

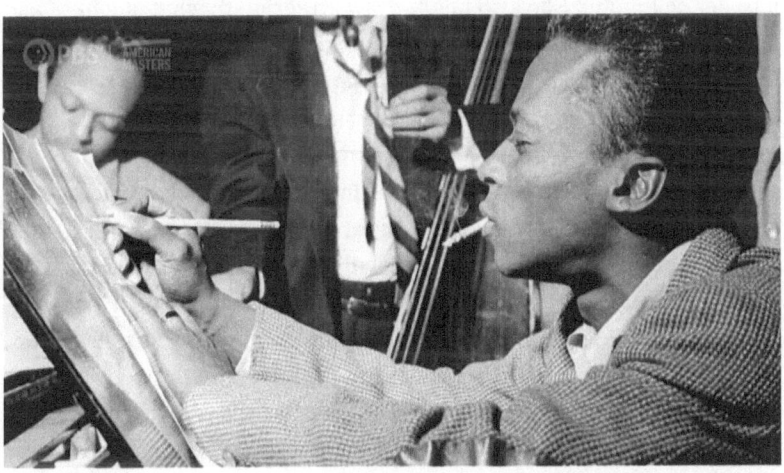

11.2 *Birth of the Cool* probes Miles Davis's complicated background.

oblique. The Cobain documentary, on the other hand, has a mix of life-like rotoscoped animation (resembling Richard Linklater's *Waking Life* from 2001), alongside more rough-hewn animations of his drawings and sketches. This meshes nicely with Cobain's prosumer autoerotic speaking into tape recorders and scribbling in notebooks. Jenn Nkiru's *Black to Techno* (2019) has a wonderful mix of high art, Matthew Barney touches, and street documentary; this is meant to reflect the techno cultures of Detroit. The brief YouTube "making of" clips, talk-show segments, and award shows rarely acknowledge the work of a director or promote a style, though they might.

Compare this to brief audiovisually intensified material on the web. For dreamy and committed fans, Miley Cyrus's music video "Slide Away" (2019), moment-for-moment, gives more than a long-form music documentary. We could even imagine the traditional documentary's voiceover narration. Here's the moment in Miley Cyrus's career where she's stuck in the Hollywood hills, partying too hard while taking too many drugs. Her relationship of ten years has fallen apart, and her ex has returned to Australia. Rather, in this music video we receive this content threaded through more multisensorial, richly affective content. Some narrative information is conveyed through the song's lyrics, as they momentarily jut out and submerge. Shaped by recent music production techniques, these songs differ from earlier pop. They're more autobiographical. Today it's common for studio producers to mess around with tracks, while the star enters and exits, offering tales of her recent life's events, bits of melody, fragments of lyrics, and how she's feeling, all facilitated by her singing and tapping into her cellphone. She also might draw attention to what she likes and doesn't about individual recorded elements—and her ear is sharp. This more collaborative and syncretic process enables a musician-performer to personalize her songs and to give her music a stamp (and she collects royalties as well—perhaps much comes down to the money).

My guess is that hermetically sealing in performers and producers from the start may be beneficial. With lyrics, for example, some stars, most famously Beyoncé, have shifted to including special fan-oriented puzzles and hints that detail lived events. These make the songs seem like autobiographies on steroids. Miley Cyrus's lyrics, like "we're not seventeen, we're grown now," point to her marriage: the line "slide away, back to the ocean" is what really happened. Her ex goes to Australia to surf. There's more: "Slide Away" shows Cyrus in some unfolding time, and it encourages us to follow her reactions to her setting, like the pool and the partygoers passed out and strewn around her in this Hollywood mansion. Simultaneously we hear her voice from the original recording, so two senses of time are suggested. We're aware that Cyrus was in some sort of state when she wrote and recorded this song. Now we witness her through the camera's eye. As she lip-syncs to playback, we might guess what she thinks about her song now, alongside her initial experiences of it. There are multiple layers of time. The composition and the images' flow against the music are gorgeous. This video conveyed a mood that a long-form music documentary wouldn't be able to capture as effectively.

There's also auxiliary material to consider. Cyrus has performed "Slide Away" on several live stages, a practice embraced by many artists. Cyrus's VH1 Awards performance of "Slide Away" is more a departure from than a repetition of the music video. Shot in black and white, with a more stripped-down, acoustically-based arrangement (several violinists perform), Cyrus sings with additional country-rock grit and twang (the music video was more pop). The VH1 Awards set is somber and schematic—lines of lights trace what resembles the pool's edges, and as beams bounce off the shiny black floor, a shimmer makes the cordoned-off space suggestive more of dangerous tar or poison than water. The setting feels monumental and austere. Is the awards show more solemn because it was recorded after the music video? Why does Cyrus want the song and setting stripped down here, and why the shift from pop to rock and roll and country? What sense of time does each performance convey? Are we to assume that the loss of a close relationship becomes more costly over time? Earlier, I noted how the "Slide Away" music video suggested multiple layers of time. The new performance adds a few more. What does this mean (figs. 11.3 and 11.4)?

I've watched many Dua Lipa's award-show-style presentations of her song "Don't Start Now" (2019–22). An attentive viewer will notice that the choreography and arrangement are already set, and Lipa's singing changes little, but the costuming, props, and lighting differ, often forming a slightly new event each time, which can be placed in relation to the others (there's a stunning one that becomes nearly pure color for the MTV VMA awards). This becomes a thing. In their music video "'ON' Kinetic Manifesto Film" (2020), BTS performs before a large cement aqueduct; later, when they reperformed it on the Jimmy Fallon show, they appear in Grand Central Station (empty, so the clip most likely was shot in a morning's early hours). One might feel tempted to chromakey one background against the other, the gestures, spacialization, and timing form a near-exact repetition. The single performance that's constant across iterations might be a good model for us. Can we bring that kind of tight game to

11.3–11.4 Miley Cyrus's music video and VH1 performance of "Slide Away" explore Cyrus's divorce.

our jobs and romances? Are we as portable? There's often something that breaks the mold. BTS also performs for James Corden's *Carpool Karaoke*. While most of the staged performances in "'ON'" feature large numbers composed of many dancers moving in angular formation, here the young men wistfully gaze out Corden's car's windows, and trade off melodic lines as if they were passing a mic.

I've started watching a music video and then going down the YouTube vortex seeking related awards shows, talk shows, and concert performances, looking for a musician's slightly different gesture, a shift in arrangement, a new backdrop. I feel I'm too old for this. I don't think I'm a fan (I don't search out every detail about a performer's life, though I was excited about Katy Perry's pregnancy, news she shared through a music video). I know Ariana's fans want her to be pregnant (that was from *Carpool Karaoke*). This feels like it's crossing into *People Magazine* territory, which I usually don't enter.

Besides the intertextuality established among music videos and award and talk shows, multiple brief genres help build a sense of musical performance that competes with long-form traditional documentaries. There's a genre of fan-authored compilation tapes, in which every instance of a star—her bitchiness, bossiness, or shadiness—is strung together into a new clip. View-counts for these can be high (Beyoncé's "Beyoncé Shadiest /Top Bossiest Moments" has 2.5 million views).[3] I assume some of these have been sanctioned by her handlers, because only a few gain millions of hits. These clips present a different vision of what it is to be human. Beyoncé's bossy moments share a family resemblance with respect to contexts and modes. It seems like character can be compartmentalized in accordance with types of behavior; within each bounded set, slight differences can occur. These compilations fracture the self, disarticulating the joints.

The performer in pain is an old trope (think Sarah Bernhardt and Bessie Smith), though depictions of pain appear rarely in the aforementioned compilation clips devoted to stars' less-than-sanctioned attitudes and behaviors. Typically a performer's pain comes from a bad romance, family, or management, and it's often wrapped up in a downward spiral of booze and drugs. I ask again, how necessary is this for our pleasure? Taylor Swift once showed off her calluses on her fingers, and the New York reporter asked if her fingers ever bled. A striking moment in Gaga's *Five Foot Two* shows her moaning in pain, prone on the couch. She discusses her large number of attendants, something she notes most sufferers can't access; one of them massages her temples.

Short audiovisual media can explore pain, too, but it's less common. One of the most jarring I've found is Swift's interview on Jimmy Fallon in 2019.[4] Fallon notes that she's just had Lasik surgery, to which she replies yes. He then tells Swift that her mother has given him a clip that he'd like to roll. Would that be okay? She agrees, and suddenly we cut to Swift with no makeup, her face swollen and tearstained. With bandages and goggles over her eyes, she can't find her way easily through her parents' home. Standing in the kitchen, she requests a banana from her mother, but frets when the one she's handed is mushy. She fumbles down the hall with her mother following, as her mother captures the star's progress on her cellphone, and then Swift crawls under her bed's covers. Has some of this been staged? Why would Swift's mother want to be in on it? Why would it be funny? (There's a laugh track.) Swift's sweater chimes with the banana's yellow and brown, so it's all a bit suspicious. She seems genuinely surprised when Fallon announces the document related to the surgery. Much like a music video, this clip's closing moments contradict earlier ones (how to put into relation Swift's shock with what must have been some careful approvals and planning). Much of this is boggling.

Like many people, probably, I enjoy *Carpool Karaoke*, and especially so when my favorite stars appear. The show's tricks have never surprised me. The series appears to be shot on a flatbed truck or in front of a green screen—more than real driving must be involved. The stars are too valuable to risk a car accident (most big film stars don't perform their stunts either, because they're too hard to insure). Plus, it's just bad driving practice. Corden never says, "Oh no, I almost hit that car!" *Carpool Karaoke*'s laugh track is the show's most contrived feature, not its flatbed truck. With sitcoms, we laugh alongside an imagined studio audience, which is next to the cameras. Where would we place all of this show's viewer-laughers—on the hood of the car? I wonder how the laugh track might be shaped to fit the car's interior's acoustics.

Many of *Carpool Karaoke*'s conceits are clever. The car's interior places performer and interviewee closer together than talk shows do (an effect enhanced by how a camera makes people look further apart than they are). James Naremore discusses the contrived performative aspects of talk shows. Features like the positionings of bodies are much more artificial than those employed in ordinary life: watch closely for stars' fiddlings with hands, markings-off of torsos, and anglings of heads. *Carpool Karaoke* has its own presentational modes. Performers reach out across the coffee-holders in ways that aim to appear natural, even while the stars wear seatbelts (Madonna spoofs this by crawling out of her seatbelt and twerking her buttocks up, filling the screen). At other moments interviewer and guest look ahead, but still seem connected. And of course, Corden doesn't always drive. The car frequently stops, and both hands occasionally leave the wheel, even when the car is in motion. Much is attractive. There are qualities of privacy and intimacy as each person turns forward and apart (similar to when we zoom or work from laptops). In a car, experiences can be intimate and familiar; one often has one's own thoughts, or, with a friend, engages in low-stakes chitchat or listening to music. Watching the show is almost like being with someone who's singing in the bathroom. Some of the shows draw out this silliness (Corden and Britney Spears engage in a lot of joshing, for example). Other public contexts can also give us this kind of privileged access. I love looking at people as they exit a museum; their dazed expressions stem from having projected a focused, outwardly directed stare for so long, and I can suddenly sneak an uninvited one back at them. *Carpool Karaoke* makes this possible too.

Some of the show's guests blossom in new ways. I especially love the episodes with Ariana Grande, Billie Eilish, and Miley Cyrus. They can sing. Supposedly the show is shot with miniature cameras taped within the car's windows, but how were they recorded so well, and why are their voices so excellent? It's true that Corden sings beautiful harmony—he's a skilled performer too, but it's all a bit surprising. *Carpool Karaoke*'s shoots comprise a full day, and there's much editing. There's probably a good bit of sweetening in post, too, but the show still feels like a feat. The performers are excited, vibrant, and in love with their music, and their call and response with Corden feels palpable. And where else would we see this? Perhaps the car's flow, alongside the song's momentum—a double sense of movement—helps bring this out. With many of these shows Corden might get out of the car for a minute to visit the studio, the star's home, or a coffee shop, or he might pause the car for a moment to lock hands with his guest or accept a gift (Justin Bieber gives him a rose; he gobbles down chocolates with Ed Sheeran). Often, Corden tears up.

These heightened moments may be designed to reconnect the star with her fans in ways different from long-form documentaries. In those, as I've mentioned, we might experience envy and pity. In the long-form docs there's a moment backstage, with a fake backdrop, handlers, and a camera, and a chosen fan gets to come up momentarily to give the star a hug. The star might tear up a bit, but the exchange is primarily shot at a distance with a telephoto lens, and feels remote. Here, we get to watch in close-up how each star relates to Corden and vice versa in a deeply proprioceptive

11.5 James Corden and Adele share an intimate moment with us.

way. Corden really likes Adele, we can see; Harry Styles and Ed Sheeran, too. It's the goosebumpy quality of them singing together, or some of the premusical moments, like both stars drawing a breath together before a song begins, that's affecting (though in this context we're not supposed to read Corden as a star, and there's often a lot of joking about this). In *Carpool Karaoke* Corden serves as a surrogate fan, and he gets to say directly to her what we're so hungry to articulate. In this way he completes the circle for us (fig. 11.5).

Sam Smith's eight-minute documentary about working on the choreography for "How Do You Sleep?" (2019) is another ancillary YouTube clip. Smith and the dancers leap up and trace the song's lines in slow motion, and there's something gorgeously musical about it. The video is fantastic: if one is going around collecting peak moments just from drifting along and surfing on the web, this might be one. Smith also shares intimate details about his relation to his body and being gay, what the rehearsals were like, what he admired in the director, and what the two wished to achieve through their collaboration. This brief clip is packed with material. It's much denser than one might find from a documentary, and I'm sure dance's lens helps here.

Vogue's *73 Questions* could be seen as some of the most moment-by-moment, envy-inducing clips of all. We visit the star's home or, sometimes, for a change, a rental or the home of a family member who hasn't yet stepped up in the world. We're allowed through the door. The star appears, and she's witty, vivacious, warm, and gorgeous—beyond what we'd imagined. We follow her through her home and gardens in a single take. The spaces are stunning. Everything's also minutely timed, so a prop, like a toy, husband, or parent, pop up at just the right moments, as the star leads us on her tour. These clips are hybrid forms that draw from music video and the musical. The rhythm of the interviewer's questions, some delivered slow and languorously and others as a series of rapid bursts, alongside the star's movements, the props' appearances, and the attractively shifting backgrounds, becomes musical. It's like *Carpool Karaoke* in that the chatter and movement allow for intimacy and flow.

The *73 Questions* series is a music documentary in miniature. Look at the one for Troye Sivan (2019). He addresses us at the door to begin the clip. We enter the kitchen and hear about his Australian roots, which dovetails with his tales of world tours. He's making an espresso, which he holds up for us—we imagine readying for travel. Next we cross into the living room and meet his boyfriend and dog, who sit close to Sivan on the couch. We imagine what this romance is like, as the three of them before us look perfect for a family portrait. Next we shift to a bedroom, as Sivan sorts through items. (We assume this is how he packs.) He discusses his T-shirts as he gets ready to move past our shared narrated childhood and present domesticity, to a future-oriented career. Outdoors we hear about his manager and his recent songwriting experiences. A small detail, like the discussion of the exterior bathtub (a swanky touch), can spark a range of fantasies. What about Troye creating music in new environments, like in hotel rooms and on Skype, and getting cozy with

11.6 Troye Sivan welcomes us into the kitchen in *Vogue*'s *73 Questions*.

famous people, from Rufus Wainwright to Ariana Grande? The bathtub seems to help here. We then head to the backyard proper, and the clip shifts into something more akin to traditionally staged performances. The interviewer asks Sivan about his experiences with modeling, and Troye shows them off, strutting toward the camera along the concrete patio's lip that rims the pool. As often transpires in *73 Questions*, Sivan is dared to close the clip with a feat: the interviewer asks him to cannonball into the pool with his clothes on (we've already had some talk about sunscreen, for Troye has fair skin). The star does this with aplomb: these stars are special; they can perform on cue (fig. 11.6). We've gotten a compressed story about Troye Sivan's life's experiences and history, but we've also spent every single moment of it with him, and with a lot of audiovisual excitement as well. It's a mini-documentary—who needs the long form?

12

TikTok and Costume-Drama Mashups on YouTube

I STAY AWAY FROM TIKTOK because I don't want to be tracked. I do very little on Facebook, but I'm sure it's capturing my data. I've got an Amazon account, and I watch a lot of YouTube, so I'm well documented by them and other corporations. But still, something about TikTok's surveillance bothers me. Nevertheless, it attracts me. As Berenike Jung has noted, it hasn't become as professionalized as YouTube.[1] When I started watching YouTube I always saw the most popular amateur videos, but now the algorithm has taken control and delivers corporate-funded clips, including film trailers, music videos, and *Saturday Night Live* excerpts.

On TikTok I prefer the figures dancing with music, the amusing animals, and the little kids. There can be a lot of cleverness in the ways people find emotional and intellectual density in thirty seconds. The ones that make it to the top can have beautiful formal qualities. Elements in the background chime with the foreground, and a few odd details jut out, like Roland Barthes's puncta.[2] Jung has argued that while we tend to empathize with the figures in music video, we do this less so with TikTok.[3] Wanting to check, I watched a good bit. I noticed that figures can take on a bit of puppet-like or animatronic qualities, or their biological rhythms can seem to come forward (slow, erratic, or fast). Movements often become rhythmized and so seem both predictable and musical. Clips seem to have "hit points" or "juttings out" that are often reiterative. These work well with TikTok's foregrounding of moments of humor or surprise that unfold within a compressed timeframe. But still. "No, these bodies most often still are like people," I thought. And it's worth remembering that though music videos have always had empathetic stars, the background figures can seem alienated—those stony mannequin-like people, service workers, or figures dancing in formation, moving like robots.

TikTok has its snarkiness. There are a lot of beautiful teens in gorgeous, empty, rich people's homes. Those kitchen counterspaces! And then a lot of mayhem with household mush and liquids. A lot of it seems like a reboot of *Jackass* or *Candid Camera*. Many of these clips have charming audiovisual relations—ventriloquism, where you pin the sound to a likely candidate, but the sound is incorrect (like when a duck seemingly sings a Bollywood musical or twerks to Cookiee Kawaii). Their formal rhythms vary: some build slowly, and others suddenly provide a denouement: splat! (Tom Gunning might claim that TikToks share early cinema's attractions—views fascinating because of "their illusory power."[4])

TikTok showcases a bit of Tinder's sadism. There's a lot of swiping to get past, and the swipings down feel even more hostile than a dating app's rightward swipe. "You get 2.1 seconds!" The bodies often share something with GIFs. They morph into vaguely inhuman animatronics, jiggly, wiggly, jerky, puppet-like. The performers cross over into what's been called "the uncanny valley."[5] The dynamics and sensations of tapping to start and move past clips are worth noting. Do I feel like I'm inducing someone's epileptic seizure? And do I feel powerful doing so?

Let me consider one exemplary TikTok video: Doggface's clip in which he's skateboarding alongside a highway listening to Fleetwood Mac's 1977 "Dreams" and drinking a large bottle of Ocean Spray cranberry juice. Why has this been engaging for so many viewers? We might be charmed that Doggface likes a throwback song. He leans back a bit on his board, as if he's a session player who gives room to the singer. Drawing from Nicholas Cook, I claim that the image can work on many levels both with and against the song.[6] What is congruent? Both Doggface and Stevie Nicks could be said to feel slowed down—loping, sleepy, dreamy. Doggface looks like some cats—somewhat pleased and a little scruffy. That connects with Nicks for me. Perhaps both singer and skateboarder present a working-class affect. Doggface's car broke down, so he rode his board to work. Stevie Nicks was a secretary. Some elements rub up against one another. A friend described Nicks as one of America's sexiest women. Within the stream of spinoff TikToks, there's one with a gorgeous young woman skateboarding, and in honor of Doggface she wears feathers. Her setting matches her beauty, with the sunlight glinting behind her and redwood trees shading the side of the road. Though this clip is handsome, it doesn't call out to me. Maybe Doggface's clip gains allure from the timing of its details—how he turns his head and for a moment we see a tattoo across his neck that resembles an eagle's feather. Does this contribute to the clip's feeling of flying? I think so. Another correspondence between music and image comes when Doggface cuts a beautiful line through the screen, and guitarist Lindsey Buckingham's melody pierces through the song just as cleanly and sharply.

Details in Doggface's clip puzzle me. I can't quite believe he's moving so quickly. He's not supposed to be tethered to the back of a car. Why a large plastic bottle of red liquid? Would something else work as well? A Coke bottle? No! Is the plastic container a trophy? Perhaps. Doggface seems to hold it that way. He opens his chest for a moment, and if you perceive the image as a still, it feels like sheer bliss. I guess all of us would like to catch moments like this. There are details that have likely been sweetened in post. The sky's blue appears oversaturated. The song may have been replaced after the visuals were shot (there's no street noise). The red cars rhyme with the cranberry juice. Songs can relate to images on many registers. In an audiovisual context the song can suggest the clip's essential truth. Here we could see Doggface acting out Nicks's lyrics, "well there you go again," as if the skateboarder, in response to Nicks or his lover, nonchalantly shrugs off a relationship. I think we'd all like to be able to do this. We'd also like to seemingly live life with such equanimity. So much is churning around Doggface, but he's found a moment to be in time in a rich way (fig 12.1).

I like the TikTok challenges—a musical snippet, a camera scheme (glitches, slo-mo, or track in) and another for movement (a run into the frame, hands cover the face while hips sway). For searches I've resorted to YouTube for "TikTok challenge" and a song title, or a Googled song

12.1 Doggface's moment of bliss.

title with hashtag. (Why are there no Troye Sivan challenges, but plenty of Halsey?) Those with two components seem special—we see the young people prepping, and then dropping into performance, or a single character who's then replicated by multiples. Perhaps it's partially the verticality of the phone, but loud, ostentatious drum and bass sounds and lanky, attractive performers with long hair work well. Performers who move faster or slower than the song are expressive—for fast, they overarticulate some of the song's features, such as blunt, sharp gestures against Megan Thee Stallion's "Savage" or Earth Wind and Fire's "Let's Groove."[7] Another is to glide more slowly across the music, like in Halsey's "Without Me" or Ed Sheeran's "Beautiful People." With these, the viewer needs to bring sonic elements into relation with visual ones—and reweight elements' importance.

Halsey's "Without You" is sometimes performed by three teenagers. A couple enters the frame and another reaches between them and steals the girl. She falls into the new suitor's arms in slow motion. Why do I find these brief clips emotionally affecting? Halsey's opening phrases are punctuated and declamatory, and then her voice elongates and becomes more legato, wavering between two pitches as the girl falls. Halsey's singing is now achingly expressive, but still measured—as if poured steadily from a cup. Described more closely, Halsey's opening singing is punctuated and declamatory, and then it elongates and becomes more legato. It is also auto-tuned at the beginning, and then ends with an echo/reverb effect that accentuates that difference. The voice is altered/amplified by technology, the same way a lot of the visuals are worked.

While we hear Halsey's song, we experience the image of the teenage women's slo-mo descent as smooth and slow. Am I engaged here because two processes, musical and visual, unravel at different speeds? Do we have a new emotional composite here—Halsey, as a voice, plaintive and raw, the falling girl on screen, vulnerable and at risk? Does the voice wish to achieve the briefer trajectory of the woman falling? Do I enjoy guessing if any of the onscreen characters might feel similarly (or if I as a viewer do)? It's a social media thing: I have to watch a lot and suddenly I come across a fragment that feels like it's just for me. I sense no one is watching it right now (though some would have done so at a different moment). I also couldn't possibly share about my feelings with someone else—for the clip is so fleeting (unfolding in an odd moment of time). Strange that this would constitute for me a life's peak experience.

Scholarship on TikTok has been thin. Black dancers haven't received proper credit.[8] TikTok's algorithm can segregate us into cul-de-sacs of vulnerability (depression, political extremism) and shape, in insidious ways, how we envision ourselves. When music video first came out, scholars offered interesting but not quite accurate observations (Ann Kaplan called music videos schizophrenic, and Marsha Kinder, dreamlike).[9] TikTok aesthetics, I sense, hasn't yet been properly described—Samantha Hautea's and Zizi Papacharissi's notions of discursive, intertextual, and memetic linkages that propagate "affective publics" is helpful.[10] I'm hoping to participate in that conversation. As with other media, we need to be proactive. Show us your algorithms.[11] Let's engage in a conversation.

I've become devoted to a surprising genre: YouTube's prosumer mashups of period romance films. Fans edit up clips with excerpts from *Pride and Prejudice*, *Little Women*, or *Anna Karenina*. The videos are accompanied by contemporary pop stars like Lana Del Rey and Taylor Swift Some of these are accompanied by Taylor Swift songs with Spanish subtitles. This genre, which I believe started in the early 2000s, can be hard to find—the titles often list only characters' first names (e.g., "Jo and Laurie" signals that a clip draws from *Little Women*), but the community of producers and viewers is huge: thousands of clips and millions of views.

These mashups nearly always feature a star and her paramour walking together, kissing, or dancing. They lack the sturdiness—the sense of craft, line, and form—that encourages multiple viewings, but some have given me affectively rich experiences. The glossy film excerpts look fabulous, but because they're disjunctive, they edit poorly. The prosumer quality of many of these clips link them to TikTok, and all of these mashup fans tend to gravitate to the same collection of images, and later edited versions often feel like riffs on earlier ones. With all of these, the performers don't move in perfect sync with the song. Each cut destabilizes me, and then I wait for the song to fill in the faces. Within these confines I seek a connection—and for an instant it's there—in a glance or head turn. Suddenly the music colors the characters and I witness an intense emotion I wish I could possess. I assume I share this sensation with others but have the best access to it; its sharpness would break the arc of an actor's performance across a scene. The actors also can't hear the song, and the song drives the experience. A different song, color grade, or edit would suggest a different mode of inhabiting the world.

Essenciais Swift has produced some of the most beautiful mashups. My favorite, "August," using a setting of *Call Me by Your Name* (fig. 12.2), is tainted by the Armie Hammer scandal, so readers may choose to watch others, including Swift's mashups of *Bridgerton* or *500 Days of Summer*.

12.2 Actor Timothée Chalamet expresses yearning.

The actors' expressions and gestures reflect distilled, often romantic emotions. But the incompletely witnessed rupture against unfolding processes suggest that beauty is continuously lost, tossed into the past, and the text creates additional losses. I've claimed that in music videos, lyrics fragment into isolated totems. The yellow Spanish subtitles unfold as a constant, dogmatic partner. They seem prescient; they're marking some upcoming point, both unavailable to me (as a non–Spanish speaker) and to the performers. Past, present, and future are all out of reach unless I can hold onto these tiny shards and find them again in my life.

To come to a better understanding, I run experiments on "August." Is it the yellow of the subtitles that are so beguiling, or is it the language? (Yes: yellow, not white; Spanish, not English or Chinese.) The text's placement? (Yes, not center frame—the text then can suggest characters' thoughts.) The period costumes and settings? (Yes, not current.) The actors? (Yes, not *Gone Girl*'s opaque Rosamund Pike; the song embosses these actors' open, chiseled faces.) The singing? (Yes, not Lana Del Rey or Billie Eilish.) Now I see Swift's craft more fully. It's blank, beautiful, empty, yet fragile, like the performers and the subtitles; she could make lovely ASMR recordings.

Looking more closely at these clips can help us reconsider our concepts of audiovisual relations including notions of diegesis and congruity as well as the ways viewers identify with audiovisual media. Film-music scholars like Anahid Kassabian, David Neumeyer, Holly Rogers, Jeff Smith, Robynn Stillwell, Ben Winters, and James Buhler have written extensively on the nondiegetic/diegetic divide, but their focus has been film music. (A simple definition of musical diegesis is sound and music that emanates from the film's world, as against superimposed scored music. Some scholars describe diegesis as music the characters can hear.)[12] At many levels, the sound and image within these mashups offer gaps, break away, and recombine. These mashups' fragmented images prevent a viewer's consistent engagement in a film's world, and a music video–like pop song may not pull viewers fully into the diegesis. Rather, a music video viewer is a partner in search of a path through the image alongside the music. This experience differs from narrative film's passages that elicit absorption.[13]

I've found the concept of diegesis little helpful for understanding music video. (Well, it looks like the band's playing but they're lip-syncing to playback; is this the kind of a place where the song might appear?) Perhaps I need new terms. "Immersion" is useful; "absorption" could work nicely too.[14] Sometimes I'm aware that there's both a soundtrack and visuals or I'm considering the production team's artifice, and at others I'm swept into the world of audiovisuality, fully interpolated. With these mashups I start with noting, "Here's another attempt to place a song against these edits," and then suddenly the music's describing the character's interiority—pulse, blood flow, sentiment. Then I'm out again. "Focalization" might be a useful term for when I'm so close to the characters, but focalization describes the characters' feelings, attitudes, and perspectives. I sense that the characters and I are creating a shared moment together. The character is coming into being. This is different.[15]

Artifice is also a good descriptor. Whether sound and image are synced or asynchronous, they can still share a common approach. Film director Jean-Luc Godard explores such Brechtian relationships extensively. (For example, in Godard's *Prenom Carmen* from 1983, sound and image are often unsynced. At one moment a string quartet saws away violently on their instruments; at another, the characters run around and collide in the manner of Buster Keaton-inspired slapstick, and I think viewers form a connection.)[16] Immersion and artifice are measures for "Apeshit," "Paparazzi," and "Tints" (chapters 6, 7, and 10, respectively). Do these images depart far from a perceived center? How well does the music inhabit this space? Does the image and music do this similarly?

The performers' entrancing faces play a vital role with facilitating immersion. They can illuminate a range of songs as the music drapes over them. Barthes grieved that the handsomest faces were of the past—Greta Garbo, Marlene Dietrich, Louise Brooks.[17] But it's not true. Today's stars—Phoebe Dynevor, Regé-Jean Page, Keira Knightley, and Matthew

Macfadyen—can be as bewitching as anything we knew. Many songs work well against the same shots and edits of performers' expressions and gestures. Each one encourages me to form a new picture of what the actors are feeling—their heartbeats and bloodflow, their levels of anxiety, feelings of attention, attitude, and corporeal weight—what neuroscience calls valence and intensity. How is it possible that *Pride and Prejudice* can work well for a sultry cover of Beyoncé's "Crazy in Love," which is slowed down to 30 beats per minute, Taylor Swift's rushing, sprightly "Goldrush," and the flippant, nonchalant "Thank You, Next," by Ariana Grande? Even Børn's glamrock "Electric Love" resonates (fig 12.3). I'm mapping all this onto the figures, even though I know that these varied states can't be simultaneously true for what the actor is feeling! I gauge that we have no idea about what people we encounter are feeling—though in each case I believe the music captures the actors' feelings as the clip unfolds. I suspect we are multiple and that we also fail to fully grasp what we're projecting. Our notions of ourselves and others might be reassessed: they may be but guesses.

Mashups can foreground gaps between the faces and the songs. Prosumers tend to draw on the same excerpts, like *Pride and Prejudice*'s Elizabeth standing on a cliff, releasing Darcy's hand, gazing moonily at him, or looking up at a chandelier. These same clips are cut repeatedly against similar songs, most often with an alternative or pop singer (of either gender) keen-

12.3 Ariana Grande's song and the cut-out text make the clip jaunty.

ing in a neutrally gendered falsetto. With such similar content, slight deviations can be compared. Overall, the actors' faces within these filmic melodramas are more consumed by heightened emotions than we expect in ordinary life; they're also far from musicians' expressions as conveyed in music video. My guess is that there's a difference between accessing emotions as an actor and when performing as a musician. In a narrative context the actor responds directly to a character or object (a faithless lover or a letter that portends ill); the actors have real targets to fixate on, and their expressions are sharply etched. It's unclear whether music can evoke emotions like grief, jealousy, or anger that bind to real people and objects.[18] Susan Langer and some musicologists have claimed that music can elicit quotidian emotions, but with a difference—music's patterns and intensities work as abstractions.[19] Nicholas Cook has suggested that music's emotional messaging may either be too specific, or that music is too vague in its pointings for us to be certain what's really going on.[20] When a pop song washes over these actors, with both expressing different kinds of intensified emotions, there may be a mismatch that the viewer tries to breach.

Which songs work particularly well with particular films? Again, there are so many mashups that we could conduct a quantitative survey (the corpus includes thousands of clips). There seem to be only one or two that baldly replicate the song's affect, and I find them less evocative. (Consider Rhodes's "Let It All Go" for *Pride and Prejudice*—the singer's anxiety matches that of the actors, and I feel if I cross my eyes I can see the actors rehearsing in everyday clothes.) If we take this observation as a bare ground, then a song not only brings out something in the characters, but also colors them as well. Sometimes a star musician's full catalog cleaves to a particular film. Lana Del Rey works beautifully with the film *Anna Karenina*, but less so with *Pride and Prejudice*, though both star Keira Knightley. My guess is that Del Rey's songs present a flattened melancholy that resonates with the doomed Russian adulterers Anna and Count Vronsky. I think connections here bind through local parameters—Lana Del Rey's lush, heavy arrangements drape well over *Anna Karenina*'s sets, which are stuffed with furs, silks, and satins. There's a texture and line to these costumes, a sense of thickness, and a color palette (*Karenina* is cool and densely saturated). Try to imagine something thinner, more translucent, and brighter here, like Taylor Swift. Likewise, Swift plays well with *Pride and Prejudice* but not *Anna Karenina*. Swift and Del Rey both strike me as projecting similarly older kinds of femininity but different vulnerabilities. Many critics have noticed that Del Rey mines a 1950s zeitgeist. Interestingly, *Karenina*'s costume designer said she drew inspiration from 1950s couturists, who at the time were incorporating styles from *Anna Karenina*'s 1870s moment.[21] Is it too much to claim that the music and image of *Karenina* mashups both reference the 1950s, but each medium does so from a slightly different angle?

Lana Del Rey is the favored accompaniment for these mashups. Is it her retro sense? An "I'm not playing along," which acknowledges the audiovisual breach? Or, romantics are also melancholics?

My perspective on audiovisual aesthetics has shifted since working with these assemblages. I might describe music and image as often glancing. I've chosen to study mashups drawn from four costume dramas: *Bridgerton*, *Little Women*, *Pride and Prejudice*, and *Anna Karenina*. All have a core set of elements, which may help to explain why they cut so well: close-ups of lingering, yearning faces, hand-holding, kissing and embracing, brisk walking, and dancing. Most often these mashups present the same shots ordered differently, with offset edit points, and somewhat similar soundtracks. In one instance a song against the images projects an overall attitude toward a setting; another might foreground characters' micro-expressions; another focuses our attention on general bodily comportment. Audiovisual relations bring forth new aspects. Music and image seek one another out, and each, now joined, illuminates something new about both the song and the images. Focusing on congruence and incongruence as a measure of music–image relations here seems too blunt, even gauche. Every clip contains both congruity and incongruity, and the proportions are not easily measurable.

There's a sizable group of scholars who have explored questions of congruence and incongruence, including David Ireland and Philip Tagg.[22] Much of their work emphasizes incongruity, especially when they turn to close analysis. Examples include the use of "Singing in the Rain" in Stanley Kubrick's *A Clockwork Orange* (1971), when hoodlums terrorize an elderly couple in their home; the torture scene in Quentin Tarantino's *Reservoir Dogs* (1992) with Stealers Wheel's "Stuck in the Middle with You"; the use of Vivaldi's *Winter* concerto from *Four Seasons* during the scene of dental torture in Park Chan-wook's *Oldboy* (2005); and the moment in Tarantino's *The Hateful Eight* (2015) with David Hess's "Now You're All Alone," when an aged loner hunts down a victim hiding in a shed. Since these are all violent, and I rarely enjoy such depictions, I don't wish to dwell for long with these clips, regardless of Tarantino's claims that they're the best part of movies (though I have analyzed an exuberant and bloody car crash from Tarantino's *Grindhouse*).[23]

I experience all these clips as congruent. All exude a balletic air. With "Stuck in the Middle with You," the pop song's music box wind-up sounds work nicely with Mr. Blonde's driven, sadistic nature. It can be oddly comforting that the music sounds a little crazier than he appears (as if the soundtrack marks an upper limit). Mr. Blonde also dances appropriately, shuffling with a bit of jauntiness. The lyrics also match: Mr. Blonde has created his own micro-world with his victim, and he can imagine everyone on the outside ("clowns to the left of me, jokers to the right").[24] The "Singing in the Rain" sequence from *Clockwork Orange* depicts someone who vacillates between joyous singing and dancing to merciless kicking and beating. I don't engage much with true crime (except for David Fincher's films and streaming series like *Zodiac* and *Mindhunter*), but I know that murderers can relish abusing their victims. In *Hateful Eight*, the killer who trundles outside in the snow to find a last man to shoot could be paired with "Now You're All Alone" to draw attention to a repressed side of himself. Perhaps when younger he may have wanted community; perhaps some part of him still wishes to be back inside with the other men. The techniques I've used for schematizing, mixing, and matching across this book help here. The solitary mood established through *Hateful Eight's* imagery of gray sky and lonely walking alongside snow dabbed with blood resonates with the song. Spring with grass and dandelions and buttercups would create a different effect.

Scholars may describe these scenes as incongruent because they disrupt decorum and sanctity, but real life doesn't follow these rules. We're multiple, and what comes forward is contingent. Everyone possesses a range of potentialities, from the vile to the virtuous. If one part is not in play it's in reserve, and the music can access that. Some theorists have argued that perceived incongruous sounds and images are attractive because the viewer must work harder to find a connection and create a synthesis.[25] But I don't think I need that; I just see these scenes as reflecting potentialities of a self. My analysis of Matt Mahurin's video for Peter Gabriel's "Mercy Street" (1986) makes the point that the song sounds like a lullaby, but the images are horrific: drowning, electrocution, abandonment, and suicide. One can make up all kinds of stories: the protagonist is reverting to fantasies of childhood, is having a bad dream, is finding solace in death and suicide.[26] Kendrick Lamar's and Anderson .Paak's music video "Tints" (chapter 10) also has a strong affective mix. The song is ebullient, yet many images are painful.

These mashups can create complicated depictions of experience, perspective, and especially time. As mentioned, when they work, the songs seemingly describe characters' thoughts and feelings; I catch glimpses of expressions incompletely experienced by them. The characters are moving forward too quickly for them to fully register these instantaneous glints, and the same is true for viewers and the production team. Note how in a *Pride and Prejudice* mashup Darcy's triple eye twitch plays against his repeated call of "I love you" to Elizabeth. And while the song describes the characters' internal emotions, it can also capture something synoptic about the context: the era, the full set of characters, the larger narrative arc. The song faces two ways—toward a bird's-eye view and an expression's flicker, though everything is fading fast.

Some pop songs could be said to possess two or more temporal streams. In Billie Eilish's "Ocean Eyes" and Taylor Swift's "August" and "Willow," the singers seem to bob above the arrangement, not quite taken up by it, with the accompaniment flowing along at a temporally slower pace. A visual correlate might be a swimmer moving more quickly than a river's current. The two senses of time create a fragile sense of nostalgia, because nothing can be perceived from a single vantage point, and time continues to unfold. For there are in truth three perspectives—the song's arrangement, the singer's voice, and the viewer's own rhythms.

This phenomenon becomes even more complicated and potent with these film mashups because music seems to seek out both the characters' states and a more synoptic point of view. Consider "Willow" and "Ocean Eyes" as part of mashups with *Pride Prejudice* and *Anna Karenina*. These clips feel dense and saturated. Then ponder clips with songs that could be described as temporally more one-dimensional or simultaneous, like Lana Del Rey's "Summer Nights" (*Anna Karenina*) and Ellie Goulding's "Love Me Like You Do" (*Pride and Prejudice*). Lyrics' associations with time help shape our sense of it: in the flattened versions, these lyrics point to a distinct moment. Again, in all of these, whether temporally more complicated or simple, the music can powerfully color the bodies and suggest what's going on inside the performers—feelings, the heartbeat, the skin's flush, and so on.

Three formal strategies help place sound, lyrics, and text in relation, thereby solidifying the mashup's structure. First, dialogue. In these clips, a phrase or two from the film's original recorded dialogue can jut out repeatedly. Perhaps these repetitions work as moments to bind streams together—arrangement, lyrics, dialogue, and image—bringing all of them into momentary focus, and thereby providing a kind of resting place or spot to reset. ("Oh yes," senses the viewer, "I know Mr. Darcy.") Second, the song's lyrics also occasionally come to the fore, catching something in the image. Swift sings "Take my hand," and then Knightley's hand reaches forward. In an *Anna Karenina* mashup we hear the lyrics "I look in the mirror," and we see Knightley reflected near a mirror's border. Third, text is also often imprinted as a showy font on the image, and it might catch the lyrics, dialogue, or another aspect of the story. The placement, size, and choice of the fonts becomes an expressive element, just like editing, color, rhythm, or costume.

Color schemes also play a strong role. For *Pride and Prejudice* some prosumers push hues to deep saturation, nearly pure blacks against whites with daubs of blues and greens—a reduction—or they honey the gold and earth-toned hues so they become cloying. Periodically over- and undersaturating color is common (at certain moments light, others dark). There can be an emphasis on texture. In a Rihanna "Love the Way You Lie" mashup for *Pride and Prejudice*, etched lines showing off the film's grain streak across the image like rain. All of these, lyrics, dialogue, and texture seem to carry meanings. The singer contributes here too. The voice projects equanimity. It often stays between the two romantic characters, without identifying too much with either. The music feels fluid, adopting a position of oversight. Sometimes, for example, there's a male, sometimes a female, covering Lana Del Rey's "Summertime Sadness" or Beyoncé's "Crazy in Love." The singer's gender doesn't much matter.

These mashups have also changed my relationships to performers and songs. I wasn't a Taylor Swift fan, but now I'm sensitized to her oeuvre's range and I've become enamored with several of her songs. Maybe she is like the stars' faces: her song is like a face. It's got an open architecture, which is also perhaps a bit unspecific. Her songs seem to span the frequency spectrum, coating the entire image (there's often a white-noise sound in her tracks). They also have a sense of transparency and fragility. I've learned to admire actor Matthew Macfadyen, in part due to his striking reflexes, how quickly he can dart his eyes while keeping his face immobile. Keira Knightley also has range (compare her sweet, youthful performance for *Pride and Prejudice* to the worn and jaded one in *Anna Karenina*).

Working with these mashups has helped my sense of audiovisual aesthetics. I've so learned these clips' iconography that if you give me a song, I believe I could conceive its mashup. I've been listening to a lot of Chaka Khan lately (my husband Charles Kronengold is writing about her), and it feels like a stretch, but I think I can guess which audiovisual relations might be most attractive. This tells me something about her singing and these films. I choose *Bridgerton* as best. Regé-Jean Page shares Khan's sexiness. Phoebe Dynevor seems waiflike, but with a touch of receptiveness that can pick up a lot. And I'm right! I draw on my new technique of schematizing, mixing, and matching through YouTube, running several of these mashups from my four films against Khan's gorgeous song "Clouds." My experiments teach me new things. Khan's singing now seems especially bittersweet, vacillating rapidly between joy and pain. Watch Page and Diviner closely and these emotions play quickly across their faces too. And taking a cue from Bridgerton's scene, those lyrics: "it's going to rain."

This might suggest an idea for the entertainment industry: directors once made screen tests of their actors to see how they worked on film. Now they might take a different, less costly tack: they could shoot a scene and encourage prosumers to edit it against a variety of pop songs. The actors who perform well under the widest range of conditions should be hired.

These mashups also shift my center of ground with cinema. A film must be comprised of many parameters all pointing in the same direction—gestures, color, cinematography, costumes. Each probably has an identifiable curve that meshes with others to form a voice. The same seems true for song: thus Del Rey rather than Swift works with *Karenina*, and Swift rather than Del Rey works with *Pride and Prejudice*. This may be because there are broad sweeps across surfaces that then connect sound and image. It's something about the weight of each, the frequency or height content is pitched at, gesture, deportment, feel, ineffables. It matters too that these mashups are a prosumer's art practice. It's again the details, like where the edits fall and which song is chosen, that can convey something about the author—how nervous or frightened, eager or desperate they are about relationships. A voice comes through. As with a music video director, a perspective can be gleaned.

Where might we place these mashups within existing genres? I might call most of them lyric videos, but leaving out those that don't have text on screen seems odd. It's time for new definitions.[27] I once described music video as sound and image devoted to selling a song, but now I think it's mostly an audiovisual object that draws our attention to the soundtrack. Or better still: it's an object we recognize as simply having audiovisual relations. And if "lyric videos" were originally designed to sell the song before the release of the "official" video, now we might include clips that fold in text (also heard rather than printed). Mashups, through a long chain of connections, bear a connection to text, for they originated as novels.

Recent neuroscience research can enrich our understanding of mashups and audiovisual relations. When the subtitles are in a different language (and I've encountered everything from Korean to Russian to Arabic), am I tickling the parietal lobe, a part of the brain that specializes in processing nonnative language? Or the superior colliculus, a part of the thalamus that amplifies indistinct or confusing sensory signals? Do these boosts enhance my aesthetic experience?

YouTube's algorithms have haunted me. First a *Pride and Prejudice* clip arrived, which I watched, and then the platform kept at it. Slowly, then picking up speed, more and more *Pride and Prejudice* mashups and then some *Anna Karenina* and *Little Women* popped up in my feed. Many of these had millions of hits. Over time, dolled up postclassical versions cropped up—with rapid editing, postproduction effects, sometimes the soundtracks mashed up. But why would these surface late? And why would the algorithm send me clips in clusters? I thought I had seen all of "Call Me by Your Name," but after I passed through a collection on *Little Women*, some of the most beautiful and committed "Call Me by Your Name" clips started arriving. These clips' appearances don't correlate to upload dates (whether I saw something from 2008 or 2020 seemed random).

I'm probably not Googling the right words, but I also can't find internet documentation on these romantic costume-drama mashups, though the phenomenon is huge. I've learned to use search terms like "mix," the film's name, and actor's name. I find some hashtags, such as #fanvidfeed. This hub hosts 97,000 clips by prosumers. I feel I just wandered into this corpus. But what am I not seeing because of YouTube's algorithms, and how does the algorithm envision me? What subcultures am I missing?

I hope readers become excited about these mashups. Patience is helpful. Many clips are amateurish or rote (my collection exceeds four hundred), but a few are some of the most beautiful media objects I've experienced.[28] I love them as much as any music video or film I've encountered, perhaps even more.

Brief audiovisual forms like TikTok videos and mashups can be siblings of music videos. As mentioned, a Bridgerton mashup riffs on Ariana Grande's music video "Thank U Next." Her "Monopoly" music video fits on TikTok. The mashup's and TikTok's audiovisual aesthetics are a function of their contexts: TikTok's vertical, hand-held, cellphone framing, length, prosumer interface, and platform might lead to this genre's look and feel (though there are also cross-cultural differences). TikTok and period-romance mashups are rhythmic, even musical. Elements jut out—a face with an edit, a smile, a duck's fluttering tail. Especially with TikTok I feel I'm peering in on a certain type of personhood, an American voice, and through virality, a community.

v New Modes of Analysis: Industry

13 Carol Vernallis, Jonathan Leal, Eric Weidt, and Aubrey Woodiwiss

The Art of Color Grading

> It is the business of the eye to make colored forms out of what is essentially shimmering. —Maggie Nelson, *Bluets*

COLOR IS ELUSIVE. Ephemeral, mysterious, and extravagant, it resides somewhere and nowhere—an interplay of culture, eye, brain, object, context, and light. Philosophers and artists have worked for thousands of years to understand, explain, and even mobilize its complexities, turning to color to illumine social, religious, biophysical, and technological systems, mechanisms, and processes. While recent research efforts across disciplines have produced striking new transdisciplinary knowledge claims, for contemporary media scholars interested in industry, questions still remain.[1] How does color actively *work* on viewers? How does it guide thoughts and feelings in relation to music and moving images? And how do artist-practitioners think about these questions, particularly as they work with the digital media so ubiquitous today?

This chapter offers a chance to ponder these questions and learn more about color and audiovisual aesthetics with the help of professional color grader Aubrey Woodiwiss. In the process, Jonathan Leal and I aim to address a lacuna in media studies—the discussion of color in relation to music and moving images—as well as articulate a need for more industry-engaged scholarship.[2]

As a color grader, Woodiwiss has worked in multiple genres with a wide range of performers—music videos with top-tier pop stars like Beyoncé, Jay-Z, Calvin Harris, James Blake, FKA twigs, ZAYN, and others; feature films like *Troy* (2004) with Brad Pitt; commercials for Nike, Calvin Klein, Honda, and Lincoln. Over the years, his hands-on experiences have taught him novel ways to see and engage with color. As we interviewed him for this piece, we were curious to learn: What do graders see when they view color in the world and on screen? How might everyday viewers calibrate their eyes to see things a little more richly—perhaps even as graders do?

We take up these questions in conversation with Woodiwiss by turning to three music videos he has graded: FKA twigs's "Cellophane," ZAYN's "The Entertainer," and Beyoncé's "Formation." After a brief consideration of scholarly literature on color across the arts, humanities, and sciences, we direct our attention to these three music videos and respond to their colors through audiovisual analysis. Next, we document Woodiwiss's responses to these clips. A final section, drawn from our interviews with Woodiwiss, gives a sense of his general approach to the craft. By alternating our analysis with Woodiwiss's reflections, we aim to highlight the overlaps and differences in our ways of approaching the same audiovisual materials: where our analysis provide more traditional scaffoldings on which readers can hang their own ideas, Woodiwiss's reflections focus more on individual images, which illuminate his process as an artist. These readings speak to one another through overlaps and departures, the interpretations suggesting a range of possible paths. Music videos, because they're brief and open, facilitate illumination of varied approaches to production and criticism across works.

Speaking with Woodiwiss and analyzing his work has taught us a great deal about how to track color in film, and by extension, in our everyday lives. It's our hope that by engaging with these music videos, our analysis, and Woodiwiss's insights, readers will discover their own routes through the ideas and materials—and most importantly the colors around them.

Color and Color Grading

Specialists across a range of disciplines have been fascinated by color for millennia, though perhaps particularly so in recent years. Poet-theorist Maggie Nelson, in *Bluets*, has explored the entwined intimacies of language, color knowledge, visual media, and loss, using blue as a mirror, a pivot, a unifying thread.[3] In the 1950s, painter Josef Albers argued that "in visual perception," "a color is almost never seen as it really is—as it physically is," making color "the most relative medium in art."[4] Recently, interdisciplinary artist-neuroscientist Bevil Conway has illumined the relationships between cognition, color perception, and art practice, claiming convincingly that "it is the inventiveness of the artist's solution to the problem of color that contributes to the visual interest of their work, and their lessons for neuroscience."[5] Vision scientists Stephen Palmer and Karen B. Schloss, in their collaborative work, have explored how individuals' "ecological experiences with color-associated objects and events" shape "color preferences" over time.[6] Philosophers Alex Byrne and David Hilbert have argued in their collaborative writing for interpretations of color via reflectance physicalism.[7] Cinema theorists like John Belton have studied how color, film aesthetics, and technological affordance relate to one another, pronouncedly so in cases like the digital intermediate.[8] And philosopher Ludwig Wittgenstein, in one of his last works, *Remarks on Color*, exploded notions of color as unified, easily explainable phenomena, building on earlier philosophical projects and poet Johann Wolfgang von Goethe's *Theory of Colours*.[9]

Media scholars have also helped make new sense of the reverie and transfiguration color can produce. Steven Peacock's 2010 *Colour* turns to close criticism of classical and contemporary cinema to model ways of being "sensitive to patterns of meaning found in colour, from film to film, and from moment to moment in a film."[10] Richard Misek's 2010 *Chromatic Cinema* provides a "condensed history of color in film" that advances an argument that "black-and-white and color have permeated and referenced each other throughout the history of cinema."[11] Edward Branigan's 2018 *Tracking Color in Cinema and Art: Philosophy and Aesthetics* turns to film, painting, photography, and literary writing to arrive at new phenomenological understandings of color's relationality, arguing that color in film "should be evaluated as a *temporal pattern* that may build from shot to shot and from moment to moment."[12] And the two of us, Jonathan and Carol, have each written on color as related to audiovisuality, new media technologies, race, and pop cultural production, asking what color, in combination with music and moving images, can help us see on screen and in our worlds.[13]

Nevertheless, we haven't found many accessible color studies of individual film media, let alone color-focused audiovisual analysis of films—analyses that considers color alongside the soundtrack, cinematography, and editing. We also haven't seen many one-on-one collaborations with industry practitioners that focus on how they interpret and shape the materials they work on (and that billions of people watch). In this chapter, then, we'll focus on three music videos that allow for close examination but should also be useful across media. As we watch them, we ask: How and why do sound, image, and color form relationships in our minds?[14] Why do some combinations produce the affects they do? And what can color teach us about the past, present, and future of media and popular culture—particularly as we enter a new and unruly decade of convergence and precarity?

Part of the initial difficulty in answering these questions goes back, in part, to language and media specificity. Color, like music, eludes (and therefore challenges) written and spoken text. Like music, color pushes viewers into uncomfortable linguistic situations, nudging descriptions into the ad hoc, improvisatory, and metaphorical.[15] As we seek to label the ways in which color—changed by surfaces, light, and texture—seems to mark us, imprinting affects, shades, and traces on us, we often fumble creatively, attempting to bridge everyday vocabularies and the granular subtleties of embodied knowledge. As artist David Batchelor puts it: "To work with color is to become acutely aware of the insufficiency of language and theory—which is both disturbing and pleasurable."[16]

For a professional color grader, though, the experience is a little different. As Woodiwiss explains later in this piece, graders not only work with industry parlance—proximal descriptions supplied by artists and directors—but also with precise, innovative visual technologies built to deliver fast results for clients with hard deadlines. Graders work at all scales, from single pixels to entire films. Through color they actively create and shape our senses of objects and people on screen, where they're placed in the visual field, whether or not we notice them immediately. In the digital realm, graders often have to shape objects from the ground up (e.g., making wood or stone more like the materials we recall). Color graders synthesize scientific, technical, artistic, and industry knowledges into visual works that move viewers emotionally. And graders like Woodiwiss, who often work in music video and cinema, also do so in relation to sound and music; they use color as an interpretive tool for generating meaning and affect.

So what can we learn from working to see like a grader sees? What can color grading—something for which there's scant fanfare and no Academy Award—teach us about cinematic and everyday experience? What can it reveal about how color tells us where to look, what to value, how to feel? What is the art of color grading?

FKA twigs: "Cellophane"

Jonathan and Carol's Reading

FKA twigs's "Cellophane" (2019) is a study in gradual, smooth transitions. Musically the song is slow, dirge-like, propelled by repeated melodic lines and repeated questions: "Didn't I do it for you? . . . When all I do is for you?" The arrangement is spare, driven by twigs's arresting voice, a subtly processed piano, a whisper-soft beatboxer—and, at the song's climax, a bass drum coordinated with subtle, sampled strings. Using only two chords—Dmaj7 and Gmaj7—the song's harmony is plagal, wistful, yearning (fig. 13.1).

For a contemporary music video, the setting, too, is bare. A room revolves, resembling a rotor amusement park's ride. Eventually its top and bottom drop out, and mirrored surfaces add both visual interest and spatial disorientation. A pole in the set's center invites twigs to dance. Paired with the visuals, her voice's smooth slides between notes (portamenti) create a slow, spinning feel, which is supported by the camera's circling movements. Sheer curtains partially drape the perimeter. A mechanical clicking sound rationalizes the dancer's confinement: a music box. As we watch, we're unsure where to place ourselves. Are we participants among the proscenium crowd (note the roaring applause at 0:29)? Are we voyeurs with privileged access? As twigs sings about desiring privacy, about not wanting to suffer others or be gazed upon, we see her on display in a space that at times feels miniaturized.

As the video progresses, twigs ascends her dance pole, climbing up through a mirror-like, illuminated ceiling and into the heavens (the clouds reminiscent of Giovanni Batista Tiepolo's *Olympus or the Triumph of Venus* [1764]) to greet a surreal, mechanical bird wearing several humanoid masks (fig. 13.2). As twigs looks on, the machine's masks unlatch and unfurl, revealing a single human face resembling twigs's own. On impulse, twigs tries to kick the contraption away, but it quickly absorbs her before fracturing and dissolving—note the brittle, glass-cracking audio sample—sending her tumbling downward into a void, and, eventually, into brick-red mud.

From start to finish, the video's narrative arc feels Dantesque: twigs, gazing up from purgatory toward a celestial cloudscape—Beatrice, perhaps?—then falling into a dark underworld. But unlike in Dante's *Inferno*, in "Cellophane," these depths aren't punishing, but rather cleansing, even peaceful. As twigs lies prostrate after her fall, silent inhabitants donning intricate masks and rich eye makeup crawl to her and spread thick mud across her skin, suggesting a purification ritual, an empathy rite. This scene, the last we see, feels tender, collective.

With this in mind, how does color function throughout the video and contribute to its narrative? We can hypothesize answers by following color in a few ways: through scene-based colorscapes, colors on specific objects, colors carried across objects, and color contrasts and relations.

13.1 "Cellophane," 0:50. twigs stretches skyward against a mirrored floor and sheer, green-lit curtains, her blue sash swaying at her hip.

13.2 "Cellophane," 2:23–2:31. twigs ascends skyward toward an emerald-tinted machine.

First, colorscapes. As one watches "Cellophane" one sees colors morph gradually but noticeably, which creates a sense of five distinct colorscapes: 1) umber, sienna, tawny, and ochre; 2) creamy whites and beiges with emerald green; 3) a greenscape; 4) a cooler, lightly tinted, midtone blue, pink, and black darkening into a dull, brownish red; and finally, 5) a deeply shaded orange-red, a dark rust. Each of these shapes the ways we respond to twigs's music and moving images. A different sequencing of these five colorscapes—inverting their order of appearance, for instance—would undoubtedly generate different responses.

The colors' objects make a difference, too; the objects and patches of color in one scene's colorscape often foreshadow those of the next, linking different moments and spaces, creating a sense of seamlessness. See twigs's blue sash, for example: strung across her hip, coming slightly forward in the midst of her fall, creating continuity as she spins through the video's contrasting sections. (Color and music share processes here; like twigs's blue sash, two common pitches in "Cellophane," D and F#, are sustained and recontextualized across the song's oscillating chords, bridging the music's harmonic spaces.)

The color green, in particular, also foreshadows developments and creates continuities across objects, surfaces, and scenes. During the video's opening, translucent, prismatic, green lights flash across the screen; a sheer green also projects onto the curtains' hems. As twigs starts dancing, her shoes and pole pick up the green, carrying it forward. As twigs spins, our eyes start searching within the frame for that green and find it mixed in with her red and gold lace—all of which prepares us for the glinting metallic reds, golds, and greens of the mechanical bird at 2:26. Then, as twigs begins her fall at 2:44, the background against which her body tumbles transitions from bluish-white into a sustained foamy green before slowly fading to black. Eventually, at the video's end, the healers' green-smeared foreheads and twigs's shiny green fingernail polish complete the thread and recall the video's opening.

In terms of color contrasts and relations, the broadest arc in "Cellophane" is a three-part movement: warm, cool, warm. The clip opens with a palette of brown earth-tones. In the video's second quarter, the colorscape shifts: the mechanical monster's green, gold, and red jewels shine against the white and beige clouds. twigs then briskly falls through a greenscape to midtone blacks with cooler, shiny pinks and blues, which transition to a duller, warmer, orange-red mud (fig 13.3). By the end, the oscillation between warm and cool shades has made us feel as if we've been somewhere, done something.

13.3 "Cellophane," 3:44–3:56. Healers spread thick orange-red mud across twigs's fallen body.

Interestingly, concerning color contrasts: gentle transitions and careful color grading end up softening the boundary between foreground and background, individual and setting. twigs's skin against the curtains at the clip's opening, for instance, or the rusty, reddish mud spread over her body at the end—these both play with differentiation and nondifferentiation. It's an interesting touch for a music video, given that the genre often emphasizes individuals against backgrounds, bringing them forward, close.

What do all of these color techniques do for us, to us? Why do they feel right? How does color elicit connections, sequences, foreshadowings, and recollections?

Woodiwiss Discusses His Color Grade

"Cellophane" is a linear journey. The piece starts in one place, and twigs, like Alice going down the rabbit hole, ends up in another.

Clients often tell me they want me to do my thing, but honestly, I don't know what that is. I'm more interested in responding to the piece's specifics. What room are we in? What is unique to this film? With twigs in "Cellophane," she's such a strong artist, she's the main character. Director Andrew Thomas Young was a 3-D artist before, with a background in

CG, so he's quite specific. But with color, for some reason, that's one of the hardest things for people to articulate. A few of the old British directors who had a background in telecine, like Luke Scott, could say, "I want four points exposure, two points contrast, one point yellow." But, that's unusual.

I think "Cellophane" initially comes across as simple, but actually, it's quite complex. Yes, it's about a linear journey, but I also see twigs as placed in a kind of neural link, or perhaps a brain. The whole piece breathes as if it's biometric. I played with the fact that it's like an organism.

Originally, the curtains were a single, warm monotone. The lights had no colors. And so I added emerald tones to the bottoms of the curtains. (Technically, this was difficult, as twigs goes through them.) I did this because I always try to add range to an image. Range gives it substance, and the viewer something more to hang onto. I knew I wanted to stay warm, but that I also needed to break up that warmth a bit. And the emerald not only worked tonally, but also narratively. The green adds emotion to the scene and makes us more sympathetic to twigs. It also helped connect her skin tone, which has this silky, velvety visual quality, and the video, as I previously mentioned, is like a velvety, living and breathing brain. It's like that until she encounters this biomechanical god.

A lot of "Cellophane"'s grade was technical. I had only seven hours to link the green of the drapes, pole, costuming, floor, and monster across shots. At 1:27, the lighting doesn't extend across twigs's straightened leg on the mirrored floor, because I had to protect her from the background. I think the way I did it works well, especially considering the time constraint.

Emerald, when we look at it from a scientific point of view, is a green-blue-cyan-ish tone, but when we talk about it from an emotional space, it's, well, an emerald, a gem. Because twigs is such a strong artist, and she's so heavily involved with the video's conception, the story, to me, adopts a mythical quality—she goes into the forest to discover herself. There's this magical, unobtainable, emerald stone behind her, and we need to accompany her into the forest to conquer our fears, slay the dragon, cross the threshold, and get the gold. A hero's journey.

I kept the emerald and gold going on her costume and a bit in her hair. Gold is not a color, right? It's a brightness thing, a luminance, a textural thing. Gold is like this green-y, yellow-y, red, orange; it's leaning more in those yellows, it's like a duo-tone thing, it's not one block color. It's more textured and complex. The director and I worked closely to achieve a sense of gold that's tangible.

To punch up the details of her dress, I brought up the gold again, and I bounced in some emerald. I did this with twigs's curls, too. The director and I overlaid the opening flashing lights.

And twigs's skin is great. It didn't need a lot. Often when I work on skin, I narrow the palette and sometimes blur to clean up the skin, but twigs is luminous. She didn't need it. I added a little bit of warmth, that's all.

Almost all of the time I spend grading, I'm listening to ambient or techno music (I listen to the music video's soundtrack before I start the grade), but the last 10 percent I grade for audiovisual connections. Audiovisual touches or punches give me a chance to take some poetic license. When twigs goes up the pole, the music shifts—the audio has this "ahh," there's more lift—and I turned the sky above her hazy to respond to that. My visuals have more lift, too: I've reinforced a sonic and emotional shift through this haze and the halo at the top of the pole. The pole has some touches of green that are darker than the curtains. So, again, this video is a breathing thing. The mechanical monster's greens also creep in and out, including on its wings. When the monster appears, we're in a different setting or space—not the same room—and I used this new environ to establish a new emotion.

Everything in "Cellophane" is shifting and warping. The spaces aren't hard, they're changing. Even at the end scene, there's a transition in the brick reds of the color grade—more yellows come in tonally.

This video won a phenomenal number of awards, including for cinematography, editing, and visual effects, but not for color. It's funny. On this one, as opposed to many other awards I've received, I strongly feel I deserved it. This was a really, really complicated color grade.

ZAYN: "Entertainer"

Jonathan and Carol's Reading

While "Cellophane" has a smooth arc—it begins at a midpoint, ascends toward the heavens, then falls into mud—ZAYN's "Entertainer" (2018) is choppier: flashforwards, flashbacks. Motivic threads of color bridge gaps across narrative settings and moments, creating continuities among intercut materials that help ground us. Melodic curves trace or chase undulating bodies through the frame—a hip turn, a hand passing over a body, a head turning, and another—connecting shot to shot. We're carried slowly through the video by color, gesture, and melody.

Musically, "Entertainer" is marked by a duality: a relaxed, atmospheric set of elements (warm bass tones, relatively slow harmonic rhythm, excluding the bridge), lush harmonies, long, subtle reverbs; and a driving set of elements (crisp hi-hat samples, a lightly syncopated rhythmic motif [3 + 3+2], intricate percussion flourishes). This productive tension also plays out through ZAYN's vocals: while his lyrics are hostile—"When you need me the most, I will turn you down / Never seen me comin'"—his singing is a soft patter, a murmured lullaby, all gentle melodic contours. The color, pulling us through the clip, resolves neither the harsh nor smooth elements in the song and lyrics, thus creating a three-part structure. (The drive of the color, the harsher and gentler elements.)

Slow arcs and small subdivisions, gentle versus choppy, especially help us engage with the color's contrapuntal red and blue threads (figs. 13.4 and 13.5). Picture it: at the beginning of the video, a city skyline at dusk. Red-lit towers popping against a dusty, multicolored horizon. Then a hard cut to a club's exterior, bathed in the saturating light of red neon bulbs, palm fronds near-black in penumbral half shadow. Another hard cut to a blueish-white dressing room that highlights, by contrast, the pinkish red of a gown, lingerie, lipstick. Then we're back at the club's exterior, albeit now with more in view; neon-red illuminates the club's entrance, while a blueish-white background pushes that entrance forward. The orange-red tip of ZAYN's cigarette holds our eye as we follow him; a shot of a security guard's workstation reveals a grid of red and blue rooms; and eventually, through ZAYN, we enter the club and find it illuminated by red and blue lights.

Once inside the club we notice more subtleties. Colors, shadows, and profiles combine, rendering bodies and faces sculptural: sharp cheekbones, defined jawlines. (Note the magenta on three-quarters of the club manager's face, or a triangle of green on a dancer's cheek.) The darkest corners of the club's rooms never reach pure blacks, but rather deep, dusty greys. Just as in the soundtrack, the juxtaposition of contrasting elements—reds with baby blues, oranges with deep greens—becomes an identifying feature of the project as a whole.

As in FKA twigs's "Cellophane," in ZAYN's "Entertainer," colors are also passed from object to object, linking scenes and generating interpretive possibilities. For instance: the orange goldfish, the surveillance cameras' orange pricks of light, and the red tattoo on ZAYN's neck (tracing the number 25) all converge across ZAYN's face outside the bar as he watches his lover taken away. Or, the blueish-white of ZAYN's paramour: the blue of her dressing-room colorscape, styled hair, and fingernail polish. The brief flashes of bluish-white light that illuminate her as ominous premonitions. The ocean. The eventual appearance of a blue hotel-room door—ZAYN's exit, his lover's color echo (fig. 13.6).

13.4–13.5 "Entertainer," 0:11–0:30. Blues and reds link spaces, subjects, and surfaces.

Why do these colors work as well as they do? Why, for instance, does the orange-red falling on ZAYN's face throughout the video feel heavy, difficult? Does the color foretell loss and failure? Do the video's internal logics and repetitions—its pairing of reddish-orange with sex, surveillance, and permanent marking—shape our interpretation? Or does the color's power come purely from itself—its uniqueness, or its frequential relationship to blue, which sits at the opposite end of the color wheel?

By the video's end, ZAYN's lover has vanished. He's obliterated her. ZAYN stands outside the club, his face bathed in an orange and neon-red glow and his expression pained and bewildered. (The orange-red seems bound to shame.) Eventually ZAYN stands on a pier, gazing out at a sunlit ocean, the dawn a hazy yellow. As the music fades, we're left with a sense of fraught desire.

Woodiwiss Discusses His Color Grade

Unlike "Cellophane," "Entertainer" isn't a living, breathing thing. It's a day, or a night—a set time. The contrast is also very soft. Obviously, I adjusted shots in the different spaces to match, but we wanted this gentle

13.6 "Entertainer," 1:35–3:25. Blue carries across surfaces and scenes: television, door, and ocean.

consistency and mood. The director, David M. Helman, wanted to use soft contrasts—they're emotional.

With the grade, we're trying for something more interesting than linear, straight colors. The goal was something more subtle—little ebbs and flows of color, small shifts and interesting palettes. When we do a grade, we lock into one shot to set the palette for the whole project. With "Entertainer," we started by designing the video's look from the shot where Malik (ZAYN) is on the jetty, gazing at the sea. We altered that environment's natural palette, turning it into a yellower, warmer, slightly cyan space, rather than just a warm, red, sunny, orange day. We felt there was more interest that way. It gave the video a mood. It also worked well with the colors bounced in from the ocean and sky.

The video's other locations are the club interior and outdoor nighttime scenes. These have a similar base palette. I reworked the scenes to the best of my ability, but in the end, it's one stroke, one emotion, one color point of view. And then those hard reds. This is just something I like to do—get the reds deep and strong. If you play the whole video through, whenever we see a red, there's an opportunity to move that red, to work with it. Early in the video, we're outside in a space with a very bright, luminous red. We didn't want to make it too deep, out of respect for the environment. And then there's the magenta, the purply-red, and all the other variations.

When we were making this video, ZAYN was the biggest pop star in the world. So naturally, it was important that he looked good. We talked about how to achieve this. But he looks good naturally, so he didn't need much.

Because this was an artistic piece, the director and I had some freedom; the label wasn't much involved. So we experimented together.

Beyoncé: "Formation"

Jonathan and Carol's Reading

Beyoncé's "Formation" (2016) is dense, symphonic. The video's color motifs rise and fall while crossing one another, forming an intricate weave while complementing the visuals and soundtrack.

The song is segmented and percussive, comprised of blocklike cells of sound—the coiled spring–like sample repeating throughout (C, E♭); Beyoncé's vocal fry–heavy verses that sit between speech and song; and the speaker-rattling trap beat that drops at 1:45. There isn't much melodic variation in the vocals until 2:00 ("I see it, I want it"), which keeps us focused on the song's timbres and rhythms and the performers' physical gestures.

Like the music, the video's colorscapes come in blocks, although they're offset from the song's musical form. "Formation"'s moments of audiovisual synchrony don't always follow the song's verse-chorus-verse pattern, nor a linear, narrative logic like "Cellophane"'s; instead, patterning is more subterranean and intricate. In other words the song's sections and the video's visual segments are staggered (figs. 13.7 and 13.8).

This all has implications for the ways we interpret color. Unlike "Entertainer," where patches of reds, oranges, blues, and greens carry our attention across objects and surfaces, "Formation" features disparate colorscapes linked by pivots. (One example is Beyoncé's pinkish, orange-red fingernails at 3:00, which match the crawfish in the next shot, at 3:02, even though the backgrounds have little in common.)

During the video's opening a pure, bright yellow-orange appears four times, creating its own percussive thread over the music's syncopations.

13.7–13.8 "Formation," 0:28–1:06. A milky pink color thread unites scenes, subjects, and surfaces. The color scape comes in blocks.

THE ART OF COLOR GRADING   **279**

Then, a longer, milky pink runs across surfaces and scenes: from the young girls' dresses, to Beyoncé's hair and eyeshadow, to the interior portrait paintings, to a small duplex's pink doors. Later, blue forms a much longer color thread, uniting a variety of visual elements in the second half (note the parade participants' costumes and the blue-tinted dance sequence in a shopping-mall parking lot). And as these colors are introduced and carried forward, their threads entwining, their intensities are adjusted: a richer pink here, a less saturated version there; a deeper red and then a more subdued one. At some moments the colors are hyped up—the teal with the fluorescent lighting in the wig shop; the deep, purplish-blue of the drum major; the dark blue of the parade host. Sometimes the vibrant, center-weighted colors demand attention; at others, as small patches, or at the frame's edge, catch but a glimpse. And still at others, colors quiet down, giving viewers opportunities to catch their breath.

Two-thirds into "Formation" the overall color palette shifts to a baby blue, which shakes colors loose for the rest of the video; red gets passed from Beyoncé to a feathered Mardi Gras dancer, the blue from the CCTV filter to a host on a parade float. A range of pastels then enter the video's swirl, tinting flowers, masks, lace; eventually, a pink, dusky sky over a young Black dancer and imposing, militarized riot police calls to mind the video's opening: the girls' pink dresses, the duplex's pink doors.

How do these colors—the tangled threads and intercut colorscapes, their intricate formations—work on us as we watch? How do they shape the ways we hear the music, watch the moving visuals, and see Beyoncé?

Woodiwiss Discusses His Color Grade

First and foremost, Beyoncé's an artist and an extremely high-level professional—she's an incredibly hardworking woman who is extremely good at what she does. As an artist, she has very clear ideas about how she wants to look and be portrayed. She actually even has her own specific teams who help her with different aspects of the image, including what we call contour work, where the shape of the body is modified. Many viewers don't know about this aspect of the craft. In "Formation," I think the touches were done sensitively.

And Melina Matsoukas, the director of "Formation," is very visual. She's got a favorite palette. The colors she likes using are often desaturated; she also loves pinks and pastels. But on this and other projects we've worked together on, she gave me a lot of freedom with color.

13.9 "Formation," 1:17. The wig shop gives Woodiwiss room to explore.

"Formation" was shot on 35 millimeter film, with an ARRI Alexa for visual effects. This was fun, because I like working with film. And as opposed to the linearity of a video like "Cellophane," "Formation" involved different elements, times, and days. It was all intentional. And it gave me a lot of room to explore.

The wig shop is a nice example. When I look at a shot—and this is something I was trained to do, as well as something I teach clients and upcoming color graders about—I deconstruct the shot and look at ways to build it up. Here, we have two women, their skin tones, and their hair color. That's fundamentally what's building this shot. That's our map, our playground (fig. 13.9).

First, I set the key values. Then, I can start moving colors. Again, when I grade, I like to push colors further than they would normally go, and the wig shop's fluorescents gave me a chance to lean into unnatural tones, especially the teal hair color. The hair was originally much greener, probably a little blue. So, I isolated it. I took that information and narrowed the palette down.

Specifically, when I looked at that original hair color on my vector scope, it looked like a wide ball. So, I sharpened it. And when you sharpen, you remove separation. On my vector scope, the green-y, blue-y, and cyan-y tones narrowed, which allowed me to make the color more striking. I pierced the color through. The hair became a richer character, because it no longer had this range of broader, muddier tones.

And their faces, that was a tonal thing. If we look at the woman on the right, in the middle of her face, we can see there's now more light on it. I definitely put that light there. It draws us into her a little. The level of the white on her face is also a little higher than on her hand, which results in our eye being drawn through luminance to the light on her face, to the color in her hair.

As I mentioned with "Cellophane" and "Entertainer," in my grading, I try to capture the beauty and nuances of skin tones. Sometimes, that involves a rim or bounce light, a subtle glow added to the way something was shot. In this scene, I decided to keep the fine rim of shadow around this woman's hairline and face, which framed her nicely. I also brought up the orange a bit for the woman on the left's hair—I wanted to give her more character, to make her hair a little more poppy. But the woman on the right is our main focus.

Again, as a color grader, I'm always looking for what makes an image interesting, and "Formation" gave me a chance to explore possibilities, including giving individual images their own color palettes. I often like to divide color up between warmer and cooler tones across scenes, shots, and within the frame. I also play with levels of contrast, darks against lights, too. The wig shop's teal feels cool. It felt appropriate to make those gospel scenes the warmest in the piece. It felt right emotionally. It tapped into something (fig. 13.10).

Aubrey Woodiwiss Contextualizes Color Grading

I work in all formats—music videos, commercials, feature films. With music videos, a range of people are likely to be involved. The artist or musician—and I've worked with everyone from Beyoncé to James Blake—has different expectations about how they'd like to be portrayed. The director's vision also varies greatly. The music video commissioner,

13.10 "Formation," 3:51. Woodiwiss grades the video's church scenes warmly.

as an intermediary between the music and data-analytics people, has to be dealt with. Some have strong ideas, and then there's management, too. In part because there are so many people to contend with, a lot of color graders, including me, are just trying to get the job done, in the best way.

I'd consider myself an artist. I've also directed, shot second unit, and acted as an art consultant. I'm trying to do cool and interesting work, but I'm also an employed person, and decisions ultimately depend on the brief (the project's proposal). The work is also almost invariably fast: it's not unheard of to get a brief on Friday and be asked to send something back on Saturday. With a brief, let's say it's Nike, I make assumptions about the company, their values, and what I think they stand for. I assume I'm often hired because I'm a good judge of all this. We're not all sitting around discussing, "Where in the culture does this work fit?" Often we're just trying to get over the hurdles and across the finish line. But this speed can be good for my art. The eye acclimates to a color the longer it looks at it; I find it's easier to see what's really there if I work quickly.

The production process has two parts: online and offline. Offline is where the edit happens. You put everything you've shot—all your rushes, transferred to low-res—into one bin. You might have eight hours of footage that you edit on your music video's timeline down to three-and-a-half minutes. Once you have a locked edit, you give me the hi-res imagery and the EDL (the edit decision list). I don't pull in all the rushes, because everything on my system is at source-resolution. The system's powerful, but it's not efficient with lots of content—when grading, I only point at the bits I need.

Here's an example of an image currently on my timeline. I'd describe it as dense. You can see it seems quite thick, the blacks are quite heavy. It's also rich in contrast. Now, the image is made up of luminance and chrominance. Luminance is basically brightness, and chrominance is basically color. Those things are intrinsically related. So if I add contrast, I'm actually adding chroma, too. When I add contrast, I add color saturation as well.

These are concepts and processes I've internalized as I've worked these last twenty years. Originally, I was trained in London, in an older-school way. Many of the greatest colorists lived and worked in the city, and in England generally. But before 2008 it was a very tough, brutal environment. Directors Tony Scott, Ridley Scott, Tony Kay, Luke Scott, Jordan Scott were extremely eccentric, hardnosed, originally working-class people. When you trained in that environment, you felt like a Zen teacher would rap your knuckles if you did anything wrong. But when you finished, you had an understanding of the fundamentals, of how to balance the core elements: base levels, shadows, black levels. That's what color grading was back then, before everything became digital.

The tools we used were clunkier, too. We worked with telecine, we'd take the film negative, put it up on this big machine, lace it up, color correct it, and then lay it to tape. We used to have to work with labs. If visual effects were desired, you would have to cut the images out and take the film back to the lab to redo that segment. The terminology was simple: "exposure," "contrast," and "saturation" of red, green, and blue values, and you could express these with points. Now, we're working in a digital system, so the points don't relate. The precise methodology isn't there anymore, which is unfortunate, because precision is helpful.

It's easy for us to look at an image, for example, and say, "That image is bright," or "That image is dark." It takes more skill and methodological precision to ask, "Is that isolated color bright? Is it dark?" So as a color grader, I'm constantly translating. When someone's like, "I want that color richer," really, what they're saying is, "I want that color darker." And when someone says they want something pastel-y, really, what they're saying is they want it brighter.

Here's what I mean by this. When I work, I can create any color with red, green, and blue. Everything is derivative of those three values. If I want to create cyan, for instance, I just remove the red. And if someone says to me, "Say, can we just take away some red?" I know exactly what they want. That's precise. But say someone says, "I want a dark pink," that requires some translation. Because pink isn't a color; rather it relates to the brightness of a color. It's a bright magenta. When someone wants to experiment or starts talking about pastel tones, I have to translate what they're envisioning. I grade separate objects within the frame brighter or darker, because they seem to lean this way, and subsequently, they're perceived as more aesthetic. People want trees a darker green than they naturally are. And if a client's going to have trouble with a color, it's going to be green, because it's such a high wavelength. For me, red is a color I like darker. Emotionally, it feels better. It's richer.

Ever since digital cameras and technologies were created, designers have been trying to address the distance between digital and film—and to emulate film's natural qualities. But there's a big difference, of course. Film is an organic process. Digital tries to recreate it by reinterpreting the image, but it's not so clear cut. Film—even the raw, ungraded stuff—has a charm to it.

The difference between the two often comes down to the natural roll-off. If you look at my scopes here, I've taken a digital image and made it react like film. The blacks and whites are a little soft. I'm not actually touching the 100 percent black or white point. I'm using curves, most often with two to four points. This example is more of an S-curve, which would be logarithmic.

Whatever technology you're using, though, the art of color grading is the art of looking closely. When I look at my plant in my living room with the afternoon light shining on it through my open window, my eye can quickly work out what's in the image and what's not. (And the human eye, I should say, is powerful: it resolves somewhere between 6K or 10K, way better than any camera. HD is roughly 2K.) This ability to look closely can be improved. Mine gets sharper the more I grade. And the more honed my vision gets, the better prepared I am, as a grader, to move viewers through my work. Through modulating colors, rises and falls, I aim to provide an emotional journey, to take viewers somewhere new.

Excerpt of an Interview with Color Grader Eric Weidt

Our collaboration with Woodiwiss piqued our desire to meet more graders. Are their approaches and perceptions similar? Below is an excerpt from an interview with David Fincher's color grader, Eric Weidt (EW). His work, also beautiful, has a feel different than Woodiwiss's.

CV   Does grading on a screen help bring quotidian colors—colors of the world—forward for you?

EW   For me grading every day in the studio opens up color when I get out in the real world. The blue of the evening sky, for example, feels so pure, so deep and mysterious. And there are things to think about—for example, that that blue is reflected by our own atmosphere—not the deep space beyond. By contrast, today's technologies with their matrices of light-emitting pixels try to manufacture experiences, spectacularly boosting "up to 10s" to overwhelm the senses. Though corporations woo us into desiring products with more pixels, more light, more gamut—I feel like this sometimes pushes the 'cinematic experience' towards a kind of hyper-reality, which isn't always better. Best is when we give ourselves the time and space to appreciate what's before us. This takes imagination.

CV   Have you found ways to encourage viewers to learn more about color? I think of the suddenly appearing, showy yellow beer cooler in *Mindhunters*.

EW   I've always encouraged people who are learning to manipulate images to go to museums. If something doesn't pique your interest there, maybe postproduction is not for you. Little things, like noticing the layers of paint on a canvas, or the way you stand back, or move in close to an artwork—these should stimulate your thoughts. Does the art try to provoke a reaction in you? Or does it more reflect the concerns and obsessions of the artist? That said, I sometimes find misinterpretations revealing. I like poetry for this reason—it tries to take up the space between words. Because communication is imperfect, we need unconventional means to jog deeper truths. Cinema can achieve this because it has text, color, light, movement, sound . . . all things that carry associations as much as denotations.

CV   What about developing your own interests while attending to other parameters—settings, cinematography, and so on? Do you draw from outside the field, like from neuroscience?

EW   I can't escape my own tastes. Sometimes collaborators have an excess of ideas—which can be fine. Nowadays there's an almost limitless variety to how you can sculpt or polish something on the computer. So which choice is right? I think we all need affective, irrational, or even mystical reasons for doing things—because they help you make decisions. Objective art doesn't exist, though science does. Analyzing color spectra of distant stars can help inform our tools and methods. For example, it's incredible that we can use electromagnetic spectra to learn about the chemical compositions of stars. That's hard science, but I believe color scientists, too, have vivid imaginations. Considering science, it's hard for me to dissociate color from context. Yes, some colors supposedly have cultural connotations. Trick question: Whose culture? And is color like sound? And are our color reactions natural, similar to our responses to chord changes? (Black-and-white movies can pack emotions too.) I could say I have an immediate thalamus reaction to bright phosphorescent orange, or this kind of bright lime/yellow green that for some reason advertisers or car designers assume is uplifting. For me, it's not. I love these optical

	illusions where the same color square placed against different visual surroundings appears differently colored—a magic trick that proves perception is seldom objective.
CV	Do we perceive color more than we register it?
EW	I believe reducing gamut can help you perceive more, because increasing gamut can direct how a viewer's eyes fixate and dazzle that individual. We might "register" more than we are aware of, but then again, we often can't remember details . . . so where did we put them? One wall may be purplish in an otherwise blue room. Is there a slightly disturbing feeling to the room? Or is someone wearing a shirt that doesn't quite match the rest of the outfit? Do they seem off-kilter? Small details with color can encourage audiences to feel desired ways.

Carol's Closing Thoughts

While often the last to touch films, color graders are among the first to tell viewers where to look, how to feel. Within single shots, graders create palettes and colorscapes; they situate viewers in filmic space, intensifying and dampening a shot's elements to prompt affective responses while also using color to create visual depth (e.g., making some objects on screen feel proprioceptively closer while pushing others further away). Across shots and scenes they create threads and motifs, linking often disparate visual images and narrative elements through colors that recur across objects and surfaces. And across entire projects, skilled graders like Weidt and Woodiwiss often create emotional arcs to maximize a film's potential and, in effect, to "take viewers somewhere new."

Becoming attentive to the art of color grading—particularly work like Woodiwiss's, which engages music and moving images in distinctive but ephemeral ways—can equip viewers to better understand how audiovisual media actively work on them as they watch. It can also help research specialists and color enthusiasts across disciplines as they track the importance of color in everyday life. As we all move further into a new era of increased and intensified digital mediation—the COVID-19 pandemic, after all, has already set new precedents for screen-mediated commerce, intimacy, activism, and more—it will become increasingly vital for us to be mindful, as Nelson writes, of how the eye and mind, the body and spirit, make "colored forms out of what is essentially shimmering."[17]

What can we gain by considering color in relation to audiovisual aesthetics? Color may be one of the best parameters to show off a soundtrack.

It's malleable, versatile, and inexpensive (that is, it can rely on fabric, paint, and postproduction techniques). It's evocative. And as we've shown in the analysis, color can direct our attention to a song's features like harmony, musical motives, sectional divisions, or larger-scale form. It can also create its own structures that function in counterpoint with the song.

Audiovisual studies remains thin. There are but two dedicated theorists, Michel Chion and Nicholas Cook, and much of the writing by the field's scholars remains impressionistic or unresolved. (By drawing on neuroscience, for example, Carol is troubling Chion's notion of added value.) Looking closely at individual parameters—gesture, dance, rhythm, color, timbre, and so on—we may develop greater precision and come to understand audiovisual aesthetics more deeply.

This chapter shows off what's unique about music video. Watching classical Hollywood cinema, we can become absorbed and lose ourselves in the narrative. But with music video we may be better able to follow what the performer, songwriter, arranger, and director are doing, and also attend to our own reactions, even as we're in the midst of the clip's unfolding. Music videos are heterogeneous. Pop songs are constructed out of aspects and moments that each call out for attention. In order to sell a song, music video image tends to show off parameters—melody, harmony, rhythm, and texture—almost as if it's a tour guide, while simultaneously offering several threads for the viewer to follow. Do you pay attention to chord changes, facial expressions, locations?

Woodiwiss's path through a video differs from ours. Hopefully readers can grasp both ways and choose how they wish to move through the clip. Woodiwiss appears to make initial assessments and decisions about a video before he begins to grade. For "Cellophane" he chose a large, formal concept: color to suggest a breathing organism. In "Formation," drawing on an insight about the varied content, he focused on pushing shots while respecting director Melina Matsoukas's preference for pastels. With "The Entertainer" Woodiwiss chose a single image to grade the entire video's look by, along with which reds should remain true to the original environment and which should reflect his personal taste. Woodiwiss is also drawn to individual images that present opportunities for extension or experimentation, like the fluorescents in "Formation," green against gold in "Cellophane," or his favorite reds against the more naturalistic red exteriors in "The Entertainer." Jonathan and I wish rather to create a synoptic view of color and the song: What patterns of colors bring out or work in counterpoint to which of the song's features—either seamless, spotted, or block-like and offset? Here are different ways of knowing clips. Can they be kept in relation? Can viewers track their own engagements?

We hope our collaborative approach will encourage readers to be more attentive to color. It's one of cinema's key devices—films employ color arcs and they also can be found in the videos we've looked at. The final shot with "The Entertainer" feels like a destination because the video was graded around it. "Formation"'s teals and golds against varied pastels creates a sense of flux, and "Cellophane"'s subtle shifts of orange-red brick establish flow and continuity.

Future questions include how color graders encourage us to attend to and learn about a project's color while at the same time being true to other parameters, such as settings and cinematography. And how can we use color not just when experiencing media but also in our everyday lives? I (Carol) have taken courses in painting, drawing, photography and videomaking, and I'm curious why, at least for me, through grading, the world's color comes forward most powerfully. In the midst of the process of grading for my book covers, I can become immersed with shifting the hexes—a point more or less of red, green, or blue. When I return to the quotidian, objects' and backgrounds' colors seem to hover as individualized elements, floating a bit nearer to me. This must be an illusion, facilitated by modulating delicate shifts with images. I once was cutting some red peppers in the kitchen while grading and drew my breath at their beauty. At least for me, a sense that color can come forward needs continuity and practice—it's a way of life. Some of us would like to live here. Would writing and sharing about color help us get there?[18]

Music Video Directors, Production Houses, and the Media Swirl

THE MEDIA SWIRL AIMS TO HELP readers develop skills in reading today's audiovisual objects. Its chapters serve varied purposes—to demonstrate the process of analysis, to show off a work's extravagance, to develop approaches to different forms and genres. But as we move toward harder texts—content that departs from progressive affiliations, or that is conducive to science-based approaches or big data analysis—we'll need tools from other domains. Simon Levy and other neuroscientists have claimed we accrue knowledge through tacit clues and schemes; drawing on these partials, we construct a second level of meaning that exceeds these components.[1]

This chapter on the music video, commercial, and film industry can remind us that media aren't made magically, or from afar. In interviews, directors and industry practitioners can come to seem like the rest of us; they're caught in a web of competing demands and institutions, and they experience the stresses of competition, limited budgets, and tight deadlines. They negotiate their work in ways that may shape our strategies in this late-capitalist period. We can notice that the most successful recent directors are often audiovisual auteurs, skilled at working across media and with many different types of clients. Our familiarity with production contexts gives us the means to understand and interpret clips.

More than a decade ago scholars like David Bordwell, Jeff Smith, and I began noting that directors and practitioners were producing work across multiple media: feature films, commercials, music videos, fashion photography.[2] It wasn't unusual for this transmedial work to be commissioned by production houses like Anonymous Content, Partizan, and Good Company. This chapter takes a possible first step toward capturing this phenomena. Many of today's important directors, like David Fincher and Francis Lawrence, came out of music video and developed their styles in these transmedia contexts. We can see their stylistic traits—hypercontrol, line, glide, and a sensitivity to audiovisual relations—as derived from these experiences. The roles of transmedial directors and practitioners have only intensified in recent years. The same is true of production houses, which serve as hubs for all kinds of media-making, including feature films, long-form video, streaming web series, mini-docs, commercials, music videos and fashion photography, Instagram and Facebook posts, and their accompanying commercial spots (now shot in batches with a range of durations, from fifteen seconds to seven minutes, to be distributed across multiple platforms), VR, and augmented reality.

Much of the ways work is produced has shifted as well. Filming for all types of media tends to take place in Los Angeles, not only because talent is deep, but because everyone can drive within a day's notice to almost any location—the beach, the mountains, the desert—and to different communities, including wealthy or impoverished. But a good amount is also shot in suburbs and cities like Cape Town, Vancouver, and Rio de Janeiro, because those cities can look American or European.[3] For these locations, a handful of first-line talent (the director, cinematographer, and some of the performers) can be flown in, and the rest of the talent and labor can be local. Much of the work we see today isn't of anywhere specific, and only certain types of directors succeed (those who work quickly, have interpersonal skills, and can survive jet lag). Jonas Åkerlund has bragged that he enjoys circulating globally and collecting experiences, as he drops into and out of micro-communities.[4]

Practitioners across a wide range of disciplines from color timing to editing also engage with a range of media practices. Many work in film and television (with its potential for world-building and sense of the past and future), music video (with its audio and visual aesthetics and rhythm), commercials (with their ability to project a message quickly), the internet (with its refreshed concepts of audience and participation), and in spaces like restaurants and amusement parks (with their brick-and-mortar materiality alongside today's digital aesthetics).[5]

These directors and practitioners, working alone and collaboratively, have shaped a new generation of makers. They encourage us to reassess concepts of authorship, assemblage, transmedia, audiovisual aesthetics, and world-building. What role has music video played in all this, and how does music video function transmedially today? How has the form changed in light of new platforms, modes of distribution, economics, and audiences? And how have directors and production houses responded to accommodate these shifts?

Music video, I've claimed, is a prime driver for today's content—it's a central generator of the intensified audiovisual aesthetics that constitutes what I've called "the media swirl."[6] Marco Calavita has suggested that our new audiovisual aesthetics is attributable to European art cinema, Hong Kong action films, and American musicals, but I've claimed that it's not about speeding up Godard and slapping some pop music against it. The music video industry was and is the laboratory for audiovisual experimentation, and I've given a more detailed history for this.[7] But it's hard to make strong arguments when there has been little recent work on the music video industry, especially with a theoretical underpinning. We need a new approach to audiovisual studies that treats the relation between the soundtrack and the image as a primary focus.[8]

Music video is the most viewed content on YouTube, and the most common way young people consume popular music. We haven't yet studied how music video–oriented directors and production houses have achieved preeminence. Perhaps traditional advertising firms weren't fleet enough to cross over to the web, and media was becoming audiovisually intensified. Perhaps the variety of advertising content and platforms made these multipurpose production houses attractive. Celebrity musicians, film stars, and athletes often request to work with music video directors, because these directors are attuned to fashion and youth culture.[9] To learn more, scholars might embed within the industry to track production, go to shoots, interview personnel, explore archives like the internet, and so on.

Music Video Directors: Negotiating the Industry

In 1994 the preeminent music video director Marcus Nispel complained that many of his colleagues had no plan when making music videos. One might throw together a woman in a flowing dress, a bunch of ninjas, a castle, and some lights, and be done with it. (I think he was grousing about Bonnie Tyler's "Total Eclipse of the Heart.") Since speaking with Nispel I've interviewed many directors about their craft—lighting, choreography, costuming—and I've gotten the sense that they've become more reflective about the genre. I recently complimented music video director Emil Nava on eliciting a nuanced performance from Charlie Puth in "Attention." A few years earlier Marc Klasfeld had confided in me that Puth seemed so awkward before the camera in his video with Wiz Khalifa, "See

You Again," that Klasfeld had instructed him to just stand there, draped in Klasfeld's leather jacket. Nava said that he and Puth had hired an acting coach for rehearsals.

Other examples of recent attention to the parameters of music video include the directors Dave Meyers, Joseph Kahn, and Nava, who create informed collaborations with choreographers with distinctive, nuanced styles. I was impressed when Kahn shared with me his and J Lo's video for "Dinero," and directed my attention to the finely wrought layers of dancers. In Nava's video for Dua Lipa's "One Kiss," he and his choreographer provided insect- and dinosaur-like gestures for the dancers stationed in the background (which complemented a giant flying paper insect). The same is true for many other aspects of production, from color timing to editing.

Also new is how much musicians and performers know more about music video production. When Marcus Nispel directed Kanye West in the early 2000s, West kept insisting that Nispel capture performers in a tight moving escalator shot with a wide-angle lens, because he assumed it was cool. (Nispel obliged, and then left out the shot.) West has since become a skilled director and collaborator. Joseph Kahn has noted that many young musician/performers are wonderful to work with, because they grew up on music video and have sophisticated notions of what's possible. He fondly describes Taylor Swift as a kind of collaborator; she's "weaponized."

Breaking Into the Music Video Industry

In the 1990s, an aspiring music video director might break into the industry by shopping a showreel, with the hope that a production-house rep would offer a contract. This possibility remains today but has become less common. Perhaps production-house staff now have many sources for finding talent and lack the time to review materials. A showreel, however, is still standard: a reel comprised of videos for a band one knows, or for musicians one wagers might break, directed for free. Friends are often enlisted to help out with crewing or editing. If the band breaks, the director's and bands' collaborations might continue throughout their careers.

Another means of entry is through a kind of "mailroom," such as PAing or assisting an editor, director, or a grip. (I haven't heard strong support for film school from the directors I've interviewed, though several have benefited from college.)[10] Emil Nava developed his skills as a director's assistant: seated next to that director while tasked with switching out recorded tapes, he listened in on how contested moments were negotiated.

Nava just listed a gig for an AD in Los Angeles with a starting salary of $45,000, which, if one lives at home or splits a low-cost rental, may be enough to live on.

Today the industry is more porous. It's just as likely a music rep might spot someone's work on Instagram (like Tierra Whack's discovery of Thibaut Duverneix and Mathieu Leger, or Mark Pellington's learning about Kate Parsons, who now teaches at Pepperdine and has done some handsome work in VR). A director might identify someone on her own and recommend her to a production house (like Janelle Monáe's request that Partizan, a renowned production house, hire Emma Westenberg).

A director's first gig is likely to be underfunded (shot for, say, $20,000). A collective of directors shared with me their story of being hired by Partizan. They had just made a viral video that riffed on Kanye West's "No Church in the Wild." A rep had seen it, tracked them down, and called, and the member who answered the phone thought she was playing a prank. The collective noted they had just been given enough money to trash one car.

Starting out in a production house has many advantages and a few drawbacks. There might be staff to help assemble treatments and budgets for the project's initial bid. The house might have a roster of practitioners, like grips and editors, available to help if the project has a rapid turnaround. There's an office, and hanging out with other practitioners can help hone one's skills. (Anonymous is legendary for the period when Spike Jonze, David Fincher, and Michael Bay, all on its roster, shared ideas; Fincher put a sticky note line drawing on Jonze's door saying, "CGI-face, bodies-puppets" for Jonze's filmic reimagination of the children's book *Where the Wild Things Are*.) Most importantly, there are reps who will call corporations and remind them of their talent, pitching names for projects.

Abteen Bagheri shared that when he was getting started, he had made a promo for Iceland (the travel board wagered a Persian American might offer a new point of view). The rep said, "We know it's not quite a commercial, but he's advertising Iceland!" His reel opened with a couple of hip-hop videos, most notably for ASAP Rocky's "Peso." When he added a narrative music video for Delta Spirit, coinciding with signing to Somesuch, Tim Nash, the production-house's head, danced around the office in London saying, "I knew he could do it!," joyful for his director's commercial viability. As a drawback, the production houses take a sizable percentage of the budget (25 percent), depressing directors' salaries. There's also a shared agreement that one doesn't find and produce one's own gigs apart from the production house, though directors are frequently exchanged among production houses, as projects need to be completed quickly. Membership within a production house includes bigger budgets, higher day rates, and a Directors Guild of America affiliation.

Treatments and Budgets

For a new director there's much to learn that won't have been gathered from film schools—norms and ways of doing tacitly shared rather than codified things. Musicians often choose their own hairstyling and costuming, which one might guess would detract from the video's overall look, but there's a long tradition of this. (Rihanna's moonsuit in Nava's "This is What You Came For"; Azealia Banks's beaded bodice in Marc Klasfeld's "Chasing Time"; and Charlie XCX's bob haircut with a touch of red in Ryan Staake's "1999" unfolded this way.) Corporations don't necessarily need to handle a music video's legal representation (such as insurance), and the production houses don't need to finesse the budgets, but this is how tasks are generally divided. Well-crafted treatments are essential, because they're one of the first steps to securing contracts. Music video directors are not compensated for them, though film and commercial directors often are (it's also mandated that commercial projects should only solicit three proposals, four as an exception). The more rapacious music companies solicit tons of music video treatments, contributing to an anxiety that uncredited ideas get poached and woven into projects without attribution. The norm, however, is three to seven, in part so that not too many people remain uncompensated. There's a shared sense that if you've got talent and you write a lot, you'll get a commission. Music video commissioner Lorin Finkelstein valued Chris Black's work and coached him to be patient. After a few tries, a project came through.

In the 1990s, directors would receive a packet containing the recorded song, its lyrics, and a picture of a band from which to design a treatment. Now, an additional element is added: directors might also receive a description of the record company's and band's favored ideas. The ways projects come in are more various than in the past. While hanging out at the office on a Wednesday at Pomp&Clout, I read a just-arrived, two-sentence email for a music video shoot that weekend, with one big and one lesser-known artist, and one elaborately storyboarded Sunny D commercial with a strong music video component.

Directors have different ways of developing ideas. When Floria Sigismondi writes treatments, she lights candles and keeps sheets of paper at her bedside so she can jot down emergent ideas. Emil Nava takes long drives, because this process seems to present the song in some sort of raw potentiality. Directors often say that a line or two gathered from a conversation with the artist often helps. Jonas Åkerlund likes to ask musicians questions like "What were you thinking when you wrote this song?" or "What are the lyrics about?" Sometimes a small comment can trigger an idea, like "I was thinking black and white." Nava shared that producer Calvin Harris felt his song "Giant" felt "muddy." It's subtle, but that feeling's present in the music video.

Treatments, then and now, consume real resources. (In the early 1990s Matt Mahurin worked hard to organize directors so they'd be compensated for their treatments, but without success.) In the 1980s and 1990s, directors might submit two or three typed pages of what resembled stream-of-consciousness prose, along with what were called "tear sheets," images pulled from magazines and fashion photography books.

Directors' responses to treatments vary widely today, too, but the push is for treatments to be more extensive. Bagheri's and Nava's treatments resemble full scrapbooks, sometimes with extensive text. Ryan Staake now incorporates moving GIFs in Google Docs for his treatments. Directors keep seeking new ways for conveying ephemeral concepts, and, just as music video works well with a hook, so does a treatment. Ryan Staake suggested in his XCX's "1999" treatment that he'd use inexpensive, out-of-the-box facial capture technology (called "deepfake") to sub in multiples of the lead singer's and Troye Sivan's heads. This would be cheaper (one didn't have to do as much image capture through greenscreen), but it was also a new device that kept stakeholders curious about how the video might unfold. And good evidence that treatments have become their own art form—Staake now teaches a course at the School of Visual Arts in New York focused on writing music video treatments.

Directors I've spoken with seem rueful about treatments that weren't greenlighted (production houses' offices often leave out folders of unaccepted treatments for interns to read). They seem to try to reinsert this material where they can, as if the imagery had become a kind of idée fixe. Marcus Nispel wanted to have elephants march down New York City streets with planes overhead, and Francis Lawrence cathected to the image of a UFO landing in a suburban house. Both images appear later in their oeuvres, though transformed.

Pitching a savvy budget is crucial. Record companies may receive several bids, and if one is markedly higher than the others, that director most likely won't get the contract. If the director underbids, the costs come out of her or his pocket. Directors see a music video as both an artwork and an act of self-expression, and they constantly underbid, to find themselves in postproduction shelling out their own money, yet with the hope that this video will surpass others.

Mark Romanek's experience with Jay-Z's "99 Problems" is a good example. He had hundreds of hours of footage, but no one was able to produce a decent edit. He returned to editor Robert Duffy, who had been contracted elsewhere when the video started, and said, "I'm out of money. I need you to cut it for free." Emil Nava tells stories of suddenly needing thousands of dollars for more fake blood or a redo of the floor, because what the camera captures isn't good enough.

Budgets are moving targets for everyone. What's too much or too little to ask for at the current moment? Right now production houses want attractive, glossy music videos, often shot on location, because these attract corporations. (One director calls these the "faded Terrence Malick" look, since Malick is a director renowned for his skill with the magic hour.) Commercial clients often look for music video directors, because they like their ads to include celebrities, musicians, and other performers, who often request to collaborate with music video directors. The reps who visit production houses' websites find the music videos helpful because it's hard to assess a director's style through ads alone. For this reason, too, production houses underwrite and post short docs, experimental films, work in VR, and so on.

Budgets for music videos have long been in transition. Michael Jackson's "Scream" was shot for $7 million in 1995 (adjusted for today, that's $11.5 million).[11] In the early 2000s, when MTV stopped showing music videos and the internet had not yet gained traction, a large proportion of directors left music video (the joke was, "I'm taking a holiday; I directed a video"). Budgets had plummeted to almost nothing, in the range of $5,000 to $10,000. Location shoots were often judged too expensive, and greenscreen was substituted. Sigismondi did beautiful work during this period, but she said the long hours under the edit suite's artificial lighting became wearing.

One would think that at this point music videos would be lucrative. Most of the big directors have made videos with view-counts on YouTube of several hundred million; Emil Nava's "Thinking Out Loud" has 2.7 billion. Music videos help sell many things—products that pepper the clips, music downloads, concert tickets, click views (which underwrite the advertising appearing alongside the video)—as well as the musician's increased fame, which pays off through commercial and film contracts. Music videos matter because YouTube is the most common way music is consumed by young people today. But budgets remain depressed, in part because industry personnel know that many talented and well-trained young directors are eager to make them.

Directors receive no compensation for YouTube views or iTunes sales (even for videos that garner millions or billions of hits or downloads), nor do they receive much for product placement. Ryan Staake received a nominal amount for foregrounding Lyft in his Charli XCX and Troye Sivan "1999" music video. I noted that this was curious considering the clip had received 29 million, but Staake wryly pointed out that a number of entities (perhaps record-company personnel, for example), had probably skimmed off a percentage.

As mentioned, the first treatments, budgets, and gigs can occur within tight constraints. But these limitations serve many purposes for both production companies and directors. Most obvious is a winnowing process (as directors decide music video directing isn't for them, and the production companies gauge whether the new hires have talent, stamina, and skills). Music video shoots most often unfold in no more than a day or two, partly because the musicians and performers are always touring, and unforeseen setbacks such as bad weather or the artist refusing to come out of the trailer require nimble readjustment (the not-coming-out-of-the-trailer problem is surprisingly common—why, I don't yet understand). A common midrange music video might run $200,000+, which is less than a commercial. But music video budgets are rising, and commercial budgets are plummeting as corporations demand content for multiple platforms like Instagram and Facebook (and these often come in various sized products—fifteen seconds, thirty seconds, two minutes—all from a single project).

A few music videos are budgeted at more than $800,000, and these are generally reserved for a few senior directors, like Dave Meyers, Joseph Kahn, and Mark Romanek. Meyers and Kahn have both told me they might be brought in by the industry for "something special." Speed is as important as an ability to work within a budget. Kahn noted that only three to five directors know how to execute a big-budget video, prepped quickly and shot in a two- to three-day window (he likes to say he's "one of the gladiators, and competition feels stiff").

Making a Name for Oneself: The Shoot and the Edit

A striking video can catapult a director. Companies and musicians start calling the production house, asking for them. Jonas Åkerlund's break was for Prodigy's "Smack My Bitch Up." As one of his first videos, he sent the edit to the band for what was his first paid gig, but the band faxed him back stating they didn't like it and he was dropped from the project. He then spent several months reediting the video with his own money. When the band received his revised edit, they changed their minds, and it released big on MTV's "After Hours." Ryan Staake's Young Thug "Wyclef Jean" video had a similar buzz, in part because he embraced the fact that the rapper never made it to the shoot. The same with director Emma Westenberg's "Pynk" and her friend's vagina-inspired pants. All these videos have memorable, risqué hooks.

Strong directors like to work quickly and cheaply, and many find ways to cut corners. Emil Nava and Kahn edit their own videos, and Kevin Kerslake operates his own camera. Kahn has developed a technique in which he runs quickly between the camera, which may be capturing the star, and a laptop, which has the just-transferred footage. He immediately slots the captured image into place alongside the song, and then races back to the camera again (he stays physically fit to be able to execute this). Jonas Åkerlund shoots with two primary cameras and a third second-unit camera that can grab cutaways or inserts—anything from a sunrise to an insert of an eye to something falling on the ground. He seeks opportunities within each setup to gather several shots. For Beyoncé's and Gaga's "Telephone," he had Beyoncé cross a door, sit down in the chair, walk and then jump around, lie down on the floor, stand up, and then sit down again. This way he gets five cuts out of a setup. Dave Meyers, too, prides himself on his speed, producing expensive, elaborate videos quickly. He stays nimble by exploring an updating set of motifs and themes. Mark Pellington has developed a technique of shooting tons of footage, and then quickly dragging the most eye-catching images onto the editing timeline.

Successful directors tend to be good at working with talent. Each artist seems to call for their own approach. Nispel couldn't figure out why Chrissy Hynde of the Pretenders didn't want his helicopter shot, but he knew to quickly let it go. (He then realized that it would most likely mess up her trademark hair.) Jonas Åkerlund has done well with Madonna because she's supportive of criticism (once in a board meeting he blurted out "That's a bad idea!," for which he forever gained her respect). Lady Gaga's ideas are wonderful, but sometimes need shaping. She works too hard, in Åkerlund's opinion. Melina Matsoukas said that Beyoncé is a consummate performer; because she's always producing wonderful material, the director will often turn on the camera between takes. Her cutting for Beyoncé and Rihanna differs: Beyoncé likes a fast-playing shot with well-shaped movement within it, and Rihanna is supportive of fast cuts.

One of a successful music video director's most important skills may be functioning without sleep and other biological necessities. Shoots commonly run overtime and editing can continue until minutes just before launch. Kahn told me that for most of his career he's only slept six hours a night, and he's very good at sleeping on planes. Marcus Nispel won't eat during a shoot, so that he doesn't lose time. I asked Emil's rep whether Nava was more of a morning or evening person, and she replied that he's a "24," which elicited the director's smile—this was the right answer.

Directors have different responses to deadlines and budgets. Nispel felt that a director's survival depended on careful planning: if the budget was small, the musician would receive a sketch rather than an oil painting. But most directors I've spoken with seem compelled to give more than what they've proposed. Perhaps a video becomes a personal artwork or statement; one hopes it will get noticed.

Music video directors like the genre because it provides a lot of room for creativity, innovation, play, and self-expression. Directors Alan Ferguson and Melina Matsoukas both embrace the form because they can engage so fully with colors, textures, movement, gestures, and sound. Commercials are commonly considered an antipode. They're most often heavily storyboarded and controlled by the advertising firm. At a commercial shoot, reps often sit in what's called a "video village" with stopwatches, making sure the images mimic the storyboards. (Sigismondi has said that commercials funded by Asian or European companies tend to be more open to the director's vision, and this shows; her ads for Samsung's flatscreen TV and Thierry Mugler's "Alien" are stunning.)

For music video, on the other hand, it's tacitly understood that the final video can diverge from the treatment. Directors often go out to locations without any supervision, where they'll improvise. Directors employ a range of approaches to handle the shoot. Kahn's videos can be heavily storyboarded (he can use a lot of CGI, while Nava likes to shoot a ton of footage without storyboards). Most directors use audio playback. (Nispel shared the difficulties of making a live music video with singer Tony Bennett.) Most don't have the performers enact the whole song, but rather have them perform sections of it repeatedly within appropriate locations. Some like to bring trucks full of props so that a number of different costumes, furniture, cups, and so on can be filmed on site. Things can come together in an editing suite in serendipitous ways—sound, image, and lyric relations are always a bit unpredictable, as well as one shot's relation to the next—and it's good to have options. Much equipment, especially cameras, have gotten cheaper, lighter, and better, but the recent breakthrough with LED colored light panels, where color can be dialed up and down like musical instruments, is a major shift (in the past, one had to swap out colored gels in front of the lights; Emil Nava's recent gorgeous work with color is enabled by this new technology). Extensive time is commonly invested in editing and postproduction. The record company, performers, and the director will frequently negotiate their way through several drafts and minor changes before the final video is realized.

Tensions common among a director, performers, and the music company concern whose artistic vision the video should follow and if the video should be treated as commerce or art (directors will often try to align with performers against management). The music company often wants to release the video quickly. Director Alan Ferguson told me that when he was working on Cee Lo's "Double Happiness," Coca-Cola had threatened, perhaps not completely teasingly, to lock him out of the postproduction suite (they knew he'd been slipping in after hours). Though the video was still lovely, I noted that the background characters' faces looked a bit strange. He agreed that this aspect grieved him; the CGI hadn't yet been completed before the clip's release. Nispel directed me to his video for Janet Jackson's "Runaway" and an airplane window he never got to finesse in postproduction. Åkerlund shared that for Beyoncé's "Haunted" video, Parkwood (Beyoncé's company) kept repetitively emailing him: "Where is it??!" Since the project was top-secret, hidden under the term "Code Lilly," he didn't know he was holding up her magnum opus. Moments after he uploaded his video, the film album released, and iTunes crashed.

For all of a director's devotion, they often experience heartbreak. Music video directors have no final cut, and it's common for videos to get shelved simply because the song didn't break, or the band's or the record company's interest waned. Often the band or the manager gets ahold of the footage and edits the work, diminishing it. Sigismondi reported that she had wanted a clip to be a continuous moving painting, and the released version contained intermittent shots of the star appearing against a black background. Kahn relayed the story of receiving a list of suggestions from Britney Spears for their video "Toxic" that would have botched it. Fortuitously, she had just gotten married overnight in Las Vegas, and the record company, busy tracking the paparazzi's distractions, allowed Kahn to release his cut. Kahn often shoots videos to protect himself from an artist taking control, but I recently received an email from him saying something like, "Never, ever again a hard rock band, especially one that espouses religious values." Often the problem is that the bass player feels he doesn't make a strong enough appearance.

The industry tolerates directors presenting their own directors' cuts on their portfolio showreels and websites, and committed fans can find these. I like Åkerlund's edit of Lady Gaga's "Paparazzi," with a long stretch of Gaga sitting on a mythical Pegasus (she asked during the edit, "What's with the horse?"). Some of the video's threads, such as Gaga's costume when the diva poisons her beau, and her dancers' ruffles that flutter in the choruses, make more sense in light of this image.

The industry has some Horatio Alger stories, where artists with little training or background become big directors through hard work and perseverance. Joseph Kahn's immigrant family remained poor throughout much his youth, for example. Kahn had little artistic training as a child, but he fell in love with the movie theaters' enormous projected images and decided film would be his vocation. He got accepted to NYU Film School, but was forced to drop out in his freshman year because he couldn't pay the tuition. He then started over in Houston, shooting low-budget hip-hop videos within neighborhoods he judged few outsiders wanted to visit. The more common story, however, is different: a fortuitous background grants a tremendous advantage. Some of today's greatest music video directors have parents who were artists. This includes Sigismondi (whose father and mother worked in opera), Romain Gavras (whose father was film director Costa-Gavras), Åkerlund (whose father was a professional photographer), Fincher (whose father worked for *Life* magazine in editorial), Michel Gondry (whose father was a professional Jazz organist), Francesco Carrozzini (whose mother was editor-in-chief of Italian *Vogue*), and Bagheri (whose father is an architect and consistently produced art).

Those who head production companies have often had illustrious childhood backgrounds and careers, starting out as practitioners with preexisting links to the entertainment industry, then going on to direct feature films during which they launch these organizations, so legacy factors are in play here, too. David Fincher and Michel Gondry head some of the biggest production companies. Ryan Staake's trajectory suggests a different story (though he has his brother Kevin as a partner, which is another kind of endowment). He shared starting his own company before he became a successful director was almost unbelievably hard. Looking back, he marvels at his contingent path (if his video with chains of dominos falling through a bungalow hadn't caught the attention of some Asian companies' reps; if Young Thug had turned up for his video shoot). His experience can be celebrated as a fortuitous, yet hardscrabble story. In a recent interview he gleefully told me that the production house Caviar, which had failed to hire him based on his early showreel, had just lost out for a couple of commercials to his production company Pomp&Clout. Nava and Ferguson are both launching what they call "360-degree companies," which include a wide array of specialists from architects to Instagram designers on their rosters. Perhaps such configurations will suggest new models for the major production houses.

Most practitioners aspire to be more than just music video directors. Few can support themselves on just music video; most supplement their income with commercials, fashion photography, and short experimental films, narratives, and documentaries, with most of their revenue coming from commercials. Music video directors still often want to direct Hollywood films or streaming online series. At one of Nispel's shoots, a production assistant pointed out to me that most of the people on set wished to direct but were instead sending faxes, handling walkie-talkies, and curating audio playback. The director, on the other hand, wanted to direct films, so everyone was in a state of attenuated desire.

Beyond Music Videos: Transmedia Directors

It used to be that music video directors would put cars on their showreels so they'd get car commercials, but now directors add more dialogue and narrative with the hope of landing a film directing gig (Emil Nava noted that his Eminem video "River" is an example). Beyond music videos and commercials, there aren't many ways to break into the film directing industry. One might land a small-budget film for one of the majors, but several music video directors I've spoken with have described such experiences as frustrating. Kahn directed Warner Brothers' *Torque*, but wasn't in sync with the producers—he imagined the film might include comedy, and they envisioned a straight-ahead action genre film. New pages of dialogue were faxed in daily, and by the time he'd wrapped the film, his credit card was more maxed out than when he started. Dave Meyers shot *The Hitcher* with producer Michael Bay, but with a stock script and limited actors, there was little room for him to show off his talents. Äkerlund's films have stayed small and independent, but he's been able to control content to a great extent, and he's moved into scriptwriting. Before directing *Constantine*, Francis Lawrence waited for several years, reading through many scripts before finding a decent one. *The Hunger Games* and *Red Sparrow* followed.

Kahn's response to all of this is the most creative. He shoots tons of commercials and some music videos, and banks the money. Every five to six years, he then directs his own independently funded film with a predicted loss of several million (such as *Detention* and *Bodied*). Now that he has a family, however, he wonders if he can continue this way. Right now he's working on several funding possibilities, including directing a pilot about a rebellious, medieval teenaged girl who wishes to be a witch rather than a princess (he has a lovely trailer for it). If he secures the initial show for the streaming series, royalties continue throughout the episodes. There seem to be primarily two ways to break into the film industry as a director. One is to write a great script, and the other is to have a strong music video or commercial showreel (which might also include experimental work and documentaries), and music video is easier to break into than commercials.

Becoming a music video director is hard. It comes down to contingencies, a kind of lottery, and talents that are both measurable and ephemeral. But it remains one of the few professions that allow individuals to experience a range of facets of the self; to explore the kinesthetic, tactile, oneiric, cognitive (especially problem-directed), and the future- and past-oriented; and the private and communal. We don't all get to be music video directors, so perhaps we might all work to make aspects of this special profession available to us all.

VI New Modes of Analysis: Neuroscience

15

Music Video's Multisensory

SO THAT WE SHARE some common ground (as well as a review of it), I'd like to begin this chapter with a brief discussion of music video aesthetics, what makes the genre unique, and some of its history and socioeconomic contexts. The bulk of my discussion will be devoted to new ways of looking at music video that I've gathered recently from neuroscience.

First, a bit about my background. The first music video I ever saw was Steve Winwood's and Chaka Khan's "Higher Love." It was 1987, and I was at a friend's who'd just gotten cable. I was blown away. It seemed like one of the most beautiful things I'd ever seen. I thought "Capitalism should be dismantled, but this is special—so entrancing" (fig. 15.1).

This video still holds up, if you know how to watch. Like many music video directors, directors Valerie Faris and Jonathan Dayton went on to make films. Their biggest hit was *Little Miss Sunshine*. As a doctoral student in the late 1980s, I was interested in film music (I wanted to be a director or composer), and I became curious about films' and music videos' relation to sound and image. Life would take me from production to scholarship, yet I stayed with music video studies in part from fondness for the genre. After submitting my dissertation video studies would blossom, but few have pursued this line, even in thirty years. At that time I kept saying to people, "Music videos are musical. The image shows off the chorus and the verse. The vocal melody's contours are often traced by the image. The colors within the image seem to reflect the song's timbres." And people would respond by saying, "What? That's strange." Now everyone shrugs their shoulders and says, "Sure, of course."

I've long been interested in a viewer's experience of sound and image across media, genres, and platforms. With feature film, I find music tends to be but one of several elements that are devoted to a single goal, which is immersing a viewer in a narrative. With a good music video, however, you really hear the song. Music video's main task is to sell the song, so the image does everything it can to make the song memorable. Music videos can't say

15.1 Music video's audiovisual beauty: Steve Winwood and Chaka Khan's "Higher Love."

much, but they can point: "Wow, what an impressive hook"; "Hey, check out that trumpet line!" Their limited resources shape them. Often comprising only three to five minutes, they lack dialogue, the characters can't speak, and the lyrics don't necessarily relate to the song's temperament. They're asked to showcase the star. Music video can point to some sort of tantalizing elsewhere. It's also designed to be watched many times, to be captivating and perplexing. Helpful notions I've developed for thinking about music video include that the clip's background actors often seem mute and uncanny, not only because they don't have any dialogue, but also because they're picking up the slowest rhythms of the song. Glitter and flowing fabrics might pick up the fastest. The genre's characteristic figures framed partially, torqued, and on an angle, help turn our attention to the sound to gauge size, weight, and depth.

Here's a bit on "Higher Love." A viewer can sense that all the elements—image, lyrics, and music—drive toward peaks in counterpoint with one another. The image's content becomes higher in the frame, the melody rises, the lyrics say "Make me a higher love, way high." The viewer is asked to hold onto phantom threads as they build toward these peaks. Studies have shown that visual objects high and low in the frame can help show off a melody's contour. Music, image, and lyrics all seem to ask: Where is this higher love? The image also offers a shorthand for the song's most memorable features, encapsulated by four emblematic gestures: 1) Winwood's swung forward, clenched fists; 2) the women's arms swirling back with their gauze and scarves; 3) the performers' inching steps forward with knees and feet; 4) and finally the musical and visual halts ("I will wait"). These all come in and out, not necessarily synced to the music. As the elements rise to find that higher love, a second process unfolds at the same time: a move toward slowness and then stillness, which is also often depicted as a drop in the frame, and forms a kind of shadow story.

My mid-era clip, Lady Gaga's "Paparazzi" (see chapter 7) is indebted to an audiovisually intensified style of filmmaking. This often frenetic aesthetic includes rapid edits and framing that's decentered, with the shots varied through changing lens lengths, from telephoto to wide angle. The camera can seem constantly in motion through dollies, cranes, or a steadycam. There might be an obvious, blustery soundtrack, perhaps with swishes and swooshes punctuating actions. Studies have shown that every year, the average shot length of Hollywood films has decreased.

David Bordwell has called this style postclassical Hollywood cinema. Some of its features, he claims, derive from television's small frame and constant refresh rate, and from digital editing systems. The smaller screens of the multiplex, as well as big-budget film shoots in far-off locations with too many cameras, which then give editors surplus material and the temptation to cut too rapidly, all contribute to the style.[1] But I think music video plays a major role in freeing up the image. In the 1980s MTV needed a lot of content, and the entry bar was low. You didn't have to put a lot of money in it to get your work screened—you were shooting on 1-inch videotape. You might try anything: turn the image upside down, make it blue, import a stolen image, whatever. MTV and the record companies recruited avant-garde filmmakers to direct clips, like Chris Marker. Marco Calavita has claimed that the new cinematic style comes from Hong Kong action films and European art cinema.[2] But discovering how to put sound and image together demands experimentation and trial and error. Music video is the only genre that afforded this kind of experimentation.

When "Paparazzi" appeared in 2008, music video had undergone a fraught fifteen-year stretch. Entering the 1990s, music video started to have a more recognizable style, and film companies wanted to participate in the new look. Music video directors who crossed over to cinema include Michael Bay, Spike Jones, and David Fincher. In the 1990s budgets could be huge, because MTV was so popular and it chipped in for music video's production costs. Michael Jackson's "Scream" from 1995 cost seven million.

But with Napster and contraband digital downloading, the industry crashed. MTV also shifted from music videos to teen-oriented sitcoms. This was the time of cheap, one-day shoots, like for Ok Go's "Treadmill" videos.

But then online platforms like YouTube took off, and *Billboard* started counting YouTube views of music videos as a part of sales. Music video budgets started rising again. Today, more young people find out about new music by watching music videos on YouTube than any other venue, including radio. The other big change was that directors didn't have to worry about the narrow tastes of the MTV board of twelve who vetted clips. Back then, you couldn't include long openings before or breaks during the song. You couldn't include product placement, sex, or guns. And I think this is partly why music videos weren't strongly narrative. Now, with this additional material and loaded signifiers, MTV could become more narrative and resemble other content. A music video might be enlisted not just to sell the song, but to ensure that the star would be hired for a commercial, or to increase her merchandising sales.

"Paparazzi" has a long intro and breaks, lots of sex, violence, and product placement, and it conveys a narrative. New ways of placing sound and image in relation contribute to a clip where I support Gaga's revenge murder.

The Carters' "APESHIT," I feel, is a good example of what might be called music video's late, ultra-self-reflective, and intertextual style. An upper limit of density and self referentiality has been reached. The artisans who collaborated on "APESHIT" have skills in audiovisual aesthetics and can produce within an array of genres—music videos, commercials, documentaries, streaming series, and even films. Production companies that house these multitalented artists like Anonymous, Caviar, and Reset also drive this new aesthetic. Think of Gaga at the Superbowl, and the surprising cuts, from extreme close-ups of her face to overheads of the arena. Beyoncé made the TikTok-like video "7/11" early on, and TikTok has been influencing music video.

With "APESHIT," I've started moving away from analyzing music videos by myself. My collaborative approaches reveal new insights, but I'd like the scholarship to move more quickly. There isn't enough that's adapted to music video's changing aesthetics.

I'd like to show how neuroscience can deepen our understanding of how we experience audiovisual media and hopefully contribute to a future disciplinary shift. This includes music video. Compare an excerpt, perhaps from a *Mission Impossible* film to a moment from Steve Winwood's "Higher

Love." Disparities between the ways we attend to a film's soundtrack and a music video's song are so marked that I wonder how much our experiences are biologically driven.

Hopefully there will be more interdisciplinary research on the neuroscience of audiovisual relations. Annabel Cohen has produced some noteworthy publications, though mostly focused on film.[3] In audiovisual studies, the work of Michel Chion and Nicholas Cook stands out; both of their research, I believe, could be troubled through an encounter with neuroscience. Chion claims that in film, sounds relinquish their autonomy and are subsumed by the image. But neuroscience studies have shown that the brain reacts differently to sonic and visual events, depending on their locations in space and in time. When events occur synchronically they're often experienced as fused, unless the inputs seem unrelated (for example, a human with a dog's bark). The more temporally distinct or separated in space, the more sound and image each become single sensory phenomena. Placed within a certain range, an image can capture the sound through ventriloquism (as when a performer who has a puppet speaks, and we attend not to her but to the doll's moving lips, or those TikTok videos with animals accompanied by incongruous, amusing sounds.)[4] Sound can also shape our experience of an image's occurrence within a temporal flow, especially if the image is less determined.[5] In these cases our sense of the image's timing will shift so that it comes closer to that of the sound.

Scientists have identified a number of audiovisual illusions, some striking. If two identical circles come toward one another silently, from different sides of the screen, they will seem to pass through each other. If a sound appears when the circles meet, they will seem to bounce off one another.[6] If we hear a synchronized beep and flash, and a beep quickly follows, we'll often see a second visual flash.[7] Sound can wield power over images.

Chion may have come to his notion of added value because his focus was primarily on narrative film, where filmic parameters avoid calling attention to themselves in the service of spatial and temporal continuity and the narrative. In music videos, however, the image attempts to showcase the song's features—"look at this hook!" "Wow, hear that shift to the chorus." Often there's a hovering percussion track in the foreground of the mix, which feels proprioceptively close. In a music video this sound can seem to sit in front of the image, dangling out there, floating in isolation, as if in front of a painted background (or at least that's the way I experience it).

Cook's multimedia model too could be revised. Cook stresses the concept of metaphor—the emergent qualities of sounds and images—as well as audiovisual relationships that can be characterized as conformance, complementation, contest, and gap filling. Here, Cook looks to gestalt-based, affective, and cultural features. Sometimes we might read an audiovisual moment as simply *sync or not*. When multiple perceptual streams—vision, touch, sound—are confusing and opaque, and the brain reads the stimuli as low-intensity, the superior colliculus may enhance them all.[8] We might describe this process simply as a signal boost. An example might be an array of gray blotches against a blur of white noise. This initial moment doesn't seem to need as full an apparatus as Cook describes. It's less about relationships than about amplification.

My intuition is that a signal-boosting process is central to how music video functions. I'd appreciate it if neuroscientists ran experiments to test this hypothesis. With music videos the image often occludes itself, so that the densely worked, initially ungraspable pop song comes to the fore. Performers and supporting characters are often torqued or displayed on an angle toward the camera, making them harder to perceive as whole. Actions are rendered incompletely, edits occur at odd moments, and spaces are partial or confusing. The soundtrack is overworked and separate from quotidian soundscapes. What's most important is the amplification or boosting of the audio signal. Cognitive processing, both early and late, also affects our aesthetic experience of audiovisual relations. Some aspects of the image and the song may first reach us quickly and sharply through the thalamus. These signals tend to be associated with risk: think stricken, pained, or angry faces; booming bass lines; bodies disturbingly disposed; percussion hits and sudden horn blares; perhaps deep red hues. These can also be softened or heightened through our preexisting knowledge—what's described as "priors"—that are calculated through Bayesian inference (derived from a known mathematical formula) in higher cortical processing: "I recognize this genre—it's heavy metal." Early stage affective processing in the thalamus used to be considered as separate from later Bayesian calculations in higher cortical regions, but now neuroscientists are starting to understand them as parts of complex feedback loops.

In what follows I'll look at excerpts from two music videos, Demi Lovato's and Sam Smith's "I'm Ready," and Lapalux's "Without You." I'll talk about the ways in which neuroscience can shift an audiovisual analysis. I should note that what I'm sharing might soon become outdated. Neuroscience studies are often limited to small domains—for example, black and white-striped rotating circles or flashes accompanied by beeps. Subjects' responses might be quantified through fMRI, EEG, skin conductance response, or stroop tests. Such studies may not carry over to material as dense as a music video. But even if these descriptions aren't accurate, the findings give me new ways of considering music videos. Functioning like beams and poles we can balance against, they help bring previously unviewed features to the fore.

With the start of Lovato's and Smith's "I'm Ready" (2020) I wonder if something first comes through for the thalamus, which responds to affectively charged stimuli—most strikingly when we sense danger. Drawing on fMRI studies, I now attend to the song's opening, which features a repeating cry or scream. There's also a percussive, jabbing sound on the quarter notes. The metallic rotating logo and glitter seem to attenuate these sonic effects, but I think the music still pierces at a gut level, even if I recognize the song falls within the genres of nu-disco and techno. Edited against this opening is Smith's voice, which sounds gravelly, and his face, framed horizontally. Studies show we're most skilled at reading visuals with a vertical or horizontal orientation—presumably due to our environmental histories (these facts were determined from studies of kittens).[9] Off-angle is harder, and Smith's face crosses the frame both diagonally and horizontally. We're so cued to vertical faces—we have a brain patch just for faces—that it's possible this shot transfers the image's unease to the soundtrack (fig. 15.2).[10] Some studies have shown that audiovisual elements can convey relationships not only through synchrony, but also through objects and events past their borders. It's as if instances and their effects project halos. I'll read Sam Smith's face this way.

Music and image perceived simultaneously tend to be linked to better recall and stronger emotions. "I'm Ready" shifts from a prechorus to a chorus that resides in a different harmonic region. Music videos often show off a song's features. Here the chorus offers a new visual scheme: characters running with flowing capes, and then Tinder-swiping on a cellphone. This running and swiping situates us differently experientially. I'll pass on engaging deeply with the overvalorized notion of mirror cells, but I do think this motion engages different parts of the brain (both the dorsal and ventral streams are always chugging away, but here the dorsal stream really kicks in). Apart from neuroscience, I'd claim that the chorus's upward-stepping harmony, along with the images, suggests greater freedom (fig. 15.3).

The next verse lies in a higher register than verse 1, and the image reveals men wearing high heels. Our body-brain likes to connect smaller objects located spatially higher with higher frequencies (this seems to be

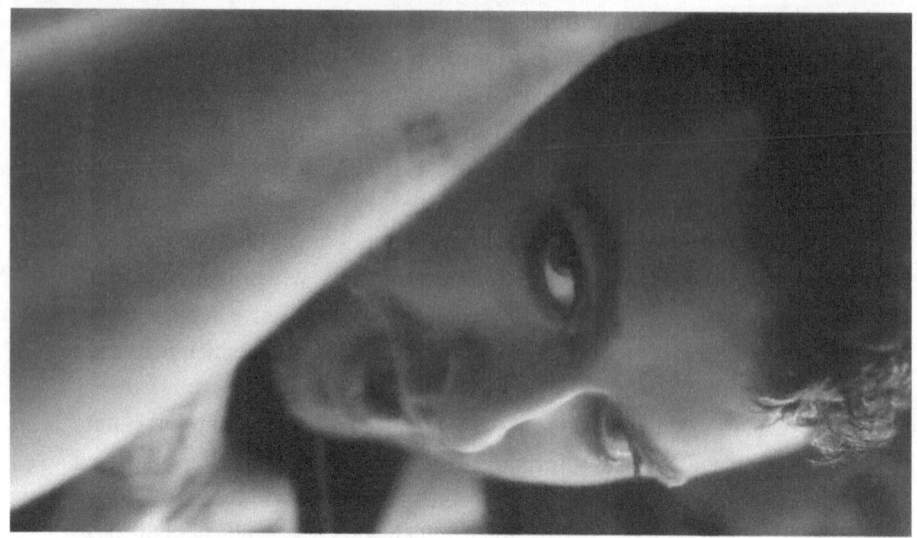

15.2 Sam Smith's head is horizontal and more difficult to cognitively process.

15.3 Male sprinters with beards, flouncy hats, and floating capes.

15.4 Demi Lovato, centered, projects.

how we perceive objects and sounds in our natural environments; think tweeting birds and bellowing panthers).[11] I seek out Sam Smith's mouth to better place his melody.

And then let's return to the super colliculus, which boosts all these signals. "I'm Ready"'s soundtrack is a dense, yet-unknown object. The image is obscured—it's shot as if through a veil of smoke, fog, or steam—and the film's grain comes forward against the oddly muted colors. But I think the images' opacity helps a viewer better hear the song. Imagine the video with a different visual treatment: shot high-key, with clarity. Such a visual scheme would likely draw attention away from the soundtrack. Keeping with that ambiguity, I like how Demi Lovato, on the diving board, leans back, but when her melody nears its apex in the chorus, she's centered and straight on. Her voice projects in an expansive chorus. "I'm Ready" builds gradually to this moment of audiovisually synchronous affective charge (fig. 15.4).

In "I'm Ready" a number of details depart from our common schemes. The video shifts from a wrestling match to the dancing, and from a race to billowing rainbow-colored fabric. Studies have shown that we have preconceived schemes for what people should do and how spaces should appear; we access these quickly. Deviations capture our attention. If I show you a photograph of a kitchen counter with a laser printer instead of a toaster, you'll hone in on that detail. "I'm Ready" has a lot of these attractors: the wrestlers in high heels, the male divers wearing lipstick and femme bathing suits, and the male sprinters wearing large flouncy hats and long capes with beards and mustaches. These are eye-catching. They support the soundtrack's stingers.

With so many streams of stimuli coming at us, we need to decide what to attend to, what binds with what, and which materials form groups and event-segments. (I'm grateful here to Jeff Zacks's innovative work on a viewer's perception of event segmentation.[12]) How to do this tends to be determined by events in relation to immediate space and time, and to priors. As I mentioned, when sound and image appear simultaneously in space and time, the signal tends to be amplified, and even more so when we have learned cultural associations to place these events together; a nearby dog with barking from the same direction, for example. Many music videos play with this. In Lapalux's "Without You" (2013), the female lover holds out a shiny key embossed with the number seven, as a bell sounds. What are we to make of this, and how does this moment relate to the clip's unfolding? Thus far the video has carefully shown that sounds connect with objects and events (fig. 15.5). (For example, the fan's whir enters whenever the appliance is revealed visually from behind the hotel clerks at their desk.) We're also prepared for the key's importance through an earlier reveal. But this lover's bell-like sound, flash, and key, I think, is more complicated than a simple correspondence. We may have some priors for such a sound belonging to a similar object. Perhaps we access a distant, learned connection between the "zwank" and a *Star Wars* light-saber. We can learn an audiovisual connection from a single occurrence. Something about the way the female lover holds the key with the bell-like sound suggests this magical object and its sound are important,

15.5 A woman holds an illuminated key and raises questions about audiovisual sync.

so we should wonder what they do. Lab studies have shown objects have odd audiovisual entanglements. As I've mentioned, if you show a flash tied to a beep and a subsequent beep close enough together, participants will see two flashes and hear two beeps, even though the second flash never occurred. Are we hungry to see the second flash? I think so. I feel like I'm waiting for it. The video reveals isolated pointillistic effects, sparsely distributed across its landscape. Maybe I understand the flash's and key's importance retrospectively. Later, the bell, lights, and key seem to set the protagonist in motion as a dancer. Next there'll be physical blows and light to suggest the character's death, and finally its metamorphosis into spirit (fig. 15.6).

Early on I asked whether sounds that float untethered to the image might work in contradistinction to Chion's claims. I mentioned that if there's a visual and auditory stream, and the visual track appears less certain, the auditory stream can suggest what's unfolding temporally: the image can seem to fold in closer to the audio event.[13] A motorhythmic, accompanying riff emerges, and, because it suggests automation, I believe it seems to drive events. When I see the car I think of its being set in motion, and when it tries to drive away I feel it's being squished a bit, as if pulled back by the soundtrack. And one last detail: neuroscience gives me a better appreciation for why the clip's opening stays with the figure loping slowly down the hall. It can take a lot of cognitive processing to decipher a song's rhythmic arrangement—its tempo, accents, and beat patterns. This is especially so for "Without You," with its sometimes syncopated, sometimes indistinct articulations, and portamenti in its lower register. The song can sound murky and even a bit impaired, as if the next beat might not arrive. In this context the character's steps may help viewers place themselves in

15.6 Lapalux's protagonist is enigmatic. What does sound mean for him?

relation to the song's rhythm arrangement. But we viewers may be quick learners. As soon as the character breaches the office door, the character moves in counterpoint to the rhythm arrangement. Perhaps our focus is more challenged here, because (as Zacks points out) going through a door often creates the perception of a new event, soon to be segmented.[14] Such shifts are common in music videos—first Mickey Mousing and then a transition to moving in complement. Neuroscience, through its wealth of studies, reassures us—we music video fans can mostly participate in this. We've become adept at sound and image.

This chapter suggests we should revise our understanding of audiovisual relations. Chion claims that sound becomes a property of the image; Gorbman says the soundtrack is heard as if under anesthesia. Both of these descriptions target narrative film. But many of today's media, like TikTok and music video, are organized along different principles. Neuroscience research provides insight. Sound often shapes the image and takes the predominant role. Of particular relevance to music video is the law of inverse effectiveness, where image is occluded or obscure, and the brain then increases the audio signal, often rendering it more striking than the image. U2's "With or Without You" and Kanye West's "Can't Tell Me Nothing" use slo-mo with added and dropped frames. Bono and West are often in darkness, and the footage is grainy, so cognitive processing boosts the sound. Sound then becomes the throughline. The Weeknd's "Sacrifice" works similarly. Neuroscientists Saul Quintero and Ladan Shams have shown that the binding properties of sound and image are fluid and malleable. With a bit of practice we can bind sound and image together differently.[15]

Tracing the Asset: Humanistic and Quantitative Approaches to Cybercrime Film Trailers (Snowden and Bourne)

THIS CHAPTER COMES OUT OF A collaboration between Unruly Media (a company that advises businesses like Unilever and Pepsi on the placement and messaging of their ads), and some media theorists, including me. We sought to discover whether sharing our methods could assist both businesses and humanities scholars. Unruly Media draws on data analysis from large audience surveys and psychometric software like facial recognition. We humanists do close readings.

The Unruly staff and I selected the project—an analysis of some cybercrime film trailers. Unruly hoped to turn the results into an industry white paper, and I to publish a chapter or article in an academic context. I developed much of the project's design, acted as a liaison (including on-site visits to the company), synthesized the results, and contextualized the findings. Media theorists, Dani Oore, Jim Buhler, and I gathered the facial tracking data. Dani and I presented some of our findings at a Society for Cinema and Media Studies conference.

I felt some trepidation about such a project, but I also thought it important to participate. We as a public are likely accelerating into socioeconomic and technological configurations we're unprepared for. Vectors with steep trajectories include the information sciences—artificial intelligence, robotics, big data, psychometrics, and biogenetics. Predictions include a 40 percent unemployment rate thanks to robots, CRISPR editing that will create pressures for engineered babies, corporations that can bypass resumés because Big Data and AI will have already quantified us, advertisers that will more aggressively direct our attention, privacy that steadily diminishes and an environment that deteriorates, dark money that will increasingly corrupt politics, and a resistance that will end up broken.[1] Imagining dystopian and utopian futures may prove helpful.

Hopefully our potentially world-changing information technologies will also provide us with tools to help us respond. New research in neuroscience can encourage us to see ourselves as biological machines. With this knowledge we may become more curious about and engaged with the ways we and others are multiply articulated and constructed through inheritances and genetics, as well as memories and experiences. To face a dystopian future, it's surely also essential for us to more fully understand the workings of capital, neoliberalism, and who the wealthy and powerful are. Together, these shifts could soften some of society's great myths—of God, the will, and individualism; fissures might appear in Neoliberalism and post-Taylorist structures.

My participation begins with a disadvantage. My research centers on audiovisual aesthetics—the ways sounds and images function in music video, YouTube, and postclassical cinema. But I've been taking a lot of neuroscience, philosophy of mind, and computer science courses at my university. I've published a collection titled *Cybermedia: Explorations in Science, Sound, and Vision*, comprised of musicologists, media theorists, neuroscientists, computer scientists, artists, and philosophers of mind.[2] In the *Cybermedia* collection, my coeditors and I were emboldened by recent neuroscience research on embodiment. While conceptual knowledge may be stored in one part of the brain, visceral experiences are elsewhere, and they may carry more weight. Media and literature may enrich our knowledge of our possible futures. I find Alex Garland's *Annihilation* (2018) a fruitful example of the ways we can affectively grasp a potential future (an interview with Garland appears in *Cybermedia*).[3] In this film, everything within the "shimmer" is refracted—plants, people, radio waves, and time. *Annihilation* encourages us to ask, "What might genetics, machine learning, and symbolic systems share?" The film's final question, "Does the shimmer learn?" seems similar to our concerns that AI might learn in ways we'll fail to recognize, outstripping us before we can respond effectively. Scholars, government agencies, and media outlets have called out for a more educated public. The collection aimed to make such an intervention (fig. 6.1).

Working with Unruly excited me because then president Sarah Wood (who reached out to me) and I share similar progressive commitments. She believes that corporations can strive for transparency: consumers and companies should engage in conversations about content, sourcing,

16.1 *Annihilation*'s shimmer refracts everything—plants, people, radio waves, and time.

politics, and labor practices. Sarah has made a commitment to Unruly's hiring 50 percent women and providing childcare for parents (including on-site). Ian Forrester, global vice president of insight, with whom I worked closely, was open to discussing our work's social ramifications. But perhaps I should have included late capitalism's volatility into my calculations. When Rupert Murdoch bought out Unruly in late 2016 Ian assured me the new contract stipulates that the company could still be "unruly," but I was concerned. While Murdoch's empire is bigger than Fox News (and Fox Searchlight Films has produced some progressive work, like *12 Years a Slave* and *The Shape of Water*), their news show scares me. Through subtle aesthetic means, outside voices are encouraged to participate on the show but are quickly discredited (through the taunts and grimaces of hosts, scale and placement in the frame, and pacing, lighting, and graphics). Much of the public discussion about global warming, the widening gap between the rich and the poor, accountability and the White House, and issues of representation go missing.[4] Fox, a handful of bad players, and psychometrics feel like a potential threat to me. I'll return to these issues.

Sarah, Ian, and I chose the *Bourne* and *Snowden* trailers as our study's focus. Cybercrime films seemed promising because they are particularly self-aware, able to explore issues of privacy and surveillance. Their characters employ both close reading and quantitative analysis and seem to encourage interlocutors. Unruly gathered and analyzed data from large, quantitative surveys, facial-recognition studies, and music-software algorithms, and we produced complementary close readings, along with our facial scans. This chapter discusses these materials—our facial scans and those of Unruly, Unruly's quantitative surveys, and my more in-depth close readings. It took several months for me to provide these close readings, for I wanted to learn the trailers' images, soundtracks, and audiovisual relations. We then compared Unruly's data with our analysis.

First, a bit about Unruly as a company. Unruly helps corporate clients gauge whether their content—whether an ad campaign, film trailer, or new product—will succeed in the marketplace. One of Unruly's primary tenets is that our desires to share emotional experiences with others are the strongest predictors of brand loyalty and purchase (fig. 16.2). To quantify these measures, they've broken down emotions into eighteen categories, like fear or joy. Big data and Facebook patterns help them identify audiences, and they've devoted more attention recently to the controversial project of helping corporations target populations outside of their traditional reach (rural gun aficionados coupled with urban- and feminine- hygiene products, for example). Similar techniques have also been applied to political advertising, including by Cambridge Analytica.

My interest in psychometrics, including Affectiva, began with the 2017 *New Yorker* profile "We Know How You Feel," which detailed the soft-

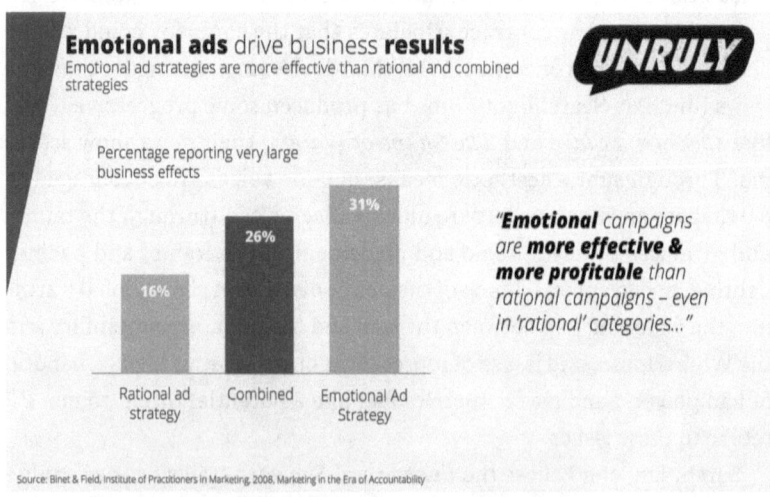

16.2 Unruly's claim that audience's emotions drive successful ads.

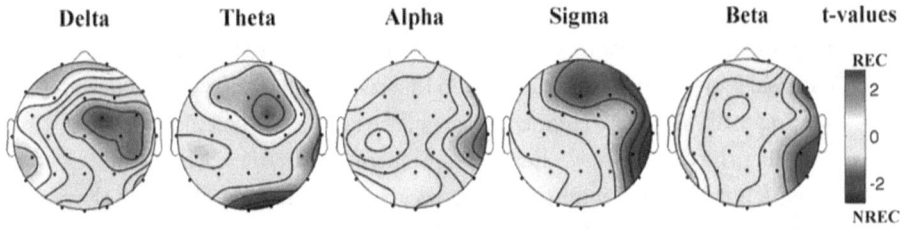

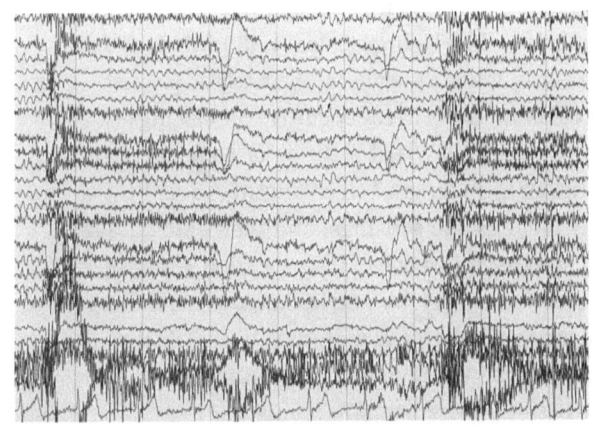

16.3 Topological EEG graph.

16.4 Sample EEG graphs.

ware's capabilities of capturing a moment from Spike Jonze's *Her*.[5] When the interest of viewers lagged, the software caught details that had proved inaccessible to the film's producers and practitioners. More recently, when taking a course on music, the brain, and EEG, I felt beguiled by the beautifully, finely spun brain wave patterns and splotches of colors blooming across simulations depicting superior views of the brain (figs. 16.3 and 16.4). These gave me the illusory sense that I could, at least for a while, more attentively experience the gap just before a music video chorus's highest peak. My heightened awareness felt like a more conscious version of a photographer's catching the "perfect moment," because neuronal signals traveling across brain modules at subcortical levels had caught hold of and mapped the emergent progress of a detail. Such quantitative methods might enable a cooperative endeavor we haven't yet seen, where nearly every visual and sonic nuance was accounted for. I have an image of other analysts and me hovering over data and content. In a nonexploitative world in which we didn't have to worry about corporate greed, class differences, and the controlling of our opinions and identity, psychometrics might have liberatory effects. We might gain a richer and deeper knowledge of ourselves and one another.

I'm drawn to this project out of self-interest (and worry that this taints my perspective). At some profound level, I've become bored as a media critic. The field is an art, not a science. (When I sense that I, as a media scholar, am making a difference, I imagine I'm part of the last stages of a film's production; like the color timer, I help viewers focus on what's worth attending to, which paths they might take across a work, and what attitudes they might take in relation to it.) Little about media criticism feels systematic. Insights come out of hundreds of hours of thoughtful viewing and the emulation of fellow scholars (like George Toles, Will Rothman, and Robin Wood). But for all the discipline's fuzziness, the analytic process—built up through decades of below-the-surface cognitive processing—has become rote for me. I'll ask questions: What if the color were different? If the gender were male rather than female? Or of another race? I try to chart the landscape of my feelings and sensings, and then I fabulate an explanation for it. A slow process, this mode of interrogation often yields the same kinds of answers. What if psychometrics acted as a mirror or interlocutor, giving me new perspectives and material? With political advertising and nonprogressive content (homophobic, racist, ageist, classist, and so on), would we better understand how it hails us?

In the following sections, I'll discuss our findings, but I'd like to note here that through collaborating with Unruly my engagement with psychometrics, neuroscience, and media has continued to sharpen; I've also, however, come to feel more strongly that corporations would have disincentives for enlisting humanists like me. I'm vocally on the Left; lack the streamlined, team corporate temperament; and can't reliably produce work synced to their rapid turnarounds. Matt Strafuss, director of customer success from Affectiva, the facial recognition company that collaborates with Unruly, told me that corporate reps mostly want bottom-line, single digits: "Is it a 7? Let's release! Only a 4? Scrap it!"[6] Still, my experiences with Unruly have been rewarding, especially when I've been able to pinpoint ways an ad produced for a well-intentioned company might be made more progressive. For example, in a Dove ad, everyday women on the street were featured as a way of celebrating average beauty types. I noted that the editing's rhythm coupled with the soundtrack's musical peaks worked to overemphasize the most attractive women, undercutting the clip's message (fig. 16.5).

Before moving into a description of the project proper, it's worth considering some frames for thinking about ads. I take seriously Sut Jhally's argument that commodities and advertising, as products and processes in themselves, narrowly focus our attention on the short term, distracting us from what's most crucial, including global warming.[7] But Unruly's Ian

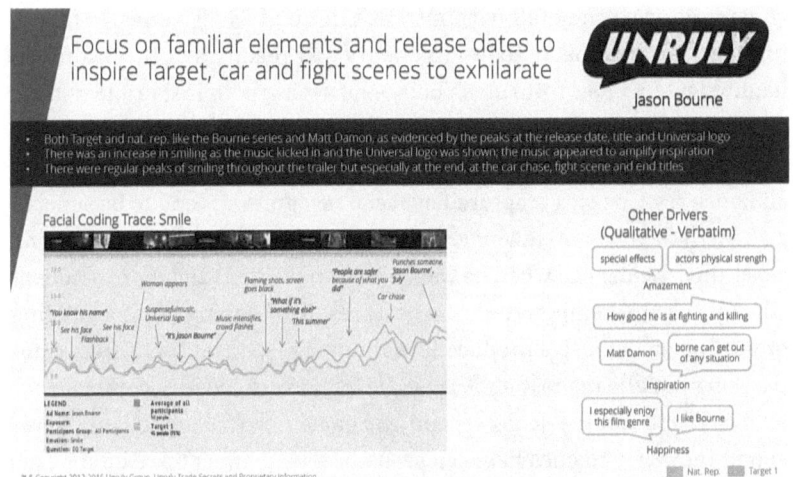

16.5 An example of what Unruly would share with clients: Affectiva's facial coding for Unruly's survey subjects who watched the *Bourne* trailer.

Forrester proposed that content analytics could facilitate more engaging ads, thereby enriching our lived experiences. Ads will be with us. Those we enjoy might spur a more varied media ecology.[8] We can imagine why oversight and discussion can sometimes be a positive good. For example, someone might have gotten to Pepsi before they released their Kendall Jenner Pop Power Commercial, which many felt cynically attempted to co-opt the messages and sentiments generated by the women's march. At Affectiva, too, I've heard pro-new-technologies claims. The software was first developed by MIT to help autistic children (tracking the ways disabilities are used for sanctioning technical advances interests me; Facebook, for example, has been touting their AI as a way to bring more content to the blind).[9] Matt Strafuss confided that facial recognition might make us more sensitive, and a good boss, one he'd wished to work with, would respond positively if he revealed dissatisfaction.[10] I've had the momentary sense that after participating in a series of scans I'd become a better judge of other's expressions, and hopefully their experiences too.

Facial Recognition: *Bourne*

I'll first discuss facial recognition scans of viewers of the *Bourne* trailer, and then consider the large data sets of surveys (primarily in relation to the *Snowden* trailer). Facial recognition analyzes the face's muscular contractions as they fall within what's defined as "T zones."[11] These findings can then be linked to EEG and fMRI readings of the brain. I'm haunted by this new form of visibility—of seeing both inside and outside of a person.

Unruly's insight director, Becky Waring, shared with me that initial audience responses, as captured by facial recognition, tend to be superficial. With the *Bourne* trailer viewers responded strongly to Matt Damon's close-ups, feeling sad when he was in a down position and more ebullient when he seemed empowered. Big gestures like jumping off of a building or hurling an explosive produced heightened responses too. Direct comparisons can't be made, but because we humanists chose to complete our analysis first and the scans second, we gauged we'd be less likely to respond intensely to cues like a close-up or a leap off a clip. And it's true that our scans tended to be flatter, with smaller, momentary fluctuations. My scan corroborates my analysis of the clip. Jason Bourne, for me, as the film's main character, is simply reactive, only one node within a larger system. This circuit, for me, most resembles a smooth line of neurons firing, first instantiated by the CIA. Bourne is captured, pinned between firm audiovisual boundaries—on the top, a high-pitched bell-like synthesizer tone and below, a rumbling low bass line. He is but a pawn—the consummate neoliberal subject.

After completing my close analysis of Bourne, I found reviewing our facial scans informative. Mine exhibit four small, telling markers: 1) A small dip in the graph coincides with an image of a van, filling the screen with white momentarily. At this moment, my brain may have little to grasp. 2) A node in the timeline for grief appears when an early oboe fragment that our contributor calls "the humanity theme" comes forward as Bourne broods, recumbent on a bed. I can feel emotion welling up in me, replicating the oboe's contour. 3) I experience pleasure at the clip's close, when Bourne slugs a competitor, his fist against a chest, sounding like a resonating metal slab. My response may also say "thank goodness I made it through this scan," but I believe most influential is the way the mournful oboe's attributes subterraneously unfold, finally liquidating during the fist's punch, thereby heightening its affective power. 4) I exhibit a startled response when a Black male CIA agent bursts through the door, and I'm concerned that my response here might be racist. I doubt I'd jolt as much if a blonde, white male came through the door (though confounding factors include a preceding flurry of rapid editing, a frenzied soundtrack, and a half-minute time point, a key turn for trailers).

All of the markers I've described are ripe for more thinking about our relation to media. How long can our attention remain sustained? Can a white out be used at just the right moment to elicit a switching of a viewer's brain systems?[12] What is the relation between the oboe and that closing, heroic theme? Is it true that an aural "down" moment at a clip's beginning helps the hero at the end, both sonically and visually? Here, am I subconsciously building patterns of connections that link across a sustained passage of convoluted material?

And am I racist? Additional studies have softened my anxiety about this (including results from a racial implicit bias test), but worries linger. Exploring whether viewers have a racial bias in relation to these films might warrant further study. One means for corroboration might be found if director Paul Greengrass shared with us screen tests with a range of actors substituting for one another in this segment. I wonder if my freighted response to Greengrass's characters' ethnicities is shaped by a wider array of aesthetic choices. The scene has an ominous, chillingly bluish cast, and the CIA character's shot at a distance, with obscured features (what would a close-up do?). Greengrass's actors of color are often called upon to convey a sense of blankness (Alicia Vikander as Heather Lee and Joey Ansah as Desh). Given my age and gender, this blank obscurity may heighten anxiety (fig. 16.6).

Additional psychometrically based studies might inform the way ethnicity functions in the films of Oliver Stone and Paul Greengrass films. Stone's background characters are often depicted with great warmth (such as the guard at the CIA's security checkpoint and city folk in *South of the Border*). These might be compared with Greengrass's. While many fMRI studies have been run with still images, scenes like these within movies could tell us much. Through fMRI, Anthony Wagner has shown that our brain's prefrontal cortex poorly encodes people from another race or group different from our own.[13] From this it can be inferred that

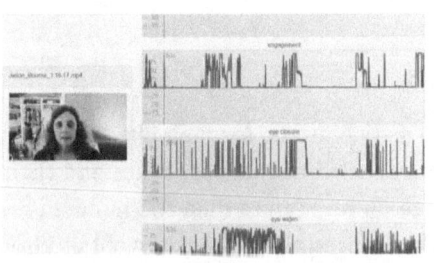

16.6 Surprise when *Bourne*'s Black CIA agent barges through the door.

people have a thinner sense of someone outside their clique. Much about the brain is run on predictive calculations, like Bayesian formulas, which are more automated than directed.[14] Other studies show that the brain is pliant, able to lay down new associations tied to imagery and sound. A recent one, for example, shows how, when various bird shapes and songs are algorithmically distorted and then mixed and matched, subjects can quickly learn new associative patterns.[15]

The scans of my male colleagues and friends differed from mine. Dani and Jim momentarily experienced some irritation with the male protagonist (perhaps linked to male competition?). A Black male student ran the Affectiva scans, and his response was markedly different from ours (he responded strongly to the images of guns, which makes sense as a member of a targeted group). The scans gave me a sense of empathy for the ways we're constructed differently, a sense that couldn't have come only from reading a study.

I have a few explanations for our nearly flat responses during facial recognition scans, which has relevance for teaching media studies. 1) We're practicing what I call "the symphony face." Like stuffy art patrons, we're performing a form of Kantian disinterested interest: we sit quietly. We don't clap or sing. 2) We're on the hunt, with a focus on tracking details. Subsequently, there's little room for oscillating emotions. 3) Our brains have assimilated the clip's patterns. Encoded data has passed into long-term memory, and our minds devote scant resources to reexperiencing the clips. (In my neuroscience courses, I've learned brains like to head off on their own computations.) When my cinema students express concern that close analysis will end their love for a film, I've reassured them that though their relation to a single film might shift, their bond to the field as a whole would deepen. Now I wonder if I'm misleading them. I'm just practicing sadistic hermeneutics—mercenarily driven modes of extraction. But I also strongly believe that through close-reading practices, and a deeper education in neuroanatomy and the politics of power, we can become more critical of and less swayed by political or commercial advertising.

Snowden and the Compound Numbers

For each trailer, Unruly provided us (as they do for their clients) with a cluster of emotional scores that revealed primal responses and their relative weights. Drawn from large surveys (more than two hundred respondents), this data suggests a kind of certainty difficult to obtain elsewhere. Reviews from aggregators like Rotten Tomatoes and Metacritic and the short responses underneath YouTube clips give a critic only contradictory and vague content. (A *New Yorker* blurb for *Annihilation*, for example, uses terms like "ponderous," "silly," and "sublime," but these are emotionally and cognitively conflated, without clear relation.) For *Bourne*, Unruly gave us a body of data drawn from many subjects, with weighted measures, and these aligned with clear categories like incredulousness, inspiration, surprise, and opinion seeking. Only after the long process of close reading did I come to realize that Unruly had captured some essentials. Yes, *Bourne* projects a simple, proprioceptive joy. The fleet, linked gestures that run across shots, along with flying objects, in tandem with warm colors, contribute to a kinesthetically infused experience of pleasure (fig. 16.7). After considering Unruly's findings I was able to reaffirm some aspects of my experiences of the clip, most particularly its long lines of energetic, synaptic-like pull and release.

Even more so than with the *Bourne* trailer, Unruly's analytics, especially with the large data sets, for *Snowden* feel on point. Becky Waring describes the *Snowden* trailer as cognitively challenging (much more so than *Bourne*), and it provokes fear and pride, as well as a strong drive to share the clip with others. This particular affective mix is unusual and hard to achieve.[16] My analysis suggest how the *Snowden* trailer achieves these effects. I note the *Alice in Wonderland*-like qualities of *Snowden*, even as it's a cyberthriller. Boxes nest, building up through miniature and

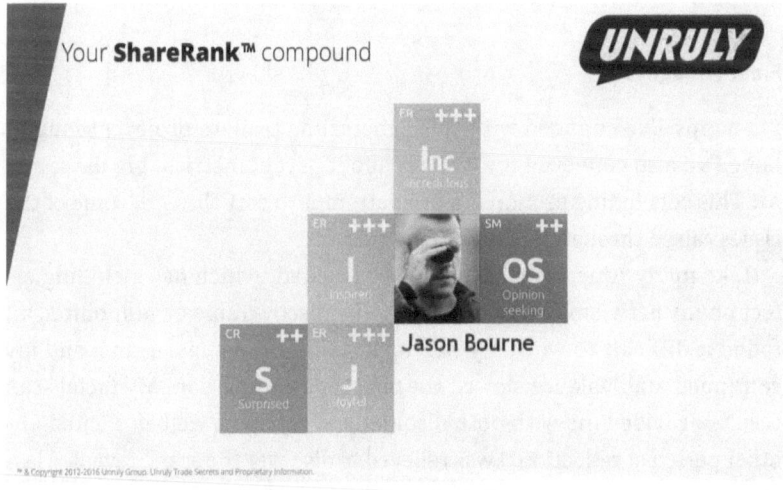

16.7 Unruly's compound numbers for *Bourne*.

hand-sized objects to larger-than-human-scaled environments. Viewed from above, the clip resembles a maze; at a mid-level, veils appear; and at the smallest level, a Rubik's cube appears. Snowden becomes both more human and Christ-like by the clip's end, and then we viewers are thrown from the clip into the darkness, as blind creatures or afterbirths; we might be called upon to be the next to lead the way.

Our analysis stresses the soundtrack's layered rhythmic patterns, and the ways these contribute to the *Snowden* trailer's cognitive challenges. During our SCMS 2018 panel, Dani Oore encouraged the audience to experience these with a proprioceptive exercise. For the clip's first 30 seconds, a span he calls a micro-trailer, he clapped the trailer's edits and stomped the soundtrack's rhythms. Patterned together, the soundtrack and image create a complexity that our speaker, drawing on the work of C. K. Ladzekpo, likened to African Ewe music (according to Ladzekpo, for the Ewe people, polyrhythms, through dance and music making, bring sense to life's complexities). Ladzekpo's analysis also points to the trailer's eleven sonic shifts of mood, each unexpected in rhythm, tempo, pitch, and/or overall texture.[17] The *Bourne* trailer is simpler, as he notes, more like a classic Hollywood musical. Jim Buhler notes the liminality of several of the soundtrack's materials—a quasi-helicopter wobble; a drum-hit that "initiates a kind of airy, trilling electronic sound," "portentous, tubby off-key hits," many reversed sounds—and moments when the editing becomes momentarily regularized but also much quicker.[18] Becky Waring finds additional materials in Unruly's data that support our claims, like viewers' responses to a musical motive aligned with depictions of data.[19]

Final Thoughts

I'm happy I've engaged with this cybercrime trailers project, though I hope I've also conveyed my worries about psychometrics, big data, and AI. This concluding section is a brief attempt to sort through some of the issues raised through this research.

Like many Americans, I fear being tracked, which has a chilling effect on my activism (I neither want to be discoverable or pinpointed). I found it difficult to work my way up to taking the facial scans, and my continued ambivalence slowed the chapter's completion. My facial scan results provided me with both disquiet and relief, as well as elicited another period of reflection. I was relieved to discover the scans revealed less about me than I guessed they might, though as part of a larger data set, they could be powerful. Additional courses on neuroscience encouraged me to feel more empowered—most helpful is the concept that the brain fires up and amplifies networks of associations it needs for a task at hand, simultaneously strengthening these connections.[20] This line of research has shown that the brain's malleable and one-off results don't necessarily reflect the brain's contents or potential, for only some of my brain's functioning is brought into play at any one moment. I think I should still be worried, however, about the kinds of assumptions facial recognition and AI algorithms make about me. This second shadow-self, which will shape my life, will likely be a poor mirror of me, directing me in ways which will not support my best potential self. If our activities help mobilize others who care about the commons, we think this project will have been a positive one.

I think other modes of participation are needed to combat psychometrics. Neuroscience research has helped us gain a better understanding about populations with the most and least status and resources. Growing up in stressful or underprivileged contexts affects both the brain and body in frighteningly deleterious ways.[21] We also understand something about those with extreme power.[22] But we don't understand those who maliciously take and who are placed in middle-tiered positions. We need better explanations for the biological, cultural, and structural causes of human greed and exploitation.

I'm unsure how much Unruly benefited from our collaboration. I hope that Unuly president Sarah Wood's commitment to transparency has been strengthened through this project, and that her staff found our insights helpful.[23] Their own research and methods have provided aesthetic constructs useful both for their clients and humanistic analysis. Unruly has its own frames for thinking about participants and media. They've noticed that a strong, intense emotion seems essential for engaging audiences with a media product. The product's visual placement at the end makes a difference. Each emotion has its own arc, and needs time to materialize and dissipate (and their advice to corporations is often to simplify and clarify). Jim Buhler and I, however, argue from a media critic's perspective—viewers' experiences of movie trailers as incomprehensible and unrelenting can prove exciting and powerful.

There are many ways to go forward. During the Q&A following Dani's and my SCMS talk, Laura Marks wondered if we were "in the belly of the beast." She has taken an alternate approach to surveillance and facial recognition: we might wear hijabs and camouflage.[24] I pointed out that except for the very rich, invisibility might be impossible. Not only our faces, but also our gait can be monitored. Our voices, the rhythms of our fingers tapping on keyboards, our biometrics when driving cars, our locations, and our web searches can all be tracked. In a later semester she shared this with students, which then sparked a lively discussion. George Lipsitz has claimed that Public Enemy's Flavor Flav wears a giant clock and flamboyant clothes in an attempt to make Blacks more visible.[25] Perhaps one strategy is for some of us to become more visible and others less. I share some things about myself that I feel are somewhat private in chapter 18.

We must come to terms with the negative repercussions that facial recognition and data-tracking systems will likely have. Simply knowing that several systems are projecting a tailored identity and social niche to an individual will feel oppressive for many, whether there's an agreement with the targeters' constructs or not. I'm hoping that many forms of individual and public engagement will help push us toward a better outcome. We might strive for public discussion, greater literacy, better regulation, and more transparency, visibility, privacy, social justice—a more robust commons.

VII New Modes of Analysis: Politics and Vernacular Culture

17

New Technologies, Social Justice, and the Future in Beyoncé's Audiovisual Albums

WE ALL HAVE ORIENTATIONS from which we respond to the world, but with our quickly shifting moment, some might be reconsidered or left aside. We're compelled to imagine a world with a 40 percent unemployment rate within the next fifteen years, intractable climate change, and the reconfiguration of personhood in light of artificial intelligence, big data, neuroscience and psychometrics.[1] As social structures continue to fail to meet these changes, we may feel adrift.

This chapter considers Beyoncé's two large-scale audiovisual works, *Lemonade* (2016) and *Beyoncé* (2013), through the lens of these accelerating shifts. It has a partly therapeutic aim. It presents several conceptual frames that seek to operate in the space of a convergence between 1) mind and framing; 2) intersectionality, with an emphasis on new and faster ways of classifying, sorting, and targeting subjects; and 3) the politics of social justice. These frames will then inform a close analysis of Beyoncé's two visual albums, which I've chosen because they are examples of popular culture that provide inspiration and, for many, project sensual and emotional weight. This dual framing/analytical approach might be incorporated within the fabric of a life—some of this chapter's aim is to spur other scholars to engage with interdisciplinary materials and to make complementary forays. We live in contentious times. Our future is uncertain. It's worth sharing our research, perspectives, political orientations, and loved media objects; we might learn from moments of commonality and difference.

This chapter tests what is called an "externalist" perspective. A strand in the philosophy of mind, externalism holds that the outside world is real, and that we and it are molded in relation to one another. Experience is a relation that includes internal sensory states, external properties, and a direct causal regularity connecting the two. Unlike much philosophy of mind, externalism draws on recent research in cognitive science and neurosciences, exploring the nature of brains and to what extent we are shaped by genetics, past experiences, and present contexts. New work on AI, psychometrics, and big data shows how *all* these factors contribute to our construction and intertwine us in a community. They also can be extrapolated into a politics of care toward others and modes of engaged connection. Embodied and emotional experiences can strengthen these understandings. We need to experience this material through more than abstract concepts: we need lived experience, and aesthetic experiences held dear. We also need a story, hence this chapter's close sonic and visual analysis of Beyoncé's two albums. Though Beyoncé's two video albums don't always match the paper's frames—and one could argue for focusing on more politically direct, documentary-based work—these projects are beloved by many, and work remarkably well. This is partly because music video, even more than other audiovisually intensified media, allows for repeated and deepening engagement.

Building a Frame

We're in the midst of what might be called the neural/AI/consciousness turn. What it means to be a mind and how a mind functions will be increasingly foregrounded. Microtargeting, AI, and big data will prod us to wonder how we make decisions. What do the corporations want from us, and how are we subject to their influence? Further, thinking about frames is cognitively productive.[2] Recent studies in neuroscience and psychology also show that reflecting on and considering our frames and embodied experiences can grant us some modicum of control over our cognitive and experiential processes (something these sections invite readers to do).[3]

How do neuroscientists describe the brain? For them, it's comprised of modular, densely interconnected systems, and its development unfolded under evolutionary pressures, with newer structures superimposed on older ones. The brain has redundancies and peculiarities—its shape is convoluted, its wiring is unusual. The brain's outer surface, a thin layer of tissue called the neocortex, is dense with interlacing nerves; a multitude of nerves also runs from the neocortex through white matter to the brain's center (which contains additional modules for processing) and back. The brain's two closely replicated halves allow for something resembling a computer's parallel processor, with greater functional preservation in the event of damage to one side. As the brain's size grew to accommodate more processing, it folded inward against the skull, a structure that couldn't expand because it needed to breach the birth canal.

The brain's strange setup can be grasped through a few additional examples. The eye's retina's neurons of cones and rods are turned away from a light's stimulus, which forces a lot of neural rewiring (fish eyes are "direct," by contrast, because light is a precious resource underwater). First crisscrossing at the mid-brain, electrical signals conveying visual stimuli from the cones and rods also take a convoluted path toward opposite sides of the occipital region, which rests against the skull's back. As the visual signal moves forward again toward the brain's front and toward greater levels of cognitive awareness, we can experience how our perception of stimuli can change. If you see the shape of an image of a dime you can tell you can't grasp it with your fingers, but once your hand moves toward it (when visual systems tied to movement come online), the dime suddenly becomes to scale. The brain's module for initially processing touch (the gyrus), is shaped like a headband that runs across the crown of the head, from one ear to the other. This gyrus's mapping of body parts responding to touch is recognizably isomorphic with the body as a whole, but also in some instances transmuted. The next gyrus forward then processes the stimuli to make more sense of it (many gyri in the brain work similarly, with higher-level processing seated one gyrus forward). Such neural relations show how *creaturely* we are—how bounded and idiosyncratic, given to particular ways of sensing and thinking. Perhaps this knowledge can encourage humility in the face of the ways we encounter and respond to materials (something that might serve us well as we approach our new pressured future).

Recent cognitive- and neuro-science research corroborates much longer culturally held notions (including Freudianism) that the mind's modes of assimilating new material are strongly influenced by previously gained perceptions and experiences. It's now understood that precepts (thoughts intended to regulate action) are shaped by processes of cognitive penetration (here, previously encoded memories shape visual and aural content directly, even at the lowest levels of the brain's processing), and through Bayesian prediction (a computation wherein data from previous and present experiences are calculated together to produce a brain's singular experience).⁴ If you've never encountered this image of splotchy blacks and whites, you probably won't make out its figures. Next, if you're told what to look for, you'll forever see its latent pattern, and the same holds true for this sound recording. These preexisting memories shape their inputs. Such processes extend to other cognitive and affective domains. A white person who considers herself to not be a racist may be flooded with negative stereotypes when encountering a person of color, which her prefrontal cortex may then work to suppress.⁵ Emotional states exert strong influence too, especially through the amygdala. If she encounters this person on the rhythm of her heartbeat and she has a gun, she will be more likely to shoot to kill; the amygdala, which among other functions triggers fight or flight, is most active on the heartbeat.⁶

Contexts shape visual and auditory experiences. In the brain's neural network, some neuronal firings are strengthened and others repressed, so that only one visual or aural experience or one memory tends to come forward. (It's why we only see a duck or a rabbit at any given time). Contexts also have effects on the single emergent experience. If I put images of Dalmatians around the above image of splotchy black and whites—an example of "priming," context-related stimuli that enable the brain to forge quicker and stronger connections with a target—you'll see the dog more quickly.

Coming from another vantage point may be difficult. It can be hard to switch frames, especially if the message comes from outside your tribal group; when content is perceived as threatening, parts of the brain tied to self-identity become more active.⁷ Conservatives tend to be driven more by hierarchy and concerns about contagion, and their amygdalas tend to be larger and more active.⁸ This chapter's egalitarian claims may ring hollow for them, for example (though recent research suggests that conservatives can be swayed by progressive arguments, especially if they feel safe).⁹ Humans aren't rational creatures. Scholars believe evolutionary pressures led us to value the opinions of our peers rather than those of an out group's, or our own surmisings, because being a tribal member improved our chances for survival.¹⁰

Intersectionality, Culture, and the Future

"Intersectionality," "inclusivity," "diversity," "social justice," "the claims of the disenfranchised," "identity politics," and "politically correct speech" are terms currently swirling in the contemporary discourse, with the Right attempting to lead the country's perception through a frame shaped by the latter terms, while progressives embrace the first. I'll stay with a frame allied with the former, though I'll circle back to counterarguments later. I'll show the ways these issues are embedded in popular culture and embodied contemporary lives; in the future, these concepts should take on even more central roles.

As defined by its Kimberlé Crenshaw, intersectionality is the theory that group identities, oppression, and discrimination interconnect and reinforce one another in a collaborative system.[11] Intersectionality has been incorporated by many groups as they struggle to gain rights, including trans, LGBTQ+, Black Lives Matter, Black feminism, Grey Panthers, and those speaking out through the #MeToo hashtag, to name but a few, with many borrowing terms and approaches from one another as they seek redress. The label comes out of the struggles of the 1980s, as Black feminists argued that the women's movement envisioned itself as predominantly white. Disenfranchised groups have multiple overlaps. The reader might envision hardships associated with being Black—you might be hetero, male, well educated, and upper middle class, and still confront threat and discrimination; it seems also possible to imagine that it'd be more complicated and tougher, or at least it might be both somewhat similar and different, to be simultaneously Black, a woman, undereducated, disabled, poor, and queer.

Many humanities departments in academia have taken up the term, with corporations eager to follow (the latter diffusing the term's power). The Society for Cinema and Media Studies—my primary professional organization—may finally have a caucus devoted to disability (the organization included a special forum focused on disability at its 2018 Toronto conference). Foregrounded during the event were a discussion of the term "cripface," which borrows from "blackface" and related terms. (For disability groups, examples of cripface include instances of hiring ablebodied actors rather than those with direct experience to perform roles exploring disability.)

The concept of intersectionality can alert us to examples emerging in new contexts, including the analyzed Beyoncé's "Pretty Hurts." The video's beauty-pageant contestants are women, minorities, and working-class; this clip both etches their forms of oppression and suggests ways of transcending them. The same might be said of the song itself, which draws on pop, rock, soul, and gospel, and interlaces these materials by the anthemic out-chorus.

Intersectionality and Social Justice: Present and Future

What does intersectionality tell us about contemporary lived experience and our shared future? Today's publics enfolded within the term are larger than what is documented by the media, corporations, or governments. Consider the number of people who enter into and exit from marginalized groups, which at different times need special considerations, services, and protections. A case might be made for women, who might want higher-paying jobs, better resources and encouragement within education (particularly for STEM), improved child care and family leave, and freedom from sexual harassment. We might extend such concerns to other groups, each possessing overlapping needs and desires: minorities (who also face racial targeting, police brutality, death, discrimination in jobs, healthcare, and housing prospects to name but a few); LGBTQ+ individuals; immigrants; those living in rural communities and in densely populated or abandoned cities; those who are ill (with health difficulties spanning from long COVID, cancer, Alzheimer's, heart disease, asthma and lung disease, mental illnesses like depression and Asperger's, to autoimmune diseases such as Parkinson's and chronic fatigue); the young, the disabled, and the aged. We might acknowledge the possibility of becoming a member of at least one of these populations at some point in our lives. Even the 1 percent, who many assume might be able to insulate themselves from others, might also wish for services and protections possible only through community—first-tier research hospitals, universities, museums, national parks, and state highways, as well as protections from environmental degradation. The 1 percent are also often connected to people who need assistance, like temporarily estranged children, less-successful family members, and service workers. If we came to terms with what is needed to ensure true opportunities and good lives, we might call for a more equal distribution of goods. The audiovisual albums *Beyoncé* and especially *Lemonade* depict a variety of subjects placed in contexts that reveal the ways their lives are marked by inequality. These albums also project some components essential to achieving social justice—receptivity, responsiveness, and desire for attunement with others, regardless of a person's station or history.

Surveillance and Psychometrics

While the United States has been able to sidestep many claims for social justice, it may be unable to withstand the fissures produced by forthcoming technological and socioeconomic shifts. Little press coverage has focused on what we might call "the great sorting." Through AI, psychometrics, and big data, workers will most likely be rated for their desirability as hires. This will create massive psychological and social upheaval. The individual as a solitary agent with responsibility for her fate is woven into our culture's fabric. Since people only reluctantly shift core beliefs about themselves, it will be hard for us to acknowledge such anonymous forces; even those firmly against such cultural constructions will be caught up, for ubiquitous patterns of thought (like religion and racism) exert a less-than-conscious influence. We may not be ready to think about wealth-concentration, robots, and the absence of meaningful work.

Unless rigorous checks are enforced, AI, big data, and psychometrics will most likely enable corporations, smaller companies, and governments to rate Americans, and this information will also be within the grasp of mom-and-pop businesses, extortionists, harassers, and grifters. Michal Kosinski has sought to trace the economic, cultural, and political ramifications of such microtargeting.[12] His research suggests that seventy Facebook likes are sufficient to determine more about you than your spouse knows.[13] His more recent work has been likened to a disturbing sort of computer phrenology: with six images, AI could determine your sexual identity better than a human could.[14] Kosinski believes this methodology can also determine your level of intelligence, religious or secular leanings, and individual temperament (including neuroticism, sanguinity, and impulsivity).[15]

This sorting is possible through an "OCEAN Score," which subdivides character into several hundred categories. To find out something about you, corporations and governments might use your web searches and Facebook likes (a fondness for curly fries, Stephen Colbert, and a Subaru rather than a Ford); so too your purchasing history, health statistics, the rhythms of your keystroke taps, the timbre of your voice in various contexts, and the places you visit (including locations Facebook records if you haven't set your privacy settings correctly). With this information, a corporation might well reject a resumé. A company might use algorithms to scrub the web in search of hires without ever announcing a job search.

This new employment scenario will most likely be twinned with a phenomenon better documented by the media: ads and content that reaffirm and direct your status, style, and worldview.[16] If you're a shy person you'll get material for introverts. If you're on the Right, you'll be deluged with content about family values and guns. The algorithms may be sloppy at times, but staff who deploy them may well trust them more than human assessments. Recently three people close to me developed serious health issues, and I searched the web for information for them. The *New York Times* then delivered me an ad for a cemetery. While writing this piece I've started getting ads for law firms skilled in arbitration. A constant barrage of such material will surely push me in a direction, just like my Facebook feed incites me to become more devoutly liberal.

Surveillance and Psychometrics, Addressing the Future

The new turn to tracking and sorting of humans is frightening, but there may be some ways we can use this data to ameliorate its worst effects. Kosinski claims it would be helpful if a sizeable number of powerful people came out of the closet, choosing to share their vulnerabilities, including all of their data, such as their warehousing of assets; with this new openness, others may experience less stigma.[17] J. K. Rowling has gestured in this direction, acknowledging an abusive relationship and a period on welfare.[18] Bill Gates, who just gave $24 million for the fight against Alzheimer's, says that close family members have succumbed to the disease, and he's frightened for his future.[19] I'm curious if the #MeToo campaign is prescient, if it prepares us for new ways of thinking about powerful men who also often have great resources and whose brains might be, as neuroscience reveals, damaged by power.[20]

In the great sorting, I doubt I'd be hired. I'm female and middle-aged. If you meet me you might not notice it, but I also have a disability. I have a back injury and a repetitive strain injury, so I have trouble engaging with the tools of my work—I don't handwrite or type much, and voice-recognition software works poorly for me. All my books and most of my email have been transcribed by assistants. In an era with a surplus of overqualified academics, employing me might be judged a too-costly risk. My spaces of intersectionality include those who are older, female, nontraditional parents, and disabled. Few academics know how poorly the ADA protects university faculty. While higher-education institutions are mandated to provide services for disabled students (often facilitated through disabled students' centers), faculty lack these protections. Rather, to receive assistance a faculty member must inform her chair of the nature of her disability and her specific needs. The money to provide that assistance typically comes directly out of the department's budget, from funds that might have been allocated instead for lecturers' salaries, faculty travel, photocopying, and so on. Before tenure, disabled faculty rightly worry they might be discriminated against by colleagues. (Are my coworkers wondering if I'll become more disabled? Or if, after tenure, that I'll cost more?) Most faculty (and this is what I've done) remain in the closet. In the closet and without support, fulfilling all aspects of the job—teaching, research, administration, and service—becomes more difficult.

Universities might hire staff who would help disabled faculty, or ensure that some target-of-opportunity hires be allocated for faculty with visible and invisible disabilities (as well as dedicated enrollment spaces for disabled students). In the universities I've taught in I can't recall seeing a visibly permanently disabled tenure-line faculty member; the few visibly disabled students I've taught were veterans who had been stationed in Afghanistan and Iraq. If people were willing to come out of the closet and align themselves with other minority groups, we might have a richer understanding of ourselves. *Beyoncé* and *Lemonade* work to portray disability, and trace the positive potentials of sharing and disclosure.

Moral Standpoints

I've talked about the mind's construction, intersectionality, and new technologies as a way of coming to terms with our vulnerability and dependence on social groups. This section adds two more components to a frame through which to see the world: the individual in relation to social structures, and an ethical stance toward others. Many conservatives downplay the negative potential of new technologies, claiming that technological change has always improved humankind's lot and that phenomena like mass layoffs should be tolerated for the sake of long-term gains. On the other hand, progressives might feel that this moment is unique, and uniquely urgent—through biological and nuclear weapons we can now annihilate ourselves in an instant, and pollution and climate change feel only a bit more slow-moving. But the possibility of better outcomes can spur our engagement. New technologies might help slow global environmental degradation and improve healthcare and longevity (though some note that the most life-enhancing drugs may only be available to the rich). A neuroscience teacher's joke, "Do you think of yourselves now as biological machines?," might carry a positive valence.

We might seek to become more aware of how we are multiply articulated, and constructed through inheritances and genetics as well memories and experiences. We're vulnerable to both the peculiarities of the ways we think and the contexts we circulate in. These potential shifts in orientation could soften some of culture's great myths—some conceptions of God, the will, and individualism; even Neoliberalism and post-Taylorist just-in-time structures might loosen their chokehold. My belief is such processes might

17.1–17.2 In *Lemonade,* figures seem to quietly witness. This encourages a viewer's curiosity and empathy. How do these characters reflect a Levinasian radical otherness?

transpire through people becoming curious about the ways they think and feel, and subsequently about others too (figs. 17.1 and 17.2).

But there are also some not-yet-mentioned negative outcomes to track, particularly in regard to technologies that facilitate new modes of surveillance, warfare, and torture. In the future, torture's trace may become less visible while its social effects are more wide-ranging. Even as an unfulfilled threat, torture can have chilling effects on populations, encouraging passivity and self-censorship. AI, fMRI, EEG, big data, and minimally invasive, untraceable brain interventions (through modes such as ultrasound, invisible sonic-attacks, and optogenetic light) make the psyche newly vulnerable.[21] Optogenetic light can trigger or ameliorate aggression.[22] Sound, it appears, can possibly destroy the brain's white matter. While international law protects the body, it doesn't yet protect the mind. Max Tegmark writes about potential techniques working bidirectionally—enabling physiological and psychological consequences—like bumblebee-sized drones that can drill into the flesh, or miniature consumables resembling worms.[23] When softer power stops working the rich might seek to insulate themselves from others through harsher, more invasive forms of bodily and psychic threat.

In the face of unpredictable futures, one might ask questions about the individual's responsibility to be good, and the kinds of social structures we might hope for. Why should one be good? Aristotle believed that only by being good could one come to know the good. Goodness is recognizable: a well-crafted bow produces what's most desired, which is an arrow's straight trajectory.[24] Philippa Foot's response to Plato's example is a thought about plants. One can judge whether a tree's roots support the tree; and just as there are ways of evaluating a plant kingdom's flourishing, so might we consider ourselves. There are also selfish reasons to be good. Principled cooperators, who signal that they can be trusted when times get rough, are among society's most prized members, and we tend to preferentially associate with colleagues, friends, and spouses who exhibit their values. It's hard to project virtues like generosity, compassion, and care for others, and then, when no one is looking, turn self-seeking. One might try, but as Baruch Spinoza pointed out, a discord in the self is a divided self. It's hard to reach a state of wisdom with parts set against one another.[25] It may also be healthy to practice care. Generosity sparks the positive neurotransmitters like dopamine, oxytocin, serotonin, and endorphins. Goodness feels good.[26] But these are only a few of many well-documented reasons.

Many progressives hope to move beyond capitalism and neoliberalism toward a social-democratic or socialist polity that embodies a thick sense of the good. Marxist and post-Marxist theory provide the most succinct and apt critiques of today's status quo. When I've taught Marx in Red states I've asked students: So you don't want the government in your life? But then who and what might take its place? Corporations? A corporation's first responsibility is to produce quarterly reports showing consistently increasing short-term profits for their shareholders. Upper management's strongest obligation is to depress wages: a company may project a veneer of care, but in truth labor is just another cost, like infrastructure and raw materials. Herbert Schiller augmented Karl Marx's analysis with social psychology, noting that the highest-ranking people tend to replicate social hierarchies (so replacing a corrupt person with a stand-in solves little).[27] Recent neuroscience corroborates this. Those with great power tend to become punch-drunk. It's possible their brains have been receiving a potent cocktail of neurotransmitters for too long, and as a result they often lose judgment, empathy, and the ability to read a group. Rich people, too, have related symptoms. The length of their gaze when looking at others is much briefer than on average, and studies also show they experience less empathy.[28]

This recent research may call upon us as community members to be more vigilant about power, and to educate ourselves about the roles of contexts, genetics, and cognition. Advances in cognitive and neuroscience may eventually help us make ethical decisions, but right now there is much we still don't know.[29] Scientists are still debating to what extent the brain is a symbols-based system or a parallel-processing neural network. Jay McClelland, a preeminent neuroscientist, gives convincing arguments for the latter: memories might be encoded as embeds, and insights might already be realized in the network before they become the focus of attention.[30] Other cognitive scientists gravitate to the work of Daniel Kahneman and Amos Tversky, who divide the brain into roughly two systems: the prefrontal and neocortex (system 1) are most responsible for deliberate, slow, analytic, and reflective thinking, and the lower limbic areas (system 2) are intuitive, immediate, and quick.[31] Others neuroscientists, like Joseph LeDoux, imagine a more integrated and emotional brain. The prefrontal cortex may choose among materials (and has its own rhythms and patterns while doing so), but the whole brain participates through networks of memory, thought and emotion.[32]

The way these questions play out may alter how we understand what it is to be human. Bill Newsome notes that we won't be that surprised if we're soon given a card containing our genome and medical history so that physicians can tailor their treatment specifically to us.[33] But we might also be granted a law card, which at any moment could measure our culpability for lawlessness.[34] Processes below our conscious perceptions—the chemistry of our gut flora, real-time genetic imprinting (including DNA from parents and fellow students not passed directly to us), affective contagion shared through group dynamics—will ideally form part of this determination.[35] People have differing capacities for blunting impulses and deciding among options; history, emotion, and context all contribute. Biology and the environment hail us and shape who we are.

John Rawls can help us extend notions of context and empathy to others. He claims that a just society takes care of the least well-off, and his thought experiment "the veil of ignorance" demonstrates its validity.[36] Imagine you and others gather behind a veil of ignorance, and past it is a container within which lives are housed. You can decide how to distribute benefits like education, healthcare, employment, housing, food, and so on. But after you have made this distribution, you must assume you might draw a lot to inhabit one of the lives within this container, including the one who is the least well-off. Most, when they consider this wager, choose to distribute resources more equitably; few opt for a social configuration like today's, with the 1 percent possessing over half the wealth, a shrinking middle class, and sizable number in poverty. Rawls allows for some inequality, especially if those who would benefit the most succeed in helping the least well-off more than if allocations were more equitable. There are good arguments regarding the limitations of Rawls's claims, but I concur with those who believe his basic construct has grip.[37]

The previous sections have offered several conceptual frames. To help forge a body of participants committed to democracy, however—to march, to make phone calls and send emails to representatives, to run for local office or support others in doing so, to stand up for rights in the workplace and common spaces and home, to follow unfolding events—requires emotional engagement, resilience, and stamina. As I've suggested, direct experiences may best provide the sustenance to keep going, but in their absence, art can help. Any readers' favorite artworks might serve. As we move toward an analysis of Beyoncé's visual albums, it will be useful to first touch on segments of *Beyoncé* and *Lemonade* that dovetail with points raised in the first half of this chapter.

Empathy

In *Lemonade*, a working-class middle-aged Black woman calls out "L-O-V-E, love, when your back's against the wall and the wall's against your back, who're you gonna call? You gotta call him, you gotta call him." Whether the viewer has religious inclinations or practices what William Connolly calls "nontheistic gratitude," she may find this woman's vibrant gospel-touched exclamations beguiling.[38] *Lemonade* has the basic materials needed for the perspectives I've catalogued, which is a sensitivity to and embrace of an array of people and their contexts. Its closing number,

17.3 "L-O-V-E, love."

"All Night," shows young families and couples located in quotidian places like the small corner grocery store, front and back yards, a strip of neighborhood park. We see a range of couples—Latina, mixed-race Black and Asian, mixed-race Black and European American, lesbian, gay, older, and younger, with children and without; we also see Beyoncé and Jay-Z as young lovers, their marriage celebrations, Beyoncé pregnant, and one of her daughter's first birthday parties. Beyoncé's "Sweet Love" reflects the desire for acceptance and community (fig. 17.3).

In *Beyoncé*'s "Blue," a song about her love for her young daughter, she sings "We can make it last forever, why don't you hold on to me." But the video, shot in Rio de Janeiro's favelas, exhibits a basic music video principle: the sentiment of the lyrics and musical accompaniment spreads, so when we see not just Beyoncé and her daughter but a range of people within the community, especially young children, the clip's tender, graceful, warm tone extends to everyone. The clip seems to claim that all these people are worthy of attention and care.

The distance between *Beyoncé's* first clip, "Pretty Hurts," and *Lemonade's* final song, "Formation," suggests a development of political awareness and the self. (We might imagine each album as half of a large arch-shaped musical form.) This is a journey we traverse with the singer. "Pretty Hurts" presents the singer considering whether she should relent to the pressures of participating in beauty pageants. She suffers demeaning coaching experiences and painful beautifying regimes. The video encourages a focus on gender and racial bias, but her questions touch on many aspects of American life. Neoliberalism extracts the maximum labor from everyone; in the chorus, Beyoncé sings "Perfection is the disease of a nation." With late capitalism, not only do Beyoncé's competitors harm themselves—successful programmers and businesspeople take cocaine and Soylent to deprive themselves of rest; no one should need to do this (see chapters 5 and 8).

Beyoncé also explores fifteen possibilities for personhood, including mother, wife, lover, sexual tourist, streetwalker, political activist, and punk. The album ends with Beyoncé as a Ra-like goddess with a clutch of babies seated on her knee and at her feet. This range of identities represents a spectrum difficult for anyone to incorporate, even a diva. Perhaps *Beyoncé*'s multiple identities became a burden, impossible to maintain. The next album, *Lemonade,* feels more through-composed and integrated. The soundtrack seems deliberately recessed so that image, music, and poetry can coincide. With *Lemonade,* Beyoncé's journey to find community and discover a history seems to come out of (or at least chimes with) a new sense of equilibrium, grace, and depth. In *Lemonade's* "Formation," Beyoncé and other women organize in the parking lot of an empty strip mall. A young person faces down a line of police, echoing the Black Lives Matter movement. Graffiti proclaims, "Stop Killing Us."[39]

The Mind

Lemonade opens with a tightly cropped image of Beyoncé's head resting against the hood of a car, and the soundtrack's concrete sound effects suggest her mind churning, reflecting, and sorting. Collective memories then seem to come forward: a low-angled shot of a long, dangling metal chain resting against a wooden wall (suggestive of a device allocated for punishment within, or a ladder out of, a slave's quarters?); an image of Beyoncé in tall rushes, possibly as a slave on the lam; and a prison's bulwark facade (perhaps a trading site for slaves?). Then there's a cut to Beyoncé, prostrate before a red curtain girding a proscenium ringed by glowing lightbulbs. A question of the mind's sorting arises: Which story might be told, and which is the truest? As is typical for the genre, the song's arrangement seems to spread across images, blurring boundaries. Beyoncé's psychological states seem sometimes to collide, and at other times, to mingle (see chapter 5, fig. 5.2).

Lemonade uses subtle priming rather than overt sound or imagery. This may be a way of making a painful history for Blacks more bearable; it may equally be a means of addressing infidelity in Beyoncé's marriage. We access these materials through several strands of imagery, including (in

Lemonade) Beyoncé driving a monster truck over parked cars and into an underground parking lot, as if in search of the unconscious, and tripping off a beauty pageant stage into deep water (to drown out stimuli and signal the horrors of neoliberalism in "Pretty Hurts"). These and other devices enable what has been recessed to feel proprioceptively understood.

Lemonade is sensitive to the ways thought works. At the beginning of each section we see text headers embossed in delicate, feminine handwriting: "Anger," "Accountability." The words quickly appear and fade away. It takes a moment until we've grasped their meanings and each section's tone. Perhaps a viewer's understanding happens only after these words appear, congealing while sound and image alternately claim our attention, both sound and image gradually accruing weight, substance, and definition. Many brain processes show a ripple effect: an impulse to direct focus or embark on an action registers in one part of the brain, and then passes on to other modules for instantiation. It's only later that we become aware of the thought or action through consciousness. The single word as embossed text here could be like this initial generator, or it could instead be an inverse of this process, here providing a flash forward to the coalescence of an understanding—first, muddled sensations which, after they've unspooled, become distinguished as identifiable thoughts or feelings. One also sometimes needs a conceptual apparatus to carry thought and emotion forward. It's only after Malcolm X's voice resounds, charging that "the most unprotected woman in America is the Black woman," that Beyoncé more fully expresses her anger about her husband's infidelity.

Technology and Neoliberalism

Shot from a moving car, a giant twister swirling at the horizon works as an unknown future coming toward us. Three videos in particular, "Ghost," "Mine," and "6 Inch" (from *Beyoncé* and *Lemonade*), could be seen as foreshadowing encroaching technologies and the alienating chill of neoliberalism. In "Ghost," Beyoncé runs in front of a white cyclorama, as if on a treadmill, against what resembles a ticking clock. She's pulled down at the waist by appendages suddenly appearing from a black void. She's coated in black oil, wrapped in diaphanous black veils or form-hugging, sheer white fabric. Her image often replicates into doubles and triples. Much suggests the punitively mechanical: there are edgy jump-cuts, disembodied high-pitched singing, cold synthesizer sounds, a five-note loop that contains two repetitions within it, and Beyoncé speaking in a low voice with a hollow echo. We might assume that Beyoncé can navigate this netherworld

17.4–17.5 Neoliberalism in "Ghost."

better than we can, but we watch as one eye zigzags as if failing to catch its target—she and we can barely catch up. Beyoncé momentarily reaches equipoise, as when she becomes centered among the billowing veils, but most of this feels like the rhythms and experiences of work speedup, not something to rejoice in: "working 9 to 5 just to stay alive, how come?" (figs. 17.4 and 17.5).

In "Mine," Beyoncé places a plaster mask in front of her face. Breaking contact with an outstretched hand, she drops into a void. Bare cycloramas and abstract landscapes contribute to an otherworldliness. Veiled figures swirl around her; at a distance, an inscrutable white-coated figure walks toward us among sand dunes while black clouds of smoke detonate around him. Beyoncé expresses hope for a monogamous relationship ("all I want is to call you mine"), but a viewer might doubt any pairing could provide solace. We see a couple kissing, hip-deep in water, but their heads are shrouded under wet cloth stamped with words like "mine." Are these anonymous lovers nothing more than branded consumer products? Has capitalism so alienated us that we can barely find another? One warmer moment near the video's end presents dancers at night, now with naked chests, dancing emphatically on a beach while African rhythms come forward; a male fist reaches around another male's naked torso to strike his chest. Visible flesh with synchronized live drumming suggests hope, but it's fragile. We see "M-I-N-E" spelled out as large signage in flames, but the letters are so far in the distance that the text feels inassimilable.

"6 Inch" is a nighttime video, filtered through a uniform cabernet red, with the darkest details muddied. A front wall of what resembles a plantation house has been replaced with a glass panel that Beyoncé presses up against; she shifts her weight back and forth stiffly on bent knees as if she were a puppet in a shop window. She's for show. In an attic, standing tall on a chair, she slowly swings a lightbulb on a rope over the heads of several seated women. (Is she summoning power?) Dressed in a flouncy white dress, Beyoncé writhes on a large brass bed while a ceiling mirror catches her image. Late at night she circles the city in a limo, pulling the plate-glass window up and down so she can gaze at stray males walking the streets. Flash-frames of shadows on a wall intimate a murder, and then the house bursts into flames. The video suggests Beyoncé pushing herself, working excessively. She sings in her lowest register with a country-tinged growl that recalls an elongated version of Isaac Hayes's cover of "Walk on By." And in response to the late capitalist demand for flexibility, with a sharp shift in the arrangement, Beyoncé jumps up an octave: she sings a serpentine rushed melody reminiscent of Joni Mitchell, while suddenly anxiously curling up in bed.[40] Does usurping a male role prove difficult? Easiest to soon be a voyeur from a limo?

Disclosure and Intersectionality

The cinematography and Melo-x's soundtrack create a sense that *Lemonade's* people both reach out to all of us and commit to their communities. The soundtrack's details—a mixture of distressed footage, concrete sounds, and figures playing live instruments, but also people with particular gazes and deportment—are probably too fine to capture quickly. Director

Kahlil Joseph's and Melo-x's intimacy becomes clearer when compared to *Beyoncé's* "No Angel," elegant in its own right, also with footage of lower-income neighborhoods. In this context, *Lemonade* foregrounds several people with disabilities who might carry a heavier cultural load: a woman with impetigo, a young girl who might be albino or white, a woman with a double mastectomy who stands partially naked and proudly erect. Most striking are the seated women who cradle photographs of their deceased sons on their laps, murdered by police, and who directly encounter the camera while holding back tears. Beyoncé calls out her positionality too ("My daddy Alabama, momma Louisiana, You mix that Negro with that Creole make a Texas 'bama").

These forms of address and disclosure may lead us to wonder about Beyoncé and Jay-Z in real life, and their relationship to this work. Beyoncé and Jay-Z are part of the 1 percent, and might be called part of the problem. Many progressives believe wealth should be limited to ten or twenty times the average salary. These performers haven't made their money through inheritance or rent-seeking, however, but rather through labor that's visible. Or so the songs suggest: in "6 Inch" Beyoncé sings "she works for the money and she earned every dollar and every minute." Both Jay-Z and Beyoncé have been public about their wealth and its relation to race and to them as a couple and as individuals. Jay-Z has pointed out that once a Black person loses money or fame, he becomes just another Black person.[41] In this light, the line in "Formation" that "the best revenge is your paper" carries weight. Blacks are poorly represented financially. Of the 2,043 people who made it to the 2017 *Forbes* list of the world's billionaires, ten are Black.[42] Today wealth buys political and social influence, and there's a long tradition of Black political thought that self-sufficiency and pooling resources are the best way forward.[43] Jay-Z and Beyoncé have made commitments to progressive work. Jay-Z has talked with media like the *New York Times* about the problems of incarceration and drugs, and he has produced a film on Trayvon Martin. The couple has also donated to underprivileged youth for education and to disaster relief.[44] Beyoncé and Jay-Z have discussed their attempts to shield themselves from some of the mental toxicity of wealth, including their labors tied to cultivating the virtues of care, engagement, humility, compassion, and the prioritizing of family, coworkers, friends, and community.[45] Most often in *Lemonade* and *Beyoncé*, wealth is portrayed as soul killing ("Jealous," "Haunted," "6 Inch"), though it might be useful for vacations or experimenting with sex ("Haunted" and "Partition"). Real pleasures can happen just on the beach ("Drunk in Love") or at the amusement park ("xo").

All the same, questions remain about who *Beyoncé* and *Lemonade* were made for. Beyoncé's biggest fan base is middle-aged, female, and white.[46] Both albums are multiracial projects, with producers, directors, songwriters, and musicians who are European American. (For *Lemonade* Beyoncé reached out to the songwriters for Chairlift and Animal Collective; we can hear Jack White and James Blake on the soundtrack.) Racial crossings and borrowings can positively shape participants.[47] But it's important too that members of underrepresented communities have formed inclusive bonds around Beyoncé's visual albums, such as Janell Hobson's website, "#Lemonade: A Black Feminist Resource List."[48]

Lemonade incorporates white viewers in ways that may be worth noting. Almost no whites appear in these films. The range of people depicted within the Black community in *Lemonade* are unusually wide for music video. bell hooks has disparaged the work for foregrounding figures who are overly beautiful, but in truth some seem average in appearance, others older and heavyset, and others strikingly handsome in ways music videos rarely show.[49] Physiognomy, build, comportment, and gait feel richly and diversely depicted. Moments of identification for European Americans might include one girl with a large blonde 'fro, and Black women who are depicted as ghosts.[50] These liminal figures form a striking relation to the soundtrack. Two European American male singers perform brief, untraditional—perhaps haunted—roles. Jack White doubles Beyoncé's singing in "Don't Hurt Yourself," and his voice projects higher harmonics than hers. They seem closely attuned in their sentiments, almost as if their vocal shudders are in sync. Blake sings a heart-wrenchingly mournful "Forward," which seems opposite to we know about white male masculinity. The fragility of his sorrow-drenched falsetto feels outside of language. His voice emerges from and recedes into the low register. At ends of phrases Blake's voice is barely recognizable because it's so highly processed, sounding almost monstrous. Summoned, it feels like *Lemonade*'s many other phantasmic elements, and, as it drops back into the mix, its potential is still felt. These visual and aural presences suggest shadowy proxies for something else, not yet named. One might recall the wish-inversion of Billy Holiday's "Strange Fruit." Here we have white men who have likely lost their white women rather than Black women who have lost their Black men—though perhaps this is an indulgent fantasy on my part.

But music videos often support threads—points of interest that cross between sound and image, spreading like archipelagos. In music videos everything seems to make contact. *Lemonade* considers the history of racial oppression, from the murder of Blacks during the Middle Passage and lynching, to the floods of Hurricane Katrina and contemporary police shootings. One thread made up of many aural and visual signs relates to lynching and its memory.[51] An experienced listener-viewer can move across *Lemonade*'s patterns, forging connections across media—from text to image to music. Because each thread is connected to distinct musical gestures, timbres, and song sections, none needs to win out or be annihilated. Like many music videos, *Lemonade* shimmers: history and current events remain co-present. As Beyoncé says, "The past and the future merge to meet us here."

Much of *Lemonade* foregrounds working-class people and the quotidian. *Lemonade* could be said to stand in opposition to Donald Trump's campaign playlist, with his 1970s, classic rock and Broadway musical numbers that exude a combative self confidence.[52] Trump's musical choices, in combination, convey an oscillation between white rage and white injury. Trump's imagery of conveyance via helicopters, airplanes, private jets, and escalators, seek to overwhelm public spaces; this stands in contrast to *Lemonade*, which often depicts people traversing their streets. In *Lemonade*, there's a sense of a multitude with an intimation of the potential for individuals to join hands and rise up.

Lemonade projects a range of dispositions and sentiments that might be useful as companions to one's own. I've mentioned the grief of Blake's performance in "Forward," the anger of Beyoncé's and White's "Don't Hurt Yourself," Beyoncé's cross-gendered assertiveness in "6 Inch," and her graciousness in "All Night." "Freedom" projects as a struggle against injustice (a drummed march becomes louder as the camera rises up and leads us to a public theater, with Beyoncé on stage, a noose behind her; Lamar's rap and a prison song curated by Alan Lomax encourages us on). The visual album also offers a moment of recession, of stepping away from the world. Against a late-day sun streaming through distant trees, Beyoncé utters "the orchestra plays but they can't hear us." This seems close to the thought-experiments of philosophers of mind: Thomas Nagel's bat and Frank Jackson's Mary who's quarantined in a room without red.[53] The visual album's many hopeful instances of rebirth, like a baby on a bed and Beyoncé softly saying "magic" alongside a Hammond organ might be embraced.

A fan might draw on *Lemonade's* moments as tools for living. Lately I've been thinking of Beyoncé's gently hopeful line "so we're gonna heal," which is spoken as many figures gather produce from a garden, prepare a meal, and come to the table.

Fox News, COVID-19, Brief Media Aesthetics, and Historical Resonances

MANY SCHOLARS HAVE WANTED to respond quickly to events, but there are obstacles. Like most academics I don't write quickly, or with the telegraphic, conversational style of journalists. (I've tried—I've sent work to the *New York Times*, *Salon*, *The Atlantic*, but I judge I'm not swift, transparent, or cool enough—finally *Salon* published me.) Few academic journals can publish quickly.[1] This book's focus now shifts from close readings grounded in entertainment to an engagement with politically oriented content. This chapter reflects my attempts to track current events. I've aimed to preserve the prismatic style we may want to adopt if we're going to intervene quickly. It includes work on the coronavirus; Fox News' media aesthetics; Grimes and DIY music videos during shelter-in-place; Donald Trump's inauguration; political advertising from 2016 applicable to 2020; The Lincoln Project's ads (TLP is a super PAC founded by former neo-conservatives who experienced an awakening of values); and my attempts to encourage others to write.

Some theorists have claimed that with neoliberalism, accelerationism, trauma, the explosion of data, and the digital turn, time becomes distorted and the past suddenly rebounds upon us.[2] At the time of this writing, living with the quarantine, murder of and violence against Blacks, and the upcoming presidential election, I'm experiencing flashbacks to 9/11, Rodney King's murder, and Trump's inauguration. I'll oscillate between now and then. This may be where we are.

Fox News, Media Aesthetics, and the Coronavirus Pandemic

I dislike Fox News, but as a scholar curious about our polarized political landscape, I want to learn more about this infotainment network, which 60 percent of Republicans watch for their single, primary source of news.[3] Especially during the coronavirus, participants other than politicians, journalists, and the wealthy might contribute to the conversation. I'll discuss Fox News' pandemic coverage and its aesthetics—and I apologize, I'm writing from what I can bear.

Fox's vitriol can be unpleasant (as is MSNBC's, though quantifiably less so). An example from Sean Hannity's commentary: "The Democrats, the media mob . . . Their rage, hate Trump psychosis . . . a virus as a political weapon . . . a shameful politicizing, weaponizing of, yes, the coronavirus . . . they are smearing the president."[4] With so many lives and livelihoods at stake, this dismissal feels painful. I followed the virus' progression from Wuhan's first cases. Why didn't I gauge that with so many government agencies dismantled or in disarray, preventative measures weren't unfolding? Fox is often described as Trump's state TV; his mouthpiece, Fox and Trump are one another's mirror.[5] With Hannity's coronavirus-is-a-hoax rhetoric and many Fox News pundits claiming coronavirus was no worse than the flu, why didn't I infer the contagion would spread, relatively unchecked?[6]

The *New York Times* noted that as Trump's responses shifted across four vantage points, Fox's coverage followed suit.[7] Graciously, for one period, I was surprised to give Fox credit. Chris Wallace and Doctor Anthony Fauci met across a table. Wallace asked, "Why don't we have tests?," and Fauci responded "I don't know" (a punt?), but a humble and sober discussion followed about risks, responses, and other nations' experiences.[8] Next, Laura Ingraham and Tucker Carlson both interviewed Fauci, the hosts unusually ruffled while Fauci maintained a scientifically assured equipoise.[9]

Fox News' interviewer-guest split screen often withdraws authority from the guest. The interviewer's placed slightly forward, elbowing out the second person; the editing's rhythm places the strong beats with the interviewer, and the stream of scrolling imagery seems to sweep the interviewee away. Subtly, this dynamic is less apparent with guest Dr. Fauci, perhaps because he's sometimes atypically granted a full-screen.

As Media Matters concurs, Fox circulates a constellation of coronavirus themes. It started in China, it's their fault, and they need to pay.[10] China's a major threat. The Left is focused on identity politics (though

Fox keeps dwelling on its attributions of their racism—gotcha).[11] Trump's doing a great job, he's responded quickly (two months!), and he closed the borders.[12] We need to preserve our way of life. We can't shut down the economy, and we need to think about letting some people die. Treatment and a cure are around the corner.[13]

Fox News highlights valuable information about the pandemic. Yes, China makes much of our products, and a break in the supply chain, especially for personal protective equipment and pharmaceuticals, would be dangerous.[14] What's not said is perilous. Experts note that border closings bought us a week or two (and couldn't Trump have envisioned risks from COVID-19-positive Europeans entering the United States?).[15] Other countries have saved more lives through better testing and tracking. How is the United States doing comparatively?[16] Many without paid sick leave will feel compelled to come to work, risking infection for many. A proactive government, less socioeconomic inequality, and a better healthcare system could have staved off this catastrophe.

Fox's aesthetics: the lines are strong and bold, chunky. The colors are deeply saturated, blues and reds. The show's lurid red grates, especially with the Chinese coronavirus imagery. The forecasters appear beefed up, sometimes pudgy, too. They're not finely drawn individuals. MSNBC's physiognomy differs, though the hosts of both stations possess androgynous features. Fox newscasters showcase a bit of a chip on the shoulder: "You want to fight with me, ma'am? I'm a fighting man!" But it resembles my memory of the school yard. Tucker Carlson appears to me as if he were just slugged in the face. Hannity looks like he's had too many lollipops (figs. 18.1–18.2). Laura Ingraham has a touch of horsiness to her, and perhaps this is unfair, but I wouldn't want to be in her clique. She resembles a bully to me. Perhaps Trish Regan's tremulousness lends variety.[17]

Fox employs finer aesthetics, too. Carlson's river of gold light or ectoplasm streaming from the frame's left side materializes the White House's and host's intimate link. The 3D-layered marquee accentuating text and pics becomes Carlson's Greek-warrior-like shield. A mid-1950s rock n' roll fanfare-bumper against the flag salutes his entrance. Rippling waves and twinkles of light bathe him in a lullaby-like oceanic plentitude. Rather than show real people suffering from the virus, Carlson reads their letters so we don't form an interpersonal connection.[18] His words are sharp. I've seen Fox, drawing on postproduction techniques, tint the B-roll of opposing speakers' faces green. The infotainment show's tone is an amalgam: forceful, brutalist, alarmist, yet reassuring (fig. 18.3).

18.1–18.2 Fox's boxy aesthetics complement Sean Hannity's physiognomy. Note the shrine to Trump.

18.3 Fox News' and Tucker Carlson's aesthetics form an amalgam—alarmist, forceful, brutalist, and reassuring.

Shifts in aesthetics matter. Compare the *New York Times* and Fox News hospital tours, what's shown and not, modes of address, cinematography and editing, soundtracks, and affect. Imagine the voiceovers delivered differently, or the soundtracks exchanged.[19]

As Fox pivots again and exhorts us to go back to work, it's failed to note that anyone can get COVID-19, and medical costs will land with the infected. Twenty percent experience extremely painful symptoms. The lungs' coating of white crystals (from fluid and decayed cells) causes organs to fail. The infected feel as if they were burning up or trying to breathe underwater. The dying in ICUs must be restrained for extended time periods as they flail, gasping, struggling to breathe. They'll die alone, without friends, family or proper funerals.

Is Fox amoral? When Hannity was calling the virus a hoax, Rupert Murdoch canceled his birthday party to avoid infection and Fox's head of staff was disinfecting its studio.[20] The *Washington Post* has posted some brief Fox News video critiques, but it's hard to grasp the show without watching a good portion of it.[21] I wish I could talk to the people at Fox and to those who depend on it. Let's participate in the COVID-19 conversation and follow Fox carefully.

Preinauguration Concerts: Trump versus Obama, 2008

I hadn't noticed, as fellow scholar James Deaville did, the press's trepidation at covering Trump's preinauguration concert, and their strategies for avoiding it.[22] (Now that I'm attuned to this, I'm more aware of the varying representations of clips online, including the most grandiose, by "Trump TV.") Nor did I know that "God Bless America" experienced a resurgence of popularity after 9/11. The heavily funded yet poorly attended inauguration event showcased many songs that were known to pull at male heartstrings. It was not a diverse performance.

Keith Olbermann and others have argued that Americans should boycott the official events. I'm writing about them because I believe it's important to see what's happening on the other side; this may give us an additional picture of what this new normal is about.

It's probably the perspective I'm viewing from, but the pre–Inauguration ceremony worried me. The discourses of staging, camera, lighting, and music, I felt, aimed to turn Trump into a demigod. It created a hierarchy of the bird's-eye (God), down through fireworks and sky, the monument, Trump and his family, the military, the attendees, and us.

The build toward Trump and his anointed place unfolded slowly, beginning in daylight from the back, and wending its way toward Trump as the nighttime culmination. While Obama's preinauguration concert and ceremonies had a woman's voiceover, Trump's male voice sounded like a gameshow host on coke or euphoria (a nod to his entertainment background). "You just can't believe this," the voice seemed to say, "we are so excited." Though the camera retracted periodically for a restart, its two most frequent gestures were a slower upward-gazing crane shot and a faster, low-arcing dolly that also looks upward. Both placed the viewer in a submissive position. It's the same rhetoric that the Metropolitan Opera has used for its Wagner simulcasts when it wants to create the sense of a singer's superhuman aspects.

The military bands, anthems, and religious songs heightened the effect, which was timed to connect Trump with Christ. The lyrics seemed to coincide with images of Trump: "The beauty of the lilies, Christ was born (Trump's and Christ's truth) is marching on." This was from Trump TV, of course, which we'd expect to be more aggrandizing than the other news shows. Listen to how the orgasmic, gasping modulation was given to the Trump family. From the helicopter's vantage overhead, the Lincoln memorial occasionally looked small and precious, God's jewel, and was shot in an alabaster glow, the same kind of celestial light Dana Gorzelany-Mostak noticed in her analysis of Jackie Evancho's performance on America's Got Talent: an ultra whiteness.[23] The fireworks above were mainly in red, like a kind of *Gone With The Wind*, the-South-in-flames image; watch for three moments that seem to suggest war. At one moment the fireworks seemed to spell "USA," and then later to represent the flag, but these images dissolved so quickly that they seemed like the last vision of all of our last hopes. But perhaps the most authoritarian touch was the placement of the military figures. Typically these performers formed tight geometric patterns of diagonal vectors leading toward Trump, or barricading lines to keep us apart. At the end, a tight triangular apex led up directly to Trump.

The ceremonies did have moments of liveliness. DJ Ravidrums, a drummer in a punk hairdo and a faux-peace-sign T-shirt in a bubble of wire mesh, was playing woodenly but with power against bagpipes. The cement fences behind him had LEDs of the names of states rising up and the stars from the flags twirling through projectors. The stage hands, in black, leisurely moving materials in and out, gave the show a bit of looseness. Ultimately the moment wasn't progressive, because we would remember

DJ Ravidrums being on one of the first lower tiers moving up through the military toward Trump (so he would remain apart). I felt that a delicate performance by the Army's fife-and-drum corps created a bit of gender-bending and vulnerability, but I wonder if Republicans read it this way.

Now compare this performance with the language of Beyoncé and others in their 2008 preinauguration ceremonies for Obama. Beyoncé walks on stage in comfortable clothing, suggesting openness and relaxation. She stands close to young people dressed in sweatshirts. She and they are just people—we don't realize just yet that these are their background singers. As Beyoncé sings the camera often turns back to the crowd, their huge numbers stretching to the horizon; but as individuals they sing along with her. Among the many are Obama and Stevie Wonder. People hug. The mood is so different—nonhierarchical and inclusive.

In comparison to Trump's ascension to office, The Women's March began for me when I saw my Facebook feed fill with pictures of friends across the country wearing their pink hats and colorful sweatshirts. A bouquet of flowers, I thought. Did Facebook know that was what I wanted to see, or had my tribe found itself? A Facebook friend argues that marchers' faces should not be shown—we need to protect their anonymity in a police state. But I was so glad to see faces of protesters on the Guardian's home-page.

I've been thinking about bodies, cameras, staging, and presentation. While Trump's and his performers' bodies appeared hard and rigid, the Women's March speakers countered with a mix of braggadocio, but also more revealing moments. Star performers can project intimacy, transparency, and truth (for example, Scarlett Johansson's speech sharing her experience with an abortion). Some say the Republicans are the party that believes there will be rich and there will be poor, and the poor will always be with us—let them sicken and die. The progressives during the march projected themselves as a coalition for inclusion—everyone should have a seat at the table. If this is true, we might see something different in the ways people are addressed—different degrees of intimacy and availability to strangers. The arts are by nature empathetic; this may be why few would sing, read poetry, or act for Trump.

Gloria Steinem spoke of this:

> We are here and around the world for a deep democracy that says we will not be quiet, we will not be controlled, we will work for a world

in which all countries are connected . . . introduce yourselves to each other and decide what we're gonna do tomorrow and tomorrow and tomorrow and we're never turning back.²⁴

Gloria Steinem hopes horizontality and recognizability rather than hierarchy might be central to the progressives' mission.

I'm struck by what Steinem's message shares with political videos like Will.I.Am's 2008 "Yes We Can," for Obama's 2008 campaign, and the Sanders campaign's "America," which used Simon and Garfunkel's eponymous song. In these two the performers turn toward viewers in open ways, as if to incorporate them. In both, there were rhetorical flourishes that called up dancing, hoedowns, nodding in rhythm.

Solange's performance at the Peace Ball (2017), viewed from spare clips on YouTube and Instagram, struck me similarly. Like Trump's, Solange and her performers make highly stylized gestures, and some of her and her singers' movements are very angular. But there's something more open and intimate about this performance, as if the background singers are reading the situation in sensitive, alert, improvisatory ways. They're vulnerable: like the grass in the way of the Tao, they'll momentarily bend and then regain their stature. These gestures depart greatly from the military's for Trump.

And then there were the constant questions of size and spectacle. Was it small, was it large, impressive or not? I should see Trump's proclamations of erroneous numbers as gaslighting, but Emily Nussbaum at *The New Yorker* encourages us to see it as part of a Borscht-belt routine in a way that's typical of Trump's humor. Many in the press said that the numbers of protestors in the streets doesn't matter, but I think they do. Legislators will know—letters, phone calls, contributions, and sit ins should be soon to follow.

I wish a novelistic writer would thread together similar experiences to those described thus far, both from people on the Right and the Left. How do these moments touch our core values? Do we sometimes put them in relation? What of this period, as it continues into the pandemic? George Floyd's murder deeply troubled me. I tried to contribute, including designing posters for safe protesting (see the mockups at https:// themediaswirl). I sent them to Black Lives Matter, Colors For Change, and others listed through Google's pages for activist groups. Putting experiences into a constellation and thinking how to act on them helped.

After Trump was elected, I became an avid newsreader. I checked four papers daily, as if to be reassured the world was still relatively whole. Now with Joe Biden in office I keep checking, and I wonder how people with different orientations are responding. With Trump, what do I remember most—as an audiovisual memory? He and Melania standing on the balcony and Trump looking straight at the eclipse (a metaphor?); or again standing on the balcony after contracting COVID, and the mash-up now accompanying him with "Don't Cry For Me Argentina"; his claim that swallowing bleach could fight COVID and coronavirus response coordinator Deborah Birx looking down; Trump's exhortation to " fight like hell [or] you're not going to have a country anymore . . . So let's walk down Pennsylvania Avenue."

Teaching Music Video in the Pandemic

My current research focuses on spectacular expansion, but with the coronavirus pandemic it seems like everything is constricting. I teach a course titled "The Art of Music Video Theory and Practice." At the pandemic's beginning, it felt brave to teach a class through Zoom while we made videos and tracked the industry and current events. It feels strange to place these experiences in the political category, but that's how it felt.

I love music video for its tightly choreographed, intertwined dancers and performers, and the play of tinsel, costumes, and intensified color. What would happen with this genre? I've watched music video die twice. In the mid-1990s my students and I sensed that ideas had been played out. (Clips would pick up around the Winter holidays, but it was too late.) Napster and teen sitcoms killed it again in the early 2000s. Music video has often resurrected itself, but this time may be harder (advertising is down, and, as E. Ann Kaplan has noted, music videos are ads plus).[25] Strong videos featuring safe distancing have already been appearing, but the possibilities may be limited: chromakey, Zoom boxes, single takes on a cellphone, and so on. At one point in my "Art of Music Video" class we compared Grimes's lovely, crowdsourced chromakey-in-your-own-background project, and we discussed whether Dua Lipa's videochat Zoom-originated dance clip on Corden's late-night talk show was live (absolutely not).[26] We watched Drakes's hybrid TikTok cellphone music video.[27] Beyond this, there might be holograms and subbed-in figures via motion control, or immersive clips that resemble videogames (with safe-distancing disclaimers).

What do I teach my students, who are charged with creating content at a distance this quarter? I sense we'll experience a bodily hunger, a just wanting to touch or be next to another, and this will drive us mad.

I'm curious whether some music videos portended our moment. Pre-COVID-19, Grimes's "Violence" has dancers wearing N-95 masks.[28] In Dave Meyers's video for Rita Ora's "How To Be Lonely," she embraces a skeleton and next a bear.[29] She then steps on eggs and breaks them.

Will our moment resemble cinema's transition to sound? Only some actors and directors will carry over? Grimes will, I believe (as will Billie Eilish; take a look at her bedroom-studio-based songs and minimalist videos). Grimes is already part avatar—witch, imp, and goddess. She self-produces. Her compositions are mostly her with her laptop. (If she needs a violin, she plays it.)[30] Her songs encompass the full frequency spectrum—they suggest an immersion in sound, an autoeroticism, a headphones experience. She has also long directed her own videos. Her audiovisual relations are sophisticated and subtle, and they often feature just her or a few other performers at a distance. She's perfect for our moment.

The class intersected with George Floyd's murder and several of my students made videos about Black Lives Matter. Many were quarantine-themed.

Dangerous Audiovisual Aesthetics: Reading The Lincoln Project

Media scholar Jonathan Leal and I can't tell if we like TLP's videos because they capture some previously unexpressed feelings we have about Trump, or they're just using high music video aesthetics. Surely it's both, but we sense our attraction mostly stems from TLP's successful meld of sound, music, and image. TLP points to a new mode of political advertising. We don't want these techniques used against progressives.

This review provides close readings of two ads: "Betrayed" and "Conservative." Director Heath Eiden himself expressed trepidation about accepting the projects. "These are swiftboat techniques straight from Lee Atwater, the architect of smear," he said.[31] The mainstream press reflects ambivalence about TLP. Are they grifters? Are they planning a Republican coup? For safety's sake, we want to show TLP's techniques at work.

These ads came together through proximity and serendipity. One of TLP's founding members, former Republican presidential consultant Stuart Stevens, has undergone an epiphany about the party's dark roots, detailed in his recent book *It Was All a Lie: How the Republican Party*

Became Donald Trump (2020). Stevens turned to his neighbor, Heath Eiden, in rural Stowe, Vermont, to direct the clips.

Eiden is a progressive. After earning a journalism degree from George Washington University and freelancing in New York City, he moved his family to Vermont to devote a decade to the insightful and revealing film, *Dean and Me* (2008). The year 2008 hit him hard. Despite political differences, Eiden and Stevens have long maintained a friendship. (As Eiden notes, the population of Stowe, 4,437, makes it a place where you can see millionaires, senators, and working-class people all at the grocery store.) Stuart wrote the ads' scripts with a collaborator. Dan Barkhuff, an Army surgeon and neighbor, played spokesperson (fig. 18.4).

TLP produces many rapid, low-budget commercials. Their aesthetics stem from Stevens's acumen: his small team is well-chosen. Eiden's *Dean* documentary reveals his directorial strengths: a quick, frontal, but warm rapport with subjects. Barkhuff excels as a strong character who could beat the shit out of Trump. He's good for the Republicans who desire strong leadership: "Let's battle."

They filmed in a back room of Stevens's home. The (unplanned) mise-en-scène intertwines masculine and feminine elements: lacy curtains, pottery, and a painting (the last embellished with imagery of women, one Matisse-ian, the other Victorian); antlers and a backyard grill, with a Paul Revere bell on the door handle. Equipment was minimal: Stevens's ringlight, Eiden's Canon XC15 camera, and lavalier mic. (Note Eiden's change in placement between shoots.)

Both shoots took two hours. For the first shoot Barkhuff read the script several times. For the second the text was read in sections, briskly. Barkhuff became more at ease for the second shoot. Notice him leaning to one side, and his pauses and cadences, especially at the end: "Trump is weak . . ." The trumpets here call and respond, helping create a musical entity.

18.4 In "Betrayed," a war veteran calls Trump a coward.

Different editors cut and color-graded the clips. "Betrayed" is meant to elicit anxiety, and it's graded blue. But with "Conservative," according to Eiden, the team wanted to denigrate Trump *and* support Biden. In "Conservative" several elements are graded warmer, yet the color schemes across videos remain similar. (Is this a TLP house-style?)

For "Betrayed," Eiden shot Barkhuff from two angles. (Eiden doesn't follow the 30-degree-rule, but Barkhuff's intense address compensates for this.) "Conservative" was shot from a fixed point, zoomed in or out. The pans and reframings are all from post.

In "Betrayed," Barkhuff's footage, interstitial material, and the soundtrack complement one another. A high-pitched, ostinato-like violin line, without vibrato, traces three pitches (3-2-1) with no lower root. (This kind of line usually appears in the bass.) A bass drum announces this line's entrance. The violin works in counterpoint with our gaze's focus, which first finds Barkhuff's eyes, high. Next we're drawn to the frame's center, which narrates surveillance, and then to a frame's lower third. The graphics connect by tracing stepwise lines. (Notice the horizontal red line drawn in real time across the frame. "Betrayed" plays with authority: which element should enter first? The music, the edit and the shot, the graphics, or Barkhuff?) The zoom-ins suggest we're probing a cover-up. Here, "Betrayed" is omniscient, giving viewers clues; the blood-red and chartreuse pencil markings and the frame's fuzzed-out areas help us find the truth. The ad breaks into three distinct sections. Rounding the form, the bass drum announces the clip's end. This ad feels like music.

The soundtrack of "Conservative" is complex. The video breaks into five sections.

1. We see Barkhuff, who drifts left but inspires trust. A ghostly, hovering, avant-gardish voice (lost!) accompanies him. We sense we'll rise (a two-tone graphic emerges from the lower right).
2. Musical and visual agitation: blurry footage from military funerals unfolds, with a soundtrack that co-opts action films' hustle themes. (Note blockbuster-style swoosh and metal-on-metal sound effects.)
3. The music shifts to ominous pedal tones: Trumpworld versus America. Color patches isolate parts of people and things. The frame's borders, blurred and over- or underexposed, render humans as totems, signs, ominous forces. Figures harden into photographic stills. (These touches serve musical functions—varied visual tempi can illustrate music's rhythmic strata.)

4   A drive to a more hopeful future. Precise, rhythmically consonant music syncs with the image (revising section 2's material). Images of Biden hugging individuals or standing before crowds, arms unfurled, suggest an encompassing warmth. An uncanny play with hands surfaces, partly because we can't see Barkhuff's.

5   Biden's fist on the podium unleashes the trumpets (slotting parts 1, 3, and 5 into a rounded ABABA form), and now we find ourselves. Focalization: the trumpets and Barkhuff mark a contrast—Trump and alienation versus Biden and community—leading to clarity and resolution. The event-igniting whip-pans shift from red to gold. At the end Lincoln replaces Barkhuff, suggesting that the surgeon is his emissary.

Richard Dyer claims that the intangibles of music, light, color, and physical gesture produce effects and carry meaning, but we don't have good ways of talking about them. It's the progressives who embrace education and media literacy—the joys of considering arguments. Hopefully progressives will have the upper hand for a bit. Now we have new techniques. Let's use them well.

Our Commons: An Academic Online Journal

Let me propose an online journal, authored by scholars, that is committed to responding to unfolding events, providing socioeconomic, cultural, aesthetic and historical readings, and enabling public responses. Tentatively called *Our Commons,* it could reach the general public.

How else to create a more robust commons? Neuroscientist Mark Reimers (faculty at Michigan State) and public health specialist Molly Magill (faculty at Brown University) and I have explored whether a technique called motivational interviewing might help a public become open to new perspectives. I've wished to have Zoom town halls between red and blue constituencies. There are so many fronts to respond to. As Sean Cubitt notes, media scholars need to consider the costs of their labor in relation to global warming.[32] There is much to be done.

Afterword: Arguments for Engaging with Audiovisually Intensified Media Now, Including Corporate- and Government-Authored Materials

HOW CAN MATERIAL DISCUSSED in *The Media Swirl* help us envision a way forward? Hope for the future seems important. Let me give it a try. In chapter 16, I discussed the ways in which Unruly Media (a predictive viral video advertising company), large quantitative surveys, neuro-marketing techniques, and computer algorithms might tell us something as humanists, and how business, science, and the humanities might collaborate for good. Let me focus here on one example that feels hopeful. Right now, industry has numbers with which they can predict whether media objects will succeed or fail. They use these data to punch up—or jettison—products, but they often do not have the time or skill to develop nuanced understandings of their materials. Media critics and scholars have theories for how media objects work, but very little with which to anchor these theories; their findings often feel like free-floating intuitions. If this information is shared, content might be constructed differently: it might be more moving, subtle, complicated, and tailored to individuals. Some of this knowledge might move out into the culture, just as some forms of media literacy are now widely shared, like Hollywood's three-act structure.[1]

Here's a graspable scenario. With the Democrats' Green New Deal, and contributions from young people who are now more critical of wealth inequality and more committed to a society structured around social justice (a surprising 70 percent of young people support projects like income redistribution and social programs that remedy inequities), we also might see a shift in thinking by the majority about who we are as individuals and a society. Among other factors, recent work in technology and neuroscience might help. We may be able to move toward a perspective that says we are not solely autonomous creatures with our own individual free wills, but also situated—constructed through a variety of forces, including the ways we are interpolated within social milieus, the fortuity and hardships of our histories (including our family backgrounds and class positions), and the ways we are subject to the idiosyncrasies of our personal biological inheritances. As such, targeted content can have a strong shaping force. We'll also be more aware of our creaturely needs to see ourselves reflected back in culture, and to imagine possibilities outside ourselves; we'll be sensitive to the ways media content becomes a means to create this awareness. This may seem like a dramatic sociocultural shift, but there are already some systems in place that acknowledge such connections. Cigarettes and other material objects are already highly regulated. The majority of the population supports gun control. Most of us acknowledge that the food we consume changes our gut, immune system, brain, overall health, and longevity in interlocking and surprising ways. We expect to see nutritional breakdowns on the packages of the food we buy, and for larger companies like Starbucks and Chipotle to both list and make available the nutritional composition of their products. Such structures and ways of thinking may spread out to media and to other social realms.

We should also come to acknowledge that we're an incredibly wealthy country. (Not all of the public knows that we have the best soil in the world—better than Russia, Europe, South America, or India—and other natural resources as well.) We may want to reward innovation, ingenuity, and hard work to a degree, but we'll also be more aware of the ways we are interconnected, and that good lives might be what many of us wish everyone has. We'll succeed at reducing the fear of precarity that many experience. (This might happen on a variety of registers. There's already a call for universal basic income to compensate for automation. Here in the wealthy city of New York, advertising claims that the state has made a commitment to provide healthcare to everyone ["let's get us all covered"] and there's now a $15/hour wage law, sufficient to live on.) And parts of society are producing and recognizing media content that is "woke," including Childish Gambino's "This Is America," which won the Grammys' Best Music Video in 2019.

As part of this new social configuration, we'll also have a changed relation to media content. Out of civic duty, an understanding of ourselves as creaturely beings, and an enhanced curiosity about ourselves and others, we might want to have access to information for media content, especially for advertising and political ads. This would combine information from close readings and quantitative data that could help us understand how this content works for ourselves and for various populations, and with which we'll derive pleasure. We'll be curious how media objects move us (and we may click instant fMRI print-outs that we might share with others, and we'll think more deeply about how our relation to media works).[2] We'll want to learn about how to build media content in schools, and we'll want to use this education to enrich both the content we produce and what we consume among ourselves.

This sounds utopian, but the other extreme is unacceptable. It may be closest to something like how China, Russia, and other totalitarian states appear to be trending, wherein the state and powerful coalitions have already grabbed power, leaving the general public with little autonomy. Instead, we might come to think that resources, labor, media content, and data are all things we have a common right to—that they're ours, and that media literacy and transparency about what our corporations, the wealthy, and governments are up to through media are essential components to a more just world. We should push for it now. If we know why a Gap or Apple ad, a Trump commercial, or a Fox News segment sways us, we may be one step closer to a conversation about ourselves and our country. Knowledge about and participation in media may be one of our best hopes.

Working Political Frame

- We're a wealthy country, with the world's best soil—enough to support everyone—as well as rich natural resources and talent.
- We're shaped by inheritances and gifts. Inheritances include biological traits, which are unique to each of us; gifts include the contexts within which we flourish or don't.
- Neuroscience will probably continue to confirm that free will plays some, but not as much, of a role as we currently believe it does.

- We're highly connected and social. No one succeeds or fails apart from the rest of us.
- Though our truths remain uncertain, we can still feel grateful that we're here. A sense of theistic and/or nontheistic gratitude can lead to a commitment to others.
- Our commitment could be to everyone having good lives.
- The ground for this includes freedom from precarity—an access to healthcare, education, economic surety, respect, community, and so on.

Notes

Introduction

1. Dyer, "Entertainment and Utopia," 20.
2. Fischer, "City of Women."
3. Flynn, "The Mutating Musical."
4. Debord, *Society of the Spectacle*.
5. Adorno and Horkheimer, *Dialectic of Enlightenment*.
6. Crary, *24/7*.
7. Heffernan, "How Hyperinflation Destroys Much More Than Just Currencies."
8. Cavell, *The World Viewed*.
9. Canetti, *Crowds and Power*.
10. Leinweber, "Why the Left Should Reject Politics-by-Mob"; McClelland, *The Crowd and the Mob*.
11. Vernallis, "Audiovisuality and the Media Swirl."
12. Lacan, *The Four Fundamental Concepts*, 86, 92.
13. Fairfax, "The Cinema Is a Bad Object."
14. See #BlackLivesMatter videos on TikTok (I took solace in many of the clips, though complaints of censorship have also arisen).
15. Cook, *Analysing Musical Multimedia*.
16. Tagg and Clarida, *Ten Little Title Tunes*.
17. Gorbman, *Unheard Melodies*.
18. Chion, *Audio-Vision*.
19. When focusing on parameters there are many ways to go deeper. Dance and neuroscience is another area to consider more fully. See Iyer, *Dancing Women*, where Usha Iyer provides an insightful and necessary global perspective.
20. See Gorbman, *Unheard Melodies*; Chion, *Audio-Vision*; Cook, *Analysing Musical Multimedia*; Cohen, "Scoring Music for Westworld Then and Now."
21. See Ireland, "Deconstructing Incongruence." I also like Dickenson's *Off Key*; Kassabian, "The End of Diegesis as We Know It?"; Stillwell, "The Fantastical Gap Between Diegetic and Nondiegetic"; Neumeyer,

"Diegetic/Nondiegetic"; Winters, "The Non-diegetic Fallacy"; Rogers, "The Audiovisual Eerie."

22 For many composers, theorists, and philosophers, including Plato, E. T. A. Hoffmann, Richard Wagner, Arthur Schopenhauer, and W. E. B. Du Bois, music expresses something beyond immediate experience—ineffable or infinite—which elicits a listener's yearning.
23 Hanslick, *On the Musically Beautiful*, 9.
24 Gill, "Entrainment and Musicality in the Human System Interface."
25 Langer, *Philosophy in a New Key*, 271.
26 See Overy and Molnar-Szakacs, "Being Together in Time"; also Mather, "Biological Motion."
27 Buckland, *Directed by Steven Spielberg*, 193–212.
28 Feuer, *The Hollywood Musical*, 3–5.
29 Vernallis, *Experiencing Music Video*, 48–67.
30 Bordwell and Thompson, *Film Art*, 482.
31 Arnheim, *The Power of the Center*, 53–55.
32 Von Trier, *Dancer in the Dark* (book), p. vi.
33 Jay McClelland, "Mind and Machines," invited guest lecture at Stanford University, Spring 2019.
34 Kaplan, *Rocking Around the Clock*, 150; Shaviro, *The Rhythm Image*.
35 I'd like to acknowledge Jim Buhler, Lori Burns, Allan Cameron, Dale Chapman, Claudia Gorbman, Thomas Grey, Amy Herzog, Caryl Flinn, David Ireland, Kay Kalinak, Selmin Kara, Mathias Korsgaard, Charles Kronengold, Jonathan Leal, Anders Aktor Liljevahl, Dani Oore, Lisa Perrott, John Richardson, Holly Rogers, Steve Shaviro, and Eduardo Viñuela, but that's just a start.
36 See Vernallis et al., "Introduction: APES**T"; Vernallis et al., "Anderson .Paak, Kendrick Lamar, and Colin Tilley," 'Get Up in Our Rearview Mirror'"; Vernallis et al., "The Janelle Monáe Dirty Computer Project."
37 Vernallis, Rogers, and Perrott, *Transmedia Directors*.
38 Vernallis, Rogers, and Perrott, *Transmedia Directors*.
39 Elsaesser, "Digital Cinema: Convergence or Contradiction?"
40 Stanford on-campus interview with Joseph Kahn, spring 2018.
41 See Landy, *How to Do Things with Fictions*.
42 Cavell, *Pursuits of Happiness*.
43 Greif, *Against Everything*.
44 Kendall Walton, in-person conversation with philosopher, summer 2019.
45 Hasson, "How We Communicate Information across Brains."
46 McClelland, "Minds and Machines."
47 Kaplan, Gimbel, and Harris, "Neural Correlates."
48 Vernallis, Rogers, Kara, and Leal, *Cybermedia*.

49   Gardner, "Optimality and Heuristics in Perceptual Neuroscience."
50   Knutson, "Inferring Affect from fMRI Data."
51   See Vernallis, *Unruly Media;* Shaviro, *Digital Music Videos*; Shaviro, *The Rhythm Image.*
52   See Adorno, *Minima Moralia*, 78–136, 199–209.
53   Baumbach, Young, and You, "Revisiting Postmodernism," 127.
54   Berlant, *Cruel Optimism*, 110.
55   Bordwell, "A Fast-Paced Cinematic Impeachment Trial."
56   Denson, Grisham, and Leyda, "Post-Cinematic Affect."
57   Denson, "Post-Cinema after Extinction."
58   Society for Cinema and Media Studies has a large special interest group devoted to industry studies, but there isn't a journal on the topic in the databases.
59   Landreville, "The Affective Density of the Post-Internet."
60   I'm writing on a Taylor Swift lyric video with Spanish subtitles that's mashed up with the film *Call Me by My Name*. Then a friend informs me that one of the film's actors, Armie Hammer, has been accused of violent abuse. I ponder this news. Showtime's *Couples Therapy* gives me a good reason to withdraw my analysis—in a therapeutic session the wife shares she's angry at her husband for making friends with her physically abusive father. She asks the spouse to end that relationship. I sympathize with her feelings and believe victims should be offered space and support. Though Hammer's case has not yet reached trial, several women have come forward with complaints. If I were them, I wouldn't want him valorized. But I also want to be true to my own background, and perhaps this might align me with the husband who's in therapy: I have my own history that keeps me sentimentally tied to the clip—a crush on a male professor, which thankfully didn't unfold further. Even with the Hammer news, the clip still chimes with a narrative I recognize; Hammer plays someone emotionally stunted and out of reach. I, like Chalamet's character, dodged a bullet. I'm also reluctant to let go of my connection because I'm not, in truth, compensated much for my academic writing, I've already done much work on the piece, and my fondness for such a media object feels unusual. Also in support of caution is the fact that community norms are shifting so quickly that tacts I take now will likely soon seem out of date, and more worrisome news about Hammer keeps coming out. (His Twitter posts seemingly align him with the iconography of right-wing patriarchy.) I recognize that my moral compass doesn't square. I know I'd feel more upset if the issue included racism and I wonder how I'd respond if the young protagonist were a woman.

And then YouTube's algorithm, which is on some bead I can't decipher, sends me some more mashups of *Call Me by Your Name*, beautifully made, and projecting such love and attention by prosumers.

Does this affect my calculation? While I'm brooding, Lil Nas X comes out with the video "Call Me by Your Name." Does it link to the Hammer/Chalamet film, or is it just again glance aesthetics? I find connections between the clip and my favorite Busby Berkeley sequence, "By a Waterfall, " from *Footlight Parade*—a reason to feel connected. Then Lil Nas X gets into a Twitter spat with the director for FKA Twigs's music video "Cellophane," which I analyze, over claims for authorship. Twigs, like Hammer's lovers, has suffered abuse at the hands of her boyfriend Shia LaBeouf. LaBeouf has acted in *Transformers*, which I've written on, and I'm glad to forgo my sense of connection to this actor. But LaBeouf also gave a wonderful performance in Lars von Trier's *Nymphomanic*. Many scholars have avoided von Trier because of his misanthropy, but I've helped publish a colleague's chapter on *The House That Jack Built*, which is a difficult film. There are also troubling intimations that von Trier acted poorly with Bjork. I wonder if my calculus of whom I'm willing to let go of is shaped by how deeply I care about the work, and for how long the participants have been out of circulation or dead. I'm pulled back in. My friend asks me to watch Lil Nas X on *Saturday Night Live* (where a costume malfunction takes me to Janet Jackson and then, with the crotch grabbing, to Michael Jackson). Lil Nas X's provocation feels good to me, though many of my students wouldn't like it. He's doing a lap dance with the devil. He's selling Nike shoes with one drop of blood. Then critic Jon Caramanica's comments seem to trivialize my concerns, noting that the elaborate song, music video, and product placement are all just so Lil Nas can have a good laugh on Twitter. That's the denouement.

What am I going to do with all this? Read more tabloids . . . This shuffling and turning over almost feels like watching the montage scene of Martin Scorsese's *Goodfellas* where bodies start to fall out of garbage trucks. A new detail emerges, and my thoughts are, "You've got to be kidding." Luca Guadagnino, who directed *Call Me by Your Name*, will now direct *Bones & All*, featuring Chalamet as a lover who's a cannibal (taking us back again to Lil Nas X and Hammer; Hammer tweeted that he was a cannibal, and Nas depicts his sexual appetites as all-encompassing, e.g., lapdancing with the devil, singing "I wanna fuck the ones I envy," and rapping "shoot a child in your mouth while I'm ridin'"). Does all of this reflect something about our era? Are these makers, as members within the same entertainment community, in the shared midst of processing issues? Or is this just a mathematical cluster? A fluke?

61   West, public talk on behalf of presidential candidate Bill Bradley, Waterloo, Iowa, 2000. See also West's *Race Matters*.

Chapter 1: Partying in *The Great Gatsby*

This chapter previously appeared as "Partying in *The Great Gatsby*: Baz Luhrmann's Audiovisual Sublime," in *Indefinite Visions: Cinema and the Attractions of Uncertainty*, eds. Martine Beugnet, Allan Cameron, and Arild Fetveit (Edinburgh: Edinburgh University Press, 2017), 180–208.

1. Tony Assness, one of the designers for this scene, has described it as arcadian. It contrasts sharply with the second party, which is depicted as dissolute (and as such, features more Black performers and extras). Luhrmann drew often on Fitzgerald's favourite phrase, "vergilis et in arcadia ego." One of this scene's inspirations was Hieronymus Bosch's "Garden of Earthly Delights." Hawker, "The Subtle Art of Staging Gatsby's Lavish Parties."

2. Lawson, "The Tragic Emptiness of *The Great Gatsby*"; Corliss, "Luhrmann's *The Great Gatsby*"; Scott, "Shimmying Off the Literary Mantle." Dana Polan was critical of the film claiming the 3D-cardboarding also flattened the characters and story. As Pam Cook notes, however, Luhrmann, drawing from the theatre, has long employed 3D-set models in preproduction. Polan, "The 'Great American Novel' as Pop-up Book," 397–99; Cook, *Baz Luhrmann*.

3. *The Great Gatsby* came out in 2013, and 2014 was the first year for a careful census of representation on film. The study found that 73 percent of actors were white. See Laura Santhanam, "30,000 Hollywood Film Characters Here's How Many Weren't White" http://www.pbs.org/newshour/rundown/30000-hollywood-film-characters-heres-many-werent-white; *Hollywood Diversity Report 2014*. Representation for Blacks since 2014 has improved, but Latinx actors are still very underrepresented. *Hollywood Diversity Report 2022*, https://socialsciences.ucla.edu/hollywood-diversity-report-2022.

4. In an interview, Luhrmann stated, "The '20s was a time . . . that there was confusion in the national moral dials so to speak. . . . Fitzgerald . . . can see that something is corrupt morally in society and it is going to come crashing down. And I think to a certain extent we have gone through that ourselves recently. Since 9/11 there has been an added slight moral rubberiness in our world . . . it is this that makes the Gatsby story especially relevant today." Ohneswere, "Baz Luhrmann Speaks on Directing 'The Great Gatsby.'"

5. As Alain Lipietz notes, "Fordism was Taylorism plus mechanization." Taylorism signified a separation between the organization of the production process (which was the task of technical offices), and the execution of standardized, prescribed tasks. Fordism implied a long-term contractualization of the wage relationship, with a monitored increase in salaries indexed to prices and general productivity. In the 1980s,

policies of "liberal flexibility" were put in place by the governments of the United Kingdom and the United States, eventually followed by most OECD countries. Workers were encouraged to practice "responsible autonomy," particularly when putting new technologies into operation, and to practice "just-in-time" labor to assist corporations in managing the production cycle. Lipietz, "The Post-Fordist World."

6 Buhler, *Hearing the Movies*; Kerins, *Beyond Dolby (Stereo)*; Ashby, *Popular Music and the New Auteur*.

7 Dyer, "Entertainment and Utopia," 373.

8 *Spectre*'s opening draws on the kaleidoscopic cornucopia of Día de los Muertos festivals, but the varied parts aren't as subtly coordinated. Bay's warring robots in *Transformers 4* present more than viewers can take in, but their visual density doesn't sweep across the entire frame. Scorsese's *Wolf of Wall Street* showcases multiple unfolding tempi, but these strata feel relatively accessible.

9 Luhrmann's first three films have been called the "Red Curtain Trilogy." All draw on motifs from the theatre: *Strictly Ballroom* emphasizes dance; *Romeo and Juliet*, prose and poetry; *Moulin Rouge!* (2001), singing and music.

10 Christiansen, "Things Gone Wild."

11 Wolf, *Building Imaginary Worlds*, 16–17.

12 My approach to analyzing music video involves considering visual, lyrical, and sonic parameters in isolation—color, harmony, props, song form, lyrics, a hook, a timbre, and then seeing how each connects with other features (music to lyrics, lyrics to image, image to arrangement, and so on). The next step involves discovering how these processes unfold temporally. With music videos, an experienced viewer can carry herself through the video as if dancing along with the song—soaring above it, anticipating a peak, collaborating in a slowdown. The *Gatsby* party sequence reveals fewer strongly demarcated experiential paths for a viewer. See Vernallis, *Unruly Media*. See also Buhler and Newton, "Outside the Law of Action"; Kronengold, "Audiovisual Objects, Multisensory People, and the Intensified Ordinary in Hong Kong Action"; Rogers, *Sounding the Gallery*.

13 With determinate chaos, stochastic behavior occurring in a deterministic space produces the highest level of dispersion within an available space. See Gorska-Olesinska. "Polish Digital Poetry," 156.

14 Tiered spaces abound in Luhrmann's *Moulin Rouge!* and *Australia* (2008) as well, each with their own narrative connotations.

15 As in *Moulin Rouge!* our location often remains indeterminate.

16 Much of the ornamentation appears overgrown (broadly striped leaves, tangled brush and butterflies), but its miniaturization gives it a storybook-like quality.

17   Note: in the pool, extras' appearances alternate between shots. Some wear calf-length dresses to accentuate the risks of immersion.

18   Here the feeling of motion is established more through music and lighting than physical distance. The music descends and accelerates, and several patches of white create a sense of passage. The ways materials cross sensory modalities makes Gatsby difficult to describe—light and sound should not feel so spatial, but here they do.

19   Geoff King has described the ways narrative can continue through spectacular scenes, most particularly with action films. King, "Spectacle, Narrative and the Spectacular Hollywood Blockbuster."

20   Two examples of added 2/4 measures include during Klipspringer's introduction and Nick's decision to get roaring drunk.

21   At the pool's center, one member of a small performing group plays a conga, but it looks like it is out of audio range.

22   In the party scene, dialogue is shaped to the soundtrack and vice-versa. After Jordan says to Nick, "Let's go find him, and you can ask him yourself," the opening of Fergie's "A Little Party Never Hurt Nobody," takes up her line's rhythm and contour. See Vernallis, *Experiencing Music Video*, chapter 7.

23   John Belton, email correspondence with author, February 6, 2016.

24   See Vernallis, *Experiencing Music Video*, 2.

25   When Nick first meets Daisy, an odd moment of running and dancing between Jordan and Daisy ("we'll put you off into boats") unfolds. Perhaps this sets a stage for these courtship displays.

26   Disco has progressive connotations, both through its inclusive group of practitioners and fans (gays, Blacks, urban working-class youth) as well as its placement within an economically less stratified era before neoliberalism took hold.

27   See Vernallis, *Experiencing Music Video*, 29.

28   See Sharff, *The Elements of Cinema*, 17, 56, 87.

29   In an interview Luhrmann explained that he wanted to use stripes even before he found a historical correlate, but he aimed to be historically authentic, so he and his team scoured the historical record, and after surveying thousands of drawings and photographs, they found their inflatable zebra toys. Looking down on the mishmash of color, tinsel and noise, it seems stripes lend cohesion. Egan, "Film Production Design."

30   The dancers wear yellow headdresses, perhaps they resemble nervous finches or parrots. They nicely integrate with the scene's flora.

31   Humphrey, *The Art of Making Dances*.

32   I have not seen dancers execute these moves. Partygoers most likely wouldn't attempt them (I don't think they read well except when captured by an overhead camera).

33   Mulvey, *Death 24x a Second*, 7.

34 Or maybe the stars are the balloons. There were over one thousand translucent, silvery balloons and a crew to keep them inflated. Perhaps the balloons stand for the extras of the extras. Hawker, "The Subtle Art."

35 Shaviro, "Post-Cinematic Affect." See Vernallis, *Unruly Media*.

36 Baz Luhrmann's reports of childhood suggest he had a rich, multidisciplinary artistic training. His mother was a ballroom dance teacher and dress shop owner; his father ran a petrol station and a cinema. He studied acting in high school and college, and in 1993, staged his first opera. He has written and produced soundtracks for several artists, directed music videos and commercials, designed shop windows and murals, and assisted in election campaigns. See Vernallis et al., *Transmedia Directors*. See also Pennington, "Wealth and Decadence."

37 See Ahnert, "A Community under Attack."

38 Consider the soundtrack's EDM elements and the ways they appear and disappear before coming to the fore. Steve Shaviro cites Robin James's claims that this style of music directly registers "neoliberal ideology." The prototypical EDM track, according to James, much like a Goldman-Sachs trader, amps up its cutting-edge technology to the point of flirting with overload, "pushing the edge of burnout and exhaustion." But in the end, this transgressive drive beyond all limits is recuperated as a new source of accumulated value; neoliberalism works through "a sort of transformation of Nietzsche's "what doesn't kill me makes me stronger" into a universalizable maxim." The process is particularly effected through EDM-pop's use of soars and drops. Together, they trace a movement of rupture followed by recuperation; the soar/drop structure mimics something like capital accumulation and depletion in the realm of finance. Shaviro, "Cyborg/Goddess" (unpublished); James, *Resilience and Melancholy*.

Chapter 2: Shattered Pleasures

1 Other good studies of Bay include Koepnick, *Michael Bay (Contemporary Film Directors)* and Bruce, *The Cinema of Michael Bay*.

2 Bordwell, "Intensified Continuity Visual Style in Contemporary American Film."

3 Dargis, "Invasion of the Robot Toys, Redux"; Scott, "Let the Mass Destruction Begin."

4 Lacan, *The Four Fundamental Concepts of Psycho-Analysis*, 184, 234, 281.

5 Dyer, "Entertainment and Utopia."

6 Savage, *American Savage*, 56–58.

7 Klein, "Transformers 4 is a Master Class in Economics."

8 Whissel, *Spectacular Digital Effects*, 14.

9   Vernallis, *Experiencing Music Video*, 21–23.
10 Bordwell, "Intensified Continuity Visual Style in Contemporary American Film."
11 Thanouli, *Post-Classical Cinema*.
12 Shaviro, *Digital Music Videos*.
13 Vernallis, *Experiencing Music Video*, 54–72.
14 I'd like to acknowledge a few of the scholars who have shaped my understanding of the soundtrack—Caryl Flinn, Kay Kalinak, Elsie Walker, Jim Buhler, Dale Chapman, Claudia Gorbman, and Frank Lehman—and who have helped with identifying genre, form, sync, and characters. Buhler, *Theories of the Soundtrack;* Flinn, *Strains of Utopia*; Gorbman, *Unheard Melodies;* Kalinak, *How the West Was Sung*; Walker, *Understanding Sound Tracks through Film Theory*; Lehman, *Hollywood Harmony*; Chapman, "Let Me Show You What That Song Really Is."
15 Brill, *Crowds, Power and Transformation in Cinema*.
16 Scott, "Let the Mass Destruction Begin."

Chapter 3: Beyoncé's Overwhelming Opus; or, the Past and Future of Music Video

1   The first wave of music video scholars in the late 1980s and early 1990s included Andrew Goodwin, Ann Kaplan, and Susan McClary. All emphasized the need for a theoretical account of music video. See Goodwin, *Dancing in the Distraction Factory*; Kaplan, *Rocking around the Clock*; and McClary, *Feminine Endings*. Vernallis's *Experiencing Music Video* provided a theory of how music, lyrics and image can be placed in relation, and detailed analysis of individual videos. A second wave of writers in the 2010s include Lori Burns, Stan Hawkins, Henry Keazor, Matthias Korsgaard, Diane Railton, John Richardson, Steve Shaviro, Joachim Strand, and Paul Watson. See Keazor and Wübbena, *Rewind, Play, Fast Forward*; Railton and Watson, *Music Video and the Politics of Representation*; Richardson, *An Eye for Music: Popular Music and the Audiovisual Surreal*; Richardson, Gorbman, and Vernallis, *The Oxford Handbook of New Audiovisual Aesthetics*; Korsgaard, *Music Video after MTV*; Arnold and Cookney, *Music/Video*; Burns, *The Bloomsbury Handbook of Popular Music Video Analysis*. I'm enjoying the work of a new generation of music video scholars. I'd like to give a shout out to Tomáš Jirsa, Eduardo Viñuela, and Anders Liljedahl. Viñuela and Liljevahl contributed to Vernallis et al., "Anderson .Paak, Kendrick Lamar, and Colin Tilley 'Get Up in Our Rearview Mirror.'" See also Jirsa, "Ascension of the Pop Icon." It's hard to acknowledge everyone. Miguel Mera wrote a beautiful analysis on Lou Reed's "Perfect Day" in *Trainspotting*. See Mera, "Reap Just What You Sow." I haven't taught

it in a while, but it's a lovely piece! I hope someone shares readings for class syllabuses.
2   Michaels, "YouTube Is Teens' First Choice for Music."
3   A definitive YouTube example might be "The Sneezing Baby Panda"; for music video it might be Lady Gaga's "Paparazzi"; a quintessential postclassical film might be *Bourne Ultimatum*.
4   See "Autotune the News #2: Pirates. Drugs. Gay Marriage."
5   See "The Duck Song," and "The Badger Song." See also Vernallis, *Unruly Media*, 147, 148.
6   As Toby Litt claims, "One of the main messages of 80s Hollywood was 'you can change your life.' Often, this was done in some astonishingly vile ways." (The pop soundtracks supported this message.) Litt, "The 80s." The 1980s were known for consumerism and materialism, including pop music.
7   Beebe, "Paradox of Pastiche," 316–19.
8   At the 2007 MTV awards show, Justin Timberlake proclaimed, "Play more damn videos. We don't want to see the Simpsons on reality television." Harris, "MTV Loses Another Music Show."
9   Interview with Matsoukas, June 2012.
10 Bordwell, *The Way Hollywood Tells It*, 21.
11 Marks and Tannenbaum, *I Want My MTV*, 26–29.
12 Let me give a shout-out to just a few of the scholars who do strong close readings and track industry practices, and technological change with sound, music, and audiovisual relations—Benjamin Wright, James Wierzbicki, William Whittington, Mark Kerins, Ron Sadoff, Katherine Spring, Danijela Kulezic-Wilson, Jay Beck, Eric Dienstfrey, Ron Sadoff, Jim Buhler. Scholarship on audiovisual aesthetics could be enriched through drawing on exemplary studies of sound. A few examples include Wright, "Sculptural Dissonance"; Wierzbicki, *Film Music: A History*; Whittington, *Sound Design & Science Fiction*; Green and Kulezic-Wilson, *The Palgrave Handbook of Sound Design and Music in Screen Media: Integrated Soundtracks*; Beck and Grajeda, *Lowering the Boom*; Dienstfrey, "Monocentrism, or Soundtracks in Space"; Sadoff, "Scoring for Film and Video Games"; Spring, "From Analog to Digital."
13 Rosen, "Beyoncé."
14 Vena, "Beyoncé Has Lady Gaga, Katy Perry 'Stanning' Out With New Album."
15 I feel Steve Shaviro and I have most concertedly written music video analysis that take into account both the music and image. I value a handful of close readings, which are suitable to assign in class, by Lori Burns, Stan Hawkins, Steve Shaviro, Anders Liljedahl, Maeve Sterbenz, Brad Osborn, Eduardo Viñuela, Tomáš Jirsa, John Richardson, Kobena Mercer, and Mathias Bonde Korsgaard. Their work suggests

where music video studies might develop, and several of these authors have also done interesting work on genre specificity. See, for example, Liljedahl, "Musical Pathfinding"; Osborn, "Risers Drops and a Fourteen-Foot Cube"; Viñuela, "Metanarratives and Storytelling in Contemporary Mainstream Popular Music"; Sterbenz, "Movement, Music, Feminism"; Mercer, "Monster Metaphors"; Shaviro, *Digital Music Videos*; Richardson, Gorbman, Vernallis, *The Oxford Handbook of New Audiovisual Aesthetics*; Vernallis, Rogers, and Perrot, *Transmedia Directors*, chs. 11, 23; Vernallis, Herzog, Richardson, *The Oxford Handbook of Sound and Image in Digital Media*.

16 In *Vertigo*, the row of heating pans at Ernie's seemed to double for Judy's breasts, and in *Psycho*, a pair of narrow Victorian inkwells at the Bates Motel's check-in counter passed for Marion Crane's.

17 Shaviro, *Digital Music Videos*.

18 Cavell, *Pursuits of Happiness*, 49.

19 See Hobson's "Feminists Debate Beyoncé."

20 Robin James claims that EDM directly registers "neoliberal ideology." The prototypical EDM track, much like a Goldman-Sachs trader, amps up its cutting-edge technology to the point of flirting with overload, "pushing the edge of burnout and exhaustion." But in the end, this transgressive drive beyond all limits is recuperated as a new source of accumulated value; neoliberalism works through "a sort of transformation of Nietzsche's 'what doesn't kill me makes me stronger' into a universalizable maxim." EDM's soar is a "sweeping, upward/forward-moving intensificatory gesture." In contrast, the drop is a movement of "deintensification": it "rapidly shifts down to bass and sub-bass frequencies and bottoms the song out." The soar/drop structure mimics something like capital accumulation and depletion in the realm of finance. James, *Resilience and Melancholy*, 21, 29, 36, 78, 79.

21 Eleftheria Thanouli and I mark the shift to postclassical film aesthetics with films from the last two decades (both consider films like *Moulin Rouge!* [2001] and *Lola Rennt* [1998]). Thanouli, *Post-Classical Cinema*, 96, 173–82; Vernallis, *Unruly Media*. See also Buckland, *Puzzle Films*; Elsaesser, "Digital Cinema: Convergence or Contradiction?"

22 As I noted earlier and will again here, Alain Lipietz observes that "Fordism was Taylorism plus mechanization." Taylorism signified a separation between the organization of the production process and the execution of standardized, prescribed tasks. Fordism implied a long-term contractualization of the wage relationship, with a monitored increase in salaries indexed to prices and general productivity. Policies of "liberal flexibility" were put in place in the 1980s by the governments of the United Kingdom and the United States and were eventually followed by most OECD countries. Workers were encouraged to practice "responsible

autonomy," particularly when putting new technologies into operation, and to practice "just-in-time" labor to assist corporations in managing the production cycle. Lipietz, "The Post-Fordist World." This turn to "flexible specialization" maximizes profits and reduces government and corporate responsibility. Not surprisingly, a Pew study released on November 4, 2015 found American working families stressed, tired, and rushed (Pew Research Center, "Raising Kids and Running a Household.") Beyoncé's album acknowledges this work speedup in clips like "Blow" and "Ghost." Her changing personas suggest a way to be responsibly autonomous and ready to practice "just-in-time" labor.

Chapter 4: Avant-Gardists and the Lure of Pop Music

This chapter was previously published as "Avant-Gardists and the Lure of Pop Music," in *The Music and Sound of Experimental Film,* eds. Holly Rogers and Jeremy Barham (Oxford: Oxford Scholarship Online, 2017), 257–82.

1. Philip Brophy, Annette Davison, David James, Holly Rogers, Juan Suárez, and others have begun thinking about this connection; they've also analyzed some of the works I'll discuss. Brophy, *Cinesonic: Cinema and the Sound of Music*; Davison, *Hollywood Theory, Non-Hollywood Practice*; James, *Rock 'N' Film*; Rogers, *Sounding the Gallery*; Suárez, *Bike Boys, Drag Queens, and Superstars*.
2. Stated most simply and broadly, experimentalists can be said to attempt new practices while avant-gardists also push the status quo. I use these terms loosely. See MacDonald, *Avant-Garde Film*, 15–16.
3. See Suárez, "The Sound of Queer Experimental Film." Also, Hawkins, *Queerness in Pop Music*, 243.
4. Frith and Horne, *Art into Pop*, 112.
5. Sitney, *Visionary Film*, xii, xiii; Mizuta Lippit, *Ex-Cinema*, 2–6.
6. Demers, *Steal This Music*, 89–91.
7. I am quoting Michael Jackson's "Slave to the Rhythm" (1991). The lyrics suggest how following music can be tied to abjection: "She dances in his sheets at night / She dances to his needs / . . . She's a slave to the rhythm."
8. Interview with Marcus Nispel, spring 1997. See also Vernallis and Ueno, "Interview with Music Video Director and Auteur Floria Sigismondi," 175.
9. Interview with Adam Sitney on December 6, 2016. Sitney reported not liking pop music, yet he cares deeply about the avant-garde. See Sitney, "Film #12."
10. Singh, "Harry Smith," 34–36.
11. This was recounted to Sitney in the 1950s, when he supplied Smith with white port for breakfast.

12　After visiting Haiti and becoming engaged with indigenous drumming, Deren started adding a soundtrack. *Meshes of the Afternoon*'s soundtrack was added twelve years after its release.
13　Such as Corey Arcangel, Chantel Akerman, and William Wegman.
14　To give a sense of each category, I will be able to discuss only segments within a work, rather than the work as a whole.
15　Rotten Tomatoes, *Scorpio Rising*.
16　Anger, "DVD commentary."
17　Brophy, "Parties in Your Head," 310. David James claims that "interactions among these [Scorpio Rising's] conflictual elements retard the major narrative, anchoring it in an ongoing present of contradictory implications." James, *Rock 'N' Film*, 21.
18　Methods for analysis include Michel Chion's concept of synchresis (the irrevocable "weld" that happens when image and sound are placed in relation) and Nicholas Cook's models of conformance, complement, contest and gap making; Chion, *Audio-Vision*, 5; Cook, *Analysing Musical Multimedia*, 98–100.
19　Carr, "Scorpio Rising."
20　Vernallis, *Experiencing Music Video*, 7–49.
21　See, for instance, Tagg and Clarida, *Ten Little Title Tunes*.
22　Tagg runs a version of these experiments in *Ten Little Title Tunes*. Here, he substitutes one genre of music for another, or alters a single parameter, like rhythm. My approach is more aggressive.
23　The choices here are intuitive. The film as a whole moves between periods of sync and nonsync (so the film's texture is not consistent).
24　Otherwise, music by Led Zeppelin and Joni Mitchell, through a shared mood, would probably "catch" more. I have written elsewhere about forged audiovisual connections where one medium acts as an amped-up version of the other, and both maintain a connection along a sliding scale of similarity (in *Experiencing Music Video*, I discuss Madonna's "Open Your Heart" [1986] video as taking musical elements and dramatically overinflating them). Nicholas Cook usefully notes that sound and image together produce emergent properties. Relations come forward when the two media share a commonality such that their connection facilitates a metaphor; Cook, *Analysing Musical Multimedia*, 57–97.
25　Zak, *The Poetics of Rock*, 78.
26　Concerning gender identity and choice, what is the relation between the female singer in "My Boyfriend's Back" and the male biker? Who is the "she" in "she wore blue velvet"?
27　Paul Morris in email correspondence with the author, December 29, 2015.
28　Paul Morris in email correspondence with the author, December 29, 2015.

29 Brakhage, interview on the DVD-ROM.
30 Rogers, "Audiovisual Dissonance in Found-Footage Film," 193–98.
31 Chion, *Audio-Vision*, 63.
32 My choices for trials are intuitive, though on reflection, they can be unpacked. Rose Hobart might be thought of as a poorer version of Greta Garbo; and Amaral of Villa-Lobos. With the new audiovisual pairings, what might be called the soulfulness, luminosity, intelligence and/or artfulness of Garbo and Villa-Lobos transfer over and infuse its thinner partner (Garbo–Amaral, Villa-Lobos–Hobart). The two strong players (Garbo–Villa-Lobos), when together, seem almost like prima donnas who drown one another out. Some aspects of these choices seem amenable to analysis with Cook's gapped relations and Chion's added value, yet they also seem different.
33 Vernallis, *Experiencing Music Video*, 93.
34 Hobart quoted in Myrna Oliver, "Rose Hobart."
35 Donnelly, "Irish Sea Power," 142. My sense is that Woolcock at least made a rough edit of the image first, so the image is prior.
36 Vernallis, *Unruly Media*, 209.
37 Audiovisual analysis might be amenable to psychoanalytic methods. Drawing on Melanie Klein and Wilfred Bion, Mitchell Morris has already used such techniques in the service of analyzing Enya's pop tunes. Morris claims Enya's songs resemble, for the listener, the engulfing breast; I wonder if her videos' depicted screens—clouds, fountains, mist—might also resemble a confining, yet comforting uterine wall. Might song fragments from "My Boyfriend's Back" spark visual associations that then activate repressed desires? The "r"s, a revving motorcycle and the skeleton puppet's "nah nah nah"s a "blitz-it!" to overrun the image's contents. Morris, "Songs of the Container."
38 David Lynch's popular *Eraserhead* (1993) and *Inland Empire* (2006) are commonly understood as experimental films; Fred Astaire and Ginger Rogers are included on UbuWeb, a site devoted to experimental media. Experimental numbers within films can reach a mass audience. Jerry Lewis was famous for taking risks with numbers, particularly in *The Bellboy* (1960).
39 Naremore, *Acting in the Cinema*, 9–14.
40 See Rogers, *Sounding the Gallery*.
41 Late, a speaker intones, "No will whatsoever." It's not clear if the speaker is the same as the opening, or this is a riff.
42 Pipilotti Rist, quoted in Harris, "Psychedelic, Baby," 74.
43 Rogers also notes the way Rist uses her own body as material and creates audiovisual ruptures. See Rogers, "'Betwixt and Between' Worlds," 537.
44 Marks, *Touch*, 2.
45 Sekula, "The Traffic in Photographs."

46 See Rogers, "Twisted Synaesthesia."
47 See Krause-Wahl, "Why Artists Make Clips," 215. See also Panera Cuevas and Rees, *This Is Not a Love Song*.
48 Gordon, "Kim Gordon's Open Letter to Karen Carpenter."
49 In Banksy's Paris Hilton CD, 2006, consumers discover they have bought some Banksy music (and possibly art) with a Hilton cover and barcode.
50 Director Floria Sigismondi said she tried the art gallery experience but felt she was ripped off. Interview with author, Spring 2016.
51 It has been often claimed that music video stole its style from the avant-garde, most notably Surrealism. Yet considering how few avant-gardists chose to participate with pop music or music video, this argument looks suspect. Many more, and more successful, music videos have been directed by Hollywood and European filmmakers. Though a large proportion of music video directors would have seen experimental films in college, they also would have been exposed to content from Hollywood musicals to foreign films. Music video's imagery and form may share a family resemblance with that of avant-garde film and video (as well as poetry, commercials, and the musical), See Vernallis, *Unruly Media*, 69–75.

Chapter 5: Beyoncé's *Lemonade*

This chapter was previously published as "Beyoncé's *Lemonade*: She Dreams in Both Worlds" by Lisa Perrott, Holly Rogers, and Carol Vernallis in *Film International* (June 2016): http://filmint.nu/beyonces-lemonade-lisa-perrott-holly-rogers-carol-vernallis/.

1 There's much strong work on Beyoncé and on *Lemonade*. Some monographs to consider include Solan, *Switched On Pop*; Iddon and Marshall, *Beyoncé*; Tinsley, *Beyoncé in Formation*; Baade and McGee, *Beyoncé in the World*; and Brooks and Martin, *The Lemonade Reader*. See also Vernallis, "Beyoncé's *Lemonade*, Avant-Garde Aesthetics, and Music Video."

Chapter 6: Tracing the Carters through the Galleries

1 See Vernallis et al., "Tracing the Carters through the Galleries"; Gunn, "The Outside Meets the Institution"; Silberstein, "Have You Ever Seen the Crowd Goin' Apeshit?"; Handley, "Representing Absence."
2 McIntyre, "Report."
3 See Burns and Hawkins. *The Bloomsbury Handbook of Popular Music Video Analysis;* Osborn, *Interpreting Music Video*; Kaplan, *Rocking around the Clock* ; Korsgaard, *Music Video after MTV*; Shaviro, *Digital Music Videos*.

4   Kaplan, *Rocking around the Clock*, 12–21.
5   Though by doing so, I contribute to a syndrome Gabrielle Lochard identifies as Black artists realizing themselves against white culture.
6   Berger, *Ways of Seeing*, 31, 32.
7   Berger, *Ways of Seeing*, 25.
8   Beyoncé, Jay-Z, and the *Winged Victory of Samothrace*, for example, seem to reign over a field of suddenly lively, once recumbent bodies.
9   Kaplan, *Rocking around the Clock*; Kinder, "Music Video and the Spectator."
10 Vernallis, *Experiencing Music Video*.
11 The song's verses, a thinking through, often a chronology; the chorus, an out-of-time summation; and the bridge, another possibility. For an example where no audiovisual instance annihilates another, see my description of Michael Jackson's "Thriller," Vernallis, *Experiencing Music Video*, 19, 167, 200.
12 An example is Tarsem Singh's and REM's "Losing My Religion," Vernallis, *Experiencing Music Video*, chapter 6, and 146.
13 A subtle detail—the ring of lights seemingly reappear in Beyoncé's sunglasses when she raps before the I. M. Pei pyramid.
14 One may recall *Lemonade*'s hallway, both yonic references.
15 European nineteenth-century collectors owned depictions of Africans as figurines. Musicologist Tom Grey notes that Beyoncé and her dancers may most resemble Matisse's figures (Matisse drew much from African culture and art as well). Conversation, Spring 2018. The dancers' hip swirls feels Egyptian and/or Arabic.
16 According to T. Carlis Roberts, "The spirituals retained the same technological function of drumming but reworked on different hardware as body percussion. The ring shout was a cultural technology that acted on the people producing it, allowing for the temporary mental and physical escape from slavery by altering the function of the body. And it was specifically a *spiritual* technology that brokered the realms of the living and dead." Slave songs, Roberts noted, also shared knowledge about the Underground Railroad. They were a technology for freedom. Roberts, "Spiritual Technologies and the Metaphysics of Enslavement."
17 Might the earlier recumbent bodies now be stacked vertically? Might these figures be witnesses to the Middle Passage?
18 Géricault drew his inspiration from the account of two survivors of the *Medusa*, a French Royal Navy frigate that set sail to colonize Senegal in 1816. It was captained by an inexperienced officer who ran the ship aground on a sandbank. Due to the shortage of lifeboats, those left behind built a raft with 150 passengers. After thirteen days at sea, with acts of murder and cannibalism, only ten survived.
19 One of Eisenstein's most famous examples, from *Battleship Potemkin*, includes a sequence of stills of sculpted lions, gradually shifting from

recumbent to more erect, as a means to convey the strikers' and their supporting crowds' revolt.

20   Rose, *Black Noise*, 78.
21   Art historian Jody Maxim notes, "Football players inadvertently strike Hellenic poses" (email conversation with author, July 2018).
22   It's notable too that Beyoncé wears a pearl-covered cowl. Starting eighty thousand years ago beads were the first "bling." Whipps, "80,000-Year-Old Beads."
23   As Beyoncé says in "Formation," "Y'all haters corny with that illuminati mess." "APES**T"'s not that kind of magic. Music video can foreground lines of force which the camera, sound, performers, and objects project. "APES**T"'s opening and ending reveal a concerted drive toward and past the *Mona Lisa*, driven perhaps by a spirit. Beyoncé conjures up dancers, swords, and warriors, and she spans epochs; Jay-Z's suit mirrors the Pei pyramid, and he summons a motorcade out of a painting. But part of this sense of magic might derive from anxieties about the rich. In chapter 6, I give the Carters' wealth a pass in part because there are so few Black billionaires, the couple's labored for rather than inherited their money, and they remain committed to social justice and progressive causes. But our brains are also structured by tribalism; we're hardwired to form outgroups. The powerful can lose empathy—their brains literally blow out from too much serotonin. The lowest ranked are shaped by cortisol, which can shorten lifespans. "APES**T"'s contrasts between those with less power (the domestic tableaux) and The Carters (who can traverse space and time). When Beyoncé sings, "250 for the Richard Mille" (I hear "250 for the rich millionaires"), she may encapsulate global capitalism. Black traditions of flight and disembodiment could be said to contest my claims here. Many studies have shown that Black lives have failed to improve, and perhaps have even worsened in the last thirty years. See Lipsitz, *The Possessive Investment in Whiteness*; Austin, "Black Americans Mostly Left Behind." See also Osnos, "Doomsday Prep for the Super-Rich."
24   "APES**T"'s harmonic stasis derives from rap and EDM; it's seeping into contemporary pop. See James, *Resilience & Melancholy*.

Chapter 7: Storytelling on the Ledge

1   Vernallis, *Experiencing Music Video*.
2   Bordwell and Thompson, *Film Art*, 482.
3   Doane, *The Desire to Desire*, 99–100.
4   Cook, *Analysing Musical Multimedia*, 3–24. Levi-Strauss, *Myth and Meaning*, 20–25.
5   Michel Chion has called this "added value" (that the sound melds with and becomes a property of the image). Chion, *Audio-Vision: Sound on*

Screen, 5. Claudia Gorbman (in "Aesthetics and Rhetoric"), cites Bernard Herrmann's famous quote, drawing on Cook's *Analysing Musical Multimedia*, 104.

6   Vernallis, *Experiencing Music Video*, 140–43.
7   Vernallis, *Experiencing Music Video*, 146–47.
8   See Žižek, *Looking Awry*, 88. His examples include a knife cradled under the family table in *Shadow of Doubt*, and a windmill that turns the wrong way in *Saboteur*.

Chapter 8: How to Analyze Music Videos

This chapter was previously published as "How to Analyze a Music Video: Beyoncé's 'Pretty Hurts,'" in *The Bloomsbury Handbook of Popular Music Video Analysis,* eds. Lori Burns and Stan Hawkins (New York: Bloomsbury Academic, 2019), 255–76.

1   Mowitt, *Percussion*, 3–5.
2   A güiro is a Latin American percussion instrument consisting of a hollow, open-ended gourd with parallel notches cut into one side. A stick or tines run along the notches produce a ratchet-like sound.
3   "Pretty Hurts" was initially written for Katy Perry and then offered to Rihanna. Perry is famous for her use of the soar, and her "Teenage Dream" provides an excellent example. The soar relies on a simple structure: a tiered chorus, which draws on principles of layering and textural builds, long a staple of electronic dance music. The song's verse begins with a relatively sparse texture, then repeats a second time with added layers, along with a propulsive dance beat. A two-part chorus drives to a rapidly building textural crescendo. The verse scales back before the beginning of the prechorus, so it can make the buildup of the chorus even more dramatic. Many musicologists don't like the soar. They feel listeners are hectored into the ecstatic high of the chorus. "Pretty Hurts" does not possess all of the soar's elements. The verse tiers with "Just another stage, pageant the pain away. This time I'm gonna take the crown. Without falling down, down, down." One might even want to hear this as a prechorus. The rhythm arrangement also thickens here. There are striking silences between sections, but the chorus pulls back a bit as well. "Pretty Hurts" is not as anthemic as Katy Perry's "Roar" (it is in a minor key), but it did well on the dance floor. Sia Furler and Ammo wrote the song—Sia sang backing vocals, and Ammo oversaw production. See Wikipedia, "Pretty Hurts (Song)," July 24, 2017, en.wikipedia.org/wiki/Pretty_Hurts_%28song%29.
4   This body bag replacing Beyoncé could be seen as a deathly image. Her earrings, shaped as a spine or fish scales, may prepare us for this (4:06).
5   I discover Matsoukas picked inner-city neighborhoods from across the country for the contestants' sashes' titles. The video was shot in a

Brooklyn high school. Greco, "'Pretty Hurts' Director Melina Matsoukas." "Shaolin" is urban slang for Staten Island. The term was popularized by The Wu-Tang Clan.

6   Greco, "'Pretty Hurts' Director Melina Matsoukas."
7   I've always seen the close-up of the contestant's face (at 1:00) as an object of tender desire. Might the hand that reaches out to Beyoncé (0:33) belong to this contestant, encouraging me to see it in this way?
8   Melina Matsoukas, interview with the author, fall 2001.
9   Crane, "What Would Beyoncé Wear?"
10 When Beyoncé sings *a cappella*, her white dress with black stars could be constructed of bandages, wrapping her like a mummy. Her dress appears confining. The star's footwear make possible different physical dispositions: the chunky high-heeled clogs at the dress rehearsals; the high heels in the chorus; the low-slung tennis shoes in verse 2; and her gangsta socks, which give her the greatest freedom. See Wikipedia, "Pretty_Hurts" (charts), accessed July 22, 2022, http://en.wikipedia.org/wiki/Pretty_Hurts_%28song%29#Charts.
11 McDonald, "The Genre Grinder's Song."
12 See Baker, "Sex, Gender and Work Segregation."
13 Weaver, "Beyoncé's Publicist Wants to Erase These Unflattering Photos."
14 Wikipedia, "Pretty Hurts (Song)."
15 A psychoanalyst might find this fragment interesting. It possesses some ululation and glottal fry, and sounds Arabic or African. Ululations are often long, wavering, high-pitched vocal sounds resembling a trilling howl. Women most often perform them during communal celebrations or grieving, for example, at weddings or funerals. The fragment may elicit some of these cultural connections. Isolated and projected, the fragment might connect with other ingested or evicted elements, like the swallowed cotton balls and the bulimic vomiting in the bathroom. The video seems to achieve some release through purging—the vocal occurrence, now healthy, cathartic, and incorporated. Finally the fragment seems to break apart or dissolve into the rhythm arrangement and Beyoncé's overdubs.
16 Feuer, *The Hollywood Musical*.

Chapter 9: Dave Meyers's Moments of Audiovisual Bliss

This chapter was previously published as "Dave Meyers's Moments of Audiovisual Bliss," in *Transmedia Directors: Artistry, Industry and New Audiovisual Aesthetics*, eds. Carol Vernallis et al. (New York: Bloomsbury Academic, 2019), 181–93.

1   I discuss the binding of sound and image in greater detail in my book *Experiencing Music Video*. Hitchcock's composer Bernard Herrmann has also made this claim.

2   It's hard to track a director's oeuvre. I believe I came across this clip by accident on the Getty website. Subsequent to writing this chapter, I discovered that artist Lina Iris Viktor successfully sued Dave Meyers for using her work in "All the Stars" without permission. I've requested interviews with Viktor and Meyers. I have thoughts on this, but I'd rather the makers speak for themselves. Viktor discusses some of her reasons for not granting permission in a lecture she gave at the University of Michigan; see Viktor, "Materia Prima." See Baron, *Reuse, Misuse, Abuse*.

3   I'm grateful to Lea Pao and her "12 Poems That Will Change Your Life" course for directing my attention to the patterns of Lamar's stressed and unstressed syllables.

Chapter 10: Janelle Monáe's "You Make Me Feel" and Anderson .Paak with Kendrick Lamar's "Tints"

1   I was drawn to Monáe's *Dirty Computer* because it seemed both aware of the genre's history and formal possibilities and, at the same time, committed to breaking preexisting models. My students liked the film's progressive politics. Brief, collaborative close readings are well suited to the genre. Because each scholar entrains differently to the clips; music videos, like pop songs, are heterogeneous with many simultaneous details. As with "APESH**T," *Lemonade*, and "Tints," this analysis came out of a roundtable I assembled.

2   O'Connor, "What Did We Do to Deserve Janelle Monáe?"; McCormick, "It Sounds Like 2018 Distilled."

3   For further discussion on the discourse of authenticity surrounding rap and hip-hop, see Williams, "Tha Realness."

4   See Vernallis, "Music Video's Second Aesthetic?"

5   See Vernallis, "The Janelle Monáe Dirty Computer Project."

6   Ngai, *Our Aesthetic Categories*.

7   .Paak, "Anderson .Paak Talks Oxnard."

8   .Paak, "Anderson .Paak Talks Oxnard."

9   See Zacks, "Cognitive Boundaries."

10 Clement, *Opera, or The Undoing of Women*, 170.

11 Lincoln, "Get Out."

Chapter 11: Who Needs Music Documentaries When There's TikTok and *Carpool Karaoke*?

1   Friedman and Caramanica, "Is Rihanna's 'Visual Autobiography' a Triumph or a Tease?"

2   *Ok!*, "10 Celebrities Who've Openly Revealed How Much They Weigh."

3   Beyoncé, "Beyoncé Shadiest /Top Bossiest Moments" (this video has been removed but YouTube still has several other clips that are similar).
4   Fallon and Swift, "Taylor Swift Reacts to Embarrassing Footage."

Chapter 12: TikTok and Costume-Drama Mashups on YouTube

1   Jung, "Ambiguous Bodies in TikTok and Reaction GIF." Right now, there's only one humanities-based scholarly article on TikTok in the databases. Earlier work on remixing may be informative. See Laderman and Westrup, *Sampling Media*.
2   See Barthes, *La Chambre Claire*.
3   Jung, "Ambiguous Bodies in TikTok and Reaction GIFs." Jung and I have touched base after the conference. We agree that in some music video genres, bodies open up as clips unfold, and perhaps we do, too, as we are carried along by them. See introduction.
4   Gunning, "The Cinema of Attraction[s]."
5   Ravetto-Biagioli, "The Digital Uncanny and Ghost Effects."
6   Cook, *Analysing Musical Multimedia*, ix
7   Complaints that white performers co-opt Black ones and then become the most popular are valid. I like Charli Damelio, but I think Keke Janajah's tops. See her dance for "Savage."
8   See Harlig, "TikTok and Short-Form Screendance before and after Covid"; for a sensitive discussion of appropriation see Baron's *Reuse, Misuse, Abuse*.
9   Kaplan, *Rocking around the Clock*, 132–33; Kinder, "Music Video and the Spectator: Television, Ideology and Dream."
10 Hautea, Parks, Takashi, and Zeng, "Showing They Care (Or Don't)"; Papacharissi, *Affective Publics*; Papacharissi, "Affective Publics and Structures of Storytelling."
11 See Goldschmitt and Seaver "Shaping the Stream"; Cook, Ingalls, Trippett, *The Cambridge Companion to Music in Digital Culture*.
12 See Kassabian, "The End of Diegesis as We Know It?"; Stillwell, "The Fantastical Gap Between Diegetic and Nondiegetic"; Neumeyer, "Diegetic/Nondiegetic"; Winters, "The Non-diegetic Fallacy"; Rogers, "The Audiovisual Eerie," 285–90; Buhler, *Theories of the Soundtrack*, ch. 6; Smith, "Bridging the Gap."
13 Meant to be watched and listened to many times, music videos present a viewer with much to attend to—momentary instances occurring across sound, image, and text. As a viewer repeatedly watches, she may draw a path through the video, a way of following and tracing it. If she likes the song and/or the imagery—she can find a moment of attunement, of well-judged comportment. Perhaps more like lyric than epic poetry, and less narrative than classic Hollywood films, relations

among music, poetry-like lyrics, performers, settings, camera movement, editing, props, and gestures fall among the viewer to be pieced out and placed in relation. Gaps, enigmatic moments, and discrepancies among lyrics, music, and image can encourage the viewer to turn within and trace her own unfolding experience, to then judge it alongside these videos' unfoldings.

14 Oudart has written on how shots and edits suture us into a film, placing us in its world. The moments I feel interpolated even though I might also maintain some critical distance, I'd like to call immersion or absorption. Oudart, "La Suture." Jim Buhler and Claudia Gorbman have written on how music sutures us into narrative film.

15 See Branigan, *Narrative Comprehension and Film*, 101; Buhler, *Theories of the Soundtrack*, 158.

16 See Baumgartner, *Meta-Film Music in the Cinema of Jean-Luc Godard*.

17 Barthes, *Mythologies*, 56–57.

18 Davies, *Musical Meaning and Expression*, 212–13.

19 Langer, *Feeling and Form*.

20 Cook, *Analyzing Musical Multimedia*.

21 "Anna Karenina."

22 See Ireland, "Deconstructing Incongruence." Tagg, *Music's Meanings*.

23 See Vernallis, *Unruly Media*, 53–56.

24 One could claim that the contexts and stakes are different here, but music video almost always takes one step away from the lyrics. I can imagine that Mr. Blonde would map some of these relationships onto this new context. He might have an attraction for his victim.

25 Mandler, "The Structure of Value: Accounting for Taste."

26 See Vernallis, *Experiencing Music Video*, ch. 13.

27 There's not a lot yet on lyric videos. I like Korsgaard's article. See Korsgaard, "SOPHIE's 'Faceshopping' as (Anti-)Lyric Video."

28 I like Julie Russo's work on video clips and fan culture. See Russo, "User-Penetrated Content."

Chapter 13: The Art of Color Grading

1 Neuroscientist Bevil Conway, for instance, has recently discovered areas of the brain that respond to specific colors in *Cybermedia*. See also Harrison, "A New Study about Color Tries to Decode 'The Brain's Pantone.'"

2 Jonathan Leal and I cowrote this piece sentence by sentence. I wrote the conclusion. The process was a pleasure.

3 Nelson, *Bluets*.

4 Albers, *Interaction of Color*.

5 Conway, "Color Consilience."

6 Schloss and Palmer, "An Ecological Framework."

7. Byrne and Hilbert, "Color Realism and Color Science."
8. Belton, "Painting by the Numbers."
9. Wittgenstein, *Remarks on Color*.
10. Peacock, *Colour*, 3.
11. Misek, *Chromatic Cinema*, 2.
12. Branigan, *Tracking Color in Cinema and Art*; Brown and Macpherson, *The Routledge Handbook of Philosophy of Colour*.
13. See Vernallis, *Unruly Media* and *Experiencing Music Video*. See also Leal, "On Color Magic: Emil Nava's 'Feels' and 'Nuh Ready Nuh Ready.'"
14. See Keidl et al., *Pandemic Media*.
15. For artists, this elision is less a foreclosure than a beginning. Consider, for example, film director and author Derek Jarman's writing on iridescence: "Lustrous with colours, we all blew soap bubbles with rainbows into a sunny sky, which burst and disappeared as they sailed away." See Jarman, *Chroma*, 145.
16. Batchelor, quoted in Wheless, "Color Is an Act of Reason."
17. Nelson, *Bluets*, 20.
18. In this project's early stages, graphic designer and information specialist Sebastian König created three color graphs for our case studies, using a tool he developed for Processing, a software sketchbook for visual developers. König's tool, Video Color Analysis, "shows the average frequency of occurrence for each color detected." His charts guided our eyes, familiarizing us with each video's color distributions by illustrating them as at-a-glance images. For more on this visual tool, see König, "Visual Color Analysis."

Chapter 14: Music Video Directors, Production Houses, and the Media Swirl

1. See Levy and Lowney, *Cybermedia*.
2. Bordwell, "Intensified Continuity"; Smith, *The Sounds of Commerce*, 199–205; Vernallis, *Experiencing Music Video*, 35–37; Vernallis, "Music Video, Songs, Sound," 277–97.
3. Conversation with Kurey, Spring 2019.
4. Vernallis, conversations with directors: Åkerlund, Spring 2016; Abteen Bagheri, Spring 2018; Joseph Kahn, Spring 2018.
5. More scholarship on the production industry is needed. Some resources include: Hesmondhalgh, *The Cultural Industries*; Banks, Caldwell, and Mayer, *Production Studies*; Caston, "The First Cut is the Deepest."
6. Vernallis, *Unruly Media*.
7. See *Transmedia Directors*.
8. See roundtables on APESHIT and Dirty Computer (JPMS and JSAM).
9. Conversations with director, Melina Matsoukas, 2001.

10 Both Dave Meyers and Francis Lawrence went to Loyola Marymount, Mark Romanek went to Ithaca, Floria Sigismondi went to Ontario College of Art & Design University, Abteen Bagheri went to Stanford, Joseph Kahn went to NYU, Mark Pellington went to University of Virginia, Marc Klasfeld went to Tisch, and Ryan Staake went to Carnegie Mellon and RISD. Marcus Nispel attended Brooklyn College and the New York Institute of Technology on a Fulbright scholarship. I noted to Bagheri that his use of a beautiful diver in The Presets "Ghosts" reminded me of Riefenstahl's *Olympia*, and he replied that he had drawn upon the image from a documentary film class. Editor/director/producer Mark Mayr, by comparison, is from a small town (Fayetteville, NC). After attending one semester of junior college, he chose to move to LA, and, as a production assistant, started hanging out with editor Vinnie Hobbs, who taught him the ropes. Mayr is one of the most engaged practitioners of audiovisual scholarship I know.

11 Wikipedia, "List of Most Expensive Music Videos," accessed June 29, 2022, https://en.wikipedia.org/wiki/List_of_most_expensive_music_videos#cite_note-mostexpensive-4.

Chapter 15: Music Video's Multisensory

1 Bordwell, "Intensified Continuity Visual Style."
2 Calavita, "'MTV Aesthetics' at the Movies."
3 Annabel Cohen has developed a model to describe the brain's audiovisual processing. Drawing on the work of Marilyn Boltz, she highlights congruence as a feature the brain cathects to. I wonder if her description works well for narrative film soundtracks, but less so for other audiovisually intensified contexts. A study of dance on film revealed that viewers most valued soundtracks that worked in counterpoint to the image. Music video seems to work similarly. Music video's allure may stem from the boosting of low-res signals in the super colliculus. See Cohen, "Scoring Music for *Westworld* Then and Now"; Morese, "Dancing in Your Head."
4 Bertelson and Gelder, "The Psychology of Multimodal Perception."
5 Morein-Zamir, Soto-Faraco, and Kingstone, "Auditory Capture of Vision."
6 Metzger, "Beobachtungen über phänomenale Identität."
7 Shams, Kamitani, and Shimojo, "What You See is What You Hear," 408, 788; Haas, Kanai, Jalkanen, and Rees, "Grey-Matter Volume in Early Human Visual Cortex Predicts Proneness to the Sound-Induced Flash Illusion," 279, 4955–61.
8 Angelaki, Gu, and DeAngelis, "Multisensory Integration," 18, 452–58.
9 Goffaux et al., "Horizontal Tuning for Faces."

10 Reales and Ballesteros, "Implicit and Explicit Memory for Visual and Haptic Objects."
11 Parise and Spence, "Audiovisual Crossmodal Correspondences."
12 Zacks, "Cognitive Boundaries," 171–87.
13 The concept of the temporal binding window applies to various levels of multisensory integration from cellular responses to human perception. Stein and Wallace, "Comparisons of Cross-modality Integration in Midbrain and Cortex."
14 Zacks, "Cognitive Boundaries," 171–87.
15 Quintero, Shams, and Kamal, "Changing the Tendency to Integrate the Senses."

Chapter 16: Tracing the Asset

1 Boffey, "Robots Could Destabilize World."
2 Vernallis et al. *Cybermedia: Explorations in Science, Sound, and Vision.*
3 Garland, "Director Alex Garland Converses with Cybermedia's Scientists and Media Scholars."
4 Many Americans don't know that some pivotal legislation changed our commons. The Supreme Court's Citizens United decision (2010) made it possible for the wealthy to buy out elections, and the dismantling of the FCC's Fairness Doctrine in 1987 ended broadcasting's responsibility to present opposing views.
5 Khatchadourian, "We Know How You Feel."
6 Conversation with Matt Strafuss, January 2017.
7 Jhally, "Advertising and the End of the World."
8 Ian Forrester, Conversation with author, July 2017. Forrester, "The Power of Emotional Advertising."
9 McFarland, "How Facebook Teaches Photos to Talk."
10 Matt Strafuss, conversation with author, January 2017. (See the Bourne and Snowden close analyses at https:// themediaswirl.)
11 Nordin et al., "Radius Based Block Local Binary Pattern."
12 Raichle et al., "A Default Mode of Brain Function."
13 Brown et al., "Cognitive Control, Attention, and the Other Race Effect in Memory."
14 Griffiths, Kemp, and Tenenbaum, "Bayesian Models of Cognition."
15 Van der Linden, Turennout, and Fernández, "Category Training Induces Cross-modal Object Representations."
16 Conversation with Becky Waring, January 2018.
17 Ladzekpo, "Drum Rhythm Principles."
18 Conversation with Jim Buhler, January 2018.
19 Conversation with Becky Waring, January 2018.
20 Bergmann et al., "Brain Activation During Associative Short-Term Memory Maintenance."

21 Sapolsky, "How Economic Inequality Inflicts Real Biological Harm."
22 Paul, "As for Empathy, the Haves Have Not."
23 Unruly Media, to my knowledge, never published a white paper on our project. Sarah Wood sold her company. The exchange between Unruly and me felt supportive and experimental. We were genuinely curious what might emerge.
24 Laura U. Marks, comment during a Society for Cinema and Media Studies Q&A, 2018.
25 Lipsitz, "We Know What Time It Is," 17.

Chapter 17: New Technologies, Social Justice, and the Future in Beyoncé's Audiovisual Albums

1 Canton, "From Big Data to Artificial Intelligence."
2 Recent fMRI studies show a larger portion of the brain is more actively involved if a task is goal-oriented. See Fransson, "How Default Is the Default Mode of Brain Function?"
3 See Vernallis et al., *Cybermedia*.
4 Vetter and Newen, "Varieties of Cognitive Penetration in Visual Perception."
5 Firat et al., "Putting Race in Context."
6 Wallentin et al., "Amygdala and Heart Rate Variability Responses."
7 Kaplan, Gimbel, and Harris, "Neural Correlates of Maintaining One's Political Beliefs."
8 Ryota et al., "Political Orientations Are Correlated in Brain Structure."
9 Brueck, "A Yale Psychologist's Simple Thought Experiment."
10 Huang et al., "Election 2016."
11 Crenshaw, "Demarginalizing the Intersection of Race and Sex."
12 See Prichard, "Is the Use of Personality Based Psychometrics by Cambridge Analytical Psychological Science's 'Nuclear Bomb' Moment?," 12.
13 See Grassegger and Krogerus, "The Data That Turned the World Upside Down."
14 Levin, "New AI Can Guess Whether You're Gay or Straight from a Photograph."
15 Levin, "Face-Reading AI Will be Able to Detect Your Politics and IQ."
16 Botsman, "Big Data Meets Big Brother as China Moves to Rate Its Citizens."
17 Kosinski, Stillwell, and Graepel, "Private Traits and Attributes are Predictable from Digital Records."
18 Gillet, "From Welfare to One of the World's Wealthiest Women."
19 Gupta, "Bill Gates' Newest Mission."
20 Useem, "Power Causes Brain Damage."

21 I've interviewed Oliver Stone and worked on his films. He's currently working on a project concerning Guantanamo. I'm a Rawlsian, who believes that a just society is one that takes care of their least well-off. Giorgio Agamben argues that the ruler's power to draw the border between who dies and who gets reprieve defines the society. See Agamben, *State of Exception*.
22 Goldman, "Brain Zap Saps Destructive Urges."
23 Tegmark, *Life 3.0*.
24 According to Aristotle: "Shall we not, like archers who have a mark to aim at, be more likely to hit upon what is right?" (*Nicomachean Ethics*, 13).
25 Spinoza, *Collected Works*.
26 Zak, Stanton, and Ahmadi, "Oxytocin Increases Generosity in Humans."
27 Schiller, *The Mind Managers*.
28 Paul, "As for Empathy, the Haves Have Not."
29 Obama's and Congress's $3 billion Decade of the Brain initiative has helped drive this research.
30 Skokowski, Minds and Machines course, lecture, fall 2017.
31 Kahneman and Tversky, *Thinking, Fast and Slow*, 13
32 LeDoux, *The Deep History of Ourselves*, 247
33 Skokowski, Minds and Machines course, lecture.
34 Skokowski, Minds and Machines course, lecture.
35 Kohn, "When Gut Bacteria Change Brain Function"; Chen, "Here's How You're Influenced by the Genes You Didn't Inherit"; Barsade, "Emotional Contagion and Its Influence on Group Behavior"; Christakis and Fowler, "Social Contagion Theory."
36 Rawls, *Justice as Fairness*, 15–18.
37 Rawls might do better with disability, including considering genetically-based and late-stage illnesses.
38 Connolly, *Why I Am Not a Secularist*.
39 The graffiti takes on even greater resonance after the flooding of Houston, Beyoncé's hometown.
40 Mitchell's mid-period (for example, "Harry's House/Centerpiece" from *Hissing of Summer Lawns*)
41 Jay-Z, lyrics for "Never Change," "Chains is cool to cop, but more important is lawyer fees." See also lyrics for "The Story of OJ." There's also the line from Beyoncé's "Formation," "best revenge is your paper." *Genius Lyrics website*.
42 Rogers, "There Are 614 Billionaires in the United States."
43 Marcus Garvey was a famous early proponent of this approach.
44 Lewis, "The 10 Not-So-Publicized Times Jay Z and Beyoncé Gave Back."
45 Baquet, "Jay Z & Dean Baquet."

46 "Beyoncé Audience Demographics"; Webster, "When Life Gives You Lemons."
47 See Ramanan, "The Video Game Industry has a Diversity Problem."
48 Hobson, "#Lemonade."
49 Hooks, "Beyoncé's Lemonade is Capitalist Money-making at Its Best."
50 Richard Dyer has written about whiteness as a kind of death. See Dyer, *White*, i.
51 Imagery and sound linked to lynching runs throughout *Lemonade*. If the too-heavy fruit of her mother's neck is the same as Nina Simone's version of "Strange Fruit?" in "Formation," her bobbing head and grasping hands alongside a "doing-doing-doing" sample might suggest a shadow memory of a hanging, now politicized.
52 David Wilson has written about Trump's appropriation of *Cats*, Adele's *Skyfall* (though she requested her music not be used), Pavarotti, and Jackie Evancho. See Wilson, "'Pub Fight' Politics"; See also Oore, "Trump the Musical Prophet"; Kasper, *You Shook Me All Campaign Long*.
53 Nagel, "What Is It Like to Be a Bat?"; Nida-Rümelin and O'Conaill, "Qualia"; Skokowski, "The Philosophy of Westworld"; Jackson, "What Mary Didn't Know."

Chapter 18: Fox News, COVID-19, Brief Media Aesthetics, and Historical Resonances

"Fox News, Media Aesthetics, and the Coronavirus Pandemic" was originally published in *Film Criticism* 44, no.4 (2020), https://doi.org/10.3998/fc.13761232.0044.402. An earlier version of "Teaching Music Video in the Pandemic" originally appeared in *Flow Journal*, April 12, 2020. "Dangerous Audiovisual Aesthetics: Reading The Lincoln Project and Music-Video's Turn" was originally published in *Film Criticism* 44, no. 4 (2020), https://doi.org/10.3998/fc.13761232.0044.409.

1 Exceptions I've discovered are *Film Criticism*, *Flow*, and *Film International*.
2 Crary, *24/7*.
3 Jurkowitz and Mitchell, "About One-Fifth of Democrats and Republicans Get Political News."
4 Hannity, "Donald Trump Jr. Slams Critics"; Hannity, "Media Using Coronavirus Coverage as Political Weapon."
5 Mayer, "The Making of the Fox News White House"; Hays and Smith, "Murdochs Failed to Rein in Fox News 'Hoax' Narrative."
6 Rieger, "Sean Hannity Denied Calling Coronavirus a Hoax."
7 Hays and Smith, "Murdochs Failed to Rein in Fox News 'Hoax' Narrative."

8   Fauci and Wallace, "On Efforts to Slow the Spread of Coronavirus in US."
9   Fauci, "Dr. Fauci: No Doubt the US Is Still in the Escalation Phase."
10 Hannity, "Once We Beat Back Coronavirus."
11 Carlson, "Coronavirus Pandemic Is a Real Fear"; Carlson, "Why Would America's Media Take China's Side?"
12 Hannity, "Left Wants You to Believe Coronavirus Is Trump's Fault."
13 Ingraham, "Contain the Virus, Protect our Freedom."
14 Taylor, "'Wake-Up Call.'"
15 Newman, "No, a Border Wall Won't Stop Coronavirus"; Kenny, "Pandemics Close Borders."
16 BBC, "Coronavirus: US Death Rates v China, Italy and South Korea."
17 Recent studies suggest we quickly judge people based on physiognomy, based upon preexisting cognitive schemes that reflect racial, gender, class, and age biases. Anthony Wagner, a Stanford psychology professor, uses fMRI to demonstrate that people poorly encode faces of other races, which likely leads to reduced empathy. Films allow us to make stronger claims partly because actors are chosen to fill types. I show students pics of the Nazi mastermind and benign butler from Hitchcock's *Notorious*. Perhaps Hitchcock chose these actors because they resemble characteristics we identify with dog breeds—the Doberman pinscher and the Labrador retriever. Richard Dyer has written that stars attract us because they're able to blend contradictory features at the same time. There's John Wayne's delicate feet, Marlon Brando's gentle hands, Michael Jackson's androgyny. We also have preferences for extremely symmetrical (Denzel Washington) or asymmetrical faces (Claudette Colbert). AI software can be trained to generate convincing faux-stars' faces. But on top of this there are learned actorly facial expressions and gestures that go back to Delsarte. They're iconic and immediate, like Jimmy Stewart's expressions of fear and rage (he brings his fist to his mouth and trembles). Tucker Carlson's snarls from behind his chubby cheeks. Most Google images of him seem to project frustration and anger.
18 Carlson, "Nurses Write to Tucker Sharing Experiences."
19 *New York Times*, "People Are Dying"; Fox News, "US Hospitals Brace for Potential Strain from Coronavirus."
20 Hays and Smith, "Murdochs Failed to Rein in Fox News 'Hoax' Narrative."
21 *Washington Post*, "Fox Hosts Shift to Emphasizing Economy."
22 This section was originally published on my Tumblr account on January 19, 2017. Also see Deaville, "The Unconventional Music of the Democratic and Republican National Conventions of 2016." Trax on the trail has some wonderful analysis of political content.

23. Gorzelany-Mostak, "Hearing Jackie Evancho in the Age of Donald Trump."
24. Steinem, "Here's The Full Transcript of Gloria Steinem's Historic Women's March Speech."
25. Hsu, "A Seismic Shock"; Kaplan, *Rocking around the Clock*, 15.
26. Grimes: "You'll Miss Me When I'm Not around"; Dua Lipa, "Dua Lipa Performs 'Don't Start Now'"
27. Drake, "Toosie Slide."
28. Grimes and i_o, "Violence (Official Video)."
29. Ora, "How to Be Lonely."
30. Grimes, "How Grimes Used Music to Confront Tragedy."
31. Eiden, Interview with author, July 2020.
32. See Cubitt, *Finite Media*.

Afterword

1. The public has recently become more attentive to features of an auteurist directors' style. One of the most persuasive disseminators is YouTube, with series like "Every Frame a Painting" with its 7.4 million hits. See https://www.youtube.com/watch?v=7vfqkvwW2fs&ab_channel=EveryFrameaPainting.
2. What is now YouTube commentary will also look much different.

Bibliography

Adorno, Theodor. *Minima Moralia; Aesthetic Theory.* Brooklyn: Verso, 2020.

Adorno, Theodor W., and Max Horkheimer. *Dialectic of Enlightenment.* Translated by Edmund Jephcott. Stanford: Stanford University Press, 2007.

Agamben, Giorgio. *State of Exception.* Translated by Kevin Attell. Chicago: University of Chicago Press, 2005.

Ahnert, Ruth, and Sebastian Ahnert. "A Community under Attack: Protestant Letter Networks in the Reign of Mary I." *English Literary History* 82, no. 1 (Spring 2015): 1–33.

Albers, Josef. *Interaction of Color, 50th Anniversary Edition.* New Haven, CT: Yale University Press, 2013.

Angelaki, Dora E., Yong Gu, and Gregory C. DeAngelis. "Multisensory Integration: Psychophysics, Neurophysiology, and Computation." *Current Opinion in Neurobiology* 19, no. 4 (2009): 452–58.

Anger, Kenneth. "DVD commentary." *The Complete Magick Lantern Cycle.* San Diego: Fantoma, 2010.

"Anna Karenina: Creating the Stunning Costumes Featurette." December 3, 2012. https://www.youtube.com/watch?v=ld5pNH3G3dI&ab_channel=AnnaKareninaTheMovie.

Aristotle. *Aristotle's Nicomachean Ethics.* Translated by Robert C. Bartlett. Chicago: University of Chicago Press, 2012.

Arnheim, Rudolf. *The Power of the Center.* Berkeley: University of California Press, 1988.

Arnold, Gina, and Daniel Cookney, eds. *Music/Video: Histories, Aesthetics, Media.* New York: Bloomsbury, 2017.

Ashby, Arved. *Popular Music and the New Auteur: Visionary Filmmakers after MTV.* New York: Oxford University Press, 2013.

Austin, Sharon. "Black Americans Mostly Left Behind by Progress Since Dr. King's Death." *The Conversation,* February 7, 2018. https://theconversation.com/ black-americans-mostly-left-behind-by-progress-since-dr-kings-death-89956.

Baade, Christina, and Kristin A. McGee. *Beyoncé in the World: Making Meaning with Queen Bey in Troubled Times*. Middletown, CT: Wesleyan University Press, 2021.

Baker, Sarah. "Sex, Gender and Work Segregation in the Cultural Industries." In *Gender and Creative Labour*, edited by Bridget Conor, Rosalind Gill, and Stephanie Taylor, 23–36. Malden, MA: Wiley-Blackwell, 2015.

Banks, Miranda J., John T. Caldwell, and Vicky Mayer, eds. *Production Studies: Cultural Studies of Media Industries*. New York: Routledge, 2009.

Baquet, Dean. "Jay Z & Dean Baquet." *New York Times Style Magazine*, November 29, 2017. https://www.nytimes.com/interactive/2017/11/29/t-magazine/jay-z-dean-baquet-interview.html.

Baron, Jaimie. *Reuse, Misuse, Abuse: The Ethics of Audiovisual Appropriation in the Digital Era*. New Brunswick, NJ: Rutgers University Press, 2020.

Barsade, Sigal G. "Emotional Contagion and Its Influence on Group Behavior." *Administrative Science Quarterly* 47, no. 4 (December 2002): 644–75.

Barthes, Roland. *La Chambre Claire: Note sur la Photographie*. Paris: Cahiers du Cinéma-Gallimard-Le Seuil, 1980. Translated by Richard Howard under the title *Camera Lucida: Reflections on Photography*. New York: Hill & Wang, 1981.

Barthes, Roland. *Mythologies*. Translated by Annette Lavers. London: Vintage, 1993.

Baumbach, Nico, Damon R. Young, and Genevieve Yue. "Revisiting Postmodernism: An Interview with Fredric Jameson." *Social Text* 34, no. 2 (127) (2016): 143–60.

Baumgartner, Michael. *Meta-Film Music in the Cinema of Jean-Luc Godard*. New York: Oxford, 2022.

BBC. "Coronavirus: US Death Rates v China, Italy and South Korea." *BBC News*, March 30, 2020. https://www.bbc.com/news/av/world-us-canada-52066105/coronavirus-us-death-rates-v-china-italy-and-south-Korea.

Beck, Jay, and Tony Grajeda. *Lowering the Boom: Critical Studies in Film Sound*. Champaign: University of Illinois Press, 2008.

Beebe, Roger. "Paradox of Pastiche: Spike Jonze, Hype Williams, and the Race of Postmodern Auteur." In *Medium Cool: Music Videos from Soundies to Cellphones*, edited by Roger Beebe and Jason Middleton, 316–19. Durham, NC: Duke University Press, 2007.

Belton, John. "Painting by the Numbers: The Digital Intermediate." *Film Quarterly* 61, no. 3 (2008): 58–65.

Benson-Allott, Caetlin. *The Stuff of Spectatorship: Material Cultures of Film and Television*. Oakland: University of California Press, 2016.

Berenike, Jung. "Ambiguous Bodies in TikTok and Reaction GIFs." Panel presentation at Society for Cinema and Media Studies conference, Chicago, March 20, 2021.

Berger, John. *Ways of Seeing*. New York: Viking, 1995.

Bergmann, Heiko C., Sander M. Daselaar, Sarah F. Beul, Mark Rijpkema, Guillén Fernández, and Roy P. C. Kessels. "Brain Activation During Associative Short-Term Memory Maintenance Is Not Predictive for Subsequent Retrieval." *Frontiers in Human Neuroscience* 9, no. 479 (2015). http://doi.org/10.3389/fnhum.2015.00479.

Berlant, Lauren. *Cruel Optimism*. Durham, NC: Duke University Press, 2011.

Bertelson, Paul, and Béatrice de Gelder. "The Psychology of Multimodal Perception." In *Crossmodal Space and Crossmodal Attention*, edited by Charles Spence and Jon Driver, 151–77. Oxford: Oxford University Press, 2004.

Beyoncé. "Beyoncé Shadiest /Top Bossiest Moments." Accessed March 17, 2020. https://www.youtube.com/watch?v=BMTnqQQOUiA&t=465s.

Boffey, Daniel. "Robots Could Destabilize World through War and Unemployment, Says UN." *The Guardian*, September 27, 2017. https://www.theguardian.com/technology/2017/sep/27/robots-destabilise-world-war-unemployment-un.

Bordwell, David. "A Fast-Paced Cinematic Impeachment Trial." *Observations on Film Art* blog, March 9, 2021. http://www.davidbordwell.net/blog/2021/03/09/a-fast-paced-cinematic-impeachment-trial/.

Bordwell, David. "Intensified Continuity Visual Style in Contemporary American Film." *Film Quarterly* 55, no. 3 (2002): 16–28.

Bordwell, David. *The Way Hollywood Tells It: Story and Style in Modern Movies*. Berkeley: University of California Press, 2006.

Bordwell, David, and Kristen Thompson. *Film Art: An Introduction*. New York: McGraw-Hill, 1997.

Botsman, Rachel. "Big Data Meets Big Brother as China Moves to Rate Its Citizens." *Wired*, October 21, 2017. http://www.wired.co.uk/article/chinese-government-social-credit-score-privacy-invasion.

Brakhage, Stan. Interview on the DVD-ROM: *The Magical World of Joseph Cornell* (Washington, DC: Voyager Foundation, 2003), published as a companion to Linda Roscoe Hartigan, Walter Hopps, Richard Vine, and Robert Lehrman, *Joseph Cornell: Shadowplay . . . Eterniday*. New York: Thames and Hudson, 2003.

Branigan, Edward. *Narrative Comprehension and Film*. New York: Routledge, 1992.

Branigan, Edward. *Tracking Color in Cinema and Art: Philosophy and Aesthetics*. New York: Routledge, 2018.

Brill, Lesley. *Crowds, Power, and Transformation in Cinema*. Detroit: Wayne University Press, 2006.

Brooks, Kinitra D., and Kameelah L. Martin. *The Lemonade Reader.* New York: Routledge, 2019.

Brophy, Philip, ed. *Cinesonic: Cinema and the Sound of Music.* North Ryde: Australian Film Television and Radio School, 2000.

Brophy, Philip. "Parties in Your Head: From the Acoustic to the Psycho-Acoustic." In *The Oxford Handbook of New Audiovisual Aesthetics,* edited by John Richardson, Claudia Gorbman, and Carol Vernallis, 309–24. Oxford: Oxford University Press, 2013.

Brown, Derek H., and Fiona Macpherson, eds. *The Routledge Handbook of Philosophy of Colour.* London: Routledge, 2020.

Brown, Thackery I., Melina R. Uncapher, Tiffany E. Chow, Jennifer L. Eberhardt, and Anthony D. Wagner. "Cognitive Control, Attention, and the Other Race Effect in Memory." *PLOS ONE* 12, no. 3 (2017). http://doi.org/10.1371/journal.pone.0173579.

Bruce, Bennett. "The Cinema of Michael Bay: An Aesthetic of Excess." *Senses of Cinema* 75 (2015). https://eprints.lancs.ac.uk/id/eprint/73962/.

Brueck, Hilary. "A Yale Psychologist's Simple Thought Experiment Temporarily Turned Conservatives into Liberals." *Business Insider,* October 21, 2017. http://www.businessinsider.com/how-to-turn-conservatives-liberal-john-bargh-psychology-2017-10.

Buckland, Warren. *Directed by Steven Spielberg: Poetics of the Contemporary Hollywood Blockbuster.* New York: Continuum, 2006.

Buckland, Warren. *Puzzle Films: Complex Storytelling in Contemporary Cinema.* Malden, MA: Wiley-Blackwell, 2009.

Buckner, Clark. "4 Chemicals That Activate Happiness, & How to Gamify Them." *Technology Advice,* June 8, 2021. http://technologyadvice.com/blog/information-technology/activate-chemicals-gamify-happiness-nicole-lazzaro/.

Buhler, James. *Hearing the Movies,* 2nd ed. New York: Oxford University Press, 2015.

Buhler, James. *Theories of the Soundtrack.* New York: Oxford University Press, 2018.

Buhler, James, and Alex Newton. "Outside the Law of Action: Music and Sound in the Bourne Trilogy." In *The Oxford Handbook of Sound and Image in Digital Media,* edited by Carol Vernallis, 325–49. New York: Oxford University Press, 2013.

Burns, Lori, and Stan Hawkins. *The Bloomsbury Handbook of Popular Music Video Analysis.* New York: Bloomsbury, 2019.

BuzzFeedCeleb. "The 'Unflattering' Photos Beyoncé's Publicist Doesn't Want You to See." *Buzzfeed,* February 5, 2013. http://www.buzzfeed.com/buzzfeedceleb/the-unflattering-photos-beyonces-publicist-doesnt-want-you-t#.ihXzDYONDq; http://knowyourmeme.com/memes/unflattering-beyonce.

Byrne, Alex, and David Hilbert. "Color Realism and Color Science." *Behavioral and Brain Sciences* 26 (2003): 3–64.

Calavita, Marco. "'MTV Aesthetics' at the Movies: Interrogating a Film Criticism Fallacy." *Journal of Film and Video* 59, no. 3 (2007): 15–31.

Canetti, Elias. *Crowds and Power.* New York: Farrar, Straus and Giroux, 1984.

Canton, James. "From Big Data to Artificial Intelligence: The Next Digital Disruption." *The Huffington Post,* December 2017. https://www.huffingtonpost.com/james-canton/from-big-data-to-artifici_b_10817892.html.

Carlson, Tucker. "Coronavirus Pandemic Is a Real Fear." *Fox News,* February 24, 2020. https://www.youtube.com/watch?v=lydWQoqDNp8.

Carlson, Tucker. "Nurses Write to Tucker Sharing Experiences Facing Coronavirus Pandemic." *Fox News,* March 27, 2020. https://www.youtube.com/watch?v=8506miurvpQ&t=53s.

Carlson, Tucker. "Why Would America's Media Take China's Side Amid Coronavirus Pandemic?" *Fox News,* March 17, 2020. https://www.youtube.com/watch?v=5W9vjsFQUUU.

Carr, Jeremy. "Scorpio Rising." *Senses of Cinema: Cinémathèque Annotations on Film* 74 (March 2015). http://sensesofcinema.com/2015/cteq/scorpio-rising/.

Caston, Emily. "'The First Cut is the Deepest' Excerpts from a Focus Group on Editing Music Videos, with Explanatory Historical and Theoretical Notes." *Music, Sound, and the Moving Image* 11, no. 1 (Spring 2017): 99–118.

Cavell, Stanley. *Pursuits of Happiness: The Hollywood Comedy of Remarriage.* Cambridge, MA: Harvard University Press, 1984.

Cavell, Stanley. *The World Viewed: Reflections on the Ontology of Film, Enlarged Edition.* Cambridge, MA: Harvard University Press, 1979.

Chapman, Dale. "Let Me Show You What that Song Really Is: Nicholas Britell on the Music of *Moonlight*." In *Transmedia Directors: Artistry, Industry, and New Audiovisual Aesthetics,* edited by Carol Vernallis, Holly Rogers, and Lisa Perrott, 305–14. New York: Bloomsbury, 2019.

Chen, Angela. "Here's How You're Influenced by the Genes You Didn't Inherit From Your Parents." *The Verge,* January 25, 2018. https://www.theverge.com/2018/1/25/16931782/genetic-nurture-nature-parenting-families.

Chion, Michel. *Audio-Vision: Sound on Screen.* Translated by Claudia Gorbman. New York: Columbia University Press, 1994.

Christakis, Nicholas A., and James H. Fowler. "Social Contagion Theory: Examining Dynamic Social Networks and Human Behavior." *Statistics in Medicine* 32, no. 4 (2013): 556–77.

Christiansen, Steen. "Things Gone Wild: The Movie Camera in the Drone Age." Panel presentation at the Society for Cinema and Media Studies conference, Seattle, 2014.

Clement, Catherine. *Opera, or The Undoing of Women*. Minneapolis: University of Minnesota Press, 1999.

Cohen, Annabel. "Scoring Music for Westworld Then and Now: A Cognitive Perspective." In *Cybermedia: Explorations in Science, Sound, and Vision,* edited by Carol Vernallis, Holly Rogers, Selmin Kara, and Jonathan Leal, 237–73. New York: Bloomsbury Academic, 2021.

Connolly, William. *Why I Am Not a Secularist*. Minneapolis: University of Minnesota Press, 2000.

Conway, Bevil. "Color Consilience: Color through the Lens of Art Practice, History, Philosophy, and Neuroscience." *Annals of the New York Academy of Sciences* 1251, no. 1 (2012): 77–94.

Cook, Nicholas. *Analysing Musical Multimedia*. New York: Oxford University Press, 2001.

Cook, Pam. *Baz Luhrmann*. London: British Film Institute, 2010.

Corliss, Richard. "Luhrmann's *The Great Gatsby*: From Jazz Age to Baz Age." *Time,* May 9, 2013. http://entertainment.time.com/2013/05/09/luhrmanns-the-great-gatsby-from-jazz-age-to-baz-age/#ixzz2SpJfRPZZ.

Crane, Dan. "What Would Beyoncé Wear? She Knows." *New York Times,* December 18, 2018. www.nytimes.com/2013/12/19/fashion/B-Akerlund-Stylist-Beyonce-Visual-Album-Fashion.html?pagewanted=all.

Crary, Jonathan. *24/7: Late Capitalism and the Ends of Sleep*. Brooklyn: Verso, 2014.

Crenshaw, Kimberle. "Demarginalizing the Intersection of Race and Sex: A Black Feminist Critique of Antidiscrimination Doctrine, Feminist Theory and Antiracist Politics." *University of Chicago Legal Forum* 1, article 8 (1989): 139–67. http://chicagounbound.uchicago.edu/uclf/vol1989/iss1/8.

Cubitt, Sean. *Finite Media: Environmental Implications of Digital Technologies*. Durham, NC: Duke University Press, 2017.

Dargis, Manohla. "Invasion of the Robot Toys, Redux: Review of Transformers: Revenge of the Fallen." *New York Times,* June 24, 2009. https://www.nytimes.com/2009/06/24/movies/24transform.html.

Davies, Steven. *Musical Meaning and Expression*. Ithaca, NY: Cornell University Press, 1994.

Davison, Annette. *Hollywood Theory, Non-Hollywood Practice: Cinema Soundtracks in the 1980s and 1990s*. Farnham, UK: Ashgate, 2004.

Deaville, James. "The Unconventional Music of the Democratic and Republican National Conventions of 2016." *American Music* 35, no. 4 (2017): 446–66.

Debord, Guy. *Society of the Spectacle*. Athens, GA: Black and Red, 2002.

De Haas, Benjamin, Ryota Kanai, Lauri Jalkanen, and Geraint Rees. "Grey-Matter Volume in Early Human Visual Cortex Predicts Proneness to the Sound-induced Flash Illusion." *Proceedings of the Royal Society* 279 (2012): 4955–61.

Demers, Joanna. *Steal This Music: How Intellectual Property Law Affects Musical Creativity.* Athens: University of Georgia Press, 2006.

Denson, Shane. "Post-Cinema after Extinction." *Media Fields Journal* no. 13 (June 4, 2018). http://mediafieldsjournal.org/post-cinema-after-extinction/.

Denson, Shane, Therese Grisham, and Julia Leyda. "Post-Cinematic Affect: Post-Continuity, the Irrational Camera, Thoughts on 3D." *La Furia Umana* 14 (2012). http://bit.ly/T3Q5rs.

Dickenson, Kay. *Off Key: When Film and Music Won't Work Together.* New York: Oxford University Press, 2008.

Dienstfrey, Eric. "Monocentrism, or Soundtracks in Space: Rediscovering Forbidden Planet's Multi-Speaker Release." In *Voicing the Cinema: Film Music and the Integrated Soundtrack,* edited by Jim Buhler and Hannah Lewis, 229–44. Champaign: University of Illinois Press, 2020.

Doane, Mary Anne. *The Desire to Desire: The Woman's Film of the 1940s.* Bloomington: Indiana University Press, 1987.

Donnelly, K. J. "Irish Sea Power: A New Version of Man of Aran (2009/1934)." In *Music and Sound in Documentary Film,* edited by Holly Rogers, 137–50. New York: Routledge, 2015.

Drake. "Toosie Slide (Official Music Video)." April 3, 2020. https://www.youtube.com/watch?v=xWggTb45brM&t=236s.

Dua Lipa. "Dua Lipa Performs 'Don't Start Now' w/ Friends on Video Chat." The Late Late Show with James Corden, March 30, 2020. https://www.youtube.com/watch?v=D6sf0LNrDss.

During, Simon, ed. *The Cultural Studies Reader 2.* New York: Routledge, 1999.

Dyer, Richard. "Entertainment and Utopia." In *Only Entertainment,* 2nd. edition, 19–35. London: Routledge, 2002.

Dyer, Richard. *White.* New York: Routledge, 2017.

Egan, Kelsey. "Film Production Design: Case Study of *The Great Gatsby*." *Elon Journal of Undergraduate Research in Communications* 5, no. 1 (2014). http://www.studentpulse.com/articles/968/2/film-production-design-case-study-of-the-great-gatsby.

Elsaesser, Thomas. "Digital Cinema: Convergence or Contradiction?" In *The Oxford Handbook of Sound and Image in Digital Media,* edited by Carol Vernallis, Amy Herzog, and John Richardson, 13–45. New York: Oxford University Press, 2013.

Fairfax, Daniel. "The Cinema Is a Bad Object: Interview with Francesco Casetti." *Senses of Cinema* 83 (June 2017). https://www.sensesofcinema.com/2017/film-studies/francesco-casetti-interview/.

Fallon, Jimmy, and Taylor Swift. "Taylor Swift Reacts to Embarrassing Footage of Herself after Laser Eye Surgery." *The Tonight Show Starring Jimmy Fallon,* October 3, 2019. https://www.youtube.com/watch?v=IZ_3FbaysHk&ab_channel=TheTonightShowStarringJimmyFallon.

Fauci, Anthony. "Dr. Fauci: No Doubt the US Is Still in the Escalation Phase of Coronavirus." *Fox News,* March 18, 2020. https://www.youtube.com/watch?v=bOGO2S5FOTc.

Fauci, Anthony, and Chris Wallace. "On Efforts to Slow the Spread of Coronavirus in US." *Fox News,* March 15, 2020. https://www.youtube.com/watch?v=zYqAYe-Nkc4&t=6s.

Feuer, Jane. *The Hollywood Musical.* Bloomington: Indiana University Press, 1982.

Firat, Rengin B., Steven Hitlin, Vincent Magnotta, and Daniel Tranel. "Putting Race in Context: Social Class Modulates Processing of Race in the Ventromedial Prefrontal Cortex and Amygdala." *Social Cognitive and Affective Neuroscience* 12, no. 8 (2017): 1314–24.

Fischer, Lucy. "City of Women: Busby Berkeley, Architecture, and Urban Space." *Cinema Journal* 49, no. 4 (2010): 111–30.

Flinn, Caryl. "The Mutating Musical." In *Oxford Handbook of New Audiovisual Aesthetics,* edited by John Richardson, Claudia Gorbman, and Carol Vernallis, 251–65. New York: Oxford University Press, 2013.

Flinn, Caryl. *Strains of Utopia.* Princeton, NJ: Princeton University Press, 1992.

Forrester, Ian. "The Power of Emotional Advertising." *Affectiva* blog, April 20, 2017. http://blog.affectiva.com/the-power-of-emotional-advertising.

Fox News. "US Hospitals Brace for Potential Strain from Coronavirus." March 12, 2020, https://www.youtube.com/watch?v=08aodVASD8M.

Fransson, Peter. "How Default Is the Default Mode of Brain Function?: Further Evidence from Intrinsic BOLD Signal Fluctuations." *Neuropsychologia* 44, no. 14 (2006): 2836–45.

Friedman, Vanessa, and Jon Caramanica. "Is Rihanna's 'Visual Autobiography' a Triumph or a Tease?" *New York Times,* October 15, 2019. https://www.nytimes.com/2019/10/14/style/rihanna-visual-autobiography.html.

Frith, Simon, and Howard Horne. *Art into Pop.* London: Methuen, 1987.

Gardner, Justin L. "Optimality and Heuristics in Perceptual Neuroscience." *Nature/Neuroscience,* April 2019, 514–523. https://doi.org/10.1038/s41593-019-0340-4.

Garland, Alex, Jay McClelland, Paul Skokowski, Simon Levy, Jeff Zacks, Carol Vernallis, Selmin Kara, and Jonathan Leal. "Director Alex Garland Converses with *Cybermedia*'s Scientists and Media Scholars." In *Cybermedia: Explorations in Science, Sound, and Vision,* edited by Carol Vernallis, Holly Rogers, Selmin Kara, and Jonathan Leal, 31–34. New York: Bloomsbury Academic, 2022.

Gill, Satinder P. "Entrainment and Musicality in the Human System Interface." *AI & Society* 21 (2007): 567–605.

Gillet, Rachel. "From Welfare to One of the World's Wealthiest Women: The Incredible Rags-to-Riches Story of J. K. Rowling." *Business Insider,* May 19, 2015. http://www.businessinsider.com/the-rags-to-riches-story-of-jk-rowling-2015-5.

Goffaux, Valerie, Felix Duecker, Lars Hausfeld, Christine Schiltz, and Rainer Goebel. "Horizontal Tuning for Faces Originates in High-Level Fusiform Face Area." *Neuropsychologia* 81 (January 29, 2016): 1–11.

Goldman, Bruce. "Brain Zap Saps Destructive Urges." *Stanford Medicine News Center,* December 18, 2017. http://med.stanford.edu/news/all-news/2017/12/brain-zap-saps-destructive-urges.html.

Goldschmitt, K. E., and Nick Seaver. "Shaping the Stream: Techniques and Troubles of Algorithmic Recommendation." In *The Cambridge Companion to Music in Digital Culture*, edited by Nicholas Cook, Monique Ingalls, and David Trippett, 63–81. New York: Cambridge University Press, 2019.

Goodwin, Andrew. *Dancing in the Distraction Factory: Music, Television and Popular Culture.* Minneapolis: University of Minnesota Press, 1992.

Gorbman, Claudia. "Aesthetics and Rhetoric." *American Music* 22, no. 1 (2004): 14–26.

Gorbman, Claudia. *Unheard Melodies: Narrative Film Music.* Bloomington: Indiana University Press, 1987.

Gordon, Kim. "Kim Gordon's Open Letter to Karen Carpenter." *Dangerous Minds,* 22 July 2013. http://dangerousminds.net/comments/kim_gordons_open_letter_to_karen_carpenter.

Gorska-Olesinska, Monika. "Polish Digital Poetry: Lack of Prehistoric Artifacts or Missing Narrative." In *Relive: Media Art Histories,* edited by Sean Cubitt and Paul Thomas. Cambridge, MA: MIT Press, 2013.

Gorzelany-Mostak, Dana. "Hearing Jackie Evancho in the Age of Donald Trump." *American Music* 35, no. 4 (2017) 467–77.

Grassegger, Hannes, and Mikael Krogerus. "The Data That Turned the World Upside Down." *Motherboard,* January 28, 2017. https://motherboard.vice.com/en_us/article/mg9vvn/how-our-likes-helped-trump-win.

Greco, Patti. "'Pretty Hurts' Director Melina Matsoukas on Beyoncé's Throw-up Scene and Casting Harvey Keitel." *Vulture,* December 16, 2013. www.vulture.com/2013/12/beyonce-pretty-hurts-director-melina-matsoukas-interview.html.

Greene, Liz, and Danijela Kulezic-Wilson, eds. *The Palgrave Handbook of Sound Design and Music in Screen Media: Integrated Soundtracks.* London: Palgrave Macmillan, 2016.

Gregory Brothers. "Autotune the News #2: Pirates. Drugs. Gay Marriage." April 21, 2009. http://www.youtube.com/watch?v=tBb4cjjj1gI.

Greif, Mark. *Against Everything: Essays.* New York: Vintage, 2017.

Griffiths, Thomas L., Charles Kemp, and Joshua B. Tenenbaum. "Bayesian Models of Cognition." In *The Cambridge Handbook of Computational Psychology,* edited by Ron Sun, 59–100. Cambridge: Cambridge University Press, 2008.

Grimes. "How Grimes Used Music to Confront Tragedy: Diary of a Song." March 20, 2020. https://www.youtube.com/watch?v=EUIAkiTYgfY&t=2s.

Grimes. "You'll Miss Me When I'm Not Around (Chroma Green Video)." April 1, 2020. https://www.youtube.com/watch?v=_IHaCyX6-Xo.

Grimes and i_o. "Violence (Official Video)." September 5, 2019. https://www.youtube.com/watch?v=M9SGYBHY0qs.

Gunn, Jenny. "The Outside Meets the Institution: The Carters' 'Apeshit' Video." *Black Camera* 11, no. 1 (Fall 2019): 385–98.

Gunning, Tom. "The Cinema of Attraction[s]: Early Film, Its Spectator and the Avant-Garde." In *The Cinema of Attractions Reloaded,* edited by Wanda Strauven, 31–40. Amsterdam: Amsterdam University Press, 2006.

Gupta, Sanjay. "Bill Gates' Newest Mission. Curing Alzheimer's." *CNN,* November 14, 2017. https://www.cnn.com/2017/11/13/health/bill-gates-announcement-alzheimers/index.html.

Handley, Agata. "Representing Absence: Contemporary Ekphrasis in 'Apesh-t.'" *Text Matters* 10, no. 11 (2020): 118–34.

Hannity, Sean. "Donald Trump Jr. Slams Critics of the Trump Administration's Response to Coronavirus." *Hannity,* Fox News transcript published March 2, 2020. https://www.foxnews.com/transcript/donald-trump-jr-slams-critics-of-the-trump-administrations-response-to-coronavirus.

Hannity, Sean. "Left Wants You to Believe Coronavirus Is Trump's Fault." *Fox News,* March 6, 2020. https://www.youtube.com/watch?v=wbqZyapMgzY.

Hannity, Sean. "Media Using Coronavirus Coverage as Political Weapon." *Hannity.* Fox News, YouTube, March 9, 2020. https://www.youtube.com/watch?v=-EQy2eawqS0.

Hannity, Sean. "Once We Beat Back Coronavirus, China Must Be Held Accountable." *Fox News,* March 18, 2020. https://www.youtube.com/watch?v=8A9lkLZd65o&t=44s.

Hanslick, Eduard. *On the Musically Beautiful*, translated by G. Payzant. Indianapolis: Hackett Publishing Co., 1986 (1854).

Harlig, Alexandra, Crystal Abidin, Trevor Boffone, Kelly Bowker, Colette Eloi, Pamela Krayenbuhl, Chuyun Oh. "TikTok and Short-Form Screendance before and after Covid." *International Journal of Screendance* 12 (March 2021): 190–209.

Harris, Chris. "MTV Loses Another Music Show, Fails to Renew 'Alexa Chung.'" *Rolling Stone,* December 11, 2009. http://www.rollingstone.com/music/news/mtv-loses-another-music-show-fails-to-renew-alexa-chung-20091211.

Harris, Jane. "Psychedelic, Baby: An Interview with Pipilotti Rist." *Art Journal* 59, no. 4 (2000): 68-79.

Harrison, Sara. "A New Study about Color Tries to Decode 'The Brain's Pantone.'" *Wired,* November 24, 2020. https://www.wired.com/story/a-new-study-about-color-tries-to-decode-the-brains-pantone/.

Hasson, Uri. "How We Communicate Information across Brains." Video posted November 19, 2019. https://www.youtube.com/watch?v=pEfBuZT5MBU.

Hautea, Samantha, Perry Parks, Buro Takashi, and Jing Zeng. "Showing They Care (Or Don't): Affective Publics and Ambivalent Climate Activism on TikTok." *Social Media + Society* (April–June 2021): 1–14.

Hawker, Philippa. "The Subtle Art of Staging Gatsby's Lavish Parties." *Sydney Morning Herald,* May 26, 2013. http://www.smh.com.au/entertainment/movies/the-subtle-art-of-staging-gatsbys-lavish-parties-20130523-2k4ok.html.

Hawkins, Stan. *Queerness in Pop Music: Aesthetics, Gender Norms, and Temporality.* New York: Routledge, 2016.

Hays, Chris, and Ben Smith. "Murdochs Failed to Rein in Fox News 'Hoax' Narrative Amid Coronavirus." *All In,* MSNBC, March 23, 2020. https://www.youtube.com/watch?v=KBBfa_wVbas.

Heffernan, Virginia. "How Hyperinflation Destroys Much More Than Just Currencies." *Terminal Madness* (October 23, 2018). https://www.terminalmadness.com/index.php/blog/how-hyperinflation-destroys-much-more-than-just-currencies.

Hesmondhalgh, David. *The Cultural Industries.* London: Sage, 2019.

Hobson, Janell. "Feminists Debate Beyoncé." In *The Beyoncé Effect: Essays on Sexuality, Race and Feminism,* edited by Adrienne Trier-Bieniek, 11–27. Jefferson, NC: McFarland Press, 2016.

Hobson, Janell. "#Lemonade: A Black Feminist Resource List." *Black Perspectives,* May 12, 2016. https://www.aaihs.org/lemonade-a-black-feminist-resource-list/.

Hollywood Diversity Report 2014. February 12, 2014. http://www.bunchecenter.ucla.edu/wp-con tent/uploads/2014/02/2014-Hollywood-Diversity-Report-2-12-14.pdf.

Hollywood Diversity Report 2022. https://socialsciences.ucla.edu/hollywood-diversity-report-2022/

hooks, bell. "Beyoncé's Lemonade Is Capitalist Money-Making at Its Best." *The Guardian,* May 11, 2016. https://www.theguardian.com/music/2016/may/11/capitalism-of-beyonce-lemonade-album.

Hsu, Tiffany. "'A Seismic Shock': Jittery Companies Pull Back on Ads during Pandemic." *New York Times*, April 3, 2020. https://www.nytimes.com/2020/04/03/business/media/ads-commercials-coronavirus.html.

Huang, Jon, Samuel Jacoby, Michael Strickland, and K. K. Rebecca Lai. "Election 2016: Exit Polls." *New York Times,* November 8, 2016. https://www.nytimes.com/interactive/2016/11/08/us/politics/election-exit-polls.html.

Humphrey, Doris. *The Art of Making Dances.* New York: Grove, 1959.

Hunt, Darnel, Ana-Christina Ramon, and Zachary Price. "2014 Hollywood Diversity Report: Making Sense of the Disconnect." *Ralph J. Bunche Center for African American Studies,* February 12, 2014. http://bunchecenter.pre.ss.ucla.edu/wp-content/uploads/sites/112/2014/02/2014-Hollywood-Diversity-Report-2-12-14.pdf.

Iddon, Martin, and Melanie L. Marshall. *Beyoncé: At Work, On Screen, and Online.* Bloomington: Indiana University Press, 2020.

Ingraham, Laura. "Contain the Virus, Protect Our Freedom." *Fox News,* March 12, 2020. https://www.foxnews.com/media/ingraham-contain-the-virus-protect-our-freedom.

Ireland, David. "Deconstructing Incongruence: A Psycho-Semiotic Approach toward Difference in the Film-Music Relationship." *Music, Sound, and the Moving Image* 8, no. 2 (2015): 48–57.

Iyer, Usha. *Dancing Women: Choreographing Corporeal Histories of Hindi Cinema.* New York: Oxford University Press, 2020.

Jackson, Frank. "What Mary Didn't Know." *The Journal of Philosophy.* 83 (5) (1986): 291–95.

James, David E. *Rock 'N' Film: Cinema's Dance with Popular Music.* New York: Oxford University Press, 2016.

James, Robin. *Resilience and Melancholy: Pop Music, Feminism, Neoliberalism.* Winchester, UK: Zero Books, 2015.

Jarman, Derek. *Chroma: A Book of Color.* Minneapolis: University of Minnesota Press, 2010.

Jay-Z. "Never Change." *Genius Lyrics.* https://genius.com/Jay-z-never-change-lyrics.

Jhally, Sut. "Advertising and the End of the World." Lecture, Media Digital Literacy Academy of Beirut, 2014, Beirut. August 20, 2014. https://shop.mediaed.org/advertising-the-end-of-the-world-p59.aspx.

Jirsa, Tomáš. "Ascension of the Pop Icon: The Creativity of Kitsch (Not Only) in a Music Video by Lana Del Rey." *Moravian Journal of Literature and Film* 6, no. 1 (2015): 5–28.

Jurkowitz, Mark, and Amy Mitchell. "About One-Fifth of Democrats and Republicans Get Political News in a Kind of Media Bubble." *Pew Research Center,* March 4, 2020. https://www.journalism.org/2020/03/04/about-one-fifth-of-democrats-and-republicans-get-political-news-in-a-kind-of-media-bubble/.

Kahneman, Daniel, and Amos Tversky. *Thinking, Fast and Slow.* New York: Farrar, Straus and Giroux, 2013.

Kalinak, Kay. *How the West Was Sung: Music in the Westerns of John Ford.* Berkeley: University of California Press, 2017.

Kanai, Ryota, Tom Feilden, Colin Firth, and Geraint Rees. "Political Orientations Are Correlated in Brain Structure in Young Adults." *Current Biology* 21, no. 8 (2011): 677–80.

Kaplan, E. Ann. *Rocking around the Clock: MTV Postmodernism and Consumer Culture*. New York: Methuen, 1987.

Kaplan, Jonas T., Sarah I. Gimbel, and Sam Harris. "Neural Correlates of Maintaining One's Political Beliefs in the Face of Counterevidence." *Scientific Reports* 6, no. 39589 (December 2016). doi: 10.1038/srep39589.

Kassabian, Anahid. "The End of Diegesis as We Know It?" In *The Oxford Handbook of New Audiovisual Aesthetics*, edited by John Richardson, Claudia Gorbman, and Carol Vernallis, 89–106. New York: Oxford University Press, 2013.

Keazor, Henry, and Thorsten Wübbena. *Rewind, Play, Fast Forward: The Past, Present and Future of the Music Video*. Bielefeld: Transcript Verlag, 2010.

Keidl, Philipp Dominik, Laliv Melamed, Vinzenz Hediger, and Antonio Somaini. *Pandemic Media: Preliminary Notes toward an Inventory*. Lüneburg: Meson Press, 2020.

Kenny, Charles. "Pandemics Close Borders—And Keep Them Closed," *Politico Magazine*, March 25, 2020. https://www.politico.com/news/magazine/2020/03/25/trump-coronavirus-borders-history-plague-146788.

Kerins, Mark. *Beyond Dolby (Stereo): Cinema in the Digital Sound Age*. Bloomington: Indiana University Press, 2010.

Khatchadourian, Raffi. "We Know How You Feel." *The New Yorker*, January 19, 2015. https://www.newyorker.com/magazine/2015/01/19/know-feel.

Kinder, Marsha. "Music Video and the Spectator: Television, Ideology and Dream." *Film Quarterly* 38, no. 1 (1984): 2–15.

King, Geoff. "Spectacle, Narrative and the Spectacular Hollywood Blockbuster." In *Movie Blockbusters*, edited by Julian Stringer, 119–25. New York: Psychology Press, 2003.

Klein, Ezra. "Transformers 4 is a Master Class in Economics." *Vox*, July 6, 2014. https://www.vox.com/2014/7/6/5873099/transformers-4-is-a-master-class-in-economics.

Knutson, Brian, Kiefer Katovich, Gaurav Suri. "Inferring Affect from fMRI Data." *CellPress*, 2014, 1–7. http://dx.doi.org/10.1016/j.tics.2014.04.006.

Koepnick, Lutz. *Michael Bay (Contemporary Film Directors)*. Champaign: University of Illinois Press, 2018.

Kohn, David. "When Gut Bacteria Change Brain Function." *The Atlantic*, June 24, 2015. https://www.theatlantic.com/health/archive/2015/06/gut-bacteria-on-the-brain/395918/.

König, Sebastian. "Visual Color Analysis" Interactive website. July 18, 2010. https://www.behance.net/gallery/584413/Video-Color-Analysis.

Korsgaard, Mathias. *Music Video after MTV: Audiovisual Studies, New Media, and Popular Music*. Oxfordshire, UK: Routledge, 2017.

Korsgaard, Mathias Bonde. "SOPHIE's 'Faceshopping' as (Anti-)Lyric Video." *Music, Sound, and the Moving Image* 13, no. 2 (2019): 209–30.

Kosinski, Michael, David Stillwell, and Thore Graepel. "Private Traits and Attributes Are Predictable from Digital Records of Human Behavior." *PNAS* 110, no. 15 (April, 2013): 5802–5.

Krause-Wahl, Antje. "Why Artists Make Clips." In *Rewind, Play, Fast Forward: The Past, Present and Future of the Music Video,* edited by Henry Keazor and Thorsten Wübbena, 207–24. Bielefeld: Transcript Verlag, 2010.

Kronengold, Charles. "Audiovisual Objects, Multisensory People, and the Intensified Ordinary in Hong Kong Action." In *The Oxford Handbook of New Audiovisual Aesthetics,* edited by John Richardson, 412–36. New York: Oxford University Press, 2013.

Lacan, Jacques. *The Four Fundamental Concepts of Psycho-Analysis.* New York: Norton, 1981.

Laderman, David, and Laurel Westrup. *Sampling Media.* New York: Oxford University Press, 2014.

Lady Gaga. "Paparazzi." Official music video. November 25, 2009. https://www.youtube.com/watch?v=d2smz_1L2_0.

Ladzekpo, C. K. "Drum Rhythm Principles of Percussion Polyrhythm from Ghana, West Africa," Lecture, University of California at Berkeley, 2012. https://www.youtube.com/watch?v=yK42w0H8rSU.

Landreville, John. "The Affective Density of the Post-Internet: Mapping Hito Steyerl's Liquidity Inc." Paper given at Society for Cinema and Media Studies conference, March 18, 2021.

Landy, Josh. *How to Do Things with Fictions.* New York: Oxford University Press, 2014.

Langer, Suzanne. *Feeling and Form: A Theory of Art Developed from Philosophy in a New Key.* New York: Scribners, 1977

Langer, Suzanne. *Philosophy in a New Key.* Cambridge, MA: Harvard University Press, 1957.

Lawson, Richard. 'The Tragic Emptiness of *The Great Gatsby*." *The Wire,* May 2013. http://www.thewire.com/entertainment/2013/05/great-gatsby-review/65020/.

Leal, Jonathan. "On Color Magic: Emil Nava's 'Feels' and 'Nuh Ready Nuh Ready.'" In *Transmedia Directors: Artistry, Industry, and New Audiovisual Aesthetics,* edited by Carol Vernallis, Holly Rogers, and Lisa Perrott, 169–78. New York: Bloomsbury Academic, 2020.

LeDoux, Joseph. *The Deep History of Ourselves: The Four-Billion-Year Story of How We Got Conscious Brains.* London: Penguin, 2020.

Lehman, Frank. *Hollywood Harmony: Musical Wonder and the Sound of Cinema.* New York: Oxford University Press, 2018.

Leinweber, David. "Why the Left Should Reject Politics-by-Mob." *Washington Post,* November 13, 2018. https://www.washingtonpost.com/outlook/2018/11/13/why-left-should-reject-politics-by-mob.

Levi-Strauss, Claude. *Myth and Meaning*. Toronto: University of Toronto Press, 1978.

Levin, Sam. "Face-Reading AI Will Be Able to Detect Your Politics and IQ, Professor Says." *The Guardian*, September 12, 2017. https://www.theguardian.com/technology/2017/sep/12/artificial-intelligence-face-recognition-michal-kosinski.

Levin, Sam. "New AI Can Guess Whether You're Gay or Straight from a Photograph." *The Guardian*, September 7, 2017. https://www.theguardian.com/technology/2017/sep/07/new-artificial-intelligence-can-tell-whether-youre-gay-or-straight-from-a-photograph.

Levy, Simon, and Charles Lowney. "(S)Ex Machina and the Cartesian Theater of the Absurd." In *Cybermedia: Explorations in Science, Sound, and Vision*, edited by Carol Vernallis, Holly Rogers, Selmin Kara, and Jonathan Leal, 45–64. New York: Bloomsbury Academic, 2021.

Lewis, Taylor. "The 10 Not-So-Publicized Times Jay Z and Beyoncé Gave Back." *Essence*, February 1, 2017. https://www.essence.com/lifestyle/do-good-brothers/10-not-so-publicized-times-jay-z-and-beyonce-gave-back/#144741.

Liljedahl, Anders. "Musical Pathfinding; or How to Listen to Interactive Music Video." *Music, Sound, and the Moving Image* 13, no. 2 (2019): 165–85.

Lincoln, Ross A. "'Get Out' Director Jordan Peele Explains 'The Sunken Place' Peele Clues You In to the Horrifying Meaning." *The Wrap*, March 16, 2017. https://www.thewrap.com/get-out-director-jordan-peele-explains-the-sunken-place/.

Lipietz, Alain. "The Post-Fordist World: Labor Relations, International Hierarchy and Global Ecology." *Review of International Political Economy* 4 no. 1 (March 1997): 1–41.

Lipsitz, George. *The Possessive Investment in Whiteness: How White People Profit from Identity Politics, Revised and Expanded Edition*. Philadelphia: Temple University Press, 2006.

Lipsitz, George. "We Know What Time It Is: Race, Class and Youth Culture in the Nineties." In *Microphone Fiends: Youth Music and Youth Culture*, edited by Tricia Rose and Andrew Ross, 17–28. New York: Routledge, 1994.

Litt, Toby. "The 80s: The Best of Times, the Worst of Times." *The Guardian*, July 29, 2010. https://www.theguardian.com/film/2010/jul/29/80s-culture-a-team-karate-kid.

MacDonald, Scott. *Avant-Garde Film: Motion Studies*. Cambridge: Cambridge University Press, 1993.

Mandler, George. "The Structure of Value: Accounting for Taste." In *Affect and Cognition*, edited by Margaret S. Clarke and Susan T. Fiske, 3–36. Mahwah, NJ: Lawrence Erlbaum, 1982.

Marks, Chris, and Rob Tannenbaum. *I Want My MTV*. New York: Penguin, 2011.

Marks, Laura U. *Touch: Sensuous Theory and Multisensory Media.* Minneapolis: University of Minnesota Press, 2002.

Mather, George. "Biological Motion." 2015. http://www.georgemather.com/MotionDemos/BioMoMP4.html. Accessed October 6, 2021.

Mayer, Jane. "The Making of the Fox News White House." *The New Yorker,* March 4, 2019. https://www.newyorker.com/magazine/2019/03/11/the-making-of-the-fox-news-white-house.

McClary, Susan. *Feminine Endings: Music, Gender, and Sexuality.* Minneapolis: University of Minnesota Press, 1991.

McClelland, J. S. *The Crowd and the Mob: From Plato to Canetti.* London: Unwin Hyman, 1989.

McCormick, Neil. "It Sounds Like 2018 Distilled into a Sci-fi Funk Pop Extravaganza—Janelle Monáe, Dirty Computer, Review." *The Daily Telegraph,* April 27, 2018. https://www.telegraph.co.uk/music/what-to-listen-to/sounds-like-2018-distilled-sci-fi-funk-pop-extravaganza-janelle/.

McDonald, Glenn. "The Genre Grinder's Song (What It's Like to Run a Machine for Sorting Music)." Panel presentation at Music and Genre: New Directions conference, McGill University, Montreal, September 27, 2014.

McFarland, Matt. "How Facebook Teaches Photos to Talk." *CNN,* December 21, 2017. http://money.cnn.com/2017/12/21/technology/facebook-ai-training/index.html.

McIntyre, Hugh. "Report: YouTube Is the Most Popular Site for On-Demand Music Streaming," *Forbes,* September 27, 2017. https://www.forbes.com/sites/hughmcintyre/2017/09/27/the-numbers-prove-it-the-world-is-listening-to-the-music-it-loves-on-youtube/#75b20c871614.

Mera, Miguel. "Reap Just What You Sow," In *Pop Fiction: The Song in Cinema,* edited by Steve Lannin and Matthew Caley, 86–97. Bristol, UK: Intellect Books, 2005.

Mercer, Kobena. "Monster Metaphors: Notes on Michael Jackson's Thriller." In *Sound and Vision: The Music Video Reader,* edited by Simon Frith, Andrew Goodwin, and Lawrence Grossberg, 93–108. New York: Routledge, 1993.

Metzger, Wolfgang. "Beobachtungen über phänomenale Identität [Observations on Phenomenal Identity]." *Psychologische Forschung,* 19 (1934): 1–60.

Michaels, Sean. "YouTube Is Teens' First Choice for Music." *The Guardian,* August 16, 2012. https://www.theguardian.com/music/2012/aug/16/youtube-teens-first-choice-music.

Miller, Clara Cain. "Stressed, Tired, Rushed: A Portrait of the Modern Family." *New York Times,* November 4, 2015. http://nyti.ms/2mjxIUi.

Misek, Richard. *Chromatic Cinema: A History of Screen Color.* Hoboken, NJ: Wiley-Blackwell, 2010.

Mizuta Lippit, Akira. *Ex-Cinema: From a Theory of Experimental Film and Video*. Berkeley: University of California Press, 2012.

Morein-Zamir, Sharon, Salvador Soto-Faraco, and Alan Kingstone. "Auditory Capture of Vision: Examining Temporal Ventriloquism." *Cognitive Brain Research* 1 (June 17, 2003): 154–63.

Morris, Mitchell. "Songs of the Container: On Enya, the Maternal Sound, and Fear of Comfort." Panel presentation at EZ Music Conference, University of California Berkeley, March 12, 2016.

Mowitt, John. *Percussion: Drumming, Beating, Striking*. Durham, NC: Duke University Press, 2002.

Mulvey, Laura. *Death 24x a Second: Stillness and the Moving Image*. London: Reaktion, 2006.

Nagel, Thomas. "What Is It Like to Be a Bat?" *Philosophical Review* 83, no. 4 (October 1974): 435–50.

Naremore, James. *Acting in the Cinema*. Berkeley: University of California Press, 1988.

Nelson, Maggie. *Bluets*. Minneapolis: Wave Books, 2009.

Neumeyer, David. "Diegetic/Nondiegetic: A Theoretical Model." *Music and the Moving Image* 2, no. 1 (Spring 2009): 26–39.

New York Times. "'People Are Dying': Battling Coronavirus Inside a N.Y.C. Hospital." March 26, 2020. https://www.youtube.com/watch?v=bE68xVXf8Kw.

Newman, Linda Hay. "No, a Border Wall Won't Stop Coronavirus." *Wired*, March 3, 2020. https://www.wired.com/story/border-wall-wont-stop-coronavirus/.

Ngai, Sianne. *Our Aesthetic Categories: Zany, Cute, Interesting*. Cambridge, MA: Harvard University Press, 2015.

Nida-Rümelin, Martine, and Donnchadh O'Conaill. "Qualia: The Knowledge Argument." *The Stanford Encyclopedia of Philosophy* (Summer 2021 Edition). Edited by Edward N. Zalta. https://plato.stanford.edu/archives/sum2021/entries/qualia-knowledge/.

Nordin, Md. Jan, Abdul Aziz K. Abdul Hamid, Sumazly Ulaiman, and R. U. Gobithaasan. "Radius Based Block Local Binary Pattern on T-Zone Face Area for Face Recognition." *Journal of Computer Science* 10, no. 12 (2014): 2525–37.

O'Connor, Roison. "What Did We Do to Deserve Janelle Monáe? Dirty Computer—Review." *The Independent*, April 27, 2018. https://www.independent.co.uk/arts-entertainment/music/reviews/janelle-monae-dirty-computer-review-today-listen-live-prince-tessa-thompson-a8324771.html.

Oden, Bryant (music) and Forrest Whaley (animation). "The Duck Song," March 23, 2009. http://www.youtube.com/watch?v=MtN1YnoL46Q.

Ohneswere, Shahendra. "Baz Luhrman Speaks on Directing 'The Great Gatsby.'" *Life and Times,* April 4, 2013. https://lifeandtimes.com/director-baz-lurhmann-speaks-on-directing-the-great-gatsby.

Ok! Magazine. "10 Celebrities Who've Openly Revealed How Much They Weigh." *Ok! Magazine,* May 8, 2014. https://stylecaster.com/how-much-does-beyonce-weigh/.

Oliver, Myrna. "Rose Hobart; SAG Official, Blacklisted Actress." *Los Angeles Times,* August 31, 2000. https://www.latimes.com/archives/la-xpm-2000-aug-31-me-13393-story.html.

Oore, Dani. "Trump the Musical Prophet." In *You Shook Me All Campaign Long: Music in the 2016 Presidential Election and Beyond,* edited by Eric T. Kasper and Benjamin S. Schoening, 263–316. Denton: University of North Texas Press, 2018.

Ora, Rita. "How to Be Lonely." March 27, 2020. https://www.youtube.com/watch?v=FS07b8EUlCs.

Osborn, Brad. *Interpreting Music Video: Popular Music in the Post-MTV Era.* Oxfordshire, UK: Routledge, 2021.

Osborn, Brad. "Risers Drops and a Fourteen-Foot Cube: A Transmedia Analysis of Emil Nava, Calvin Harris and Rihanna's 'This Is What You Came For.'" In *Transmedia Directors: Artistry, Industry, and New Audiovisual Aesthetics,* edited by Carol Vernallis, Holly Rogers, and Lisa Perrott, 169–78. New York: Bloomsbury Academic, 2020.

Osnos, Evan. "Doomsday Prep for the Super-Rich." *New Yorker,* January 30, 2017. https://www.newyorker.com/magazine/2017/01/30/doomsday-prep-for-the-super-rich.

Oudart, Jean-Pierre. "Cinema and Suture." *Screen* 18, no. 4 (Winter 1977): 35–47.

Oudart, Jean-Pierre. "La Suture." *Cahiers du cinema* 211 (April 1969): 36–39 and 212 (May): 50–55.

Overy, Katie, and Istvan Molnar-Szakacs. "Being Together in Time: Musical Experience and the Mirror Neuron System." *Music Perception* 26, no. 5 (2009): 489–504.

Paak, Anderson. "Anderson Paak Talks Oxnard, Fatherhood, Being Saved By The Church + More." Interviewed by DJ Envy, Angela Yee, and Charlamagne tha God. Breakfast Club Power 105.1 FM, YouTube, December 4, 2018. Audio, 7:21. https://www.youtube.com/watch?v=hBM7lDowLzQ&t=441s&ab_channel=BreakfastClubPower105.1FM.

Panera Cuevas, F. Javier, and Richard-Lewis Rees. *This Is Not a Love Song: Video Art and Pop Music Crossovers.* Istanbul: Pera Müzesi Yayınları, 201.

Parise, Cesare, and Charles Spence, "Audiovisual Crossmodal Correspondences." *The Oxford Handbook of Synaesthesia,* edited by J. Simner and E. Hubbard, 790–815. Oxford: Oxford University Press, 2013.

Paul, Pamela. "As for Empathy, the Haves Have Not." *New York Times,* December 30, 2010. http://www.nytimes.com/2011/01/02/fashion/02studied.html.

Peacock, Steven. *Colour.* Manchester, UK: Manchester University Press, 2010.

Pennington, Adrian. "Wealth and Decadence: Simon Duggan ACS / *The Great Gatsby*." *British Cinematographer.* Accessed April 20, 2016. https://britishcinematographer.co.uk/simon-duggan-acs-the-great-gatsby/.

Pew Research Center. "Raising Kids and Running a Household: How Working Parents Share the Load." November 4, 2015. http://www.pewsocialtrends.org/2015/11/04/raising-kids-and-running-a-household-how-working-parents-share-the-load/.

Picking, Jonti. "Badger Song (Badger Badger Badger, Mushroom Mushroom)." June 29, 2022. https://www.youtube.com/watch?v=NL6CDFn2i3I&t=1s&ab_channel=xHopelessDreamingx.

Polan, Dana. "The 'Great American Novel' as Pop-up Book: Baz Luhrmann's *The Great Gatsby* Adaptation." *Adaptation* 6, no. 3 (December 2013): 397–99.

Prichard, Eric C. "Is the Use of Personality Based Psychometrics by Cambridge Analytical Psychological Science's 'Nuclear Bomb' Moment?" *Frontiers in Psychology,* January 29, 2021.

Quintero, Saul Ivan, Ladan Shams, and Kimia Kamal. "Changing the Tendency to Integrate the Senses." *PsyArXiv Preprints*, September 6, 2022. 10.31234/osf.io/x89kc.

Raichle, Marcus E., Ann Mary MacLeod, Abraham Z. Snyder, William J. Powers, Debra A. Gusnard, and Gordon L. Shulman. "A Default Mode of Brain Function." *PNAS* (2001): 676–82.

Railton, Diane, and Paul Watson, *Music Video and the Politics of Representation.* Edinburgh: Edinburgh University Press, 2011.

Ramanan, Chella. "The Video Game Industry Has a Diversity Problem—But It Can Be Fixed." *The Guardian,* March 15, 2017. https://www.theguardian.com/technology/2017/mar/15/video-game-industry-diversity-problem-women-non-white-people.

Ravetto-Biagioli, Kriss. "The Digital Uncanny and Ghost Effects." *Screen* 57, no. 1 (Spring 2016): 1–20.

Rawls, John. *Justice as Fairness: A Restatement.* Cambridge, MA: The Belknap Press of Harvard University Press, 2001.

Reales, José Manuel, and Soledad Ballesteros. "Implicit and Explicit Memory for Visual and Haptic Objects: Cross-Modal Priming Depends on Structural Descriptions." *Journal of Experimental Psychology: Learning, Memory, and Cognition* 25, no. 3 (1999): 644–63.

Richardson, John. *An Eye for Music: Popular Music and the Audiovisual Surreal.* New York: Oxford University Press, 2011.

Richardson, John, Claudia Gorbman, and Carol Vernallis, eds. *The Oxford Handbook of New Audiovisual Aesthetics.* New York: Oxford University Press, 2011.

Rieger, J. M. "Sean Hannity Denied Calling Coronavirus a Hoax Nine Days After He Called Coronavirus a Hoax." *Washington Post,* March 9, 2020. https://www.washingtonpost.com/politics/2020/03/19/sean-hannity-denied-calling-coronavirus-hoax-nine-days-after-he-called-coronavirus-hoax/.

Roberts, T. Carlis. "Spiritual Technologies and the Metaphysics of Enslavement." The Ron Alexander Memorial Lectures, Stanford University, Stanford, CA, Winter 2018.

Rogers, Holly. "Audiovisual Dissonance in Found-Footage Film." In *The Music and Sound of Experimental Film,* edited by Holly Rogers and Jeremy Barnham, 193–98. New York: Oxford University Press, 2017.

Rogers, Holly. "The Audiovisual Eerie: Transmediating Thresholds in the Work of David Lynch." In *Transmedia Directors: Artistry, Industry and the New Audiovisual Aesthetics,* edited by Carol Vernallis, Holly Rogers, and Lisa Perrott, 285–90. New York: Bloomsbury, 2019.

Rogers, Holly. "'Betwixt and Between' Worlds: Spatial and Temporal Liminality in Video Art-Music." In *The Oxford Handbook of New Audiovisual Aesthetics,* edited by John Richardson, Claudia Gorbman, and Carol Vernallis, 525–42. New York: Oxford University Press, 2013.

Rogers, Holly. *Sounding the Gallery: Video and the Rise of Art-Music Films.* New York: Oxford University Press, 2013.

Rogers, Holly. "Twisted Synaesthesia: Music Video and the Visual Arts." In *Art or Sound,* edited by Germano Celant, 384–88. Milan: Fondazione Prada, 2014.

Rogers, Nicole. "There Are 614 Billionaires in the United States, and Only 7 of Them Are Black." *Business Insider,* September 4, 2020. https://www.businessinsider.com/black-billionaires-in-the-united-states-2020-2.

Rose, Tricia. *Black Noise.* Middletown, CT: Wesleyan University Press, 1994.

Rosen, Jody. "Beyoncé: The Woman on Top of the World." *New York Times,* June 3, 2014. https://www.nytimes.com/2014/06/03/t-magazine/beyonce-the-woman-on-top-of-the-world.html.

Rotten Tomatoes. "Scorpio Rising." Accessed July 1, 2016. https:// www.rottentomatoes.com/m/scorpio-rising.

Russo, Julie. "User-Penetrated Content: Fan Video in the Age of Convergence." *Cinema Journal* 48, no. 4 (2009): 125–30.

Sadoff, Ronald H. "Scoring for Film and Video Games: Collaborative Practices and Digital Post Production." In *The Oxford Handbook of Sound and Image in Digital Media,* edited by Carol Vernallis, Amy Herzog, and John Richardson, 663–81. New York: Oxford University Press, 2013.

Santhanam, Laura, and Megan Crigger. "Out of 30,000 Hollywood Film Characters, Here's How Many Weren't White." *PBS News Hour*, September 22, 2015. http://www.pbs.org/newshour/rundown/30000-hollywood-film-characters-heres-many-werent-white/.

Sapolsky, Robert. "How Economic Inequality Inflicts Real Biological Harm." *Scientific American*, November 1, 2018. https://www.scientificamerican.com/article/how-economic-inequality-inflicts-real-biological-harm/.

Savage, Dan. *American Savage: Insights, Slights, and Fights on Faith, Sex, Love, and Politics*. New York: Plume, 2014.

Schiller, Herbert. *The Mind Managers*. Boston: Beacon, 1975.

Schloss, Karen B., and Stephen E. Palmer. "An Ecological Framework for Temporal and Individual Differences in Color Preferences." *Vision Research* 141 (2017): 95–108. https://doi.org/10.1016/j.visres.2017.01.010.

Scott, A. O. "Let the Mass Destruction Begin: Review of Transformers: Age of Extinction." *New York Times*, June 27, 2014. https://www.nytimes.com/2014/06/27/movies/transformers-age-of-extinction-is-fourth-in-the-series.html.

Scott, A. O. "Shimmying Off the Literary Mantle: 'The Great Gatsby,' Interpreted by Baz Luhrmann." *New York Times*, May 10, 2013. http://www.nytimes.com/2013/05/10/movies/the-great-gatsby-interpreted-by-baz-luhrmann.html.

Sekula, Allan. "The Traffic in Photographs." *Art Journal* 41, no. 1 (1981): 15–21.

Shams, Ladan, Yukiyasu Kamitani, and Shinsuke Shimojo. "'What You See is What You Hear.'" *Nature* 408 (December 14, 2000): 788.

Sharff, Stefan. *The Elements of Cinema: Toward a Theory of Cinesthetic Impact*. New York: Columbia University Press, 1982.

Shaviro, Steven. *Digital Music Videos*. New Brunswick, NJ: Rutgers, 2017.

Shaviro, Steven. "Post-Cinematic Affect." In *Post-Cinema: Theorizing 21st-Century Film*, edited by Shane Denson and Julia Leyda, 1.2. Falmer, UK: REFRAME Books, 2016.

Shaviro, Steven. *The Rhythm Image: Music Videos and New Audiovisual Forms*. New York: Bloomsbury, 2022.

Silberstein, Elodie. "'Have You Ever Seen the Crowd Goin' Apeshit?': Disrupting Representations of Animalistic Black Femininity in the French Imaginary." *Humanities* 8, no. 3 (2019):135. https://doi.org/10.3390/h8030135.

Singh, Rani. "Harry Smith, an Ethnographic Modernist in America." In *Harry Smith: The Avant-Garde in the American Vernacular*, edited by Andrew Perchuk and Rani Singh, 34–36. Los Angeles: Getty Research Institute, 2010.

Sitney, P. Adams. "Film #12: Heaven and Earth Magic." In *Harry Smith: The Avant-Garde in the American Vernacular*, edited by Andrew

Perchuk and Rani Singh, 73–84. Los Angeles: Getty Research Institute, 2010.

Sitney, P. Adams. *Visionary Film: The American Avant-Garde, 1943–2000*, 3rd ed. Oxford: Oxford University Press, 2002.

Skokowski, Paul. "The Philosophy of Westworld." In *Cybermedia: Explorations in Science, Sound and Vision*, edited by Carol Vernallis, Holly Rogers, Selmin Kara, and Jonathan Leal, 207–22. New York: Bloomsbury Academic, 2021.

Smith, Jeff. "Bridging the Gap: Reconsidering the Border between Diegetic and Nondiegetic Music." *Music and the Moving Image* 2, no. 1 (spring 2009): 1–25.

Smith, Jeff. *The Sounds of Commerce: Marketing Popular Film Music*. New York: Columbia University Press, 1998.

Solan, Nate. *Switched on Pop: How Popular Music Works, and Why it Matters*. New York: Oxford University Press, 2019.

Spinoza, Benedictus de. *The Collected Works of Spinoza*. Edited and translated by Edwin Curley. Princeton, NJ: Princeton University Press, 1985.

Spring, Katherine. "From Analog to Digital: Synthesizers and Discourses of Film Sound in the 1980s." In *The Palgrave Handbook of Sound Design and Music in Screen Media: Integrated Soundtracks*, edited by Danijela Kulezic and Liz Greene, 273–89. London: Palgrave Macmillan, 2016.

Stein, B. E., and M. T. Wallace. "Comparisons of Cross-modality Integration in Midbrain and Cortex." *Progressive Brain Research* 112 (1996):289–99.

Steinem, Gloria. "Here's The Full Transcript of Gloria Steinem's Historic Women's March Speech." *Elle*. January 21, 2017. https://www.elle.com/culture/news/a42331/gloria-steinem-womens-march-speech/.

Sterbenz, Maeve. "Movement, Music, Feminism: An Analysis of Movement-Music Interactions and the Articulation of Masculinity in Tyler, the Creator's 'Yonkers' Music Video." *Music Theory Online* 23, no. 2 (2017). https://mtosmt.org/issues/mto.17.23.2/mto.17.23.2.sterbenz.html.

Stillwell, Robin J. "The Fantastical Gap Between Diegetic and Nondiegetic." In *Beyond the Soundtrack: Representing Music in Cinema*, edited by Daniel Goldmark, Lawrence Kramer, and Richard Leppert, 184–202. Berkeley: University of California Press, 2007.

Suárez, Juan A. *Bike Boys, Drag Queens, and Superstars*. Bloomington: Indiana University Press, 1996.

Suárez, Juan A. "The Sound of Queer Experimental Film." In *The Music and Sound of Experimental Film*, edited by Holly Rogers and Jeremy Barnham, 233–56. New York: Oxford University Press, 2017.

Tagg, Philip. *Music's Meanings: A Modern Musicology for Non-musus*. Larchmont, NY: Mass Media Music Scholars' Press, 2013.

Tagg, Philip, and Bob Clarida. *Ten Little Title Tunes: Towards a Musicology of the Mass Media*. New York: Mass Media Scholars' Press, 2003.

Taylor, Guy. "'Wake-Up Call': Chinese Control of U.S. Pharmaceutical Supplies Sparks Growing Concern." *Washington Times,* March 17, 2020. https://www.washingtontimes.com/news/2020/mar/17/china-threatens-restrict-critical-drug-exports-us/.

Tegmark, Mark. *Life 3.0: Being Human in the Age of Artificial Intelligence.* New York: Knopf, 2017.

Thanouli, Eleftheria. *Post-Classical Cinema: An International Poetics of Film Narration.* London: Wallflower, 2009.

Tinsley, Omise'eke Natasha. *Beyoncé in Formation: Remixing Black Feminism.* Austin: University of Texas Press, 2018.

Useem, Jerry. "Power Causes Brain Damage." *The Atlantic*, July/August 2017. https://www.theatlantic.com/magazine/archive/2017/07/power-causes-brain-damage/528711/?utm_source=nhfb.

Van der Linden, Marieke, Miranda van Turennout, and Guillén Fernández. "Category Training Induces Cross-Modal Object Representations in the Adult Human Brain." *Journal of Cognitive Neuroscience* 23, no. 6 (2011): 1315–31.

Vena, Jocelyn. "Beyoncé Has Lady Gaga, Katy Perry 'Stanning' Out with New Album." *MTV News,* December 13, 2013. http://www.mtv.com/news/1719025/Beyoncé-album-lady-gaga-katy-perry-reactions/.

Vernallis, Carol. "Audiovisuality and the Media Swirl: Campaign 2016." *Flow Journal*, October 25, 2016. https://www.flowjournal.org/author/carol-vernallis/.

Vernallis, Carol. *Experiencing Music Video: Aesthetics and Cultural Context.* New York: Columbia University Press, 2004.

Vernallis, Carol. "Music Video, Songs, Sound: Experience, Technique and Emotion in *Eternal Sunshine of the Spotless Mind.*" *Screen* 49, no. 3 (2008): 277–97.

Vernallis, Carol. *Unruly Media: YouTube, Music Video and the New Digital Cinema.* New York: Oxford University Press, 2013.

Vernallis, Carol, Dale Chapman, Gabriel Ellis, Kyra Gaunt, Jason King, Gabrielle Lockard, Eric Lyons, Dani Oore, and Maeve Sterbenz. "Tracing the Carters through the Galleries (Roundtable on 'APES**T')." *Journal of Popular Music Studies* 30, no. 4 (November 2018): 11–70.

Vernallis, Carol, Lauren Cramer, Jonathan Leal, Anders Liljedahl, Daniel Oore, Steven Shaviro, and Eduardo Viñuela. "Anderson .Paak, Kendrick Lamar, and Colin Tilley 'Get up in Our Rearview Mirror': Collectively Analyzing the 'Tints' Music Video." *Quarterly Review of Film and Video* 39 (January 2021): 1–40.

Vernallis, Carol, Gabriel Zane Ellis, Jonathan James Leal, Gabrielle Lochard, Daniel Oore, Steven Shaviro, Maeve Sterbenz, and Maxwell Joseph Suechting. "The Janelle Monáe Dirty Computer Project." *Journal of the Society of American Music* 13, no. 2 (Spring 2019): 250–71. doi: 10.1017/S1752196319000154.

Vernallis, Carol, Amy Herzog, and John Richardson, eds. *The Oxford Handbook of Sound and Image in Digital Media*. New York: Oxford, 2015.

Vernallis, Carol, Holly Rogers, Selmin Kara, and Jonathan Leal. *Cybermedia: Explorations in Science, Sound, and Vision*. New York: Bloomsbury Academic, 2021.

Vernallis, Carol, Holly Rogers, and Lisa Perrott, eds. *Transmedia Directors: Artistry, Industry, and New Audiovisual Aesthetics*. New York: Bloomsbury, 2019.

Vernallis, Carol, and Hannah Ueno. "Interview with Music Video Director and Auteur Floria Sigismondi." *Music, Sound, and the Moving Image* 7, no. 2 (2013): 167–94.

Vetter, Petra, and Albert Newen. "Varieties of Cognitive Penetration in Visual Perception." *Consciousness and Cognition* 27 (2014): 62–75.

Viktor, Lina Iris. "Materia Prima." Lecture at University of Michigan, December 8, 2018. https://www.youtube.com/watch?v=FOs yOcG1JVU.

Viñuela, Eduardo. "Metanarratives and Storytelling in Contemporary Mainstream Popular Music: *Romeo and Juliet* in the Making of the Star Persona." *Text Matters*, November 24, 2020. https://doi.org/10.18778/2083-2931.10.13.

Von Trier, Lars. *Dancer in the Dark*. UK: Filmfour Books/Macmillan Books, 2000.

Walker, Elsie. *Understanding Sound Tracks through Film Theory*. New York: Oxford University Press, 2015.

Wallentin, Mikkel, Andreas Højlund Nielsen, Peter Vuust, Anders Dohn, Andreas Roepstorff, and Torben Ellegaard Lund. "Amygdala and Heart Rate Variability Responses from Listening to Emotionally Intense Parts of a Story." *NeuroImage*, 58, no. 3 (2011): 963–73.

Washington Post. "Fox Hosts Shift to Emphasizing Economy Amid Coronavirus Outbreak." March 25, 2020. https://www.youtube.com/watch?v=PI32zdQPw70.

Weaver, Caity. "Beyoncé's Publicist Wants to Erase These Unflattering Photos from the Internet." *Gawker*, February 5, 2013. http://gawker.com/5981957/beyonces-publicist-wants-to-erase-these-six-unflattering-photos-from-the-internet.

Webster, Sina H. "When Life Gives You Lemons, 'Get In Formation': A Black Feminist Analysis of Beyoncé's Visual Album, Lemonade." Senior Honors Thesis, Eastern Michigan University, 2018.

West, Cornel. *Race Matters, 25th Anniversary ed*. Boston: Beacon Press, 2017.

Wheless, Avery. "Color Is an Act of Reason." Press Release for Baert Gallery Exhibition, Los Angeles, August 3–September 14, 2019.

Whipps, Heather. "80,000-Year-Old Beads Shed Light on Early Culture." LiveScience, June 18, 2007. https://www.livescience.com/1626-80-000-year-beads-shed-light-early-culture.html.

Whissel, Kristen. *Spectacular Digital Effects: CGI and Contemporary Cinema*. Durham, NC: Duke University Press, 2014.

Whittington, William. *Sound Design and Science Fiction*. Austin: University of Texas Press, 2007.

Wierzbicki, James. *Film Music: A History*. New York: Routledge, 2009.

Williams, Jonathan D. "'Tha Realness': In Search of Hip-Hop Authenticity." *CUREJ: College Undergraduate Research Electronic Journal* (Winter 2007): 1–15.

Wilson, David. "'Pub Fight' Politics." In *You Shook Me All Campaign Long: Music in the 2016 Presidential Election and Beyond*, edited by Eric T. Kasper and Benjamin S. Schoening, 317–46. Denton: University of North Texas Press, 2018.

Winters, Ben. "The Non-Diegetic Fallacy: Film, Music, and Narrative Space." *Music & Letters* 91, no. 2 (May 2010): 224–44.

Wittgenstein, Ludwig. *Remarks on Color*. Edited by G. E. M. Anscombe and translated by Linda L. McAlister and Margerete Schättle. Berkeley: University of California Press, 2007.

Wolf, Mark J. P. *Building Imaginary Worlds: The Theory and History of Subcreation*. New York: Routledge, 2014.

Wright, Benjamin. "Sculptural Dissonance: Hans Zimmer and the Composer as Engineer." *Sounding Out!,* July 10, 2014. https://soundstudiesblog.com/author/wrigh-tonfilm/.

Zak, Albin. *The Poetics of Rock: Cutting Tracks, Making Records*. Berkeley: University of California Press, 2001.

Zak, Paul J., Angela A. Stanton, and Sheila Ahmadi. "Oxytocin Increases Generosity in Humans." *PLOS ONE*, November 7, 2007. https://doi.org/10.1371/journal.pone.0001128.

Zacks, Jeffrey. "Cognitive Boundaries, 'Nosedive,' and *Under the Skin*: Interview with Jeffrey Zacks." *Cybermedia: Explorations in Science, Sound, and Vision,* edited by Carol Vernallis, Holly Rogers, Selmin Kara, and Jonathan Leal, 171–87. New York: Bloomsbury Academic, 2021.

Zardi, Andrea, Edoardo Giovanni Carlotti, Alessandro Pontremoli, and Rosalba Morese. "Dancing in Your Head: An Interdisciplinary Review." *Frontiers in Psychology* 12 (April 30, 2021).

Žižek, Slavoj. *Looking Awry: An Introduction to Jacques Lacan through Popular Culture*. Cambridge, MA: MIT Press, 1992.

Index

academia, 8, 342, 356, 375n58
Ackerman, Chantal, 111
acting, 59–60, 107–8, 254–55, 259, 292–93, 299, 327, 401n17
Adele, 244
Adichie, Chimamanda Ngozi, 94
Adorno, Theodor, 2
advertising, 15–16, 78, 138–40, 188, 205, 294, 300, 304, 319–25, 341–42, 364, 370. *See also* monetization; product placement
affect, 4, 17, 30, 46–47, 49, 66, 195, 248–49, 251, 255, 348
Affectiva, 322–25
affective publics, 251
Afrofuturism, 150–52, 211–12
Agamben, Giorgio, 398n21
Åkerlund, Bea, 185–86
Åkerlund, Jonas, 16, 86, 90–91, 154–60, 166–72, 194, 196, 291, 296–99, 301–3
Albers, Josef, 266
algorithms, 3, 17, 250–51, 261, 341, 375n58
"All Night" (Beyoncé), 130, 133, 348
"All the Stars" (Lamar), 196–98, 207–9
alternative music, 75
Alternative Nation, 75
Amaral, Nestor, 107–8
Ambassadors, The (Holbein), 5
America Is Waiting (Conner), 113–15
Amor Vincit Omnia, 106
Anash, Joey, 327
Anderson, Laurie, 98, 120–21
Anderson, Wes, 15

Anger, Kenneth, 98, 100–106
Animal Collective, 354
Anna Karenina, 255–56, 258–61
Annihilation (Garland), 320–21, 329
Anonymous Content, 290, 294
Anthropocene, 4
"APES**T," 138–50, 253, 310, 389n23
ArchAndroid, The, 212
Aristotle, 345
Arnheim, Rudolf, 13
art: and advertising, 138; education in, 99, 296; and moral instruction, 17, 19; and neuroscience, 266; perceptions of, 160; and politics, 139–40, 151. *See also* avant-garde
artifice, 253
ASAP Rocky, 294
Ashley, Robert, 120–21
Assness, Tony, 377n1
Atlantic, The, 45
attention, 2, 37, 46, 218–19, 315–16, 318, 323–24, 327
"Attention" (Puth), 292
audiences: attraction of, 4, 6, 10–11, 15; and gender, 52; individual paths through a clip, 215; measurement of, 30, 76–77, 82–83, 241, 322–23, 328–29, 344–45; overwhelming of, 67; and race, 354; relation to, 162, 167–68, 176, 207–10, 232–33, 236–37, 247, 350, 355–56, 358, 371
audiovisual, 76, 79, 87, 152, 160, 168, 197, 206, 209, 213, 221, 225, 255–56, 313, 355, 358, 367

audiovisual aesthetics, 21, 71, 84–85, 195, 225, 292, 307, 320

audiovisual analysis, 6–8, 23, 87, 97–102, 121–23, 175–96, 217–24, 288, 310–13, 335–36, 378n12, 386n37

audiovisual history, 310

audiovisual illusions, 311, 317

audiovisuality: contradictions in, 218; creator's relation to, 15; emergence of new forms, 74; and interpolation, 253; morals and values of, 17; and relationships, 79–80, 97, 101, 106, 118; studies of, 5–6, 8, 23, 222. *See also* media swirl; music videos

audiovisual koans, 126

audiovisual relations, 97, 142, 187–88, 196–97, 207, 248, 274. *See also* sound-image sync

audiovisual rhymes, 203–4, 214

audiovisual synchrony, 279

audiovisual theory, 311

"August" (Swift), 258

aura, 140

Auslander, Phil, 232

auteurism, 75, 86

authority, 143–44, 147, 367

autobiography, 85–86

auto-eroticism, 116

automation, 35, 62–63, 319–20, 383n22

autotune, 73–74, 145

Auto-Tune the News, 73–74

avant-garde, 97–100, 111, 117, 120–22, 309, 367, 387n51. *See also* art

Avengers: Infinity War (Russo), 4, 16

Bachianas Brasileiras No. 5, 107

backbeats, 177, 191–92

background figures, 12, 75–76, 130, 163–64, 247, 308

"Bad Romance" (Gaga), 72–73

Bagheri, 302

Bamboozled (Lee), 193

"Bang, Shot My Baby" (Scherzinger), 35

Barkhuff, Dan, 366

Baroque music, 163

Barthes, Roland, 247, 253

Batchelor, David, 268

Battle Potemkin (Eisenstein), 22

Bausch, Pina, 135

Bay, Michael, 15, 28–29, 48–54, 59–61, 66–67, 84, 95, 205, 294, 303, 309

Bayer, Samuel, 76

Bayesian predictions, 13, 312, 337–38

beat, 34–35, 130, 177–78, 191–92. *See also* rhythm

Beatles, 155

"Beautiful People" (Sheeran), 250

Beavis and Butthead, 119

Beebe, Roger, 75

Belton, John, 36, 267

Benson-Allott, Caetlin, 261

Berger, John, 140

Bergman, Ingmar, 131

berimbau, 141, 147

Berkeley, Busby, 1, 28, 375–76n58

Berland, Lauren, 22

BET, 75

"Betrayed," 365–68

"Bette Davis Eyes" (Carnes), 81

Beyoncé, 79, 85–96, 131–32, 141–55, 175–94, 233–38, 278–82, 299–301, 310, 339, 347–53, 362, 389n23, 391n10

Beyoncé (Beyoncé), 71, 74, 82, 85–93, 212, 335, 343, 347, 349, 353–54

Biden, Joe, 22, 364, 368

Bieber, Justin, 233, 236, 243

Bigelow, Kathryn, 117

"Big Poppa" (Notorious B.I.G.), 75–77

Big Sleep, The, 218

Bijou, 106

Billboard, 76–77

"Bird of Flames" (Lynch and Bell), 117

Birth of a Nation (Griffith), 22

Birx, Deborah, 364

Black, Chris, 295

Black Lives Matter, 206, 339, 349, 363, 365

Black Panther (Coogler), 196–97

Black to Techno (Nkiru), 238

Blake, James, 123, 126–27, 130, 133, 354–55

"Blank Space" (Swift), 73, 81

blindness, 46
blockbusters, 7, 48–49, 51–52, 95–96, 232. *See also* Hollywood
"Blow" (Beyoncé), 87–88
"Blue Monday '88" (New Order), 120
blues music, 223
Bluets (Nelson), 266
Blue Velvet (Lynch), 111–12
"Blue Velvet" (Vinton), 104, 109
Bodied, 304
bodies, 11, 130, 152, 169, 197, 199. *See also* gestures
"Boiler" (Limp Bizkit), 203
Bollywood, 28, 71
Bones & All, 375–76n58
"Boogie Wonderland" (Earth, Wind, and Fire), 87
Bordwell, David, 48, 58, 81, 95, 155–56, 290, 309
Børn, 254
Botticelli, 38
Bourne Ultimatum, The (Greengrass), 58, 64, 321–22, 325–29
Bowie, David, 99
Boyle, Danny, 84
Brakhage, Stan, 106
"Brand New Day" (Lovato), 23
Brando, Marlon, 401n17
Branigan, Edward, 267
"Breathin" (Grande), 2
Bridgerton, 251–52, 256, 259–60
brief media, 5–6, 8, 13. *See also* TikTok
Brill, Lesley, 66
Bringing Up Baby (Hawks), 18
Brion, Jon, 136
Brooks, Louise, 253
Brophy, Philip, 101
BTS, 239, 241
Buckland, Warren, 95
Buhler, James, 252
Buhler, Jim, 319, 330
Buñuel, Luis, 22
Burgess, Anthony, 109
Burns, Lori, 374n35, 381n1, 382n15, 387n3
Butch Vig, 76

"By a Waterfall" (Berkeley), 375–76n58
Byrne, Alex, 267
Byrne, David, 113–14

Cabaret, 111
Cabello, Camila, 208
Calavita, Marco, 292, 309
"California" (Mitchell), 103
call and response, 123
Call Me By Your Name (Guadagnino), 23, 251, 375n58
"Call Me by Your Name" (Lil Nas X), 375–76n58
Cambridge Analytica, 195, 322
camera: angles, 46, 76; and closeness, 11, 104–5, 169; movement of, 103, 118, 123–24, 128–29, 141–44, 179, 189, 221, 361–62; rhythm of, 37, 42–43; unpredictability of, 32–33, 37, 46
Canetti, Elias, 3
capitalism, 7, 21–28, 51, 55, 62, 94, 206, 290, 319–21, 323, 345, 348–49, 352
capitol insurrection, 22
Caramanica, Jon, 235, 375–76n58
Caravaggio, Michelangelo, 106
career trajectories, 15–16, 28, 47–54, 84, 100, 117, 196, 205–6, 213, 273–74, 282, 290–307, 396n10. *See also* directors; education
Carlson, Tucker, 357–58
Carpenter, John, 2
Carpenter, Karen, 120
Carpool Karaoke, 231, 233, 241–44
Carr, Jeremy, 101
Carrol, Diahann, 226
Carrozzini, Francesco, 302
Casetti, Francesco, 7
Cavell, Stanley, 3, 17, 19, 94
Caviar, 14–15, 302–3
Cee Lo, 301
celebrities, 6, 45–47, 72, 106, 205–6, 226, 233–38, 241–44, 253–54, 308, 362
"Cellophane" (twigs), 266, 268–74, 288, 375–76n58

censorship, 101, 117
Chainsmokers, 10
Chairlift, 354
Chalamet, Timothée, 252, 375n58
Chaplin, Charlie, 111
character arcs, 171, 201
Chien Andalou, Un (Buñel and Dalí), 111
Childish Gambino, 371
Chion, Michel, 8–9, 87, 288, 311
choreography, 43–44
chorus, 123, 162, 164–65, 175–77, 181, 190, 193, 223, 313
Chromatic Cinema (Misek), 267
cinematography, 29, 32, 37, 65, 83, 128, 243, 367
"Circles" (Post Malone), 218
Citizen Kane, 36, 111
Citizens United (2010), 397n4
class, 19, 27, 94, 182, 187, 191, 248, 302, 341, 345, 355, 383–84n22
Classical Hollywood Cinema (Bordwell), 155–56
Clement, Catherine, 227
climate change, 4, 17, 21, 153, 206, 321, 343, 368–70
Clinton, Hillary, 4
Clockwork Orange, A (Burgess), 109, 256–57
"Clouds" (Khan), 260
Cobain, Kurt, 234–35, 238
Cohen, Annabel, 9, 311, 396n3
Colbert, Claudette, 401n17
Cold War, 113–15
collaboration, 225, 280, 292, 296–97, 299, 303, 326, 328, 354, 366, 370
colonialism, 152
color, 36, 49, 165, 223, 259, 265, 301
Color Adjustment (Riggs), 226
color grading, 265–89, 367
color palette: analyses of, 395n18; and continuity, 86; language of, 267–68, 273, 283; limited control of, 79; in mashups, 259; and narrative, 41, 177–78; patterns of, 165–66; symbolism of, 148, 169, 223; and temporality, 267; variations in, 36–37, 107, 271–72, 279; and visual interest, 36–37
colorscapes, 269–71, 279
commercials. *See* advertising
commodification, 152
commons, 332, 368
community, 122–23, 125, 191, 211, 336, 340, 346, 349
Conner, Bruce, 98, 112–15
Connolly, William, 347
"Consequences" (Cabello), 208
"Conservative," 365–68
Constantine, 303
contagion, 40
continuity, 41–42, 86, 88, 143, 182, 203–4. *See also* post-continuity
Conway, Bevil, 266, 394n1
Cook, Nicholas, 8–9, 87, 159, 248, 255, 288, 311–12
Cook, Pam, 389n2
Corden, James, 241–44, 364
Cornell, Joseph, 106–9
costume, 45, 155, 163, 185, 295; ambiguity of, 155; corresponding to timbre, 161; and fixing attention, 46; and heteronormativity, 91; historical accuracy of, 45, 78; labor of, 295; and narrative meaning, 185–86; patterns of, 41–42, 182, 203; and racial categories, 40; symbolism of, 111, 124, 156–58, 165, 167, 209
COVID-19 pandemic, 21–22, 340, 356–60, 363–65
Crary, Jonathan, 3
"Crazy in Love" (Beyoncé), 254, 259
Crenshaw, Kimberlé, 339
crowds, 37–38, 42–46, 66–67, 362–63
"Cry Me a River" (Lawrence and Timberlake), 203
Cubitt, Sean, 368
Cukor, George, 33
cultural studies, 159
Cybermedia (Vernallis), 20, 320, 394n1
cymbals, 141
Cyrus, Miley, 238, 240

"Daddy Lessons," 125
Damon, Matt, 326
dance, 43–44, 46, 76, 91, 116, 145, 147, 157, 201–3, 373n19, 388n15. *See also* gestures
"Dancing in the Street" (Martha Reeves and the Vandellas), 109
Dargis, Manohla, 49
Dash, Julie, 135
David, Jacques-Louis, 141
Davis, Miles, 237
Davison, Annette, 384n1
Dayton, Jonathan, 307
Dean and Me (Eiden), 365
death, 164; depictions of, 58, 164, 225, 390n4; symbols of, 57, 169
Deaville, James, 360
Debord, Guy, 2
Delacroix, Eugène, 141
Del Rey, Lana, 260
Demers, Joanna, 98
Denson, Shane, 23
Deren, 385n12
Detention, 304
dialogue, 36, 56, 61, 64, 185, 245, 361; limited use of, 59, 101, 308; in mashups, 258; as repetitive, 36; strategic use of, 61–62, 303; and subtitles, 54
diegesis, 125–26, 232, 252–53
Dienstfrey, Eric, 382n12
Dietrich, Marlene, 253
digital audio production, 76, 83, 142, 200, 213–14, 238
digital cinema, 52–53, 55–58, 83, 92, 284. *See also* film production
digital composition, 40, 78, 118, 301
Digital Music Videos (Shaviro), 92
"Dinero," 293
Dior, 16
directors: compensation for, 298; distinct styles of, 75, 119, 135, 309; methods of work, 61–62; perceptions of music video genre, 292–93; reputations of, 15, 51, 81, 392n2; and self-expression, 282, 295–96, 300; working methods of, 95, 295,

299–302. *See also* career trajectories; *specific directors*
Dirty Computer, 211–12, 392n1
disability, 156, 339, 342–43, 353
discorrelated media, 23
disorientation, 29, 31–33, 40–41, 43, 46, 91, 126, 181, 201–3, 219, 269. *See also* spatiality
Dixieland, 34–35
Django Unchained (Tarantino), 132
DJ Ravidrums, 361–62
Doggface, 248–49
Dolby, 83
Donnelly, Kevin, 110
"Don't Cry For Me Argentina" (Madonna), 364
"Don't Hurt Yourself" (Beyoncé), 127–28, 131, 354–55
"Don't Start Now" (Dua Lipa), 239
"Double Happiness" (Cee Lo), 301
Drake, 364
Dr. Dre, 225
"Dreams" (Fleetwood Mac), 248–49
dreamscapes, 56
drum machines, 74–75
Dua Lipa, 233, 239, 293, 364
Duffy, Robert, 297
Duran Duran, 74
Duverneix, Thibaut, 294
Dyer, Richard, 1, 3, 47, 49–50, 368, 401n17
Dynevor, Phoebe, 253–54, 259–60

Earth, Wind, and Fire, 74, 87, 224, 250
East of Borneo (Melford), 106–7
economics, 75, 78, 81, 95, 206, 294, 297–98, 321, 342
editing, 54, 83, 88, 184, 237, 253, 279, 350; and the fourth wall, 123–24; jump-cuts, 350; labor of, 283, 297, 299, 301, 367; and layers of sound, 200; match cuts, 54, 89, 182, 185; pace of, 37, 50, 275, 330, 357; and relation to audience, 394n14; and rhythm, 83, 181; shot lengths, 192–93, 309

INDEX 433

education, 16, 213, 283–84, 293, 295, 302, 320, 396n10. *See also* career trajectories
Eiden, Heath, 365–66
Eilish, Billie, 233, 258, 365
Eisenstein, Sergei, 22, 148, 388n19
Electric Lady, The, 212
"Electric Love" (Børn), 254
electroencephalography (EEG), 30, 81–82, 313
Electronics, 120
Elliott, Missy, 205–6, 208
Elsaesser, Thomas, 95
Eminem, 303
empathy, 19
Endless (Ocean), 82, 95, 212
Eno, Brian, 113
"Entertainer, The" (ZAYN), 266, 274–78, 288
Eisenstein, Sergei, 149
Eternal Sunshine of the Spotless Mind, 58, 96
ethics, 20, 347, 360
Evancho, Jackie, 361
Exorcist, The, 163
Experiencing Music Video (Vernallis), 154
"Express Yourself" (Madonna), 88
externalism, 335–36
eye-tracking, 30, 81–82

facial tracking, 30, 82, 322, 325–28, 332
Fallon, Jimmy, 239, 242
Famous (Kanye), 95
fandom, 232–34, 236, 238, 241
Faris, Valerie, 307
fascism, 4
Fast, Susan, 232
"Father Figure" (Michaels), 13, 79–80
Fauci, Anthony, 357
femininity, 190
feminism, 123, 183
Fergie, 34, 36, 42–43
Ferguson, Alan, 6, 212–13, 215, 300–301
fetishism, 105
Feuer, Jane, 11

film production, 281, 284–85, 303, 308, 365. *See also* digital cinema
Fincher, David, 84, 196, 257, 285, 291, 294, 302, 309
Finkelstein, Lorin, 295
"Fireworks" (Perry), 22
Five Foot Two (Moukarbel), 234, 241
500 Days of Summer (Webb), 251
"Flawless" (Beyoncé), 91–92
Fleetwood Mac, 248–49
Flock of Seagulls, 74
Floyd, George, 363, 365
Flying Lotus, 99
Flinn, Caryl, 2
focalization, 253
foley, 42
Foot, Philippa, 345
Footlight Parade, 1, 375–76n58
Ford, John, 61
Fordism, 16, 27–28, 92–94, 96, 377n5, 383n22
foreshadowing, 40–41
"Formation" (Beyoncé), 132, 136–37, 266, 278–82, 288, 348–49, 353, 389n23
Forrester, Ian, 321
"Forward" (Beyoncé), 123, 131, 354–55
Four Seasons (Vivaldi), 256
Fox News, 321, 356–60
fragmentation, 112–13
Frank, Robert, 117
Frankenstein (Whale), 22
"Freedom," 127, 132–33
free will, 18, 20, 370–71
From the Sea to the Land Beyond (Woolcock), 110
functional magnetic resonance imaging (fMRI), 30, 81–82, 313, 327, 371, 398n2, 401n17
Fury (Lang), 22

Gabriel, Peter, 225, 257
Gaga, Lady, 72–73, 154–55, 157–62, 165–67, 170–72, 227, 234–35, 241, 299, 302, 310

galvanic skin response (GSR) measures, 30, 81–82, 313
Garbo, Greta, 107–8, 253
Gardner, Justin, 20
Garland, Alex, 320–21
Gates, Bill, 342
Gavras, Romain, 302
Gaye, Marvin, 89, 190–91, 194
gaze, 5, 46, 93–94, 201
gender, 52, 59–60, 123–26, 133, 143, 158, 160, 187–88, 190–91, 194, 227, 259, 340, 362
genre, 78, 82, 85 132; blurring of, 5, 12, 75, 300; conventions of, 6, 71–72, 265; definitions of, 73, 117, 188, 292; histories of, 24, 154, 392n1
Géricault, Théodore, 388n18
German expressionism, 43
Gershwin, George, 33–34
gestures, 126, 132, 150, 167; choreography of, 208, 220–21, 293; and emotion, 60, 141; patterns of, 166–68, 217–18; and sense of character, 107; and song structure, 198; stylization of, 60, 168, 199, 363; symbolism of, 126–27, 148, 150, 162, 179, 309; and sync, 189; as transmedial, 185; weight of, 200–203. *See also* bodies; dance
"Get the Party Started" (P!nk), 206
"Getting Away with It" (Marker), 120
"Get Ur Freak On" (Elliott), 208
"Ghost" (Beyoncé), 350–52
"Giant" (Harris), 296
globalization, 14–16, 21, 27–28
Godard, Jean-Luc, 54, 253
"God Bless America," 360
Godron, Kim, 119
Goethe, Johan Wolfgang von, 267
"Goldrush" (Swift), 254
Gondry, Michel, 302
Gone with the Wind (Fleming), 361
Good Company, 290
Goodfellas (Scorsese), 375–76n58
Google, 3
Gorbman, Claudia, 8–9
Gorzelany-Mostak, Dana, 361

Gothic films, 160–61
Goulding, Ellie, 258
Grammer, Kelsey, 50
Grande, Ariana, 2, 208, 233, 235, 241, 254
Great Gatsby, The (Luhrmann), 27, 29–32, 35, 43–44, 96–97, 122, 377n3, 378n12
Greengrass, Paul, 327
Grey, Joel, 111
Grey, Tom, 388n15
Griffith, D. W., 22
Grimes, 356, 364–65
Grindhouse (Tarantino), 256
Guadagnino, Luca, 375–76n58
Gunning, Tom, 95
Guns N' Roses, 164

Habermas, Jürgen, 4
Halloween (Carpenter), 2
Halsey, 218, 250
Hammer, Armie, 23, 375–76n58
Hannity, Sean, 248, 356
"Happiness Is a Warm Gun" (Beatles), 115
harmony, 89, 91, 143, 186, 200, 269, 313
Harold and Maude (Ashby), 84
harpsichord, 73
Harris, Calvin, 296
Harvey, David, 232
Hasson, Uri, 19
Hateful Eight, The (Tarantino), 256–57
"Haunted" (Beyoncé), 90–91, 93, 301
hauntedness, 141–42, 144
Hautea, Samantha, 251
Hawks, Howard, 18, 61, 218
Hayes, Isaac, 352
heartbeat, 208–9
Heffernan, Virginia, 3
Helman, David M., 278
Her (Jonze), 232
"Here it Goes Again" (OK Go), 76–77
Herrmann, Bernard, 160
Hess, David, 256
heteronormativity, 98
heterosexuality, 134, 183
"Higher Love," 307–11

"high" and "low" media, 24, 138
Hilbert, David, 267
Hilton, Paris, 121
Hirst, Damien, 117
Hitchcock, Alfred, 38, 91, 169, 383n16, 401n17
Hitcher, The (Meyers), 205, 303
Holbein, Hans, 5
"Hold On," 130
Holiday, Billy, 354
Holiday in Brazil (Amaral), 106
Hollywood, 48, 155; budgets of, 47–48, 59, 81; as dominant shooting location, 291; race relations in, 187; traditional narrative styles, 155–58, 170; working conditions in, 107. *See also* blockbusters; postclassical film aesthetic
Holocaust imagery, 67
home-movie footage, 124
homosexuality, 106, 183
hooks, bell, 123, 126
Hopper, Dennis, 111
horror films, 160–61
House That Jack Built, The (von Trier), 228, 375–76n58
"How Do You Sleep?," 244
"How to Be Lonely," 365
Human League, 74
humor, 228
Humphrey, Doris, 44
Hunger Games, The, 96, 303
Hynde, Chrissy, 299

Imagine Dragons, 64
IMAX 3D, 53
I'm Not the Girl Who Misses Much (Rist), 115–16
"I'm Ready" (Lovato and Smith), 10, 312–17
indie rock, 118
infidelity, 85, 122–23, 132, 349, 352
Inglorious Basterds, 67
Ingraham, Laura, 258, 357
Instagram, 5
instrumentation, 141, 144–45, 147, 215. *See also* song arrangement

interdisciplinarity, 5–8, 14, 20, 24, 311
intersectionality, 338–43
intertextual, 238–39, 338, 361
"In the Night" (The Weeknd), 82
intimacy, 5, 48, 118, 212–13, 220, 243–44, 353, 362
Ireland, David, 9, 256
It Was All a Lie (Stevens), 365–66
I Want My MTV (Marks and Tannenbaum), 83

Jablonsky, Steve, 54
Jackson, Janet, 86, 205–6, 301
Jackson, Michael, 158–59, 184, 218, 297, 309–10, 375–76n58, 401n17
James, Robin, 94, 380n38, 383n20
Jarman, Derek, 98, 118–19
Jawline, 231
Jay-Z, 141, 143–45, 148–52, 164, 296, 348, 353
jazz, 29, 34, 99, 125
"Jealous" (Beyoncé), 90
Jhally, Sut, 324
Jirsa, Tomáš, 381n1, 382n15
Johansson, Scarlett, 362
Jonze, Spike, 84, 294, 309, 323
Joseph, Kahlil, 353
"Joy" (Lawrence), 16
Joyce, Joshua, 60
jump-cuts, 350
Jung, Berenike, 259, 405n3
Jung, Carl, 247, 393n3
"Justify My Love" (Madonna), 90

Kahn, Joseph, 16, 293, 298, 302
Kahneman, Daniel, 346
Kalinak, Kay, 374n35, 381n41
Kant, Immanuel, 4, 328
Kaplan, E. Ann, 14–15, 138, 251, 364
Kassabian, Anahid, 252
Kaye, Tony, 117, 283
Keaton, Buster, 253
Keazor, Henry, 381n1
Keitel, Harvey, 186
Kerins, Mark, 48
Kerslake, Kevin, 299

Khalifa, Wiz, 292–93
Khan, Chaka, 87, 259–60, 299–301, 303–4, 307–8
Kinder, Marsha, 251
King, Geoff, 379n19
King of Hearts, 84
Klasfeld, Marc, 292
Knightley, Keira, 253–55, 259
Knowles, Beyoncé. *See* Beyoncé
Knutson, Brian, 21
König, Sebastian, 395n18
Korsgaard, Matthias, 381n1, 382n15, 394n27
Kosinski, Michal, 341–42
Kravitz, Lenny, 83
Kronengold, Charles, 259, 374n35, 378n12
Kubrick, Stanley, 131, 135, 256–57

LaBeouf, Shia, 375–76n58
labor, 234, 283, 300, 304, 350
Ladzekpo, C. K., 330
"La La La" (Shakira), 81
Lamar, Kendrick, 127, 196–97, 201, 207, 209, 216–30, 257, 355
Landreville, John, 23
Landy, Joshua, 17
Lang, Fritz, 22
Langer, Susanne, 11, 255
Lapalux, 312–13, 316–18
"Last Friday Night" (Perry), 226
Lawrence, Francis, 16, 72–73, 84, 95, 184, 196, 203, 291, 303
Lawrence, Jennifer, 16
Leal, Jonathan, 223, 265–89, 365
LeDoux, Joseph, 346
Led Zeppelin, 385n24
Lee, Spike, 193
Leger, Mathieu, 294
Leibnizian monads, 14
Lemonade (Beyoncé), 71, 74, 82–96, 122–37, 211–12, 335, 343–50, 352–55, 400n51
Lennon, John, 115
"Let It All Go" (Rhodes), 255
"Let's Groove" (Earth, Wind, and Fire), 250

Levey, Simon, 290
Levine, Adam, 201–3, 207–8
lighting, 141, 149, 169, 197, 217, 281, 317, 379n18
"Like a Prayer" (Madonna), 88, 188
"Like a Rolling Stone" (Dylan), 82
Liljedahl, Anders, 381n1, 382n15
Lil Nas X, 23, 375–76n58
Limp Bizkit, 203
Lincoln Project, 22, 356, 365–68
Linklater, Richard, 238
Lipietz, Alain, 377n5, 383n22
Lippit, Akira, 98
Lipsitz, George, 331
Little Miss Sunshine (Faris and Dayton), 307
"Little Party Never Killed Nobody, A" (Fergie), 34, 36, 42
"Little Susie's on the Up" (Ph.D), 74–75, 164
Little Women, 256, 261
Lochard, Gabrielle, 388n5
Lomax, Alan, 355
Longo, Robert, 117
Lovato, Demi, 10, 23, 312–17
"Love Drought," 130
"Love Me Like You Do" (Goulding), 258
"Love the Way You Lie" (Rihanna), 259
"Lucky" (Spears), 206, 208
Luhrmann, Baz, 27–30, 41, 43, 45, 47–48, 95–96, 377n4, 379n29, 380n36
Lynch, David, 15, 84, 111–12, 131
lynching, 400n51
lyrics, 9, 89, 105, 124, 148–49, 154, 166, 176–81, 201, 213, 222–23, 238, 252, 258–59, 275, 353, 375n58

Macfadyen, Matthew, 253–54, 259
"Made for Now" (Jackson), 205–6
Madonna, 13–14, 86, 88, 90, 188, 242–43, 299
Magill, Molly, 368
Mahurin, Matt, 75, 225, 257, 296
Maidza, Tkay, 21
major chords, 143, 149
Malcolm X, 128, 350

Malick, Terrence, 23, 135
Marker, Chris, 120, 309
Marks, Craig, 83
Marks, Laura, 331–32
Maroon 5, 196, 201–3, 207–8
Martin, Katherine, 29
Martin, Trayvon, 353
Marxism, 4, 345–46
Mary, Frank Jackson, 355
masculinity, 60, 94, 126, 366
mashups, 6–7, 36, 256–59, 261, 375n58
match cuts, 54, 89, 182, 185
Matisse, Henri, 50
Matsoukas, Melina, 6, 88–90, 175, 182–86, 191, 194, 281, 288, 299–300, 390n5
McClary, Susan, 381n1
McClelland, Jay, 13, 19, 346
MC Hammer, 67
Me and Rubyfruit, 116–17
"Mean What You Say" (Chainsmokers), 10
media literacy, 3, 8, 175, 196, 320, 368–69. *See also* media swirl
Media Matters, 357
media swirl: acceleration of, 1–2, 5, 16, 22, 341–42; and cable news, 357–60; and celebrities, 232–33; and hybrid forms, 122, 206, 232, 244–46; intensification of, 46, 195, 236, 291–92, 369–72; as overwhelming, 223; and paratexts, 244; and politics, 3, 17–18, 20, 206; and viewing practices, 241. *See also* audiovisuality; media literacy; spectacle
Megan Thee Stallion, 250
melodrama, 158, 255
melody, 188, 207, 308
MeLo-X, 130, 136, 352–53
Memento, 96
"Men All Pause, The" (Klymaxx), 88
Mendes, Sam, 29
Mera, Miguel, 381n1
"Mercy Street" (Gabriel and Mahurin), 225, 257
Me Too movement, 206, 339, 342

Meyers, Dave, 6, 23, 75, 196–210, 236, 293, 298–99, 303, 365
Michaels, George, 13, 79
Midnight Love, 75
Migos, 141
Miles Davis: Birth of the Cool, 236
military-industrial complex, 112–13
"Mine," 350–52
Minnelli, 28
Misek, Richard, 267
misogyny, 227
Miss Americana, 236
Mission Impossible, 310–11
Mitchell, Joni, 103, 352, 385n24
Monáe, Janelle, 211–16, 392n1
monetization, 78, 297–98. *See also* advertising; product placement
Monsted, Anton, 29
montage, 148–49, 388n19
monumentality, 53, 63
morality, 17, 20, 50, 62, 345, 347, 360
Morris, Mitchell, 386n37
Morris, Paul, 105–6
Morrissey, 118
motif, 208, 214
motifs, 56–59, 165–66, 168, 177–78, 208–9. *See also* patterns
Moulin Rouge!, 43, 58, 378n15
"Moving On," 133
Mowitt, John, 177–78
"Mr. Sandman" (Chordettes), 2
MSNBC, 357–58
MTV, 72, 74, 76, 82–83, 117–19, 164, 239, 297, 299, 309–10
MTV Raps, 75
multitemporality, 142
Mulvey, Laura, 45
Murdoch, Rupert, 321
Murnau, F. W., 22
musicalization, 83
musicals, 28
music documentaries, 231–34, 236–37, 244–46
music videos: ambiguity in, 76, 184–85; and audiovisual intensification, 291–92; and avant-garde aesthetics, 122, 125;

cultural influence of, 71, 83, 195; as a distinct genre, 15, 71–72, 78–79, 188, 309–10; evolution of, 71–72, 74–77, 81–82, 364; film allusions in, 135; and immersiveness, 9–10; modes of production, 12, 14–15, 206, 213, 234, 238, 266, 282–83, 290, 292–301, 304, 365; narrative in, 12–13, 154, 206, 208, 227–28, 269, 288, 303, 310; personal experiences of, 225–26, 241; production costs, 81, 84, 119, 183–84, 294, 297, 300, 309–10; production technologies of, 21; as promotions for the song, 30, 72–73, 160, 188, 260, 308; repeated viewings, 12, 393n13; and scale, 53–54; terms for, 9, 74, 96, 122, 211–12; theorization of, 138, 381n1. *See also* audiovisuality; *specific videos*
"Mutual Core" (Huang and Björk), 117
My Beautiful Dark Twisted Fantasy, 212
"My Boyfriend's Back" (Angels), 101, 103–6, 109
My Life in the Bush of Ghosts (Eno and Byrne), 113

Nagel, Thomas, 355
Naremore, James, 111, 242
narrative, 33, 50, 154, 156, 171, 185, 219, 226, 233, 330; and autobiography, 85–86; and color palette, 177–78; comprehension of, 50–51, 65; in lyrics, 89; in music video, 72, 154, 159, 206, 208, 227–28, 269, 288, 303, 310; and religious structures, 63; rhythm and flow, 181–82; and spectacle, 27, 33, 379n19; structure of, 46, 55–56, 64, 155–57, 160–61, 170, 233, 269, 273–74; and tableaux, 39–40; through costuming, 185–86; traditional Hollywood styles, 155–58, 170; tropes of, 156, 194
Nash, Tim, 294
Nava, Emil, 292–93, 295, 297, 299–300, 303
Nava, Jake, 86

Nelson, Maggie, 266, 287
neoliberalism, 14, 16, 18, 22, 28, 47, 51, 75, 92–94, 92 348, 151, 319–20, 326, 343–56, 380n38, 383n20
Neumeyer, David, 252
neuroscience, 11–13, 18–20, 227, 236, 254, 260–66, 286, 288–90, 310–31, 336–43, 346, 350, 368–72, 373n19, 394n1, 396n3
New Order, 120
New Orleans, 136
Newsome, Bill, 346
New Yorker, The, 322–23, 329, 363
New York Times, 4, 85, 260, 353, 357
Ngai, Sianne, 223
Nicks, Stevie, 248
"1999" (XCX), 296, 298
"99 Problems" (Jay-Z), 164, 296
Nispel, Marcus, 196, 292, 303
Nkiru, Jenn, 238
"No Angel," 353
"No Church in the Wild" (West), 294
Nomadland, 23
non-sync, 107–9, 124–25, 248, 309. *See also* sound-image sync
nontheistic gratitude, 347
Nosferatu (Murnau), 22
"No Tears Left to Cry" (Grande), 208
Notorious, 401n17
"November Rain" (Guns N' Roses), 164
"Nowhere to Run" (Martha and the Vandellas), 109
Nussbaum, Emily, 363
Nymphomaniac (von Trier), 375–76n58

Obama, Barack, 362–63
Ocean, Frank, 95, 212
"Ocean Eyes," 258
Oedipal conflict, 66
Olbermann, Keith, 360
Oldboy (Park), 256
120 Minutes, 75
"One Kiss" (Dua Lipa), 293
"1+1" (Beyoncé), 79–80
"'ON' Kinetic Manifesto Film" (BTS), 239, 241

Oore, Dani, 319, 330–32
opera, 227
Ora, Rita, 365
ornamentation, 27, 30–31, 111, 206
Osborn, Brad, 382n15, 387n3
Oudart, 394n14
Our Commons, 368
Oursler, Tony, 119

Paak, Anderson, 216–30, 257
Page, Regé-Jean, 253, 259–60
pain, 234–35, 241–42, 390n3
painterly style, 58, 112
Palmer, Stephen, 266–67
Papacharissi, Zizi, 251
"Paparazzi" (Lady Gaga), 154–72, 227, 253, 302, 309
paratexts, 232, 241, 244
Park Chan-wook, 256
Parkwood, 301
Parsons, Kate, 294
Partizan, 290
patriarchy, 112–13, 124–25
patterns, 41–42, 44–46, 55, 88, 165–66, 182, 203, 215. *See also* motifs; repetition
Peace Ball (2017), 363
Pearce, Craig, 29
Pellington, Mark, 294, 299
Peltz, Nicola, 50–51
performance art, 82
performers, 36, 43, 203, 223, 232, 241, 244, 251, 278, 363
Perry, Katy, 22, 78, 81, 85, 226, 390n3
"Peso" (ASAP Rocky), 294
P Funk, 74
phantasmagoric worlds, 11
Pharrell, 141
Ph.D., 164
Plato, 345
"Please, Mister Postman" (Marvelettes), 103–4
P!nk, 205–6
poetry, 10, 122, 131, 209, 286
Polan, Dana, 389n2
political action, 127, 140, 149, 151–52, 213

politics: awareness of, 348; participation in, 8, 17–18, 122–23, 321, 371–72; and polariation, 250–51; spectacle of, 4. *See also* public sphere
Pomp&Clout, 295, 303
Pomplamoose, 74, 82
Poole, Wakefield, 106
pop music, 12, 74–75, 97–100, 110–12, 120–21, 152, 171, 186, 213–14, 228, 236, 238
Portman, Natalie, 16
postclassical film aesthetic, 6–7, 46–47, 56–57, 95, 138, 309. *See also* Hollywood
post-continuity, 58. *See also* continuity
post-Fordism, 16, 27–28, 92–94, 96, 377n5, 383n22
Post Malone, 218
postmodernity, 34–35
post-Taylorism, 14, 343, 377n5, 383n22
"Pray You Can't Catch Me," 124
Prenom Carmen (Godard), 253
"Pretty Hurts" (Beyoncé), 88–89, 175–94, 339, 348, 390n3
Pride and Prejudice, 254–56, 258–61
privacy, 222–23, 243–44, 247, 322–23, 330
Prodigy, 298–99
production houses, 14–15, 290–91, 294–95, 302–3. *See also* transmedia work
product placement, 78, 81, 154, 298, 310. *See also* advertising; monetization
props, 60–61, 183–84, 316
Psycho, 383n16
psychoanalysis, 19, 159, 337, 386n37, 391n15, 559
psychology, 19, 171
psychometrics, 322–24, 330, 340–43
Public Enemy, 83, 331
public sphere, 122–23, 320, 368, 397n4. *See also* politics
Puth, Charlie, 292–93

Queen Is Dead, The (The Smiths), 118
quilting points, 169

race, 27, 50, 133, 187, 191, 327, 354; and art practices, 139; of audiences, 354; depictions of, 133–34, 140, 148, 150, 184, 187–88, 191; and hip-hop production, 205; influence on research methods, 123; and injustice, 85; and musical genres, 75; perceptions of, 40, 149, 227; visibility of, 332

racism, 22, 75, 85, 122–23, 132, 136, 220, 226, 326, 349, 354–58

Raging Bull (Scorsese), 193

Railton, Diane, 381n1

rap, 148–51, 207, 209, 355

Rawls, John, 4, 347

reactionary, 48, 155

Red Sparrow, 303

Reeves, Keanu, 84

"Reflektor" (Arcade Fire), 82

Regan, Trish, 358

Reimers, Mark, 368

religion, 63, 115, 199–200, 301, 361

Remarks on Color (Wittgenstein), 267

repetition, 36, 57, 170–71, 182, 186, 213–14. *See also* patterns

Reservoir Dogs (Tarantino), 256

resonance, 196–97, 199, 254

Rey, Lana Del, 255–56, 258–59

Reynor, Jack, 50

Rhapsody in Blue (Gershwin), 33–34, 40

rhythm, 37, 62–64, 83, 91–92, 116, 130, 147, 165–68, 181–82, 189–94, 209, 247, 275, 330, 350. *See also* beat

Riggs, Marlon, 226

Rihanna, 233, 235, 259, 390n3

Rist, Pipilotti, 98, 112–13, 115–16, 135

"River" (Eminem), 303

Roberts, T. Carlis, 388n16

Rogers, Holly, 106, 252

Romanek, Mark, 75, 84, 99, 203, 296, 298

Rose, Tricia, 148

Rose Hobart (Cornell), 106–9

Rothman, Will, 324

Rowling, J. K., 342

"Rude Boy" (Rihanna), 79

Runaway (Kanye), 82

"Runaway" (Jackson), 301

Saake, Ryan, 296

Saboteur (Hitchcock), 38

Sadoff, Ron, 382n12

sampling, 98–100, 113, 115

Sanders, Bernie, 4

Savage, Dan, 50

"Savage" (Megan Thee Stallion), 250

scale, 2, 31, 46, 53–55, 179, 181, 194, 201, 363

scene structure, 54, 64

Scherzinger, Nicole, 35

Schiller, Herbert, 346

Schloss, Karen B., 266–67

Scorpio Rising (Anger), 98, 100–106

Scorsese, Martin, 28–29, 193, 375–76n58, 378n8

Scott, A. O., 49, 66

Scott, Jordan, 283

Scott, Luke, 273, 283

Scott, Ridley, 283

Scott, Tony, 283

"Scream" (Jackson), 297, 309–10

"See the Light" (Kaye), 117–18

"See You Again" (Khalifa), 292–93

"Serpentine Fire" (Earth, Wind, and Fire), 224

setting, 38, 53, 96, 147, 161, 169, 178–79, 182, 187–88, 203, 207–8, 210, 212, 240, 269, 274, 352, 378n15

"7/11," 310

73 Questions, 3, 231, 233, 244–46

sex, 87–88, 156, 158, 164, 183, 214–15, 219–21, 310

sexuality, 39, 82–98, 105–6, 109, 156–58, 183, 187–91, 211–13, 339–41

Shape of Water, The (del Toro), 321

Shaviro, Steve, 14, 20, 92, 380n38, 382n15

Sheeran, Ed, 243–44, 250

Shire, Warsan, 131

"Side By Side," 84

Sigismondi, Floria, 99, 196, 295, 301–2, 387n50

signposting, 55–56

silence, 140–42, 181

INDEX   441

Simon and Garfunkel, 363
Simone, Nina, 132
"Singing in the Rain," 256–57
Sitney, P. Adams, 98–99
Sivan, Troye, 231, 245–46, 298
"6 Inch," 131, 350–53
Skrillex, 64
slavery, 136, 145–47, 354–55
"Slide Away" (Cyrus), 239–40
slurry, 23
"Smack My Bitch Up" (Prodigy), 298–99
"Smells Like Teen Spirit" (Nirvana), 75–77
Smith, Harry, 99
Smith, Jeff, 9, 252, 290
Smith, Sam, 10, 244, 312–17
Smiths, The, 118
Snowden (Stone), 321–22, 328–30
soar, 78, 390n3
social justice, 48, 94–95, 338–40, 369–70
social media, 15–16
Solange, 363
Somesuch, 14–15
song arrangement, 33, 73, 87–88, 90–91, 127, 145, 147, 161–67, 171, 177–78, 181, 190–91, 194, 199, 217, 221–22. *See also* instrumentation
song length, 128–29
song sections, 32, 35, 64, 89, 104, 150, 152, 159–61, 163, 176–77, 181, 186, 188–91, 194, 218, 222, 278
song structure, 127, 198
sonic space, 35, 131
Sonic Youth, 119–20
"Sorrow," 130
"Sorry," 136
sound: and avant-garde aesthetics, 131; layers of, 199–200, 330; relation to image, 8, 13, 63, 87, 103, 110, 135, 308, 311; resonance of, 196–97, 199; and sense of motion, 200; sources of, 27, 36
sound effects, 42–43, 46, 83, 169, 181, 213

sound-image sync, 79, 105–10, 152, 168–71, 176–79, 187–200, 255–56, 279, 311–16, 367, 385n18. *See also* audiovisual relations; non-sync
soundtrack, 34, 63–64, 252
South of the Border, 327
spatial deformations, 201–3
spatiality, 46, 53, 65, 92–93, 124, 142–44, 178–79, 201, 208, 379n18. *See also* disorientation; temporality
Spears, Britney, 206, 208, 301
spectacle, 1–4, 16–17, 27, 30–31, 33, 363, 379n19. *See also* media swirl; sublime
Spector, Phil, 104
Spectre (Mendes), 29
Spielberg, Steven, 48
Spinoza, Baruch, 345
Spring (Botticelli), 38
Staake, Ryan, 298–99, 302
stardom. *See* celebrities
Steely Dan, 74
Steinem, Gloria, 362–63
Sterbenz, Maeve, 382n15
Stevens, Stuart, 365–66
stillness, 145, 147, 218
Stilwell, Robynn, 9, 252
Stockwell, Dean, 111
Stone, Oliver, 327, 398n21
"Stonemilker" (Bjork), 82
Strafuss, Matt, 324–25
"Strange Fruit" (Holiday), 354
Strauss, Levi, 159
streaming, 85, 95, 212, 309
"Stuck in the Middle with You" (Wheel), 256–57
Styles, Harry, 231, 235
sublime, 3–4, 29, 71, 121, 329. *See also* spectacle
subtitles, 54, 252, 260–61
"Summer Nights" (Rey), 258
"Summertime Sadness" (Rey), 259
Super-8, 124
surveillance, 247, 322–23, 330, 340–43
"Sweet Love," 348

Swift, Taylor, 5, 73, 81, 233, 236, 241–42, 251–52, 254–55, 258–60, 375n58
Syles, Harry, 244
"Sympathy for the Devil" (Rolling Stones), 103
synchresis, 87, 385n18
synthesizer, 74, 160–61, 164, 166–67, 170, 197, 200
SZA, 197–98, 200–201, 207, 209
Szetela, Adam, 123

tableaux, 37–40, 46, 208–9
Tagg, Philip, 8, 87, 101, 103, 256
Tannenbaum, Rob, 83
Tarantino, Quentin, 67, 132, 256
Tarkovsky, Andre, 131, 135
Taverner, John, 64
Taylorism, 14, 343, 377n5, 383n22
technological advancement, 21, 85–86, 102, 110, 284–85, 319–20, 322, 332, 336, 343–44, 356, 370
technology, 95, 106, 116, 284, 301, 325, 344, 364, 369
Tegmark, Max, 345
"Telephone," 154–55, 299
tempo, 91–92, 129, 149–50, 152, 221, 250, 258
temporality: acceleration of, 66; and cognitive processes, 227; and distance, 178; extensions of, 106; and futurity, 37; and globalization, 15; and heterosexuality, 105; manipulation of, 92–93, 115–16, 239, 248, 258; markers of, 233, 267; and music tempo, 91–92; and non-sync, 124; and nontime, 3–4; perceptions of, 13, 397n13; and slowness, 65–66. *See also* spatiality
texture, 86, 177–78
"Thank U, Next" (Grande), 254
Thanouli, Eleftheria, 58
Theory of Colours (Goethe), 267
"There Is a Light that Never Goes Out" (The Smiths), 118–19
"This Is America" (Childish Gambino), 371
"This Is How We Do" (Perry), 78, 81

"Thriller" (Jackson), 158–59, 184, 218
Tiger and Snake (Delacroix), 141
TikTok, 5–7, 14, 23, 231, 247–51, 310, 364. *See also* brief media
Tiller Girls, 28
Tilley, Colin, 6, 218, 223, 225, 228
timbre, 141, 161, 177–78, 192. *See also* vocals
Timberlake, Justin, 203
Tinder, 248
"Tints" (.Paak and Lamar), 216–30, 253, 257
Toles, Georges, 324
Torque (Kahn), 303
Tourneur, Jacques, 61, 135
"Toxic" (Spears), 301
Tracking Color in Cinema and Art (Branigan), 267
Transformers: Age of Extinction (Bay), 28–29, 48–66, 122, 378n8
transmedia, 47, 84, 86, 205, 283, 290
Transmedia Directors (Vernallis), 15
transmedia styles, 15, 47, 185, 194, 196
transmedia work, 28, 170, 290–91, 303. *See also* production houses
Trecartin, Ryan, 117
Trier, Lars von, 13, 15, 228, 375–76n58
Triumph of the Will, 1
Trump, Donald, 1, 4, 17, 137, 153, 206, 355–57, 360–64, 366
Tsai Ming-Liang, 111
Tucci, Stanley, 51
"Tunic (Song for Karen)" (Sonic Youth), 119
Tversky, Amos, 346
12 Years a Slave, 321
27: Gone Too Soon, 236
twigs, FKA, 266, 268–74, 375–76n58

underscoring, 40–41
United States: historical depictions of, 182–83; racism in, 122–23, 132, 349; wealth of, 20, 370–72

Unruly Media, 319–22, 324–26, 328–29, 331, 369, 397n23
urbanization, 75

Vaucanson, Jacques de, 63
Vertigo, 383n16
Vevo, 76–77. *See also* YouTube
VH1, 75, 239
video games, 82
"Video Killed the Radio Star" (Buggles), 74
Vikander, Alicia, 327
Villa-Lobos, Heitor, 107–8
Viñuela, Eduardo, 374n25, 381n1, 382n15
Vinyl (Warhol), 98, 109, 112
"Violence," 365
Virdiana (Buñuel), 22
Vivaldi, 256
vocals: *a cappella*, 391n10; and harmony, 89; manipulation of, 115, 179; and sync, 189; and tension, 275; timbre of, 177–78, 192; various registers of, 141, 201, 313. *See also* timbre
vocoder, 151
Vogue, 45, 231, 244–45
voice-over, 36

Wagner, Anthony, 327, 401n17
Wahlberg, Mark, 50–51
"Wait" (Maroon 5), 196, 198, 201–3, 207–8
Waking Life (Linklater), 238
Wallace, Chris, 357
Warhol, Andy, 98, 109, 112
Waring, Becky, 326, 329–30
Washington, Denzel, 401n17
Washington Post, 360
Watson, Paul, 381n1
Wayne, John, 401n17
Wegman, Will, 117, 120
Weidt, Eric, 285–87
West, Cornel, 24
West, Kanye, 212, 293–94
Westenberg, Emma, 299

Westerns, 65
Whack, Tierra, 294
Whale, James, 22
"What You Need" (INXS), 79
Wheel, Stealers, 256
"When the Levee Breaks" (Zeppelin), 103
"Where Is My Mind (Pixies Cover)" (Maidza), 21
Where the Wild Things Are, 294
Whissel, Kristen, 55
White, Jack, 127, 131, 354
white-outs, 46
Will.I.Am, 363
Williams, Hype, 75–76, 86–88
"Willow" (Swift), 258
"Will You Still Love Me Tomorrow?" (Shirelles), 103
Wilson, Nancy, 83
Winehouse, Amy, 234
Winters, Ben, 252
Winwood, Steve, 307–8, 310–11
"Without Me" (Halsey), 218, 250
"Without You" (Lapalux), 312–13, 316–18
Wittgenstein, Ludwig, 267
Wolf, Mark, 29
Wolf of Wall Street (Scorsese), 28–29, 378n8
Women's March, 362
Wonder, Stevie, 362
Wood, Robin, 324
Wood, Sarah, 320, 397n23
Woodiwiss, Aubrey, 265–89
Woolcock, Penny, 110
world-building, 29
Wübbena, Thorsten, 381n1
"Wyclef Jean" (Young Thug), 299

XCX, Charli, 296, 298

"Yes We Can" (Will.I.Am), 363
"You Can't Touch This" (MC Hammer), 67
"You Make Me Feel" (Monáe), 211–16

Young, Andrew Thomas, 273–74
Young Thug, 299
"You're Either Mine of You're Not" (Fergie), 42
YouTube: as decontextualized, 110–11; and generic boundaries, 73, 188; influence of, 154; media landscape, 206; metrics of, 76–77; and participatory culture, 82, 85, 232–34; strategies of, 2, 16, 212, 231–32, 251; styles of, 6, 86; viewing practices, 241, 244, 260–61, 292, 297, 329, 375n58. *See also* Vevo
YouTube experiments, 101–4, 106, 109, 141, 224, 252, 255–57, 260, 324, 386n32

Zacks, Jeff, 227, 316, 318
ZAYN, 266, 274–78
Žižek, Slavoj, 169

www.ingramcontent.com/pod-product-compliance
Lightning Source LLC
Chambersburg PA
CBHW031323230426
43670CB00006B/220